Citizenship Education around the World

Though certainly not a new idea, *citizenship education* manifests in unique and often unpredictable ways in our contemporary neoliberal era. The question of what it means to be a productive and recognized citizen must now be understood simultaneously along both global and local lines. This edited volume offers an international perspective on citizenship education enacted in specific socio-political contexts. Each chapter includes a pointed conceptualization of citizenship education—a philosophical framework— that is then applied to specific national cases across Europe, Asia, Canada and more. Chapters emphasize how such frameworks are implemented within local contexts, encouraging particular pedagogical/curricular practices even as they constrain others. Chapters conclude with suggestions for productive change and how educators might usefully engage contemporary contexts through citizenship education.

John E. Petrovic is Professor of Educational Philosophy and Policy Studies and Program Coordinator for the Social and Cultural Studies in Education PhD at The University of Alabama, USA. He has written articles on a range of issues and topics from Dewey, to heterosexism, to language policy. He has published in such journals as *Educational Theory, Educational Studies, Journal of Language and Politics*, and the *International Multilingual Research Journal*. He is editor of *International Perspectives on Bilingual Education: Policy, Practice, and Controversy*.

Aaron M. Kuntz is Associate Professor of Educational Studies at the University of Alabama, USA, where he currently serves as Program Coordinator for the PhD in Educational Research. His research interests include critical qualitative inquiry, academic activism and citizenship, critical geography, and philosophy of education. Dr. Kuntz's publications appear in such diverse journals as *Qualitative Inquiry, Educational Action Research, Cultural Studies <=> Critical Methodologies*, the *Journal of Language and Politics, Educational Studies, The Journal of Higher Education*, the *Peabody Journal of Education*, and others.

Routledge Research in International and Comparative Education

This is a series that offers a global platform to engage scholars in continuous academic debate on key challenges and the latest thinking on issues in the fast growing field of International and Comparative Education.

Books in the series include:

1 **Teaching in Primary Schools in China and India**
   Contexts of Learning
   Nirmala Rao and Emma Pearson
   with Kai-ming Cheng and
   Margaret Taplin

2 **A History of Higher Education Exchange**
   China and America
   Teresa Brawner Bevis

3 **National Identity and Educational Reform**
   Contested Classrooms
   Elizabeth Anderson Worden

4 **Citizenship Education around the World**
   Local Contexts and
   Global Possibilities
   Edited by John E. Petrovic
   and Aaron M. Kuntz

Citizenship Education around the World

Local Contexts and Global Possibilities

Edited by
John E. Petrovic and
Aaron M. Kuntz

Routledge
Taylor & Francis Group
NEW YORK   LONDON

First published 2014
by Routledge
711 Third Avenue, New York, NY 10017

and by Routledge
2 Park Square, Milton Park, Abingdon, Oxon OX14 4RN

*Routledge is an imprint of the Taylor & Francis Group,
an informa business*

Library of Congress Cataloging-in-Publication Data
Citizenship education around the world : local contexts and global
    possibilities / edited by John E. Petrovic and Aaron M. Kuntz.
        pages cm. — (Routledge research in international and comparative
    education)
    Includes bibliographical references and index.
    1. Citizenship—Study and teaching—Cross-cultural studies.   I. Petrovic,
John E.   II. Kuntz, Aaron M.
    LC1091.C5244 2014
    370.11'5—dc23
    2013046242

ISBN13: 978-0-415-72106-6 (hbk)
ISBN13: 978-1-315-86361-0 (ebk)

Typeset in Sabon
by IBT Global.

Contents

Prologue: Citizenship and the Purposes of Education   ix
JOHN E. PETROVIC AND AARON M. KUNTZ

1   Citizenship Education in England in an Era of Perceived
    Globalisation: Recent Developments and Future Prospects   1
    BEN KISBY

2   Who Belongs in What Hong Kong? Citizenship Education in the
    Special Administrative Region   22
    LIZ JACKSON

3   Citizenship Education in China under Discourses of Nationalism,
    Cosmopolitanism, Neoliberalism and Confucianism   43
    JUANJUAN ZHU AND STEVEN P. CAMICIA

4   Creating Citizens in a Capitalistic Democracy:
    A Struggle for the Soul of American Citizenship Education   66
    JESSICA A. HEYBACH AND ERIC C. SHEFFIELD

5   Citizenship Education in Spain in the Twenty-First Century   87
    MIQUEL MARTÍNEZ AND ENRIC PRATS

6   Lost in Citizenship Education: Questions Faced by Amerasians
    in Japan   110
    KANAKO IDE

7   Citizenship Education and the Construction of Identity in Canada   128
    DIANNE GERELUK AND DAVID SCOTT

8 Civic Education in Israel: Between National-Ethnocentricity
and Universalism 150
ZEHAVIT GROSS

9 On Hostipitality, Responsibility and *Ubuntu*: Some Philosophical
Remarks on Teaching and Learning in South Africa 165
YUSEF WAGHID AND NURAAN DAVIDS

10 Citizenship Education in Colombia: Searching for the Political 180
ANDRÉS MEJÍA

11 Citizenship Education in Mexico 197
MARIA-EUGENIA LUNA-ELIZARRARAS

12 Tertiary Education and Critical Citizenship 220
PETER ROBERTS

Epilogue: Reading Citizenship Education in Neoliberal Times 237
AARON M. KUNTZ AND JOHN E. PETROVIC

Contributors 253
Index 259

Prologue
Citizenship and the Purposes of Education

John E. Petrovic and Aaron M. Kuntz

INTRODUCTION: THE PURPOSES OF EDUCATION

There are four broad purposes of education that are, arguably, universal
with varying degree. These include economic, social, political, and intellectual purposes.[1] While certainly overlapping, these purposes become more
or less emphasized within particular sociohistorical contexts and/or when
the more specific goals within each are accented. The emphasis or accen-
tuation depends largely upon sociopolitical and historical context. These
four purposes collude in the production of the educated citizen. Localized
contexts foreground particular manifestations of the citizen that are never
fully divorced from global discourses.

Throughout this book, chapter authors interrogate national contexts as a
means to better understand the production of citizenship education within
particular time and space. Together, these chapters provide a more globalized overview of citizenship education as both a localized and increasingly
global phenomena. It is our hope that encountering these chapters against
one another will provide readers with a dynamic understanding of citizenship education: one that refuses generic conceptions of the term. More than
individualized examples, these chapters detail how visions of citizenship
education extend from foundational assumptions about the purposes of education and address three overarching questions: (1) What is the good or productive citizen?; (2) How should citizenship education be conceptualized?;
(3) How does the local sociopolitical context affect these conceptualizations? The complexity of the foundational assumptions—how they develop
and manifest in particular power-laden policies and practices—demands
a critical and philosophical approach that lays the groundwork for inten-
tional and productive change in the future. Never in isolation, intentions
for change must necessarily encompass the economic, social, political, and
intellectual purposes for education as differently emphasized—and often
contradictory—discourses.

The economic purpose of education is to enhance the economic prosperity of the nation, the idea being that an educated citizenry is more innovative and, therefore, more productive. An accented goal within this purpose

would be providing students the skills necessary to gain employment leading to their place as productive citizens. We do not want to suggest that educating students with the skills and knowledge to support themselves economically is in and of itself problematic. The point is twofold in our contemporary neoliberal era. First, students are educated toward this as a priority in unhealthy ways, ways that direct them away from their interests and passions and flourishing lives toward economically defined lives. Second, this is because "productive" is typically cast in very limited, mainly pecuniary, terms: How much do you earn? How much do you contribute to the creation of profit? How much do you pay in taxes? Thusly embedded in a neoliberal logic, the economic purposes cast students as human capital and citizenship as productivity within that very limited frame. So how should citizenship education take shape to deal with the tensions among the received view of the economic purposes of education (education for innovation and productivity) and its corollary outcome (compliance)?

Neoliberalism, we would argue, induces compliance as one of the social purposes of education: socializing students into the proper behaviors or dispositions necessary to this economic ethos. Such dispositions include punctuality, discipline, surveillance, docility, as well as a consistent 'presence' in the economic market (through purchasing goods, say, or selling one's labor).

In addition to this compliant consumerism of neoliberalism, the social purposes have emphasized behavioral socialization, dispositions that extend from an historical view of education as behavior modification. As Robert Wiebe notes of the mind-set of reformers of the common school era in the first third of the nineteenth century, "If one could just inculcate the proper habits—those almost infallible signs of an inner morality—when the faculties were tender, the mold of the good man would be set."[2]

Finally, socialization might also include assimilation into particular cultural values seemingly necessary to national cohesion—what it means to be a citizen of a particular nation. Is the good citizen one who embraces and enacts dominant values, cultural traits, language, religious beliefs, and so on? If so, to what degree?

This assimilatory socialization also begins to name the political purposes of education. Schooling builds national cohesion and a national identity by helping to construct an historical narrative that is sometimes based in fact, sometimes myth, but always incomplete. This is enacted through civics or social studies classes, history classes, symbols (e.g., flags, anthems, mascots, etc.), and rituals (e.g., the pledging of allegiance in U.S. schools),[3] among other things. Beyond this, the political purposes include basic education in the kind of government under which one lives, how it functions, its structure, different branches and their purposes. At times—and touched upon in the chapters to follow—civics education often stands in for citizenship education; as though the most basic political functions of education are all that is needed to create a unified and productive citizenry.

Such a limited conception of education is likely to lead to an uncritical and thoughtless nationalism.

However, the political purposes of education should also include the development of robust questioning, discussion, and debate and provide students experience in these. The technical aspects of government and myth building should be considered less important than building the capacity for reasonable engagement in the public square. The political purposes here would be to inculcate the habits of thought that allow students to deliberate among competing conceptions of the good life, while respecting other reasonable conceptions.[4] Notice that the extent of the expression of this political purpose will depend on the sociopolitical context and the concomitant extent to which one emphasizes assimilatory social purposes.

Ideally, technology would enhance the public square and critical engagement. In our polarized political world, we may be heading away from this ideal. We engage by 40-character tweet that simply dismisses any legitimate concerns or by simply clicking "block," "ignore," or "delete" so as to need pay attention only to that which with one agrees. The ideal is that technology might promote substantive engagement in the cyber-public-space by increasing the means of communication. Of course, technology has served this democratic imperative to some degree—think Arab Spring. But, even then it was homogeneity of engagement to combat the power of the repressive state apparatus. The difference is that in most contexts it is the ideological state apparatus that must be addressed, remembering that education is part and parcel of the apparatus.[5]

So combine block-ignore-delete with the claptrap that passes as news today—increasingly driven by the need to compete with multimedia. This ensemble of electronic techniques (e.g., tweets) disallows little other than easy dismissal or simple-minded agreement. And, in the United States at least, what counts as the news today serves much the same purpose as, say, the NFL and other corporate entertainment: distraction. Having occupied our minds away from important issues of the day with the NFL, *American Idol, Jersey Shore*, ad nauseum, the corporate news media can simply then tell us what the important issues are, with the ultimate effects being, as Herman and Chomsky noted some time ago, a taming of the bewildered herd and the manufacture of consent.[6]

Reading through this noise, the development of the capacity for engagement in the public square through rational deliberation, and being able, as Paulo Freire suggested, to read the world through critical thinking, should be considered among the most important intellectual purposes of schooling.[7] Furthermore, these purposes should inform and, ultimately, drive the political purposes of education vis-à-vis citizenship education. Of course, learning the skills necessary to the economic purposes of schooling and the technical knowledge necessary to the political purposes might also be considered intellectual purposes. Basic numeracy and literacy are obvious intellectual purposes as well. The point here is that these intellectual purposes of education are never absent significant assumptions regarding economic, social, and political rationales for education (and yet, often, these intellectual purposes are often rendered as some isolated and/or timeless sense of intellectualism unencumbered by such sociopolitical baggage). Further, it is the critical engagement with such assumptions and rationales that are foregrounded in the intellectual purposes of schooling; mere recitation of capitalistic assumptions regarding the free market, for example, is not an intellectual endeavor.

As we have tried to make clear, these purposes of education will overlap in myriad ways and be emphasized differently, depending upon the sociopolitical context. For example, understanding the economic system and one's role within it probably subsumes all four of the mentioned purposes of schooling. "Understanding" refers, perhaps, to the intellectual purpose; that is, as noted earlier, not rote memorization but engagement and reflection on the economic system and its concomitant values, assumptions, and historical development. But this also has a social purpose to the extent that understanding the economic system is simultaneously a process of socializing children into that system. Pedagogy, for example, can reinforce or undermine capitalism by taking more competitive or cooperative forms in terms of the ways students are permitted or encouraged to engage in tasks (e.g., individually or collaboratively) or in terms of how they are evaluated (e.g., competitive letter or numerical grading procedures or portfolios). Notice, in turn, that which pedagogical choice to make here is already a political decision for this, at least partially, defines the role one should play. Furthermore, when we emphasize one or more of these three purposes—social, economic, or political—in particular ways, we are saying something important about the intellectual purpose and this will serve the interests of some over others. We can take the social studies curriculum in Texas which stresses the superiority of American capitalism as a case in point.

In the Texas curriculum standards, not only are non-capitalistic economic models absent in the K–8 standards, but also the ability to critique, an important intellectual capacity in a democracy supposedly based on rational deliberation among competing ideals, is missing. For example, students are expected to "explain how government regulations and taxes impact consumer costs," but not how the profit motive does. Students are to "identify historical figures, such as individuals, past and present, including Henry Ford, and other entrepreneurs in the community such as Mary Kay Ash, and Wallace Amos, Milton Hershey, and Sam Walton, and ordinary people in the community who have started new businesses." At the high school level, "The student understands the historical origins of contemporary economic systems and the benefits of free enterprise in world history." But, unlike the K–8 standards, socialism is mentioned in the high school standards, namely in the goal to "formulate generalizations on how economic freedom improved the human condition, based on students' knowledge of the benefits of free enterprise in Europe's Commercial Revolution, the Industrial Revolution, and 20th century free-market economies, compared to communist command communities" (p. 25). Cleary, the Texas standards emphasize not just economic purposes of schooling, but a very narrow economic ideology, undermining critical intellectual purposes of schooling, if those are to be something other than socialization, indoctrination, and simple regurgitation. What kind of citizen does one become with such an education? In this volume, Chapter 4, which focuses on American citizenship education, addresses such concerns quite poignantly. These general purposes of education, explicated above and contextually rendered via the Texas case, intersect to produce the 'educated citizen' in particular ways and within the sociohistorical contexts that gives them their meaning. In this sense, citizenship education takes on both formal and informal dimensions as it extends from the assumptive educational practices of students, teachers, and administrators alike.

CITIZENSHIP AND CITIZENSHIP EDUCATION

Georgi Dimitrov and Pepka Boyadjieva define citizenship as "the system of values, efforts and institutionalized practices required for creating and maintaining conditions for living together in a complex society."[8] Contextual factors of the particular "complex society" shape the very idea of citizenship to be pursued. What are the values necessary to maintain which specific conditions given extant political beliefs in a given society? Here it is necessary to recognize two conditions. First, citizenship is conceptualized, we hope only initially, through the frame of the modern nation-state. That is to say, the nation-state is the complex society generally referred to, sometimes exclusively but certainly prior to, say, the global society. Contrary to the "imagined community" of the modern nation-state,[9] diversity within these states helps define them. This is particularly evident in the chapter that focuses on Canada (Chapter 7). Thus, second, conceptualizations of citizenship also address—sometimes as collusions with, sometimes as reactions against—the fact of diversity within nation-states. Given this, the notion of "living together" might lead to a more specific conceptualization of citizenship such as "shared-fate citizenship." Such a notion not only recognizes diversity but also stability in terms of how and why individuals are civically bound. As Sigal Ben-Porath defines it, shared-fate citizenship is "the visions, practices, and processes that make up the civic body through engaging individuals and groups in the continuous process of designing, expressing, and interpreting their membership in the nation."[10] The complex political machinations of developing such a conception is evidenced in the chapter on Hong Kong (Chapter 2).

While Ben-Porath explicitly invokes a liberal democratic framing of citizenship, we cannot (1) assume that all nation-states embrace liberal democracy and that (2) all of those that do, do so in identical ways. Different political values may be more or less promoted or protected within different states as well as different economic systems or priorities. Given such variation among nation-states and broad understandings of citizenship generally, the notion of citizenship education, while most directly situated among the political purposes, incorporates all of the purposes of education discussed. This is because education is a multidirectional information process. From one direction, for example, the sociopolitical context certainly informs the nature, purpose, and content of citizenship education, as the case of Texas illustrates. Furthermore, extant political institutions are both products and producers of the sociopolitical milieu. As such, they may not only inform but explicitly direct citizenship education. From the other direction, education should not merely reflect the larger sociopolitical context—even as it must to some degree—but also inform and challenge it; this is education as critical engagement. The claim, then, that citizenship education manifests in unique and often unpredictable ways should be uncontroversial.

While the case of the Texas curricular standards does not strike of citizenship education for democracy properly conceived, it does illustrate the driving purpose of this volume: to conceptualize citizenship education, understand and illustrate how it is affected by the larger sociopolitical order and historical contingencies, and to make recommendations as to what a humane, intellectually driven citizenship education might look like in the service of democracy both locally and globally. What does citizenship education look like around the globe? What are the specific philosophical or ideological commitments that affect the purposes of citizenship education? How do these manifest in educational policy and practice? The authors in this collection of case studies describe the given political context and the political values that tend to drive educational policy and curriculum. Building on this descriptive analysis, the chapters herein also make normative claims around an ideal of citizenship education and recommend changes given the sociopolitical context of their study.

This said, it is our position that discussions of citizenship education cannot be left at the local level. If Ben-Porath's notion of shared-fate citizenship, for example, is reasonable, does a shared fate really end at national borders? Or, is there or should there be a larger political project? As national boundaries are rendered increasingly porous or blurred through processes of globalization, the question of what it means to be a productive and recognized citizen must now be understood simultaneously along both global and local lines. Can and in what ways should citizenship education include a global perspective? Thus, the focus of the epilogue is to make explicit the overarching themes and shared sociohistorical contexts that might inform such a global perspective.

GLOBALIZATION AND CITIZENSHIP EDUCATION

Globalization might refer to any number of political, cultural, or ideological phenomena. But the most obvious form of globalization is economic globalization within a neoliberal ethos via multinational corporations who need not respect in any significant way national borders. How has the increasingly neoliberal social order, which seems to be, as many of the chapters suggest, one characteristic of this globalization, changed ideals of what it means to be a citizen and, in turn, how citizenship education is formalized? As we noted earlier, the productive citizen, in this vein, takes on pecuniary connotations: The good citizen is productive and productivity means contributing to the local economy and participating in global capitalism. Given that this excludes a large slice of the citizenry—the very old, the very young, the infirmed, the disabled, the incarcerated, to name a few groups—are there not saner interpretations of a productive citizen that we might/should embrace? What does it mean to be a citizen and what does it mean to citizenship education in this new corporate order, a corporate order that can, in large part, either ignore or set national policies according to their profit-driven need? How do these overarching and ever strengthening economic forces affect the purposes of education generally and citizenship education specifically? Have the scales weighing the various purposes of education been irrevocably tipped away from the intellectual and toward the economic? What does this mean to citizenship?

The globalization of neoliberalism creates economic change, mainly by increasing the gap between rich and poor nations and individuals. This creates uncertainty and anxiety about the ability of nations to provide or maintain a degree of economic security in increasingly interconnected economic times that often downplay the otherwise defining boundaries of the nation-state. People across the globe lead increasingly tenuous economic lives. Such economic forces help to set the stage for neoconservative, protectionist backlash. This backlash is couched as patriotism, an inward looking ideal of citizenship. In contrast to the neoliberal citizen who thinks of his or her own economic well-being first, the neoconservative citizen is asked to give teleological priority to a fairly narrow ideal of his or her community (nation) in the name of patriotism. As a consequence, we might justifiably ask, how should citizenship education approach patriotism? How should it teach patriotism while disallowing it to move into its more insidious ideal: nationalism? Should we think about being global citizens instead? And, what would a citizenship education that seeks to balance patriotism and global citizenship look like?

This inward (national) and outward (global) push and pull raises similar kinds of questions within diverse nation-states. In this case, it is not economic protectionism that comes into play but a retrenchment of nationalist cultural projects, as reflected in draconian anti-immigration legislation in the United States or the recent resurgence of the Golden Dawn Party in Greece. How, then, should citizenship education be shaped to promote social stability and national unity on the one hand while recognizing internal diversity on the other? In other words, to what degree should an ideal of citizenship value the *unum* over the *pluribus* or vice versa and how does such differential valuing inform the meaning of the "good citizen?"

In the end, we think that a conceptualization of citizenship education must start with a theory of interest and a theory of experience. Whose interests do extant conceptualizations of citizenship education serve? Whose interests should they serve? Do they serve the interests of robust local and global democracy? What kind of experiences must students have in school to understand what it means to be a good citizen? Citizenship is practice, not commodity; engagement, not isolation; caring, not self-preservation. While citizenship education is rightly informed by and speaks to each of the purposes of education, at its best it is conceived of in terms of the intellectual purposes of education: those purposes that require students to ask deep and difficult questions about how societies function and to engage the philosophic method in attempting normative claims as to how they should function.

OVERVIEW OF CHAPTERS

The contributors to this volume were chosen for their expertise in the field of citizenship education and with the aim of providing a culturally, politically, and economically diverse set of case studies. The epilogue, by the coeditors, will consist of a cross-analysis of the case studies in order to provide the reader a concise summary of common themes, an analysis of how sociopolitical forces play out educationally in different contexts and why, and a discussion of the overlapping recommendations on how to engage in citizenship education that is globally responsive with local practices. In the end, the editors aim for this volume to offer readers a nuanced and grounded interrogation of citizenship education as a philosophically informed yet practical approach to change and learning.

In Chapter 1, Ben Kisby explores the role and meaning of citizenship education in a British context. Unlike in the three other home nations, citizenship lessons in England have been compulsory in secondary schools since 2002. But Kisby notes the "considerable concern. . .expressed by citizenship education campaigners that new proposals to cut down the citizenship curriculum" are "underpinned by a highly individualised, consumerist agenda." Such an educational agenda stems from what Kisby identifies as a "hyperglobalism." Arguing that it is not at all clear that the world has reached anything that can be cast as a new era of globalization, radically distinct from other periods, Kisby notes that a discourse of hyperglobalisation, one that sets in dire tone the diminution of national sovereignty, has taken hold and has been made coterminous with neoliberalism. This may make it very difficult to establish the kind of global citizenship education that Kisby defends, one that respects diversity, commits to social justice, and requires critical thinking.

In Chapter 2, Liz Jackson examines the challenge of citizenship education in Hong Kong. Hong Kongers are experiencing an identity crisis related to citizenship since the handover from the United Kingdom to the People's Republic of China in 1997. This has been exacerbated by current debates over the government's 2012 proposal for "moral and national education." Though the curriculum in Hong Kong has always emphasized cultural ties with the mainland, new calls for political allegiance to China in education worry members of society who are proud of their Western political traditions and liberal civil rights. Jackson posits that "Hong Kong's colonial legacy as a transitory, depoliticized international community places it at odds with historically isolationist mainland China." Nevertheless, through a vision of intercultural education and a multitiered notion of citizenship, Jackson argues that Hong Kongers can learn to see themselves as Hong Kongers first and Chinese second.

In Chapter 3, Juanjuan Zhu and Steven Camicia underscore that given the social changes in China, citizenship and citizenship education are gaining traction in both official and popular parlance there. As the authors discuss *gaige kaifang zhengce* (the reform and opening up policies) begun in the late 1970s and leading to Chinese entrance into the World Trade Organization in 2001, globalization seems to be a key element in social change. Educationally, *gaige kaifang zhengce* raised questions about how to balance this new albeit limited openness with the need to maintain control, social cohesion through nationalism, and stem the social tensions resulting from neoliberal reforms. Citizenship education, of course, is implicated in this balancing act. Sorting through official policy documents and curricular standards, Zhu and Camicia argue that citizenship education has taken shape through four, sometimes competing but always interrelated, discourses: nationalism, cosmopolitanism, neoliberalism, and Confucianism. "Instead of enabling Chinese citizens to thrive towards emancipation," the authors conclude, "these conceptions facilitate the society's most powerful group to maintain the status quo and hegemonic control."

In Chapter 4, Jessica Heybach and Eric Sheffield assert that "citizenship in America is equated with economic imperatives of the global economy and not indebted to questioning what it means to be a citizen, and how to best address human societal problems." This has come about, they argue, via two politico-ideological reconstructions: conservativism into neoconservatism and liberalism into neoliberalism. These two reconstructions then become conflated such that the overriding educational ethos, couched as the making of good citizens, is to promote unquestioning patriotism as support of the free market. In this way, what is called citizenship education becomes paralyzingly aesthetic as opposed to intellectually driven towards an emancipatory notion of citizenship and citizenship education. Heybach and Sheffield discuss the recently outlawed Mexican American studies program in Arizona as an exemplar of this emancipatory vision.

In Chapter 5, Miquel Martínez and Enric Prats note that citizenship education has been a focus of educational reform in Spain since 2000. To be expected, these reforms have been caught up in the ideological and political debates in a country that has had governments ranging the political spectrum from right-wing liberal to socialist and back to conservative in a short period. During this time, citizenship education has occupied a complicated legal position in the education system: first, as a cross-cutting curricular dimension; then as a key competency and specific compulsory subject; and now, removed from the curriculum altogether. Further, these political divisions have led to two distinct educational approaches: civics education vs. educating for citizenship. Drawing on a more communitarian model that recognizes not only the role of Europe in citizenship but also local constituencies, Martínez and Prats argue that the Spanish education system should recover the centrality of citizenship education in the curriculum. This requires a democratic model of school governance such that the sensitivities and diversities present in the educational community, teachers, students, families, local communities, unions, and social, cultural, civic, and economic organizations are accommodated.

In Chapter 6, Kanako Ide argues that current attempts to "foster globalized Japanese citizens" may help to perpetuate the myth that Japan is culturally monolithic, a misperception that carries through to educational policy (mis)informing notions of citizen and citizenship. While recognizing a number of cultural minority groups in Japan, Ide focuses on revealing the voice of a silent minority that finds itself between national boundaries: Amerasians born in Okinawa to U.S. military fathers and Japanese/ Okinawan mothers. It is questionable whether it is reasonable for Japan to expect both mainstream Japanese and Amerasians to have the same educational needs, and also questionable whether it is morally acceptable for the U.S. to be indifferent to the educational issues of Amerasians, who owe their existence to the historical realities of U.S. foreign policy. Ide argues that the conspicuous absence of Amerasian perspectives on citizenship education is caused by the subordination of education by the political debate. The case of Amerasians reveals a possible reconciliation of the global-citizen approach with a multicultural-citizen approach which Ide frames through a combination of liberal and communitarian political philosophy.

In Chapter 7, Diane Gereluk and David Scott focus on a key theme in citizenship education: how to promote social cohesion and diversity simultaneously. They point out that provincial jurisdiction over education in Canada emerged from a reconciliation of contentious issues defined by two dominant groups related to issues of national culture and identity and how Confederation addresses this. Specifically, tensions

between the perceived rights of French and British colonialists to preserve their cultural heritage and identity expressed through language
(French and English) and religion (Catholic and Protestant) and to have
these rights reflected in the Constitution Act of 1867 (formerly called the
British North American Act). Silent in the Constitution was the voice
of First Nation peoples and constitutional concessions to preserve their
language, culture and traditions. Such diversity presents challenges in
not only developing a Canadian civic identity but also in determining
how to frame this identity in the first place. This chapter discusses two
frames—multiculturalism and interculturalism. While pointing out how
neoliberalism has detracted from the ideal, Gereluk and Scott defend
liberal multiculturalism as the preferable frame from which to develop
Canadian civic identity.

In Chapter 8, Zehavit Gross examines citizenship education in Israel.
Gross identifies the historical tension between teaching about Israel as
a Jewish state (i.e., a state for Jews) or as a democratic state, provocatively intimating an important conceptual difference here, asking whether
Israel is a state for Jews or a democratic state. As she notes, "each option
embodies a different interpretation of the Jewish elements of the state,
and places in doubt the feasibility of a democratic regime with a civil
character that is intended to include all citizens of the state." To address
this concern, Gross draws on distinctions among apolitical, political, and
ideological education. Recognizing that education is always already political and indoctrinary, she defends a political approach, one that identifies
key interests and underlying assumptions. Pedagogy for effective political education, as citizenship education, must be reflective as opposed to
instrumental. Similar to Martínez and Prats, Gross alludes here to the
important distinction between civics education and citizenship education.
She argues that the latter will draw from both a particularistic discourse
of identity and from universalistic discourse of rights. Such an approach
recognizes both difference and inclusivity.

In Chapter 9, Yusef Waghid and Nuraan Davids argue that schools
in post-apartheid South Africa are dysfunctional because of attempts
to divorce them from their history and social context. As they note,
the particular educational and political discourse that permeated and
shaped these schools was essentially one of remonstration, dissent, and
violent objection to the social situation of the time. This now manifests
in other unhealthy ways. In order, then, for democratic citizenship to
take hold, cosmopolitan education must embrace a culture of "hostipitality" in South African schools. Hostipitality requires respectful provocation that makes teachers and students alike distrustful of dystopias in
such a way that the dysfunctionality that has come about in post-apartheid South Africa might be disrupted and dealt with. This requires, they
argue, the nurturing of *ubuntu* (human interdependence) and responsibility in schools which must begin with teacher education. In the sense of

ubuntu, citizenship must reflect the idea that a person becomes a person in relation with other persons. From this framing, Waghid and Davids examine recent attempts in South Africa to promote moral education in the public schooling sector and advance a critical understanding of learning and teaching vis-à-vis the promotion of moral education qua citizenship education.

In Chapter 10, Andrés Mejía notes that Colombia declares the values of a liberal democracy in its Constitution. Nevertheless, he argues that there is a tension between liberalism and democracy. Liberalism is formulated within rationalism and individualism and, therefore, requires no political activity beyond securing one's negative freedoms. On the other hand, democracy is political and requires engagement with the other. Thus, there is always tension between liberalism and democracy and it is in this tension that a space opens for political action. Mejía Delgadillo then traces the development of citizenship education as it alternately reflects or deflects the liberal or democratic. One such deflection of the political is the entrance of standardized assessment into Colombian educational policy, especially assessment of the National Standards of Citizenship Competencies. Assessment policies, he argues, problematically drive a conception of citizenship "that can be described as psychologistic, formalistic, and largely apolitical."

In Chapter 11, Maria-Eugenia Luna-Elizarraras argues that recent political changes in Mexico (e.g., the electoral defeat in 2000 of Partido Revolucionario Institucional which had provided authoritarian rule for seventy years) have led to reconceptualizations of "citizen" and "citizenship." Even as government corruption continued, local social movements and market liberalization (resulting in increased economic disparity) required a more robust notion of citizenship as participatory (as opposed to the historically nationalist conception) and demands of accountability from government representatives. Luna-Elizarraras notes that educational reforms since 2000 have "included topics related to a participative democracy, in which a more active role is conferred to the citizen in democratic societies" and a trajectory toward a more cosmopolitan notion of citizenship. Nevertheless, pedagogical challenges remain due to an authoritarian school culture that does not reflect the more democratic vision represented in the curriculum. In the end, a community approach that involves all stakeholders in the decision-making process is required to move school culture. As Luna-Elizarraras concludes, "citizenship formation requires appreciation in schools as an opportunity to analyze the dynamics of social life and the school itself."

In Chapter 12, Peter Roberts, drawing on policy developments in New Zealand, provides an important redirection of our attention toward the role tertiary education can play in fostering critical citizenship. Roberts points out that emphasis in recent government policy has been on performance, accountability, relevance, and economic advancement or, as he puts it, on "the ontological construct homo economicus." Knowledge is, then, treated as a commodity, and competition within and between tertiary education institutions has been encouraged. Roberts problematizes these trends, arguing that they rest on a narrow, largely neoliberal conception of citizenship. Here we might say that Roberts rehearses for the tertiary level, the purposes of education discussed previously and mainly with K–12 education in mind. For example, echoing the overlap between, say, political and economic purposes, Roberts importantly points out that critical thinking, even at the tertiary level, has come to refer to a skills-based activity as opposed to involving critique, which is necessarily and importantly political. Furthermore, academics must be prepared to turn this critique upon ourselves and our institutions given that "the university is a political institution [and this] has never been more obvious, with commercial interests playing a more dominant and intrusive role in determining what forms of teaching and research are supported than ever before." We, as editors, set this chapter as the last from our contributors, hopefully provocatively, for it is with ourselves, perhaps, that we should begin.

Finally, in the Epilogue, we make the case for why citizenship education matters given our contemporary times. We begin by considering citizenship as an ongoing practice, requiring critical examination at local and global levels simultaneously. As the contributions to this volume illustrate, interrogations of citizenship education must consider how immediate contexts intermingle with larger socio-historical processes that can never be contained by national boundaries. As such, we expand on manifestations of citizenship education as presented in this volume through the lens of globalization generally and the production of the neoliberal citizen more specifically. Drawing on specific examples from the various chapters, we argue that the neoliberal citizen takes center stage in policy discussions, curricular formations, and pedagogical practices; citizens become visible and are defined by their adherence to neoliberal values and practices. As a point of resistance, we call for a rethinking of citizenship and citizenship education—one that moves beyond the commodification of knowledges and subjectivities into products meant for patriotic consumption. We, instead, offer the possibility of citizenship education as an intervention into the (re)production of the neoliberal order in our globalized times. Acts of citizenship cannot always be governed by the assumptive frame of neoliberalism—alternative practices of citizenship do exist even if they are not always made visible by the interpretive eye. These newly emergent critical practices might, in the end, be the means by which we read through dominant discourses, activated by the possibility for progressive social change.

NOTES

1. This is not to suggest an exhaustive set of purposes and we thank anonymous reviewers for adding others. For example, we might also include "personal purposes" to include moral and aesthetic development, health, physical fitness and the pursuit of happiness beyond the pecuniary. In this regard, Brighouse

argues for "educating for flourishing," not only in a self-interested way but also in ways that promote the flourishing of others. See Harry Brighouse, *On Education*, New York, NY, Routledge, 2006. For a similar discussion of these particular four purposes see Joel Spring, *American Education (16ᵗʰ ed.)*, New York, NY, McGraw-Hill, 2013.

2. Robert H. Wiebe, The Social Functions of Public Education. *American Quarterly, 21*(2), 1969, 150.
3. In U.S. schools, students stand to salute the flag with a pledge of allegiance. The wording of the pledge has changed several times over the decades, most importantly to add the words "under God" at the beginning of the cold war to distinguish from godless communism.
4. Cf. Amy Gutmann, *Democratic Education*, Princeton University Press, Princeton, NJ, 1999. For discussions of "reasonable" see John Rawls, *Political Liberalism*, Columbia University Press, New York, NY, 1996 and Brighouse, *On Education*.
5. Louis Althusser, *Lenin and Philosophy and Other Essays*, Monthly Review Press, New York, NY, 1971.
6. John E. Petrovic, "In Search of Equality of Educational Opportunity for Harrison Bergeron," in Jessica A. Heybach and Eric C. Sheffield (eds.), *Dystopia and Education: Insights into Theory, Praxis, and Policy in an Age of Utopia-Gone-Wrong*, Information Age Press, Charlotte, 2013, 181. The NFL is the National Football League in the United States; *Jersey Shore* is a reality television program; and *American Idol* is a televised reality singing competition.
7. Cf. Paulo Freire and Donaldo Macedo, *Literacy: Reading the Word and the World*, Bergin & Garvey, Westport, CT, 1987.
8. Georgi Dimitrov and Pepka Boyadjieva, Citizenship Education as an Instrument for Strengthening the State's Supremacy: An Apparent Paradox?, *Citizenship Studies, 13*(2), 2009, 156.
9. Cf. Benedict Anderson, *Imagined Communities: Reflections on the Origin and Spread of Nationalism*, Verso, New York, NY, 2006.
10. Sigal Ben-Porath, Citizenship as Shared Fate: Education for Membership in a Diverse Democracy, *Educational Theory, 62*(4), 2012, 382.

1 Citizenship Education in England in an Era of Perceived Globalisation
Recent Developments and Future Prospects

Ben Kisby

INTRODUCTION

This chapter[1] examines the development of citizenship education in England in the context of discourses of globalisation.[2] In particular, it discusses the notion of global citizenship education, which has gained prominence in the UK and elsewhere in recent years, especially amongst academics, teachers, and campaigners, in significant part as a result of the prevalence of debates about the meaning, nature, and impact of globalisation. The chapter argues that both the previous Labour government and the current Conservative-Liberal Democrat coalition have tended to view the requirements of globalisation and the requirements of neoliberalism as one and the same.[3] When last in power, Labour introduced a form of compulsory citizenship education into secondary schools in England that had a significant participative element, but at the same time the Labour government often advanced a very business-focused view of educational skill acquisition, especially with the international environment in mind. This chapter argues that this emphasis has intensified under the coalition government. It has adopted a lukewarm attitude toward citizenship lessons, proposing a very problematic, slimmed down citizenship curriculum, underpinned by a highly individualised, consumerist agenda. Moreover, it constructs the "international" in education largely in terms of young people as future workers and consumers in a competitive global economy, rather than as citizens acquiring knowledge, skills, and values that enable them to reflect on important historical and contemporary issues and to engage in forms of civic activity at both national and international levels. In light of these competing impulses, this chapter starts by asking: What is citizenship education?

WHAT IS CITIZENSHIP EDUCATION?

Citizenship is an "essentially contested concept" and, as such, citizenship education is a contested subject.[4] At a basic level, citizenship can be defined in terms of an individual's membership of a state or of a political community of some kind and the legal and moral rights and duties that this membership gives rise to. Citizenship then has legal dimensions, relating to both national and international law, defining who are and who are not citizens and who are and who are not accorded legal and other rights, and normative aspects, being concerned to specify how an individual citizen should behave and what it is about their behaviour that should be regarded as admirable or worthy of criticism. It can also be seen as relating to individual and group identities, to citizens' possession of particular values and virtues, and their rights and responsibilities, broadly conceived. Citizenship is a concept regularly invoked in discussions surrounding globalisation, immigration, asylum, and nationality. It is possible to understand modern conceptions of the citizen and debates about the meaning and nature of citizenship as deriving from two historical traditions: liberal and republican citizenship, with the former emphasising citizens' individual rights and the latter citizens' civic duties.[5] There are important contemporary debates around, for example, cosmopolitan, communitarian, multicultural, ecological, and feminist conceptions of citizenship, which seek in different ways to critique and/or build on these two core traditions.

Leaving aside those who are against citizenship education,[6] there are considerable differences of opinion regarding the appropriate content of citizenship lessons and modes of delivery to students among those who are in favour. The chapter is concerned principally with citizenship lessons in secondary schools and colleges,[7] as opposed to primary or higher education, or to forms of citizenship education for immigrants that are designed to enable non-citizens to become citizens. Whilst empirical studies can shed important light on the effectiveness or otherwise of particular forms of citizenship education, these issues are clearly, to a large extent, normative, since any attempt to address them necessarily relies on various assumptions about what the aims of citizenship education should be and how these objectives should manifest themselves in the citizenship syllabus; the role of schools, teachers, and students; and so on.

From the perspective advanced in this chapter, democracies need active and informed citizens, willing and able to play a part in the democratic process so as to safeguard and bolster democratic principles. Citizenship education seeks to address issues of general concern through collective action. It is important as a means of connecting young people to the political system, helping them make sense of a complex political world and thereby strengthening democracy. As such, citizenship education can be defined as a subject that is or ought to be concerned to provide students with knowledge and understanding of political ideas and concepts,[8] and local, regional, national, and international political processes and institutions; to develop students' skills so as to enable them to engage in decision making, critical thinking, debate, and (in ways of their own choosing) to participate effectively in political and democratic activities inside and outside school; and to instil in students particular values that make it likely they will want to engage in such activities.[9] It is not about attempting to create "perfect" or "model" citizens. It should certainly be very concerned with issues around rights and pluralism in the contemporary world—key liberal preoccupations. But if the aim is to promote a form of citizenship education that enables and encourages students to think critically about contemporary issues and to engage actively in political and civic participation so as to address such matters, as well as to protect and promote rights rather than to merely be aware of already existing legal rights, then it ought also to be informed by a conception of citizenship that owes a great deal to the republican tradition, in which citizenship is conceived of primarily as an activity rather than a status. The next section provides an overview of how citizenship education in England has developed in recent years.

CITIZENSHIP EDUCATION IN ENGLAND

Since 2002, citizenship education in England has been part of the non-statutory personal, social, and health education framework at primary level and a statutory subject in secondary schools. Prior to this, citizenship lessons had never been compulsory in English schools, although citizenship had been one of five non-compulsory, cross-curricular themes of the National Curriculum since 1990.[10] In fact, the history of citizenship education can be traced back much further than this—perhaps to 1934 and the formation of the Association for Education in Citizenship, which aimed to teach the children of ordinary people, and not just public school elites, about the merits of liberal democracy and the dangers of totalitarianism.[11] Indeed, some scholars trace political education in Britain back as far as the late eighteenth and early nineteenth centuries, to the university education of aspiring elites, which included some instruction in political leadership and patriotism.[12]

The decision to introduce citizenship as a statutory foundation subject in the National Curriculum was made clear by the incoming Labour government in its first education white paper, *Excellence in Schools*, published two months after the general election in May 1997. The white paper announced the formation of "an advisory group to discuss citizenship and the teaching of democracy" in schools.[13] Later that year, David Blunkett, Education Secretary at the time, announced that the group would be chaired by the political theorist and commentator, the late Bernard Crick, one of the leading figures who had been pushing for the different but related concept of political education in schools since the 1970s. However, Blunkett's view was that political education had too narrow an emphasis,[14] being preoccupied with political literacy,[15] and that citizenship education ought to be concerned more generally with how children should be taught to be citizens.

The Advisory Group on Citizenship (AGC) published its report, *Education for Citizenship and the Teaching of Democracy in Schools*, in

September 1998 and was one of the immediate causes of the inclusion of citizenship in the National Curriculum. The AGC's report provided the framework for citizenship education in England. It defined citizenship education in terms of three strands:

1. Social and moral responsibility—learning from the very beginning self-confidence and socially and morally responsible behaviour both in and beyond the classroom, both toward those in authority and toward each other;
2. Community involvement—learning and becoming helpfully involved in the life and concerns of their communities, including learning through community involvement and service to the community;
3. Political literacy—learning about and how to make themselves effective in public life through knowledge, skills, and values.[16]

Citizenship education was introduced in England principally because of concerns held by a range of actors, including politicians, academics, and pressure groups constituting an ideational policy network, about what they perceived as a decline in levels of social capital in Britain.[17] Such individuals and groups were particularly influenced by the neo-Tocquevillian conception of social capital advanced by the US political scientist Robert Putnam, for whom the concept refers to the social networks, such as networks of friends and neighbours and organizations like trade unions, churches, and schools, and the norms and trust that such networks give rise to, which allow citizens to work together to achieve collective goals.[18] Concerns about levels of social capital were a key driving force behind the development of New Labour's third way philosophy both in opposition and government, and senior Labour Party figures explicitly linked worries about stocks of social capital with the need to introduce citizenship lessons in schools. For example, Blunkett argued that the state must enable citizens to lead autonomous lives, especially through citizenship education. For Blunkett,

> it is clear that weak civic engagement and an absence of social capital deprives democracy of its vitality, health and legitimacy. A fully participatory democracy depends on sustained dialogue between free and equal, socially committed citizens . . . The State . . . can facilitate and provide the framework within which the greater strength of community and society can be brought to bear to support people in reaching their full potential . . . autonomy requires a rich and rounded education . . . If autonomy is dependent on education, and a fully autonomous person is also by definition an active citizen, then there needs to be explicit education for citizenship in the school and college curriculum.[19]

The impact of the concept of social capital on the citizenship education initiative can also be seen in the normative presuppositions underpinning the

AGC report.[20] Putnam does not detail the model of citizenship he believes most enhances levels of social capital. Nevertheless, the outlines of such a model can be discerned from his analysis. One of Putnam's key concerns is with political participation and arguably the biggest single influence upon his work is that of Tocqueville, usually regarded as a major thinker in the republican tradition.[21] However, Putnam's interest in civic virtue and emphasis on the extent to which this is reliant on community membership suggests that his thinking is also underpinned by a communitarian conception of citizenship. The normative model of citizenship that best corresponds to Putnam's concerns can then be described as a "republican-communitarian" model, broadly of the kind developed by Michael Sandel.[22] In Sandel's conception of citizenship, community membership is viewed as the pre-political, primary constitutive attachment upon the individual citizen, but he also conceives of citizenship as an activity, whereby citizens are concerned with achieving common goods.[23] Similarly, the principal aims of citizenship education in England are to teach young people to become well-informed, responsible citizens engaged in mainstream political and civic activities, such as voting, and undertaking voluntary work, in particular, at a local community level.[24]

The AGC report also marked an important shift away from the Marshallian conception of citizenship that had exerted a strong influence over the Labour Party in the postwar period until the late 1980s/early 1990s.[25] Although making reference to T.H. Marshall,[26] the report relied more on the key concerns of social capital theorists such as Putnam than the rights-based schema advanced by Marshall, focusing not on Marshall's conception of civil, political, and social rights but rather on "the interrelationships between norms and values, community, networks, civic engagement and democratisation."[27] The AGC report argues that welfare (Marshall's social rights) should be not only an instrument of the state but something that should also be provided by community organizations. In emphasizing the importance of social and moral responsibility and community involvement, defined in the particular ways that they are, the AGC report is, in effect, arguing that citizens have a moral obligation to undertake voluntary activity in the community and to take responsibility for their own individual welfare provision.[28]

Following Keith Ajegbo's review of diversity and citizenship in the curriculum,[29] published in January 2007 and welcomed by the Government,[30] from September 2007, governing bodies had a new duty to promote community cohesion and since September 2008 the secondary curriculum for citizenship education has included a new fourth strand: "identity and diversity: living together in the UK," which was introduced to go alongside the three initial strands, with school children now also taught about national, regional, ethnic, and religious cultures (and their connections), and to explore the concept of community cohesion. The Ajegbo report was consistent with New Labour concerns around patriotism and national identity and it marked an important shift of emphasis for citizenship lessons in England.[31] The call by Gordon Brown and others for a greater focus on "Britishness" and "British" values,[32] sparked a debate about the meaning of citizenship in the UK and led to the Goldsmith report on citizenship, which provided a relatively sophisticated approach to understanding multiple identities and citizenship, although its reform proposals focused on symbolic measures to strengthen British citizenship, such as citizenship ceremonies, and efforts to support volunteering.[33] However, it also led to the establishment of the Youth Citizenship Commission, which has undertaken much needed research on young people's understandings of citizenship and on increasing levels of political participation.[34]

At the time of writing, the final consultation on the UK government's revised National Curriculum for schools in England is coming to an end. The updated curriculum for citizenship will then be finalised and published and will be taught in schools from September 2014. The current Education Secretary, Michael Gove, has expressed concern about the country's position in international school league tables and argues that: "If our schools, and young people, are to become internationally competitive again we must learn from the best in the world."[35] For a long time after the Conservative-Liberal Democrat coalition government came to power in May 2010, it looked as though citizenship would be removed as a compulsory subject in the National Curriculum. Indeed this was the recommendation of the Curriculum Review Panel set up by the coalition government in January 2011. The panel's report was published in December 2011 and it took the (very questionable) view that citizenship is not a distinct subject as such and therefore its compulsory status in the National Curriculum should be revoked.[36] Given that the stated purpose of citizenship lessons was to increase levels of civic engagement and given that the evidence clearly suggests it is having some success in this regard, the logic of the panel seems rather peculiar.[37]

To the surprise of many, Gove rejected the panel's recommendation in February 2013 and made it clear that citizenship would be retained as a statutory foundation subject at secondary school level,[38] although unfortunately a great deal of momentum that had previously built up behind citizenship education was lost during the two years of uncertainty, as it was widely believed Gove did not support citizenship lessons. Indeed it was reported in the press in October 2012 that the government had considered removing citizenship education from the National Curriculum, but decided against this so as to avoid having to introduce new legislation to do so.[39] In fact, despite it remaining a compulsory subject, it is likely that significant numbers of young people will not receive any citizenship lessons because, at the time of writing, about 40 percent of secondary schools in England have become Academy schools (and were strongly encouraged by the government to do so),[40] and thus have the freedom to, among other things, opt out of following the National Curriculum. This stands in strong contrast to previous Conservative party policy; it was, in fact, a Conservative government that in 1988 introduced the National Curriculum, which was intended precisely to promote the idea of universalism, of all children being taught some of the same core subjects. Moreover, considerable concern has been expressed by citizenship education campaigners that the proposed new slimmed-down citizenship curriculum[41] is, in any case, very problematic, underpinned by a highly individualised, consumerist agenda—focusing on teaching about personal finance and financial services and products but not providing students with knowledge about public finance and economic decision making more broadly, for example.[42] It also seems to regard active citizenship as entirely synonymous with volunteering and is very unclear in its guidance about human rights teaching, among other issues.[43] It remains to be seen if an improved citizenship curriculum will emerge after the end of the consultation process.

WHAT IS GLOBALISATION?

The development of citizenship education in England has taken place against the background of significant debates about the meaning and nature of globalisation, which have impacted on how the UK government constructs the "international" in education. So what is "globalisation"? The term is pervasive in contemporary society but is hard to define. It is often viewed as relating to issues around interdependence between countries and the permeability of state borders, the development of supra-national organizations and global information and communications technology, the internationalisation of capital and culture, advances in transportation, and the impact of these trends on governments, businesses, and ordinary citizens, particularly as regards the exchange of resources and ideas, and forms of international interaction and integration. As a starting point, it can be said that the concept refers to an increased interconnectedness and interdependence of individuals and societies across the world affecting economic, social, cultural, environmental, security, and political matters and aspects of life. More precisely, Held et al. define globalisation as

> a process (or set of processes) which embodies a transformation in the spatial organization of social relations and transactions—assessed in terms of their extensity, intensity, velocity and impact—generating transcontinental or interregional flows and networks of activity, interaction, and the exercise of power.[44]

For theorists labelled "hyperglobalist" by Held et al.,[45] globalisation is defined in terms of such developments leading to a diminution of state sovereignty, whereby national borders are increasingly open to the flow of goods, services, capital, people, information, and ideas, and to the growing importance of the international institutions that promote these developments. For Ohmae, for example, putting forward what can be regarded as an American business school hyperglobalist perspective, the nation-state is becoming outdated as a "borderless" world emerges as a result of the development of information and communications technology, the geographical flexibility of large firms in terms of their ability to source capital and information from around the world, to locate and relocate in different countries and to sell products globally. Ohmae argues that the era of nation-states is ending with important economic decisions now being made at the regional level. He argues that "the modern nation-state itself—that artifact of the eighteenth and nineteenth centuries—has begun to crumble."[46] For Ohmae, the activities of large multinational corporations should be seen in a positive light and they must not be overburdened by regulations. In fact, for him, national level regulatory regimes and uneven regional development are unfortunate barriers to globalisation. The limitations of state power make the implementation of a neo-liberal policy agenda largely inevitable and certainly desirable. Ohmae's vision is one in which individual consumers can ensure all of their needs are met in the global marketplace—ignoring the important role that is or ought to be played by states in the provision of all sorts of important non-market, public goods—and where multinational corporations enjoy a great deal of power and are subject to very limited control by, or accountability to, national governments or international organisations, let alone ordinary citizens through democratic fora.[47]

Hyperglobalism has been strongly criticised by globalisation "sceptics," as they have been termed by Held et al.[48] Theorists such as Hirst and Thompson, for example, strongly reject hyperglobalist arguments of the kind put forward by Ohmae on both empirical and normative grounds. They question the extent of contemporary levels of international interdependence and integration when examined in historical terms. Indeed, they argue that in some respects the international economy may be regarded as less global than before 1914. They stress that businesses are still for the most part based nationally, even where they trade multinationally, and argue that there has not been an intensification of truly global economic interaction but rather a regional concentration of such activity, with international flows of capital concentrated within the core "triad" of Europe, North America, and Pacific Asia. Hirst and Thompson argue for the continued importance of nation-states at national and international levels of governance, both as a matter of fact and as something that is normatively desirable, emphasising that governments continue to retain significant political and economic power. For Hirst and Thompson, there is nothing inevitable about greater international economic integration. Rather, it is brought about by governments making particular political choices: neoliberal policies do not need to be introduced because of some irresistible forces of globalisation as claimed by some hyperglobalists.

A third perspective has been advanced by a number of theorists which Held et al. describe as "transformationalist."[49] Held et al., for example, agree with the hyperglobalists that there are real sets of processes taking place in the contemporary world that are appropriately labelled as representing forms of "globalisation." However, unlike the hyperglobalists, rather than positing a final destination to which states are headed, they argue that the outcomes of globalisation are uncertain and unpredictable. Held et al. conceive of globalisation as significantly more complicated and multidimensional than hyperglobalists claim. Unlike the globalisation sceptics, Held et al. argue that structural power has shifted to a significant extent from national governments to global markets and firms. They argue that the international economy is becoming an interconnected global economy. For Held et al., globalisation has a number of important political, cultural, and economic dimensions, which are seen as being transformed in global terms but which must also be viewed contextually: some states, societies, and communities are increasingly entangled, while others are excluded. Their view is not that nation-states are in terminal decline but rather that their nature and role is changing and that the division between domestic and international affairs is no longer clear.[50]

There is little doubt that the claims of hyperglobalists such as Ohmae are greatly overstated. Hirst and Thompson advance a powerful critique, making clear that the functioning of the contemporary international economy does not render national governments as weak and with as few viable policy options as hyperglobalists such as Ohmae believe. Nor are there good reasons for thinking that the world is moving inevitably toward a single, world market, in which nation-states will disappear and be replaced by global corporations. On the contrary, state power has been reasserted considerably in recent years so as to address the global financial crisis[51] and prevent the collapse of banks and the money markets.[52] However, Held and his co-authors make a persuasive case that there are significant differences between the international economy in the pre-1914 era and the situation over the past few decades. In particular, they argue strongly that there has been a general increase in international economic activity and greater trade and financial integration than in the past, and that markets are more open and that nation-states have less control over them. As such, Hirst and Thompson arguably underplay the limitations placed on national economies and states. Nevertheless, whether the differences Held and his colleagues point to should be seen as adding up to a qualitatively novel epoch of globalisation, distinct from earlier forms of international integration, is questionable. While real economic and, for that matter, social, cultural, and political changes do seem to be taking place, along the lines they suggest, it is perhaps an exaggeration to view these as significant enough to mark a new era as such—at least as yet.[53]

What is particularly important in a British context, in any case, is that politicians across the major parties have tended not only to accept globalisation as an empirical reality, but in fact to embrace to a large extent a hyperglobalist discourse. This, in turn, offers a justification for the imposition of neoliberal economic policy: there is no alternative in a globalised world it is argued; and, indeed, globalisation can be analyzed not only in terms of referring to a set of empirical forces and processes but also as a discourse relating to these forces and processes.[54] Certainly, under New Labour, globalisation tended to be presented as an inexorable force, with the concept constructed as a non-negotiable exogenous economic constraint, significantly limiting the boundaries of political choice open to governments. New Labour believed that in an era of increased capital mobility the policy choices open to it must be strictly in line with macroeconomic orthodoxy. The discourse of globalisation adopted by key New Labour figures, such as former UK Prime Minister Tony Blair, posited the exigencies of neoliberalism and the exigencies of globalisation as being one and the same. As such, it was the rhetorical articulation of a particular understanding of globalisation, rather than real changes in the international economy that the discourse employed by New Labour was attempting to represent, that made various policy choices "necessary" that were, in fact, contingent, thereby making the hyperglobalisation thesis, which predicts the spread of such financial and monetary orthodoxy, a self-fulfilling prophecy.[55] For Blair,

> the world has changed in a more fundamental way. Globalisation has transformed economies and our working practices . . . Many of our domestic problems are caused on the other side of the world. Financial instability in Asia destroys jobs in Chicago and in my own constituency in County Durham. . .We are all internationalists now, whether we like it or not. We cannot refuse to participate in global markets if we want to prosper . . . Any Government that thinks it can go it alone is wrong. If the markets don't like your policies they will punish you.[56]

The current UK Prime Minister, David Cameron, has sought to distance himself from an often uncritical rhetoric on globalisation deployed by key New Labour figures. In some respects, such as in relation to immigration and the UK's relationship with the EU more generally, he has sought to reassert the role that can be played by the nation-state. Nevertheless, in economic and social policy, the underlying message he has advanced has been similar to that put forward by Labour: that in the contemporary world, the UK needs to be more "competitive" than ever before and this necessitates the implementation of various policies to help ensure this. For Cameron, this means that the UK ought to engage to a greater extent with the fastest growing economies, the size of the British state should be reduced, public spending, especially social security or welfare spending, needs to be cut, and changes to the education system must be made so as to enable young people to "succeed" in the "global race." Cameron argues that there is simply no viable alternative to these policies in a "rapidly changing world," "a world that would be barely recognisable to previous generations" and in the context of an "era-shifting change in technology."[57] Cameron thus avoids some, but not all, of the hyperglobalist discourse deployed by Blair. But even where he adopts a more cautious tone than Blair with regard to globalisation, in reality the justifications he advances for the desirability of a fundamentally neoliberal agenda—which is being pursued by the current UK Conservative-Liberal Democrat coalition government to an even greater extent than under Labour—are essentially the same.[58]

WHAT IS GLOBAL CITIZENSHIP EDUCATION?

In the context of debates about globalisation, in recent years the notion of global citizenship education has gained prominence in the UK and elsewhere, especially among academics, teachers, and campaigners. What is global citizenship? Cosmopolitan or global conceptions of citizenship can be defined as relating to the idea that all human beings belong, or ought to see themselves as belonging, ultimately, to a single, world community. For example, Held envisages a democratic order in which citizens have rights and responsibilities both as national and cosmopolitan citizens. Held reaches this conclusion through an analysis of different aspects of globalisation, which, he argues, have given rise to a variety of developments, such as new forms of international decision making and the increasing scope and range of international communication systems, and to a range of problems, such as instability within the world economy, the proliferation of arms, and increasing levels of environmental degradation, that are necessarily transnational in nature. It follows for Held that if such international or global issues are to be tackled effectively there needs to be a development both of transnational political institutions and processes and transnational citizenship, in which individuals ought to be seen, and see themselves, both as citizens of particular states and as cosmopolitan citizens able to engage in different kinds of national and international political participation.[59]

As with citizenship and citizenship education, cosmopolitan citizenship and cosmopolitan or global citizenship education are contested concepts and subjects respectively. This chapter is treating cosmopolitan citizenship education and global citizenship education as one and the same, although global citizenship education is sometimes viewed as a broader notion, linking with various different forms of education, such as development education, anti-racist education, and peace education, whereas cosmopolitan citizenship education is sometimes regarded as being more narrowly focused on democratising international institutions. Global citizenship education can also be distinguished from global education, which can be seen as covering a more extensive range of forms of education.[60] Forms of global citizenship education[61] are underpinned by the notion of the interdependence of individuals, communities, and societies across the world and are concerned to provide students with knowledge, skills, and values that encourage and enable them to reflect on international issues, such as social justice, peace, diversity, discrimination, and the environment, and to engage in active global citizenship. That is to say, to engage in forms of civic and political participation so as to address such matters. In the UK, the idea that education should help promote a greater understanding of the wider world can be traced back to internationally minded teachers in the 1920s following the First World War and to later work in the post-Second World War period.[62] Subjects such as world studies, development studies, and peace studies have been taught in some British schools since the 1970s.[63]

More recently, Osler and Starkey have advanced a well-developed cosmopolitan approach to citizenship education. They are critical of national citizenship education programs because they do not adequately attend to the multiple identities and loyalties of young people living within culturally diverse communities, and instead rest on the notion of citizenship as exclusively relating to loyalty to a particular nation-state. This, Osler and Starkey believe, is especially problematic for members of minority groups who face particular formal and informal barriers to citizenship.[64] Adapting UNESCO's framework,[65] Osler and Starkey argue that "educated cosmopolitan citizens will be confident in their own identities" and will be willing and able to strive toward the goals of "peace, human rights, and democracy" at local and global levels[66] by:

- Accepting personal responsibility and recognizing the importance of civic commitment;
- Working collaboratively to solve problems and achieve a just, peaceful, and democratic community;
- Respecting diversity between people, according to gender, ethnicity, and culture;
- Recognizing that their own worldview is shaped by personal and societal history and by cultural tradition;
- Respecting the cultural heritage and protecting the environment;
- Promoting solidarity and equity at national and international levels.[67]

Oxfam has also developed a similar framework for global citizenship education that seeks to help students to develop the knowledge, skills, and values it believes are "needed for securing a just and sustainable world in which all may fulfil their potential."[68] Oxfam argues that in "a fast-changing and interdependent world" education for global citizenship "can, and should, help young people to meet the challenges they will confront now and in the future."[69] For Oxfam, global citizenship education "gives children and young people the opportunity to develop critical thinking about complex global issues in the safe space of the classroom" and encourages them "to explore, develop and express their own values and opinions, while listening to and respecting other people's points of view."[70] Oxfam identifies three main areas that are essential for the development of global citizenship: knowledge and understanding; skills; and values and attitudes. Knowledge and understanding, for Oxfam, relates to:

- Social justice and equity
- Diversity
- Globalisation and interdependence
- Sustainable development
- Peace and conflict

Oxfam defines skills in terms of:

- Critical thinking
- Ability to argue effectively
- Ability to challenge injustice and inequalities
- Respect for people and things
- Cooperation and conflict resolution

By values and attitudes, Oxfam is referring to:

- Sense of identity and self-esteem
- Empathy
- Commitment to social justice and equity
- Value and respect for diversity
- Concern for the environment and commitment to sustainable development
- Belief that people can make a difference.[71]

The next section suggests that such frameworks offer the clear potential to contribute greatly to young people's education for citizenship.

CONCLUSION

A key challenge to the notion of cosmopolitan or global citizenship is that it is principally focused on rights and on political participation rather than civic responsibilities, and that the republican virtues required of citizens are much more likely to be developed within national borders, where citizens have communal ties and relations of reciprocity and mutual trust, than where the only thing binding cosmopolitan citizens from different countries together is a shared commitment to addressing a particular issue in a certain way.[72] Nevertheless, while this chapter has questioned whether a qualitatively novel epoch of globalisation can be said to exist, the increasing importance of supranational political organizations, the internationalisation of capital, and advances in information and communications technology, are clearly very significant developments. The chapter has argued that the claims of hyperglobalists are greatly exaggerated, but given that there are good grounds for believing that there are economic and other processes at work in the contemporary world that are having real (if highly contested) impacts on states and citizens, to which "globalisation" is the label usually attached, given the prevalence of discourses relating to these forces and processes, and given the normative desirability of young people gaining a greater understanding of the wider world, it is entirely appropriate that pupils and students in schools engage with notions of the interdependence of individuals and societies and with issues that can be viewed as international in nature as part of their education for citizenship.

As such, while the 1998 AGC report has many merits,[73] not least its commitment both to pluralism and to participative democracy, it can reasonably be criticized, among other things, for containing within it little sense of the potential "international dimension" to citizenship education.[74] The clear, almost exclusive, emphasis in the AGC report is on developing a conception of citizenship that is situated within a specifically UK context rather than also making a strong case for viewing citizens as having rights and responsibilities both at a national and international level and being able to engage in forms of political participation beyond the level of the nation-state—although the 1999 Citizenship Order, which set out the programs of study for school pupils, does refer to pupils being taught about "the opportunities for individuals and voluntary groups to bring about social change locally, nationally, in Europe and internationally."[75] Moreover, during Labour's period in office some useful documents were published that sought to demonstrate how, for example, the "global dimension" could be incorporated into the school curriculum and in terms of schools developing partnerships with the wider community,[76] and which outlined the government's view of the "knowledge, skills, and understanding" it believed UK citizens needed "to live in and contribute effectively to a global society and to work in a competitive, global economy," albeit *Putting the World into World-Class Education* has a very business centred view of educational skill acquisition.[77]

As with the form of citizenship education advanced under Labour, the current UK government's proposed new citizenship curriculum is also very much focused on the UK, although it does contain brief references to students learning about action they can take "in democratic and electoral processes to influence decisions locally, nationally, and beyond" and to pupils being taught about "local, regional and international governance and the United Kingdom's relations with the rest of Europe, the Commonwealth and the wider world."[78] So, while the proposed curriculum is certainly very seriously underdeveloped from a global citizenship education perspective, there should continue at least to be scope for schools and teachers to address some pertinent issues. Nevertheless, the overriding focus of the coalition government, as set out in its white paper, *The Importance of Teaching*, is on improving the country's position in international surveys of educational attainment. Just as Labour emphasised the importance of students gaining particular skills so as to be able to "work in a competitive, global economy," so the PM and Deputy PM make clear in their foreword that, for them, "what really matters is how we're doing compared with our international competitors" in these league tables.[79] The white paper has nothing to say about citizenship or citizenship education. Consistent with Gove's and Cameron's comments highlighted earlier in this chapter, the only concern with the "global" in education here is that young people are "internationally competitive" and "succeed in the global race."[80]

Neither Labour during its last period in government nor the current Conservative-Liberal Democrat coalition have sought to systematically advance global citizenship education. Given the developments noted earlier, its prospects in England appear rather bleak at present, at least at the level of governmental support. There are, of course, teachers and schools that are very committed to global citizenship education, and aspects of it will continue to be taught in some schools. And as work by Osler and Starkey, Oxfam, and many others makes clear, the subject has the potential to make a significant contribution to young people's education for citizenship. It can, for example, highlight links between patterns of consumption by citizens in some countries and problems of various kinds—relating to the environment, workplace conditions, low wages, etc.—elsewhere. It can tackle misinformation and ignorance about the lives of people living in different parts of the world. It can address important issues around identity, social justice, and human rights. But unfortunately the UK government's almost exclusive focus is on what it sees as pupils and students as future workers and consumers in a competitive global economy, rather than on ensuring that schools inculcate in young people knowledge, skills, and values they need as citizens to reflect on matters of significant historical and contemporary concern and to engage in forms of political and civic activity at personal, local, regional, national, and international levels.

NOTES

1. I would like to thank the editors for their helpful comments on an earlier draft of this chapter.
2. The UK government has control over education policy only in England and citizenship education provision differs in the four UK home nations. At the time of writing, citizenship education in Wales is not a separate, discrete subject, but is delivered through Personal and Social Education (PSE), Education for Sustainable Development and Global Citizenship (ESDGC), and the Welsh Baccalaureate. PSE became a statutory component of the Welsh curriculum in September 2003 for ages 7 to 19. The future of ESDGC and citizenship education is being considered as part of a curriculum review that is taking place during 2013–14. In Scotland,

citizenship is a non-statutory component of the Scottish Curriculum for Excellence. It is not a separate subject but a cross-curricular theme that is supposed to pervade both the curriculum and also processes and practices of school life. In Northern Ireland, since September 2007, citizenship education provision for primary schools has been established as a strand within "Personal Development and Mutual Understanding." Secondary schools have seen the introduction of "Local and Global Citizenship" as a statutory component of the revised Northern Ireland Curriculum as part of "Learning for Life and Work." See Ben Kisby and James Sloam, "Citizenship, Democracy and Education in the UK: Towards a Common Framework for Citizenship Lessons in the Four Home Nations," *Parliamentary Affairs*, vol. 65, 2012.

3. By "neoliberal" I am referring to an ideology that advocates free market competition and private sector control of the economy through policies such as trade liberalisation, deregulation, and privatisation, and which argues against, and is keen to reduce, state intervention in the market and specifically is against state level measures aimed at reducing the high levels of economic inequality that inevitably result from such policies. For a more detailed definition and discussion, see Colin Hay, *Why We Hate Politics*, Polity, Cambridge, 2007, pp. 97–99.

4. Bernard Crick, *Essays on Citizenship*, Continuum, London, 2000, p. 3; Ruth Lister, *Citizenship: Feminist Perspectives*, Macmillan, Basingstoke, 1997, p. 3; David Miller, *Citizenship and National Identity*, Polity, Cambridge, 2000, p. 82. For a discussion of essentially contested concepts, see William Connolly, *The Terms of Political Discourse*, Martin Robertson, Oxford, 1983 [1974], ch. 1.

5. Derek Heater, *What is Citizenship?*, Polity, Cambridge, 1999, p. 4; Dawn Oliver and Derek Heater, *The Foundations of Citizenship*, Harvester Wheatsheaf, Hemel Hempstead, 1994.

6. For a free market libertarian critique of the state imposition of such education, see James Tooley, *Reclaiming Education*, Cassell, London, 2000, pp. 139–160. For an effective rebuttal, see Terence McLaughlin, "Citizenship Education in England: The Crick Report and Beyond," *Journal of Philosophy of Education*, vol. 34, 2000.

7. In England, this refers, from September 2013, to compulsory schooling for 11–17 year olds. This will rise to 18 from 2015; previously education was compulsory until age 16.

8. I define "politics" broadly as being concerned with the expression and resolution, or at least mitigation, of significant differences between people—differences of opinions, ideas, interests, and values, for example, and about finding ways of cooperating to achieve collective action and decision making. Politics relates to what happens in a wide range of institutional and non-institutional settings, and formal and informal groups and organizations; to activities in both the "public" sphere of the state and civil society and the "private" realm of personal relations, and arises because of the inevitability of disagreement about profoundly important matters, relating to how lives should be lived, how societies should be organized, how resources should be allocated and so on. Politics is concerned, in particular, with issues around power and the consequences for individuals and society of the distribution and exercise of power. For a discussion, see Colin Hay, *Political Analysis: A Critical Introduction*, Palgrave, Basingstoke, 2002, pp. 2–5.

9. Ben Kisby and James Sloam, "Revitalising Politics: The Role of Citizenship Education," *Representation*, vol. 45, 2009, pp. 316–319.

10. The National Curriculum Council, *Curriculum Guidance 3: The Whole Curriculum*, NCC, London, 1990; The National Curriculum Council, *Curriculum Guidance 8: Education for Citizenship*, NCC, London, 1990.
11. Guy Whitmarsh, "The Politics of Political Education: An Episode," *Journal of Curriculum Studies*, vol. 6, 1974.
12. Gordon Batho, "The History of the Teaching of Civics and Citizenship in English Schools," *The Curriculum Journal*, vol. 1, 1990; Derek Heater, "The History of Citizenship Education: A Comparative Outline," *Parliamentary Affairs*, vol. 55, 2002; Andrew Mycock, "Restricted Access: A History of National Political Education in Britain," unpublished paper, presented at the Political Studies Association Annual Conference, University of Lincoln, April, 2004.
13. Department for Education and Employment, *Excellence in Schools*, DFEE, London, 1997, p. 63.
14. Stephen Pollard, *David Blunkett*, Hodder & Stoughton, London, 2004, p. 262.
15. Bernard Crick and Derek Heater, *Essays on Political Education*, Falmer Press, Lewes, 1977; Bernard Crick and Alex Porter (eds.), *Political Education and Political Literacy*, Longman, London, 1978.
16. Department for Education and Employment/Qualifications and Curriculum Authority, *Education for Citizenship and the Teaching of Democracy in Schools*, DFEE/QCA, London, 1998, pp. 11–13.
17. For an alternative analysis of the introduction of citizenship education in England, which is rather more equivocal about the significance of the concept of social capital, see Jon Tonge, Andrew Mycock and Bob Jeffery, "Does Citizenship Education Make Young People Better-Engaged Citizens?" *Political Studies*, vol. 60, 2012. In the course of their important contribution to the debate about the impact and utility of citizenship education in England, their discussion, in my view, understates the significance of social capital for the citizenship education initiative. They do not draw enough attention to the vital influence of Putnam's particular conception of social capital on a range of key New Labour figures; they do not distinguish between the relative importance of Blunkett and Crick in the policy's development—Blunkett, in fact, was the single most important actor, the key policy entrepreneur, whose interest in social capital was deep and abiding; they do not discuss the major role played by various individuals and organisations outside of the AGC, which constituted an ideational policy network that was also principally motivated by concerns about perceived declining levels of social capital in Britain; nor do they sufficiently emphasise the extent to which these concerns were reflected in the normative presuppositions underpinning the AGC report. See Ben Kisby, "New Labour and Citizenship Education," *Parliamentary Affairs*, vol. 60, 2007; Ben Kisby, *The Labour Party and Citizenship Education: Policy Networks and the Introduction of Citizenship Lessons in Schools*, Manchester University Press, Manchester, 2012.
18. Robert Putnam, *Bowling Alone: The Collapse and Revival of American Community*, Simon & Schuster, New York, 2000; Robert Putnam with Robert Leonardi and Raffaella Nanetti, *Making Democracy Work: Civic Traditions in Modern Italy*, Princeton University Press, Princeton, NJ, 1993.
19. David Blunkett, *Politics and Progress: Renewing Democracy and Civil Society*, Politicos, London, 2001, pp. 26–29.
20. Ben Kisby, "Social Capital and Citizenship Lessons in England: Analysing the Presuppositions of Citizenship Education," *Education, Citizenship and Social Justice*, vol. 4, 2009.

21. Per Mouritsen, "What's the Civil in Civil Society? Robert Putnam, Italy and the Republican Tradition," *Political Studies*, vol. 51, 2003.
22. Michael Sandel, *Democracy's Discontent: America in search of a Public Philosophy*, Harvard University Press, Cambridge, MA, 1996; Michael Sandel, *Liberalism and the Limits of Justice*, Cambridge University Press, Cambridge, 1998.
23. Sandel, *Democracy's Discontent*, p. 117.
24. Kisby, "Social Capital and Citizenship Lessons in England."
25. David Marquand, "Half-way to Citizenship? The Labour Party and Constitutional Reform," in Martin Smith and Joanna Spear (eds.), *The Changing Labour Party*, Routledge, London, 1992.
26. DFEE/QCA, *Education for Citizenship and the Teaching of Democracy in Schools*, p. 10; see Thomas Humphrey Marshall, *Citizenship and Social Class and other essays*, Cambridge University Press, Cambridge, 1950.
27. Eva Gamarnikow and Anthony Green, "Social Capital and the Educated Citizen," *The School Field*, vol. X, 1999, p. 119.
28. Kisby, "Social Capital and Citizenship Lessons in England."
29. Department for Education and Skills, *Diversity and Citizenship Curriculum Review*, DFES, London, 2007.
30. See, for example, Alan Johnson, "New Citizenship Classes to emphasise British Identity," 25 January 2007, accessed 18 March 2007, http://www.24dash.com/content/news/viewNews.php?navID=48&newsID=15731.
31. See, for example, Gordon Brown, "Speech by the Rt. Hon. Gordon Brown MP, Chancellor of the Exchequer," the British Council annual lecture, 7 July 2004; Gordon Brown, "The Future of Britishness," Speech to the Fabian Society New Year Conference, 14 January 2006; The Stationery Office, *The Governance of Britain*, TSO, London, 2007.
32. For a discussion, see Rhys Andrews and Andrew Mycock, "Dilemmas of Devolution: The "Politics of Britishness" and Citizenship Education," *British Politics*, vol. 3, 2008.
33. Peter Goldsmith, *Citizenship: Our Common Bond*, Ministry of Justice, London, 2008.
34. Youth Citizenship Commission, *Making the Connection: Building Youth Citizenship in the UK: Final report of the Youth Citizenship Commission*, YCC, London, 2009.
35. Michael Gove, "Review of the National Curriculum in England," statement by the Secretary of State, Department for Education—Rt Hon Michael Gove MP, 19 December 2011.
36. Department for Education, *The Framework for the National Curriculum: A Report by the Expert Panel for the National Curriculum Review*, DFE, London, 2011.
37. Paul Whiteley, "Does Citizenship Education Work? Evidence from a Decade of Citizenship Education in Secondary Schools in England," *Parliamentary Affairs*, advanced access, 2012, p. 19.
38. House of Commons, Hansard, column 446, 7 February 2013.
39. Jack Grimston and Liz Lightfoot, "Children to be taught about 200 British Heroes," *The Sunday Times*, 14 October 2012, features, p. 2.
40. Paul Bolton, "Converter Academies: Statistics," Standard Notes: SN06233, House of Commons Library, London, June 12, 2013.
41. Department for Education, *The National Curriculum in England: Framework Document*, DFE, London, 2013, pp. 185–187.
42. Michael Grimes, "Teaching Economics Teaches Young People Who to Blame for their Problems," *New Statesman*, July 17, 2013, accessed July 25, 2013, http://www.newstatesman.com/business/2013/07/teaching-economics-teaches-young-people-who-blame-their-problems.

43. See Citizenship Foundation, "19 Days to make the Citizenship Curriculum Better," July 19, 2013, accessed July 25, 2013, http://www.citizenshipfoundation.org.uk/main/news.php?n1068.

44. David Held, Anthony McGrew, David Goldblatt and Jonathan Perraton, *Global Transformations: Politics, Economics and Culture*, Polity, Cambridge, 1999, p. 16.

45. See, for example, Kenichi Ohmae, *The Borderless World: Power and Strategy in the Interlinked Economy*, Collins, London, 1990; Kenichi Ohmae, *The End of the Nation State: The Rise of Regional Economies*, HarperCollins, London, 1995; Martin Albrow, *The Global Age: State and Society Beyond Modernity*, Polity, Cambridge, 1996; Robert Reich, *The Work of Nations: Preparing Ourselves for 21st century Capitalism*, Simon & Schuster, London, 1991; Susan Strange, *The Retreat of the State: The Diffusion of Power in the World Economy*, Cambridge University Press, Cambridge, 1996.

46. Ohmae, *The End of the Nation State*, p. 7.

47. For a perspective that could be defined as hyperglobalist but which views globalisation in profoundly negative terms, see Hans-Peter Martin and Harald Schumann, *The Global Trap: Globalization and the Assault on Prosperity and Democracy*, Zed, London, 1997.

48. See, for example, Paul Hirst and Grahame Thompson, *Globalization in Question: The International Economy and the Possibilities of Governance*, Polity, Cambridge, 1999 [1996]; Robert Gilpin, *Global Political Economy: Understanding the International Economic Order*, Princeton University Press, Princeton, NJ, 2001; Stephen Krasner, *Sovereignty: Organized Hypocrisy*, Princeton University Press, Princeton, NJ, 1999; Robert Wade, "Globalization and its Limits: Reports of the Death of the National Economy are Greatly Exaggerated," in Suzanne Berger and Ronald Dore (eds.), *National Diversity and Global Capitalism*, Cornell University Press, Ithaca, 1996; Linda Weiss, *The Myth of the Powerless State: Governing the Economy in a Global Era*, Polity, Cambridge, 1998.

49. See, for example, Held et al., *Global Transformations*; David Held and Anthony McGrew (eds.), *The Global Transformations Reader: An Introduction to the Globalization Debate*, Polity, Cambridge, 2003; Manuel Castells, *The Rise of the Network Society*, Blackwell, Oxford, 1996; Anthony Giddens, *The Consequences of Modernity*, Polity, Cambridge, 1991. Despite its usefulness, the Held et al. typology does have the effect in some cases of understating important ontological, epistemological, methodological, and normative differences between particular authors placed under the same label, while sometimes overplaying such differences between writers labelled differently.

50. Also of note has been work by those advancing a "new institutionalist" perspective on globalisation, who have argued that the forces and processes of globalisation are mediated by national institutions—see David Marsh, Nicola Smith, and Nicola Hothi, "Globalization and the State," in Colin Hay, Michael Lister and David Marsh (eds.), *The State: Theories and Issues*, Palgrave, Basingstoke, 2006, pp. 175–176. For example, for Weiss, globalisation is viewed as being embedded in the institutions of nation-states and either advanced or opposed by governments within the context of distinct national capitalisms, and Garrett argues that globalisation does not necessitate deregulated free market capitalism but rather requires policy coherence, whether neoliberal or social democratic; capital will not flee different kinds of regime, providing efficient policy combinations are advanced. See Weiss, *The Myth of the Powerless State*; and Geoffrey Garrett, *Partisan Politics in the Global Economy*, Cambridge University Press, Cambridge, 1998.

51. An important topic for discussion in citizenship lessons, one might think, but not, it would seem, according to the proposed new citizenship curriculum.

52. See Helen Thompson, "The Character of the State," in Colin Hay (ed.) *New Directions in Political Science: Responding to the Challenges of an Interdependent world*, Palgrave, Basingstoke, 2010.

53. As Martell argues, there is, in fact, quite a lot of common ground between the "sceptical" position advanced by Hirst and Thompson and the "transformationalist" perspective of Held et al., with some differences really matters of emphasis and characterisation. For example, Hirst and Thompson accept that there have been some significant changes in the international economy in recent decades and Held et al. accept that territorial boundaries continue to be important and that some nation-states may be able to be reconstituted in a globalising world in such a way that leads to a preservation or even an increase in powers. See Luke Martell, "The Third Wave in Globalization Theory," *International Studies Review*, vol. 9, 2007, pp. 185–192.

54. See, for example, Colin Hay, *The Political Economy of New Labour: Labouring under False Pretences?*, Manchester University Press, Manchester, 1999; Colin Hay and David Marsh (eds.), *Demystifying Globalization*, Palgrave, Basingstoke, 2000.

55. Matthew Watson and Colin Hay, "The Discourse of Globalisation and the Logic of No Alternative: Rendering the Contingent Necessary in the Political Economy of New Labour," *Policy & Politics*, vol. 31, 2003; Colin Hay, "'Taking Ideas Seriously' in Explanatory Political Analysis," *The British Journal of Politics & International Relations*, vol. 6, 2004.

56. Tony Blair, "Doctrine of the International Community," speech to the Economic Club of Chicago, Chicago, US, 22 April 1999. For Gordon Brown's similar views on financial markets, see Eric Shaw, *Losing Labour's Soul? New Labour and the Blair Government 1997–2007*, Routledge, Abingdon, 2007, p. 161.

57. David Cameron, "Plan for Britain's Success," speech given at DP World, London Gateway, June 10, 2013.

58. For a discussion of New Labour's ideology when it was in government, which argues that it is best viewed as a hybrid of social democracy and neoliberalism, see Kisby, *The Labour Party and Citizenship Education*, ch. 4.

59. David Held, *Democracy and the Global Order: From the Modern State to Cosmopolitan Governance*, Polity, Cambridge, 1995.

60. Lynn Davies, "Global Citizenship: Abstraction or Framework for Action?," *Educational Review*, vol. 58, 2006; Harriet Marshall, "Developing the Global Gaze in Citizenship Education: Exploring the Perspectives of Global Education NGO workers in England," *International Journal of Citizenship and Teacher Education*, vol. 1, 2005.

61. See, for example, Davies, "Global Citizenship: Abstraction or Framework for Action?"; and Nel Noddings (ed.), *Educating Citizens for Global Awareness*, Teachers' College Press, New York, 2005.

62. Derek Heater, *World Studies: Education for International Understanding in Britain*, Harrap, London, 1980, ch. 2.

63. Davies, "Global Citizenship: Abstraction or Framework for Action?", p. 6.

64. Audrey Osler and Hugh Starkey, "Learning for Cosmopolitan Citizenship: Theoretical Debates and Young People's Experiences," *Educational Review*, vol. 55, 2003, p. 244.

65. United Nations Educational, Scientific, and Cultural Organization, *Integrated Framework of Action on Education for Peace, Human Rights and Democracy*, UNESCO, Paris, 1995.

66. Osler and Starkey, "Learning for Cosmopolitan Citizenship: Theoretical Debates and Young People's Experiences," p. 246.

67. Osler and Starkey, "Learning for Cosmopolitan Citizenship: Theoretical Debates and Young People's Experiences," pp. 246–247; see also Audrey Osler and Hugh Starkey, *Changing Citizenship: Democracy and Inclusion in Education*, Open University Press, Maidenhead, 2005.

68. Oxfam, *Education for Global Citizenship: A Guide for Schools*, Oxfam, Oxford, 2006 [1997], p. 1.

69. Ibid.

70. Ibid., p. 2.

71. Ibid., p. 4.

72. Miller, *Citizenship and National Identity*, pp. 89–96.

73. DFEE/QCA, *Education for Citizenship and the Teaching of Democracy in Schools*.

74. Osler and Starkey, *Changing Citizenship*, p. 92.

75. Department for Education and Employment/Qualifications and Curriculum Authority, *Citizenship: The National Curriculum for England key Stages 3–4*, DFEE/QCA, London, 1999, p. 15.

76. Cathie Holden and David Hicks, "Making Global Connections: The Knowledge, Understanding and Motivation of Trainee Teachers," *Teaching and Teacher Education*, vol. 23, 2007, p. 15; see, for example, Department for International Development/Department for Education and Skills, *Developing the Global Dimension in the School Curriculum*, DFID/DFES, London, 2005.

77. Department for Education and Skills, *Putting the World into World-Class Education: An International Strategy for Education, Skills and Children's Services*, DFES, London, 2004, p. 1.

78. Department for Education, *The National Curriculum in England: Framework Document*, p. 186.

79. Department for Education, *The Importance of Teaching: The Schools White Paper 2010*, DFE, London, 2010, p. 3.

80. Gove, "Review of the National Curriculum in England"; Cameron, "Plan for Britain's success."

2 Who Belongs in What Hong Kong?
Citizenship Education in the Special Administrative Region

Liz Jackson

INTRODUCTION

The Special Administrative Region of Hong Kong grapples with an unusual challenge in conceiving of national identity and citizenship education today. From the perspective of global citizenship, it would seem to possess a unique advantage, as a community and culture which has developed for over a century with an outward-looking face. Historically and today, legal rights in Hong Kong have not been tied to ethnicity, language, or culture, but to residency and employment. Hong Kongers are, on the whole, proud to represent a liberal, cosmopolitan society: "Asia's world city." However, in having been "returned" from Great Britain to the People's Republic of China (mainland China) in 1997, the challenge of integrating legally and culturally with a larger nation-state at odds with liberal democracy is undeniable. That there is friction between the two entities is clear when it comes to mainland immigration policy and in stereotypes of mainland Chinese people ("New Arrivals") as less clean, civilized, and orderly than Hong Kongers. Ideological conflicts between the two related to ideals of citizenship are evident in debates about citizenship education in Hong Kong, which have increased in intensity over time.

This chapter focuses on challenges in developing citizenship education in Hong Kong today. First, I give an overview of the sociopolitical context of Hong Kong and the evolving question of the nature of Hong Kong national identity. I show how part of Hong Kong's colonial legacy as a transitory, depoliticized international community places it at odds with historically isolationist mainland China. This creates a challenge for citizenship education that aims to integrate Hong Kong with mainland China today, as Hong Kongers hold a multitiered conception of civic identity, affiliating meaningfully at local, national, and global levels. As Lee argues, this multitiered citizenship concept implies competing tensions in Hong Kong citizenship education, between "delocalized nationalization" and "localized internationalization," as Hong Kong's historical culture is much more globally oriented and pluralistic than that of mainland China.[1]

Then I examine additional issues related to the meaning of Hong Kong citizenship and its implications for education which have arisen more recently, in connection to the local government's 2012 push for "moral and *national* education" as a reform of existing "moral and *civic* education" (implemented in 2000). Though similar in tone, "moral and national education" (MNE) aims to bolster its precursor, "moral and civic education" (MCE), by making citizenship education a formal, timetabled subject within Hong Kong curriculum for the first time, thereby systematically increasing attention to mainland China. While the term "national" is key here, today's debates are not simply about whether or not more attention or affection to China is warranted, but about the nature of the relationship between China and Hong Kong, and about what kind of society Hong Kong is, as a form of ethnic-Chinese assimilationism has emerged in this context, that challenges a multicultural, multiethnic view of Hong Kong society.

I conclude by recommending intercultural civic education, which can enhance Hong Kong's outward-looking face with an orientation toward local-global diversity, and a focus on dialogue for the development of an expansive notion of shared-fate civic identity. Hong Kong and China lack the "shared histories, struggles, institutions, languages, and value commitments"[2] Ben-Porath suggests should be utilized and promoted in developing a sense of shared fate through citizenship. Indeed, Hong Kong internally lacks such homogeneity. Yet Ben-Porath's emphasis on citizenship education that connects "understanding of an individual's relations to the state with discussions of his or her relations to other members of the nation"[3] is nonetheless critical to Hong Kong's path forward in citizenship education, as diverse Hong Kongers must first develop mutual understanding and mutual recognition internally across different segments of society, in order to approach the tough questions they face about greater integration with mainland China in the future.

WHO IS HONG KONG?

Perhaps nowhere exemplifies the view of political entities as tenuous "imagined communities"[4] better than Hong Kong does today. Its colonial history plays an important role in present-day challenges in conceiving of citizenship education there, since the handover in 1997. Hong Kong was a transitory location for much of its history. When it was ceded from China to Britain in 1842, approximately 5,000 people lived there;[5] its population rose steadily thereafter, as people from nearby parts of China came for work or to avoid unrest, for temporary refuge rather than to make permanent homes. Local Chinese-colonial liaisons were not always facilitated by the British, but emerged pragmatically as they were in the interest of both parties, each of which was in Hong Kong for economic opportunities arising with the colony.[6] Highly diverse from the start, colonial Hong Kong never had assimilationist policies, in education or elsewhere. Sweeting thus describes Hong Kong as more *wok* than melting pot, as "various separate ingredients are rapidly and briefly stir-friend in a very heated and high-pressured atmosphere. . .their tastes rarely mix."[7]

The "transitization" of Hong Kong—its colonial development as a place to make money, but not a home—discouraged long-term, large-scale educational development. As the first director of education E.A. Irving wrote in 1905, "What becomes of the hopes of those who aspire to raise the standard of education in Hong Kong to a uniformly high level? As well hope to raise the standard of education in Charing Cross Hotel!"[8] His successor likewise compared his work to that of running a school at Victoria Station. At the turn of the twentieth century, schooling followed a British model which was minimal in local intervention. Local Chinese educational institutions were tolerated alongside colonial, missionary, and private schools, though their leadership was sometimes altered to provide more pro-Christian orientations.[9] The society emerging at this time was not only Chinese and British, but also Portuguese and Indian, as this 1924 report points out:

> The number and circumstances of British children in this distant Colony make it at once feasible and desirable to provide them all with an education . . . as nearly as possible equal and similar to what they could find *at home* . . .
>
> Other communities for which separate provision for education is needed are the Portuguese and the Indian . . .
>
> The problem of Chinese children is different. Their numbers are so large that it is impossible for the Government to take charge of the education of all. . . .[10]

As Chinese nationalism against colonialism flared from time to time, schools were prohibited from engaging in education which was seen as "in any way political" until 1990.[11] This "depoliticization" was seen as necessary to neither promote nor defame mainland China, as the British colony depended on China for food and natural resources, but also wished to avoid any social instability in Hong Kong arising from local ideological identification with China. In 1971, this policy was crystallized in Educational Regulations as follows:

> No instruction, education, entertainment, recreation or propaganda or any activity of any kind which, in the opinion of the Director, is in any way of a political or partly political nature or prejudicial to the public interest or the welfare of the pupils or of education generally. . .shall be permitted upon any school premises. . .No salutes, songs, dances, slogans, uniforms, flags, documents or symbols which, in the opinion of the Director, are in any way of a political or partly political nature shall be used, displayed or worn. . . .[12]

Socially oriented education focused on basic laws and commercial and industrial goals, shared by colonialists, Chinese residents, and other immigrants and refugees increasingly coming from Europe and elsewhere in Southeast Asia, for short and long stays. Moral education was seen as relatively unproblematic by colonial authorities, as different communities were largely free to teach according to diverse cultural and religious values while living under Hong Kong Basic Law. "Civics" focused on responsibilities to larger legal entities, and loyalty to family, friends, school, and employers, but no attempt was made to suggest belonging to Hong Kong or to conceptualize Hong Kong as a complete or independent, permanent entity.[13] While Hong Kong as a law-based liberal society was emphasized, the historical sense of Hong Kongers as a temporary and incidental collectivity of people not bound by shared values, customs, or cultures thus precluded early development of notions of shared-fate citizenship, the view of Hong Kong as a community or independent entity with a distinctive orientation to the rest of the world.[14]

In the 1970s and 1980s, Chinese people in Hong Kong and non-Chinese expatriates (usually British) began to see themselves as Hong Kongers, identifying Hong Kong as their home for the first time, despite the government's historical efforts toward depoliticizing the society. Given increasing political instability in mainland China, many Chinese people in Hong Kong in this same time period became "astronauts," taking steps to move outside Asia, to Australia, Canada, or the United States, in anticipation of the handover, to be completed in 1997.[15] Approximately one-sixth of Hong Kong's residents moved abroad during this period, and one-third of this group has since returned.[16] The process of the transition of sovereignty officially began with the Sino-British Joint Declaration on the Question of Hong Kong in 1984. In 1985, the Hong Kong government published new guidelines on civic education, which emphasized for the first time loyalty to large-scale political entities: Hong Kong and mainland China. Though it was agreed at this time that Hong Kong would continue to follow liberal democratic legal traditions within the "one country, two systems" policy, there was also a sense that effort would need to be put into integrating Hong Kong culturally and conceptually with China after a century of increased separation. The 1985 guidelines emphasized the following:

- Sense of national identity and belonging
- Love for the nation and pride in being Chinese
- Respect for Chinese culture and tradition
- Willingness to contribute toward the economic development of China
- Appreciate the need for interdependence
- Appreciate the importance of the role of China in maintaining stability and prosperity in Hong Kong
- Appreciate the contribution of Hong Kong toward the modernization programs of China[17]

One sees in these early guidelines attention to China and Hong Kong's interdependence for their future success. That Hong Kong and China must work together to mutually benefit aligns with Ben-Porath's view of shared-fate citizenship, as the guidelines suggest that "one's fate is shared with that of his or her compatriots [in] the nation (rather than subgroups or the global community)."[18] After the publication of these guidelines, the government provided subsidies to implement changes through development of new curriculum, and in 1988 a new school subject on Hong Kong and China was introduced. However, many saw these changes as superficial, as new subjects were offered in less than 20 percent of schools, and were then often elective, unpopular, and studied by only a handful of Hong Kong students.[19] What the guidelines required was the inclusion of civic education elements into the total school environment as local educational leaders saw fit, within the highly decentralized educational system that had developed over the decades of colonial rule. Typically, adding civic elements to formal education involved extracurricular rather than content additions, such as school assemblies, field trips, and exchanges.[20] Educators were not provided with training or formal assistance to provide civic education, and most were unenthusiastic at the time about educational reform in general, as government interventions were numerous during the transition, to increase global competitiveness.[21]

Many see early attempts at developing civic education as intentionally weak on the part of a tentative and transitional government which aimed to avoid controversy during the transfer of sovereignty. In general, Hong Kongers were anxious about their national status at the time of the handover: uncertain how to identify with mainland China politically, without aligning with the Communist Party of China, which many have very negative attitudes toward. The distinct regional legal status of Hong Kongers also precludes any easy political identification with mainland China for most, who still remain citizens only of the Special Administrative Region, not entirely free to travel in mainland China, or liable to its laws. Surveys conducted in the late 1990s and 2000s show fluctuations in Hong Konger identification with mainland China when asked to give their nationality or preferred nationality.[22] In a survey comparing Hong Kong and mainland students' political attitudes after the handover, Fairbrother noted that in all dimensions of national attitudes mainland students were much more positive.[23] Both groups were patriotic in the sense of having a general pride in Chinese culture, including the language, history, philosophy, and art. In Hong Kong this can be explained in part by a course in Chinese history which remains prevalent today, which avoids the modern era or questions of identity in favor of a more abstract, historical approach. However, when it came to the Chinese nation, Hong Kong students were ambivalent or outright negative about the modern country and its symbols, such as the national anthem.

In this context, citizenship education which focuses on cultural distinctions of China or the Chinese people is more palatable to Hong Kong students than nationalistic approaches which focus on the modern nation-state of China. Lai and Byram thus argue that Hong Kong is similar to other Asian societies in prioritizing a "cultural" national identity in citizenship education.[24] National identity in Asian societies, they write, is "based on particular exclusive cultural legacies," and citizenship education is thus conceived as a framework of cultural distinction, in courses such as Chinese history.[25] However, Hong Kong is different from many other Asian societies in having a longstanding foundation in rule of law, without a historical or permanent cultural community before the British colonial period. Thus, in Hong Kong today, most ethnic-Chinese Hong Kongers conceive of Hong Kong national identity and culture as a blend of Chinese and British/Western liberal democratic components. "Liberal Studies," Hong Kong's secondary-level social studies subject of today, stresses this blend of cultures as foundational to Hong Kong. As one textbook notes,

> Yuanyang is probably the most endemic beverage of Hong Kong . . .
> It is a product created by integrating several food cultures: tea from China served the British way with milk and blended with coffee from Africa. It fully reflects Hong Kong's unique cultural diversity as well as the ability of Hong Kong people to create their own unique local culture from different cultures.[26]

Here national identity seems aligned with a cosmopolitan view, and Hong Kong society is clearly marked as a melting pot, a place where something distinct arises out of heterogeneous materials. This is not a culturally Chinese or Chinese-facing depiction of Hong Kong.

Furthermore, given China's relative isolationism during Hong Kong's colonial period, Hong Kong's culture is distinct from mainland China's and more globally oriented. Lee emphasizes tensions within a multitiered conception of Hong Kong citizenship (as local/territorial, national, and global), which simultaneously involves "delocalized nationalization" and "localized internationalization."[27] As proponents of citizenship education in Hong Kong makes strides toward conceptual integration with mainland China, they ask teachers to orient student allegiance from the local/regional level of Hong Kong to a nation-state level, deemphasizing local distinction in favor of national commonality (although mainland China is hardly homogeneous in reality, itself). On the other hand, it is traditional in Hong Kong to identify oneself with a global level of citizenship, with laws of free trade and personal freedom regardless of culture, nationality, or ethnicity, so this latter form of citizenship education is favored for its connection with values perceived as more Hong Konger than Chinese, such as pluralism, democracy, freedom, tolerance, equal opportunities, and human rights.

Thus, while in many countries globalization seems to be the alternative to local or regional agendas which might overemphasize global economic concerns about free trade over local needs, in Hong Kong global and local economic and political values converge and contrast with those of nation-state citizenship, with the latter representing to many Hong Kongers a regression in political development, to a less just, unequal civic environment. There is little apparent conflict in Hong Kong today over globalization's impact on education (aside from educator fatigue due to ongoing reform), as Hong Kong has historically been seen as a place for global trade, capitalism, and entrepreneurship. Yet the idea of Chinese political tradition, which clearly conflicts with capitalist economics historically, is hard for Hong Kongers to embrace or even tolerate, indicating nationalism versus regionalism as a larger educational challenge. Identities in Hong Kong remain multifaceted and multilayered today, existing meaningfully within local, national, and global dimensions.

THE CHALLENGE OF MOVING FROM "CIVIC" TO "NATIONAL"

Since the 1985 guidelines, mainland China "elements"—mostly cultural discussions—have been gradually increased within a civic education framework and in the Liberal Studies curriculum. In 1995, revised civic education guidelines were published, which focused more on developing "positive attitudes and values conducive to the development of a sense of belonging to Hong Kong *and* China, so that [students] are ready to contribute to the betterment of society, the state, and the world."[28] The guidelines took a pluralist orientation toward differences between the two systems, stating that critical thinking and valuing democracy were important, while students should also learn to understand the ideologies "the Chinese government is upholding, i.e. socialism and communism; the economic system . . . the administrative system, especially the fundamental mechanism of democratic centralism and the Party."[29] In 2000, "moral and civic education" was made an overall aim of education in the reform *Learning for Life, Learning through Life*. The government continued to promote a "whole school" approach to the subject rather than conceiving it as a separate course, however, leaving educators to do what they pleased, which was often very little apart from perhaps studying controversial issues related to Hong Kong-China policies as part of current events.

Teachers who have been active in developing and teaching moral and civic education in the twenty-first century have focused on local, global, and moral elements, often avoiding politics or the Chinese nation-state, encouraging students to compare the values of Hong Kong and China but not discussing ideas of Hong Kong or Chinese citizenship. This is in alignment with traditional approaches to civic education in Hong Kong, as political education was banned in the colonial period, and perhaps also reflects ambivalence of educators during this time about issues of nationality and political identity. As Lai and Byram document, within a yearlong civic education program, educators discuss China rarely, and even then focus on political aspects apart from the functioning of the government examining, for instance, child poverty in poor regions, but not commenting on its relation to national or party activities or lack thereof.[30] Extracurricular elements also supported political learning with a local or global rather than national orientation, such as a democracy wall on campus, the encouragement of student governance organization, and philanthropic engagement with countries worldwide facing financial or other disasters, highlighting localized internationalization rather than delocalized nationalization, as discussed previously.

Despite the government's expressed hopes, such a curriculum could hardly promote a pluralistic, optimistic approach to mainland Chinese political ideology in schools, as most Hong Kong educators do not relate favorably to mainland Chinese political issues and will therefore teach about them (*if* they teach about them) in an outsider, ethnocentric way, in relation to teaching competing local values of democracy and human rights. Most local educators are Hong Kongers who have never lived in mainland China, but might have lived in Australia, Canada, or the United States. Thus, ambivalence and avoidance of controversy comingled for the first fifteen years of "one country, two systems," and pluralistic integrationist citizenship education was on the whole sporadic and ineffective in this context.

In early 2011, the Hong Kong government's Education Bureau announced a new subject would be implemented starting in the 2012–2013 school year, "moral and national education" (MNE). The Education Bureau Curriculum Development Council released a consultative document of the proposed curriculum and invited conversation and dialogue within all of Hong Kong on the content. From an outsider perspective, the document contained little that was new or surprising. It again stressed the inclusion of Chinese elements, including Chinese history and an understanding of contemporary society, politics, and ideology. It maintained that students should appreciate that they are a part of Hong Kong, China, and the world, and strive to have a positive, participatory role within each sphere. It emphasized developing student "affection" for mainland China and a sense of shared fate, which have been part of the government's formal position on civic education since the 1980s, repeating to a large extent the content of historical guidelines discussed previously.

Nonetheless, MNE opened the floodgates to anxieties across diverse subsections of Hong Kong, which had grown over the last few decades, about Hong Kong's status and preservation of its way of life within mainland China. Loud criticisms and protests of the proposed curriculum emerged rapidly and developed into a large-scale movement of students, parents, and educators, which culminated in mass protests in the summer of 2012. According to the Education Bureau (EB), in four months it received 1,000 comments on the document, in areas related to curriculum, implementation, and assessment.[31] Issues with the new proposal related to (a) concerns over brainwashing, assessment, and implementation; (b) its symbolism of wider social fears about the mainland Chinese government's imposition in

Hong Kong; and (c) its implications for describing and defining Hong Kong national or cultural identity. I describe these concerns in turn.

Concerns over Brainwashing, Assessment, and Implementation

A first issue related to curriculum involved a recent handbook published by the National Education Services Centre, a private pro-China organization which receives funding from the EB. Entitled "The China Model Handbook," this text was the EB's worst enemy when it came to MNE, for many people conflated the handbook with MNE curriculum, and remained suspicious of the relationship between the two, despite repeated government attempts to distinguish them and distance themselves from the "China Model."[32] The handbook, only published in Chinese, promotes Chinese socialism, the Communist Party of China, and the one-party system, arguing that Western-style democracy is divisive, unjust, and ineffective. The handbook describes the Communist Party as "advanced, selfless and united," and defends the government's actions in the July Fourth Incident of 1989. This is an incident many Hong Kongers feel deeply about, as many personally supported Chinese student leaders of the democratic movement, which ended in violent repression and defeat in Tiananmen Square with hundreds if not thousands killed.[33]

In this political context, many of those protesting the new curriculum emphasized its intention to white-wash modern Chinese history and "brainwash." Hong Kongers are deeply suspicious of any citizenship education that promotes allegiance to a government or political entity because of (a) their own experience of often thoroughly depoliticized civic education, and (b) their knowledge of patriotic education in mainland China, where the Communist Party has focused a great deal of effort on national education, which originally emphasized memorization of quotations by Chairman Mao and the related development of affective attachment to Mao and the party. Such fears have been further exacerbated by a now-infamous public statement made by a mainland Chinese official based in Hong Kong, Hao Tie-chuan, in defense of "brainwashing," although he seems to understand the term here as indicating a basic, content-oriented education, rather than an education that permanently harms student autonomy:

> Some people say that the moral and national education in primary and secondary school in Hong Kong is brain-washing, if you take a look at the education systems in western countries like the United States and France, such brain-washing is a necessity and international norm. Some say it is necessary to develop critical thinking among primary and secondary school children, but the common practice in international society is to cultivate critical consciousness in university education.[34]

In this Chinese/party context, Hong Kongers thus reasonably worry that the Hong Kong government is asking educators to promote affective feelings instead of critical thinking in Hong Kong schools, representing to them a political and ideological regression, in moving away from education for liberal democracy. The Hong Kongers thus argued against the proposed curriculum that mainland Chinese people suffer from brainwashing, although studies suggest that mainland students today are often quite skeptical and think critically about national politics and governance, while in Hong Kong students commonly lack a critical orientation or curiosity about current politics and events.[35] Nonetheless, political repression in mainland China at a larger scale, such as the historical ban of religions by the Communist Party in its early leadership, no doubt also fuels popular perception in Hong Kong that people are brainwashed in China.

The relationship between critical thinking and teaching of affection and appropriate moral values is also confusing as it is elaborated in the proposed curriculum. Splitter contrasts the guidelines' lofty references to students making independent judgments and engaging in personal values clarification, with highly specific discussions of the values and virtues MNE *intends* to cultivate, including "Chinese virtues," such as wisdom and filial piety, and "universal values." Given this, Splitter argues that the curriculum might reasonably be accused of brainwashing, for its intended affective learning outcomes of loyalty and a strong sense of national allegiance. On the other hand, teaching for affective changes in the very academically focused Hong Kong of today is no straightforward task, despite common fears about brainwashing; even if teachers attempted to teach in order to brainwash, many students would likely remain apathetic, given the lack of substantial mainland Chinese affection on the part of ordinary educators.[36]

Speculation about modes of assessment also reflects the broad fear of emotional brainwashing as an intended outcome of MNE, as an August 2012 EB document on "concerns and clarifications" summarizes:

Concern 9: MNE requires teachers to assess "students' change in their perception of values." This is a reform of their mind.

Concern 10: Students can only gain marks in the MNE assessment by showing that they are "moved."

Concern 11: National education only places emphases on "instillation of emotions and recognition of China," but ignores facts.[37]

To address these concerns, the EB responds that teachers should not mark students on or aim to instill any particular values, that independent thinking is prioritized over emotional changes, and that teachers should simply provide for and encourage student self-reflection about China's strengths and weaknesses. Yet the concerns remain justifiable in light of the specific examples and aspects of Chinese society the curriculum documents encourage teachers to deal with. While no topics are explicitly censored, there are few negative references to China apart from vague discussions of "strengths and weaknesses" and "development challenges," but a lengthy list of specific neutral and/or positive things identified as potential classroom topics. For instance, the four proposed learning objectives for the national domain (the curriculum considers the local, national, and global domains) for grades 1–3 include:

- Appreciate the richness and beauty . . .
- Cultivate national identity . . .
- Trace traditional Chinese customs . . .
- Learn the admirable character and virtues of outstanding figures . . .[38]

Only twice are challenges that mainland China faces mentioned, and this is at the secondary level:

- Understand the opportunities and challenges facing the country through rendering concern for its important developments and plans
- Probe into significant historical events in the country from a holistic perspective and draw comparison with major work events of the age, understand the course of internal hardships and external challenges facing the country prior to its reform and opening-up, and realize the adversities, struggles, development and accomplishments during the course[39]

While there are negative things about mainland China one can identify and could teach, doing so is not explicitly promoted, while references to positive aspects of China worth teaching seem endless in the curriculum guides. Given the overall social and political context, it is understandable that people would be wary about this reform. Even Lai and Byram, who are optimistic about citizenship education in Hong Kong, describe the government's policy as "giving a free hand for schools to do anything they like as long as they are not doing things anti-governmental, un-patriotic or anti-nationalistic."[40] Yet in practice one cannot avoid being anti-governmental in Chinese Hong Kong under "one country, two systems," without simultaneously endorsing and denigrating democracy, liberalism, and the rule of law. Thus a common sentiment among some faction of protestors, particularly students, is that the curriculum precludes examining what they need to know about mainland China, which should be historical and contemporary facts and events, rather than feelings of concern and affection, which seem more strongly emphasized by the EB.[41]

There are additional practical concerns related to the overall reform context of Hong Kong. Liberal Studies was introduced only in 2009, and mandates significant coverage of Hong Kong, globalization, modern mainland China, and the nature of student identity. Thus, there is significant overlap of the proposed MNE with Liberal Studies. Additionally, little time was given to prepare for Liberal Studies, and so teachers are still playing catch-up, while they are being asked to introduce the new MNE. There does not seem to be any direct answer to questions of how such a new subject will be added into full timetables, or monitored, resourced, or assessed. Some also express discontent with the consultation and implementation schedule originally proposed, suggesting that if the Education Bureau and Curriculum Development Council truly wanted to encourage the public to express their views and develop consensus on the subject, the consultation period would have been made longer and more systematic.[42] These concerns speak to challenges within the larger reform environment of Hong Kong education, wherein educators are exhausted by continuous change and skeptical about the potential of new ideas coming from above.

Concerns over Mainland Chinese Interventions

Local political issues also lead many to fear inappropriate mainland Chinese intervention in the educational system and elsewhere, which is another cause of protestation of MNE. Anti-mainland and anti-"New Arrival" sentiment have risen since the handover, particularly in the last five or so years, related to a number of political, economic, and cultural factors. For example, politically, pro-Chinese political factions have been increasingly well organized in electoral politics, with people suggesting they are engaging in voting fraud, and the mainland government is understood to have delayed universal suffrage of the chief executive of Hong Kong, which was promised at the handover.[43] Economically, property costs have risen while salaries remained the same amidst efforts to integrate the two economic systems. Linguistically, the use of Putonghua (Mandarin) has increased in institutions over the locally used Cantonese, though many Hong Kongers have little ability with the former. And culturally, incidences of smuggling milk powder (baby formula) from Hong Kong to China, resulting in milk powder shortages in Hong Kong, and the rise of mainland women giving birth in Hong Kong are further trends which grate on local sensibilities.

Chou also observes that increased interpersonal contact between Hong Kongers and New Arrivals (the majority of whom arrive to Hong Kong as economically disadvantaged) has generated culture shock among Hong Kongers, as "the difference in hygiene, manner, and other personal habits triggered much public discontent, especially in cyberspace in which abrasive words were often exchanged."[44] Though the local media can be seen to fuel such cultural shock in focusing on the controversial aspects of integration and movement of New Arrivals to Hong Kong, this complex mix of political, economic, and cultural concerns creates a setting where MNE is the tip of a political iceberg, rather than an isolated incident of the public responding unfavorably to a curriculum proposal.

What Kind of Citizens?

A final series of concerns comes from the point of view of "ethnic minorities," or non-Chinese Hong Kongers. To the extent that moral and civic education has so far been tolerated and successful in Hong Kong, it has relied upon the idea that Hong Kong shares ethnic ties with mainland China: that Hong Kongers are at a basic level "Chinese." This commonality rings true when one considers that despite a century of political separation, mainland China is a pluralist nation-state today (with many ethnic minority groups), and ethnic-Chinese Hong Kongers continue to follow Cantonese and other traditions which might be held at a general, global level, as "Chinese." As mentioned earlier, there has been a kind of compromise position strived for by educators who focus on common culture to arrive at common nationality, regardless of the political tensions between Hong Kong and China. This sentiment is dramatically employed in some instances by emphasizing a "blood relation" between all Chinese people, uniting (Chinese) Hong Kongers and mainland Chinese. For instance, consider this quote from a current Liberal Studies textbook which focuses on Hong Kong national identity:

> The most unforgettable moment was when the Chinese national flag was raised and the British one lowered. At that time, I was stirred. On the one hand I did not want changes to the current situation under British rule and felt sad about their departure. On the other hand, I was more worried that the development of Hong Kong would fall behind. Today, when I watched the memorial activities for the 10th anniversary of the Handover on television, I was similarly stirred when the national flag was raised. But this time I was touched by *the blood relationship with the motherland*. . .All of the sudden, I felt so proud of being Chinese.[45]

For many protestors of MNE this common cultural and ethnic "Chineseness" is assumed; indeed, many see this common culture and ethnic background as a starting point for developing mutual understanding of Hong Kong with the mainland through a *better* form of MCE or MNE. However, Hong Kong is not a homogeneous society from an ethnic or cultural standpoint. Just over 90 percent of the population is ethnically Chinese today, but this number is decreasing while ethnic/national groups including Indonesian, Indian, white, Filipino, Pakistani, and Nepalese are on the rise. For these populations, who often also regard Hong Kong as their home, orientations such as that employed in the above textbook extract and learning outcomes encouraging students to see themselves as fundamentally Chinese are disturbing. Those who are not Chinese feel invisible in such statements, as if they do not belong, though permanent legal residency is not based on ethnicity, language, or culture in Hong Kong. No doubt, focusing on shared cultural and ethnic elements has been seen as an easy path toward further integration, but it also leads to alienation of some Hong Kongers, and an increasingly exclusive view of Hong Kong nationality and identity, as delocalized nationalization conflicts with localized internationalization at the level of civic identity.

Often the MNE curriculum guide emphasizes diversity and multicultur-alism at a general level, which is another common thread between moral and civic/national education and Liberal Studies, which was seen previously to symbolize Hong Kong culture as like a tea with British, Chinese, and African essences. Under the theme of the national domain, MNE guidelines give the following examples of diverse cultural learning outcomes:

- Understand the customs of traditional festivals and their cultural meanings (e.g., Mid-Autumn Festival symbolizing family reunion, Dragon Boat Festival praising the patriotism of Qu Yuan, and cus-toms such as family visits during the Chinese New Year reflecting harmony among people); thereby realizing the characteristics and inheritance of Chinese culture from the festivals
- Appreciate the different local customs, respect the culture of ethnic minorities such as their architecture, clothing and accessories and liv-ing habits, and cultivate broadmindedness[46]

Though token representation and toleration is provided for here, for non-Chinese Hong Kongers such emphases on exotic differences, and being described as "ethnic minorities" to be "respected," reflects a wider hidden curriculum in Hong Kong of prioritizing Hong Kong-Chinese integration (doubtless an important concern) at the cost of recognizing Hong Kong as a multicultural society, and ethnic minorities as authentic Hong Kongers. This issue is also related to larger challenges faced by disadvantaged non-Chinese speaking youth in education. Currently many non-Chinese speak-ing low-income youth face severe educational obstacles in learning Chinese and integrating with Chinese students in schools, both of which are seen as essential to their social mobility. Studies show that integration of non-Chinese and Chinese students in public schools is rarely encouraged by educators, resulting in formal and informal segregation within schools.[47] Everyday racism against disadvantaged minorities coming particularly from southwest Asia is so commonplace as to be acknowledged simply as part of living in Hong Kong as a minority in the Liberal Studies textbooks, and in many cases educators do little to discourage this type of prejudice.[48]

From the perspective of non-Chinese Hong Kongers then, "national" education has come to imply assimilationist "Chinese-ethnic" education, which excludes non-Chinese parts of society. One concerned British Hong Konger, whose children are dual citizens, identifies numerous references in guideline documents to Chinese culture which assume students are Chi-nese, for instance:

Study the relationship between festive customs and geographic loca-tions, starting from one's student's ancestral home. For example, ingredients and flavours of moon cakes vary in different regions, reflecting features of local food cultures. Embrace the diversified

Chinese culture through studying the characteristics of festive customs of different regions.[49]

The parent argues that "the authors of the document appear unaware of the numbers of non-Chinese or multi-national children in Hong Kong's schools," conflating ethnicity and nationality to suggest that "ethnic minority students" are only 1 percent of the population, when many more Hong Kongers have international parents and/or dual nationality, including "'pure' Chinese families that have become citizens in other countries, with, in some cases, their children born abroad, who have returned to Hong Kong."[50] Hong Kong national identity is equated here with Chinese culture and ethnicity over other valid factors in the MNE proposal and related documents, resulting in a conception of citizenship education moving away from the multicultural local and global to a Chinese orientation that excludes Hong Kongers without Chinese ethnic or cultural heritage or affiliation. This trend toward Chinese nationalization of Hong Kong can also be seen in today's Liberal Studies textbooks, which denies localized internationalization in favor of Chinese nationalization, as in this focus on globalization:

> Cultural globalization can in fact be seen as a double-edged sword—it can eliminate the world's cultural boundaries by the global spread of information and cultural attitudes, but its uniformity may lead to the elimination of cultural diversity. Localization is thought to be an effective means of countering globalization. It refers to resisting the influence of globalization by reviving and preserving the characteristics and values of the local culture, while also raising one's consciousness about the local culture. For instance, many Chinese restaurants still offer traditional Chinese dim-sum every day.[51]

Read in the context of the MNE debate, it seems a hidden curriculum denying (possibly out of ignorance) the legitimacy of non-Chinese communities in Hong Kong is an important point to consider in adding national and Chinese elements to the Hong Kong curriculum, if Hong Kong truly sees itself as a plural, liberal democratic society.

Given these various problems, few were pleased with the MNE proposal. For those worried about Chinese patriotic education and the undue influence of the mainland government in Hong Kong, introducing anything positive about China was problematic, while for many student protestors, challenges related to not learning *enough*, as curriculum documents avoided negative discussions in favor of affective development and values, raising eyebrows on both sides regarding assessment and brainwashing. Scheduling and implementation were concerns, as much of the content overlaps with Liberal Studies. Finally, the proposal was disturbing from the viewpoint of non-Chinese Hong Kongers, who recognized that the curriculum focuses almost exclusively on shared cultural values, traditions, and values with mainland China, despite the fact that Hong Kong has a proudly diverse, multicultural and multinational liberal democratic society, wherein being Chinese has never been and should not become essential. The question of who is a Hong Konger, what kind of person they are, has proved challenging to answer, but seems necessary to develop a citizenship education that can satisfy diverse Hong Kongers today.

As August of 2012 arrived, protests became impassioned. Students participated in hunger strikes and mass rallies, and parents sent letters to schools demanding that they not engage in MNE, or that they at least provide the proposed curriculum of the school to parents beforehand, for parental approval. In September, the government "shelved" the proposal indefinitely, in response to the visible, loud public demonstrations against the curricular addition, and in recognition of the insurmountable challenge implementation would place on local educators. Moral and civic education, previously under the public radar, has become in this context controversial as well. Moral education, which has always been noncontroversial, is no doubt proceeding today as values education across Hong Kong's religiously and culturally plural schools, while civics emerges only as basic social rules and laws, as MNE or any other kind of more substantive national or citizenship education has become taboo: an issue which teachers must take sides on, and about which there seems to be no good answer.

THE NEED FOR INTERCULTURAL CITIZENSHIP EDUCATION

As discussed here, a major challenge for developing citizenship education in Hong Kong relates to Hong Kong national identity. Many permanent Hong Kong residents, Chinese and non-Chinese, see themselves as dual citizens, in a sense, in a Hong Kong that has never required singular loyalty before. Though today Hong Kong residents of Chinese descent are considered Chinese nationals, laws and rights remain vastly different between the two entities; Hong Kong residents require "home return permits" to visit the mainland, while China residents also require two-way permits to go to Hong Kong, or must apply for residency. It makes sense in such a context that any citizenship education program would be multitiered, addressing multiple sources of identity and affiliation, from a local or regional level (Hong Kong), to the national level and beyond. However, it must also be, at the lower levels, multicultural and multiethnic, to not exclude some Hong Kongers or preclude the positive development of diverse hybrid identities which are often both Chinese and international at the personal level or family level. There should be a place for both localized internationalization and delocalized nationalization in Hong Kong, and other pathways of delocalized internalization (recognition of diverse, non-Chinese "New Arrivals") and localized nationalization (recognition of local Hong Kongers and diverse, permanent "New Arrivals").

Yet so far the first binary, of localized internationalization and delocalized nationalization, has been the norm, with increasing attention paid to the latter (to Hong Kongers as part of mainland China). In relation, Hong Kong's more general multicultural education today is woefully lacking. Despite lip service given to multicultural topics within the Hong Kong local context in curriculum guides, mentions of "ethnic minorities" are an add-on in textbooks, while most discussions describe Hong Kong as Chinese, or as a hybrid of East and West, normally elaborated as Chinese and British. As mentioned previously, discussions of globalization emphasize that Hong Kong's traditions are Chinese, though content about integration with mainland China contrasts the two in terms of their politics and civic norms. Though there are occasional references to Hong Kong's international environment, non-Chinese Hong Kongers are most visible in textbooks, curriculum, and in school environments overall, as problems of the society, disadvantaged foreign workers from the Philippines, Pakistan, and Bangladesh, though this hardly reflects the diversity of Hong Kong's non-Chinese residents.[52] For instance, in a typical textbook discussion, it is noted:

> Hong Kong is mainly populated by Chinese people. According to the Hong Kong 2006 Population By-census, 95% of Hong Kong's population is Chinese. Those who participate in local social and political affairs are mainly Chinese. Hong Kong is also the home of people of other ethnicities, but they receive less social support than local Chinese because of their different languages and lifestyles, so their sociopolitical participation rate is lower.[53]

Such a discussion hardly invites conversation about the diversity of Hong Kong, so happily articulated elsewhere in terms of *yuanyang* tea, portraying non-Chinese Hong Kongers almost as a minor irritation: an unimportant group that is tolerated but not celebrated, and an inconsequential part of society politically. This does not square with promoting the British foundation to Hong Kong basic law or enable understanding of different cultures in Hong Kong.

Intercultural education is needed in this context, which focuses on non-Chinese and Chinese students working together and learning from each other, among other mutually alienated communities, such as "New Arrival" children and Hong Konger children. Those interested in non-Chinese students' educational opportunities have been recommending systematic cultural integration for decades, as non-Chinese students can face disadvantages in Hong Kong without cultural adaptation. However, intercultural education can also be more broadly conceived in relation to citizenship education as a means for preparing all students to engage with diverse others in dialogue, not just across different parts of a society, but also across global and territorial/national divisions.[54]

In Hong Kong, one's local, national, and international identities can be split such that each person has a truly hybrid civic or sociopolitical identity inside and outside Hong Kong. These hybrid identities can be a source of division and alienation in society, as different groups do not know each other and may not even know that each other exist in Hong Kong (i.e., that whites and Indians have lived in Hong Kong for many generations, while many Chinese Hong Kongers have also lived in Western societies for significant periods of time, and therefore relate as much or more to Western cultural values than Chinese ones). Developing dialogue within and across different groups can prepare students to better understand the makeup of Hong Kong society and help prepare young people as Hong Kong residents to participate in decision making informed about others' various communities of affiliation.

Intercultural education is increasingly seen in Europe today as education for dialogue across international borders, between immigrant groups and mainstream citizens.[55] In still-transitory Hong Kong, the line between these two is far less clear than it is elsewhere, as localized internationalization is one mode of citizenship there today, which orients students toward understanding Hong Kong as a dynamic, international place. Intercultural education in this context can help meet the needs for Chinese and non-Chinese Hong Kongers, and Hong Kongers and New Arrivals to develop mutual recognition and understanding. Such mutual recognition is necessary to develop norms of toleration and nondiscrimination that are often overlooked given Hong Kong's dynamic political status, as educational opportunities for both disadvantaged New Arrivals and non-Chinese students can be highly unequal today.[56] Mutual understanding can help pave the way toward a future consensus on an expanded vision of shared-fate citizenship education from that proposed by MNE, not just for Chinese people in China and Hong Kong, but for all people in China and Hong Kong.

CONCLUSION

Education has never had an assimilatory role in Hong Kong as it has had in many other societies. Private education is a longstanding tradition, apart from the British system of schooling. In Hong Kong it is seen as parents' rights to educate their children according to their (parents') abilities, which include financial capabilities, as monthly fees for high-quality schools can exceed median incomes. Different schools have different orientations toward moral or values education, and may socialize students to Hong Kong or global communities depending upon the student population. In this context, it has been easy to sanction civic education which focuses on laws, technical processes, and globalization, instead of requiring that education deal substantively with trickier issues such as national identity and patriotism.

The debate over MNE exposed a lack of foundation in place in society about what it means to be a Hong Konger, however, apart from regulations about residency and nationality. *Who* is Hong Kong is never meaningfully addressed or discussed fully in curriculum or textbooks; it is a question that has gone unanswered for far too long. To state that Hong Kong is Chinese is insufficient, as national and local identities among this large-scale cultural/ethnic/national group vary widely, and as the rift between New Arrivals and Hong Kongers has been broadening for decades. Attending to this rift may be a starting point. Yet Chinese Hong Kongers are also diverse in their attitudes and affiliations. Families and individuals are increasingly mixed in their sense of identity in Hong Kong, affiliating themselves with Hong Kong society and that of various other countries as well.

The question of citizenship education in Hong Kong also opens up many concerns Hong Kongers have related to Chinese nationality and the implications of the handover for Hong Kong's future. Hong Kong people overwhelmingly desire peaceful integration between the two entities, with preservation of the political ideologies seen as native to Hong Kong today. Yet how to teach for both in schools, and in such a politically challenging time in Hong Kong's history, is no simple task. It is unsurprising that the focus of specific educational debate has mainly revolved around how to teach about China, historically and today, as this hints at larger issues about what kind of political and cultural place Hong Kong is and will become.

At this juncture in Hong Kong's ongoing debate over citizenship education there is no simple solution. Cultural assimilation and integration with the mainland comes at a cost to the important Hong Kong tradition of localized internationalization, while on the other hand the society faces alienation with its "motherland" today, and many also see global citizenship increasingly as a weak and questionable concept. Though by no means a cure-all, intercultural education which promotes dialogical encounters across these rifts of nationality, culture, and ethnicity can play a productive role in developing and reforming a more substantial form of citizenship education in Hong Kong in the future, where mutual understanding and mutual recognition are prerequisite to educational officials and the public working together productively to develop a curriculum which can be seen by all as helpful and reasonable.

NOTES

1. Wing On Lee, "The Development of Citizenship Education Curriculum in Hong Kong after 1997: Tensions Between National Identity and Global Citizenship," in David L. Grossman, Wing On Lee, and Kerry J. Kennedy (eds.), *Citizenship Curriculum in Asia and the Pacific*, Springer/Comparative Education Research Centre, Hong Kong, 2008.
2. Sigal Ben-Porath, "Citizenship as Shared Fate: Education for Membership in a Diverse Democracy," *Educational Theory*, vol. 62, no. 4, 2006, p. 385.

3. Ibid.
4. Benedict Anderson, *Imagined Communities*, Verso, London, 1991.
5. Mark Bray, "Hong Kong Education in an International Context: The Impact of External Forces," in Gerard A. Postiglione (ed.), *Education and Society in Hong Kong: Toward One Country and Two Systems*, Hong Kong, Hong Kong University Press, 1992, p. 84.
6. Anthony Sweeting, "Hong Kong Education within Historical Processes," in Postiglione, *Education and Society in Hong Kong*.
7. Ibid., pp. 65–66.
8. Ibid., p. 67.
9. Bray, "Hong Kong Education in an International Context."
10. Qtd. in Sweeting, "Hong Kong Education within Historical Processes," p. 43.
11. Gregory P. Fairbrother, *Toward Critical Patriotism: Student Resistance to Political Education in Hong Kong and China*, Hong Kong University Press, Hong Kong, 2003.
12. Qtd. in Fairbrother, *Toward Critical Patriotism*, p. 37.
13. Ibid., p. 38.
14. Ben-Porath, "Citizenship as Shared Fate."
15. Sweeting, "Hong Kong Education within Historical Processes," p. 67.
16. P.K. Kee and Ronald Skeldon, "The Migration and Settlement of Hong Kong Chinese in Australia," in Ronald Skeldon (ed.), *Reluctant Exiles? Migration from Hong Kong and the New Overseas Chinese*, Hong Kong University Press, Hong Kong, 1994.
17. Qtd. in Fairbrother, *Toward Critical Patriotism*, p. 41.
18. Ben-Porath, "Citizenship as Shared Fate," p. 385.
19. Fairbrother, *Toward Critical Patriotism*.
20. Ibid.
21. See Wing-Wah Law, "Globalization as Both Threat and Opportunity for the Hong Kong Teaching Profession," *Journal of Educational Change*, vol. 4, 2003.
22. Lee, "Development of Citizenship Education Curriculum in Hong Kong after 1997."
23. Fairbrother, *Toward Critical Patriotism*, pp. 80–83.
24. Pak-sang Lai and Michael Byram, *Re-Shaping Education for Citizenship: Democratic National Citizenship Education in Hong Kong*, Cambridge Scholars, Newcastle upon Tyne, 2012.
25. Ibid., p. 37.
26. Tai Mei Har Hui, *Liberal Studies: Hong Kong Today, Book 1*, Hong Kong Educational Publishing Company, Hong Kong, 2009, p. 77.
27. Lee, "Development of Citizenship Education Curriculum in Hong Kong after 1997."
28. Qtd. in Fairbrother, *Toward Critical Patriotism*, p. 49.
29. Ibid.
30. Lai and Byram, *Re-Shaping Education for Citizenship*, pp. 67–69.
31. Education Bureau, "Concerns and Clarifications about 'Steamrollering the Implementation of Moral and National Education (MNE) by the Government," Public Statement of August, 2012, p. 3.
32. Ibid., p. 1.
33. Kwok Ping Chou, "Hong Kong's National Education Controversy," *EAI Background Brief No. 753*, September 13, 2012, pp. 4; 8.
34. Oiwan Lam, "Hong Kong: Brainwashing Education," *Global Voices*, May 12, 2011.
35. Fairbrother, *Toward Critical Patriotism*.

36. Laurance J. Splitter, "Moral and National Education: The Underlying Issues," lecture delivered at the Hong Kong Institute of Education, November 2012.
37. EB, "Concerns and Clarifications," pp. 3–4.
38. Ad Hoc Committee on Moral and National Education, *Consultation on Moral and National Education Curriculum*, Curriculum Development Council, Hong Kong, 2011, pp. 11–12.
39. Ibid., pp. 12–14.
40. Lai and Byram, *Re-Shaping Education for Citizenship*, p. 18.
41. Joshua Wong Chi Fung, "Scholarism," lecture at the University of Hong Kong, January 2013.
42. EB, "Concerns and Clarifications," pp. 2–3.
43. Chou, "Hong Kong's National Education Controversy," p. 10.
44. Ibid., p. 12.
45. Tai Mei Har Hui, *Liberal Studies: Hong Kong Today, Book 2*, Hong Kong Educational Publishing Company, Hong Kong, 2009, p. 133. Emphasis added.
46. Curriculum Development Council, *Moral and National Education Curriculum Guide (Primary 1 to Secondary 6)*, Education Bureau, Hong Kong, April 2012, p. 31.
47. See Kelley Loper, "Race and Equality: A Study of Ethnic Minorities in Hong Kong's Education System," *I.C. Paper No. CB(2)2559/04–04(01)*, University of Hong Kong Faculty of Law, Hong Kong, February 2004.
48. Liz Jackson and Yanju Shao, "Where Are Ethnic Minorities in Hong Kong Curriculum?" lecture in Hong Kong, July 2013.
49. Qtd. in Allan G. Dyer, "Extended Submission to the Consultation on the Moral and National Education Curriculum," republished on *Is This a Blog?* August 31, 2011.
50. Ibid.
51. Pak Kui Ngai, *Liberal Studies: Globalization II*, Longman, Hong Kong, 2010, p. 37.
52. Jackson and Shao, "Where Are Ethnic Minorities in Hong Kong Curriculum?"
53. Hui, *Liberal Studies, Book 2*, p. 13.
54. Michael A. Peters, "Western Models of Intercultural Philosophy," in Tina Besley and Michael A. Peters (eds.), *Interculturalism, Education and Dialogue*, Peter Lang, New York, 2012.
55. Tina Belsey, "Narratives of Intercultural and International Education: Aspirational Values and Economic Imperatives," in Besley and Peters, *Interculturalism, Education and Dialogue*.
56. See also Celeste Y.M. Yuen, "Education for New Arrivals and Multicultural Teacher Education in Hong Kong," *New Horizons in Education*, vol. 45, 2002.

3 Citizenship Education in China under Discourses of Nationalism, Cosmopolitanism, Neoliberalism, and Confucianism

Juanjuan Zhu and Steven P. Camicia

INTRODUCTION

The past two decades has witnessed "a revival of interest"[1] in citizenship worldwide. A confluence of social, economic, cultural, and political changes may have called for this rethinking and reimagination of citizenship. In tandem with this revived interest in citizenship is a renewed emphasis on citizenship education. Indeed, since the 1990s, a plethora of government policy documents and curriculum standards have been published in a number of countries, such as the United States, England, Australia, and China. In addition, "exponential growth in scholarship on citizenship education both within and across national borders"[2] serves as another powerful manifestation.

This chapter examines the underlying ideologies and hidden agendas of citizenship education in present-day China by articulating the ways the country's citizenship education is influenced by discourses of nationalism, cosmopolitanism, neoliberalism, and Confucianism. Policy documents and curriculum standards for China's citizenship education issued since 1991 are critically dismantled through relating the text to other texts and to the contexts from the lens of our theoretical framework. We ask, in this chapter, "How do the discourses of nationalism, cosmopolitanism, neoliberalism, and Confucianism influence the production of citizenship education in China?"

CONTEXT

Before the dawn of the twentieth century, China had been known worldwide as a long-established civilization. However, in the first half of the twentieth century, the Chinese people experienced a series of natural disasters, internal strife, and military failures to foreign powers. The founding of the People's Republic of China (PRC) in 1949 brought an end to this turbulent modern history.[3] As a regime of proletarian dictatorship, PRC is a one-party state ruled by the Communist Party of China (CPC). During PRC's early history from the 1950s to 1970s, the focus of the government had centered on "establishing [CPC's] legitimacy as the new ruler of the Chinese nation,"[4] "consolidating the party's ideological and political control,"[5] and accomplishing the country's socialist transition.[6]

At the Third Plenum of the Eleventh CPC Central Committee in 1978, *gaige kaifang* (reform and opening up) was formulated as a long-term state policy, which represented a major shift in CPC's working emphasis from class and ideological struggles to social and economic development.[7] Since then, China has experienced dramatic changes in multiple aspects.

One of the most noticeable changes occurred in the economic sphere. Official records showed that China's economy skyrocketed after the implementation of the *gaige kaifang zhengce* (the reform and opening up policy) in 1978. The economic growth in this country was even more remarkable after Deng Xiaoping's visit to South China in 1992, which marked further economic liberation in China. As officially endorsed by the 14th CPC National Congress that was also held in 1992, CPC's overall goal in terms of economic reform was to gradually shift China's economic system from a planned economy to a market-oriented economy, or a "socialist market economy" in official terms. The implication of this economic system shift for the development of China's citizenship concept is significant. Lee and Ho argued that the rise of a socialist market economy has required the Chinese to take on new citizenship qualities, such as a global perspective, an orientation toward achievement, open-mindedness and democratic awareness, which are substantially different from what was expected from them in Mao's times.[8] Besides these landmark events, China's entry into the World Trade Organization (WTO) in December 2001 seemed to have ushered in another phase of economic change. In the face of the increased competition stimulated by WTO, it was clear that "China could only opt for further marketization and privatization,"[9] which brought about the increased acceptance of the opening up mentality and global outlook in Chinese society.[10]

In addition to these economic changes, shifts in the political climate have occurred. Class struggle was no longer at the top of CPC's agenda, though enhancing its legitimacy and maintaining its control has always been CPC's most essential concern. Oscillating between expanding freedom of expression and setting boundaries from 1978 to 1989,[11] CPC nevertheless reasserted its authoritarian control through the June 4th Incident at Tiananmen Square in 1989. In the years to follow, several events took place which had far-reaching impact. One was the return of Hong Kong and Macau to Chinese sovereignty in 1997 and 1999, respectively. Lee and Ho argued that the handover of these two places brought about the revival of nationalism in China.[12] Similarly, an event happening seven years later, namely, the 2008 Beijing Olympic Games, also promoted China's openness to and interconnection with the rest of the world, though Law contended that "the Chinese state continues to be a key actor in defining citizenship and citizenship education by promoting nationalism and nation-specific elements of citizenship education while linking its people to an increasingly interconnected world."[13]

Alongside the massive economic reform and some political shifts, there have been enormous social changes in China. On the one hand, people's living standards and conditions have been greatly advanced as evidenced by possession of more material products and more openness to the outside world. On the other hand, however, social tensions have been worsening in an era of rapid domestic GDP growth and globalization. For instance, the widening economic gap and the uneven and unfair distribution of wealth has become an acute social problem over the years.[14] Also, while people in China were enjoying the benefits brought about by reform and globalization, they were increasingly plagued by unemployment, increased crime rate, poisoned food, deteriorated environment, an inadequate social security system, and rampant government corruption.

Moral decline has been a major social phenomenon in post-reform China. Encouraged by Deng's famous saying "White or black, as long as the cat can catch mice, it is a good cat," more and more Chinese preoccupy themselves with no other life goals but money making, the result of which is "the weakening of individual character, family ethics, occupational ethics (the society filled with fake goods), collectivism, social ethics, patriotism and sense of national dignity."[15] Thirty years after the implementation of the reform and opening up policy, Han was under the impression that "the society had lost its basic values and behavior code."[16] Such changes in China's social fabric together with those in the economic and political circumstances underscore the importance of taking new measures in the country's approach to citizenship education.

THEORETICAL PERSPECTIVES

Two perspectives guide our investigation. The first involves critical and postmodern understandings of discourse. In China, discourses surrounding citizenship education have been influential in shaping conversations and understandings about the desirable knowledge, skills, values, and dispositions that Chinese citizens are expected to possess. This chapter pays particular attention to discourses of nationalism, cosmopolitanism, neoliberalism, and Confucianism, which are the four distinct discourses in the contingency of China's context. Through a critical lens, these four discourses facilitate our analysis of how "civic education can be interpreted as an attempt by elites to maintain their hegemony in the face of demand from individuals and groups to exercise their rights"[17] in China.

The second perspective involves new understandings of how these discourses interact on the discursive field of China's citizenship education. Power relations between discourses are asymmetrical, or put another way, some discourses are more influential in determining and changing policy and curriculum than others. The degree to which a discourse such as nationalism has the power to shape policy and curriculum standards depends on the context in which the discourse operates. Each location and context in the world influences and is influenced by discourses differently, resulting in not one, but a dynamic mix of discourses that shape citizenship education in that location.

In our theoretical framework, we are particularly interested in the ways that discourses of nationalism, cosmopolitanism, neoliberalism, and Confucianism influence citizenship education in China's context.

Discourses of Nationalism, Cosmopolitanism, Neoliberalism, and Confucianism

As a conceptual lens, discourse analysis helps in understanding citizenship education and reforms because it focuses on the rules of what and how speech is interwoven with social relations and ideologies. Because social relations are central to topics of citizenship education, how ideology and language influence these relations is of central importance. Citizenship education is governed by discourses that influence the way personal traits and the critical attributes of citizenship are taught, and as a result, the way that citizenship is conceptualized. Mills provides an operational definition of discourse:

> A discourse is not a disembodied collection of statements, but groupings of utterances or sentences, statements which are enacted within a social context, which are determined by that social context and which contribute to the way that social context continues its existence. Institutions and social context therefore play an important determining role in the development, maintenance and circulation of discourses.[18]

We focus on the discourses of nationalism, cosmopolitanism, neoliberalism, and Confucianism because they stand out as powerful in the milieu of China and are significant when they function within the contexts that we have already described. Other studies have pinpointed these four discourses in China's citizenship education "discursive field," a heuristic defined by Steinberg as the terrain where discourses struggle for influence.[19] For instance, both Feng[20] and Zhong and Lee[21] have attested to the established dominance of the nationalistic discourse in China's school curricula as a norm that runs counter to the irresistible trend of globalization while excluding marginalized views and encouraging ethnocentric stances. The cosmopolitan ideal reflected in the concept of global citizens, on the other hand, is a recent addition to China's citizenship discourses.[22] Law discovered that in Shanghai, one of the most cosmopolitan cities in China, teachers and students still wanted to increase the global dimension of citizenship education in their curriculum.[23] As for the discourse of neoliberalism, we believe it has become one officially endorsed and commonly recognized citizenship discourse in China because "the market is one element selected from the changing economy for defining the new socialist citizenship"[24] and also because the market in China "increasingly incorporates neoliberal elements interdigitated with authoritarian centralized control."[25] Finally, Law's erudite study on China's citizenship education called our attention to the discourse of Confucianism's unique position in the country's citizenship discursive field. In the following, we provide a definition for each of the four discourses.

The discourse of nationalism can be approached from two aspects. Within the national boundaries, the nationalist discourse is characterized as presenting a nation's culture as a monolithic, common narrative.[26] The intrinsic exclusionary nature of nationalism asserts a normative, discursive power that coerces the subjugation of varied individual identities to a national whole. In Bhabha's eyes, the narration or imagination of nationalism negates the fluidity, plurality, heterogeneity, and hybridity of every identity.[27] Outside the borderline of the imagined community,[28] nationalism has given rise to uncritical patriotism, which elevates the fatherland into "the object of the citizens' adoration."[29] In its most extreme form, the nationalist discourse can be an absolutist, ethnocentric speech that lauds the superiority of a national family to others, and establishes an antagonistic binary between those belonging to the national community and those who do not.[30] Since citizenship education has been traditionally influenced by the intent to bolster national identity, it often articulates visions that emphasize exceptionality, pride, and national unity. As is the case in other locations, the discourse of nationalism in China places the nation-state as the lens through which the world is viewed, in which all actions, both local and global, are there to strengthen the nation-state.

The discourse of cosmopolitanism has many modes.[31] For the purposes of this chapter, we operationally define cosmopolitianism as an ideal where people's allegiance is to "the worldwide community of human beings."[32] Under conditions of globalization, cosmopolitanism poses a legitimate challenge to the nationalistic rhetoric in that supra-nationally, a cosmopolitan frame of reference is cultivated among individuals as agents equally possessing human rights and sub-nationally, cosmopolitanism enables the identities and equality of diverse groups to be fostered in society.[33] As it becomes increasingly common for people to find themselves operating daily in "overlapping communities of fate"[34]—local, regional, national, and international, instead of just within their national community—cosmopolitanism is expected to guide people to exercise and orchestrate their citizenship at all levels in the principles of peace, equality, human rights, and social justice in this globalized world.[35]

A broad, and often contested label, we operationally define neoliberalism as an economic and political doctrine that extols the efficiency of open markets, private businesses, and free trade while seeking to diminish state control in economic and associated political affairs. Economic growth has been highest on the agenda of the neoliberal regime. Indeed, market growth, not quality social services, has been the primary measurement of government work, marking a shift from an egalitarian ideal.[36] In the educational arena, in particular, where government is expected to play the major role, neoliberalism featured with the implicit and explicit language of market, efficiency, competitiveness, accountability, and standardization permeates the mainstream discourse. There have been different names coined to describe the qualities of good citizens viewed from a pro-market and anti-big-government ideological stance. For instance, Apple observed that students have been trained as human capital, future workers and producers who "must be given the requisite skills and dispositions to compete efficiently and effectively."[37]According to Teitelbaum, "this kind of citizenship has a lot to do with actions at the individual level and includes primarily limited involvement in the needs of local community, with little focus on the larger social structures and institutions of which the local is ostensibly a part."[38] In other words, a neoliberal intent is expressed when citizenship education is seen as an important venue for the cultivation of competitive producers and consumers who are only concerned with "survival, prosperity, corporate viability and individual achievement"[39] in the marketplace.

Like neoliberalism, Confucianism means different things to different people.[40] First of all, concern for self-cultivation is undoubtedly one of the distinct features of Confucianism.[41] Many may question this emphasis as being reflective of an individualistic orientation. However, Lee contended that self-cultivation represents individuality, different from individualism and that the individual and the collectivity are "two sides of a coin in terms of citizenship"[42] in Asian countries. As a word that has both a moral and a collective dimension,[43] self-cultivation is Confucianism's primary tool through which "one's inner strength of assuming responsibilities for oneself, for one's family and for society at large"[44] is developed. Closely related with the feature of self-cultivation is another Confucian tradition: the emphasis on communal spirit.[45] Qualities such as consensus seeking, deference, interest in harmony, recourse to third-party mediation to avoid direct confrontation between rivals, and an expressed concern for group solidarity are more commonly seen in East Asian countries than in countries where individual rights and benefits are prioritized. According to Rozman, "familism or the extraordinary preoccupation with family solidarity and interests"[46] in East Asian societies is undoubtedly another noticeable feature of Confucianism. Unlike Western-style civil societies that are based on voluntary associations, countries of a decidedly Confucian brand are noted for the salience of family-style connectedness, which is "noncontractual, extralegal and ascriptive"[47] in nature. The final point worth mentioning here is that moral governance is a political ideal spelt out in Confucianism. By moral governance, we mean a strong government that rules with moral authority. Contrary to their Western peers who customarily harbor an entrenched distrust toward the government, people in East Asian societies consider government leadership "indispensible for a smooth functioning of the domestic market economy"[48] and responsible for translating, with high moral standard, the general will of the overwhelming majority into reasonable policies on health care, social welfare, and education, and so forth.[49]

Finally, the relative power of the discourses to one another is contingent upon what, when, and where people are speaking. Discourses are not equally powerful but embedded in a dynamic network of power relations.[50] In other words, some discourses are privileged and thus more powerful than others operating on a discursive field in a certain place and at a certain time. The competition between dominant and marginalized discourses on a discursive field is governed by power relations or "orders of discourse."[51] For instance, in citizenship education, the discourse of cosmopolitanism can be weakened by an increased sense of national security and unity that some find in the discourse of nationalism. Discourses are also fractured, and even seemingly coherent bundles of statements can be complicated by different contexts and power relations. For example, as has already been mentioned, the discourse of cosmopolitanism has multiple windows of meaning depending upon the stakeholder, theorist, and contexts.[52] Conceptually, Appiah blends the discourses of nationalism and cosmopolitanism into what he terms "rooted cosmopolitanism."[53] He emphasizes the importance of having a home country and customs while recognizing that humans are part of a larger, global community. His example shows how the power relations between different discourses are rarely a zero sum game. The discourses of nationalism, cosmopolitanism, neoliberalism, and Confucianism blend and morph in China's citizenship education, creating a postmodern condition of hybridity, fluidity, and multiplicity. In other words, as we will discuss later, the discursive field of China's citizenship education is complex, noisy, and messy where the four discourses are engaged in an intense, constant competition and entanglement.

METHODOLOGY

In this project, documents and archival materials[54] represented the sole forms of data. We collected citizenship education policy documents and curriculum standards published for both elementary and secondary schools in China since 1991 for analysis because in this country where a centralized education system is in place, such documents provide official parameters within which all schools in the nation operate. After careful searching, we gathered a data set that included various guidelines, circulars and directives issued by the CPC-led state or its educational agency to enhance students' patriotic sentiments in the 1990s, to reinforce students' behavior codes in the early 2000s, and to promote then president Hu Jintao's theory of constructing a harmonious society and a set of moral values called "Socialist

Concepts on Honors and Disgraces" in the mid-2000s. Also included in the data set were amended curriculum standards for both elementary and secondary schools in the early 1990s, the revised primary citizenship curriculum in the early 2000s and the revised secondary citizenship curriculum in the middle and late 2000s, respectively. We gave emphasis to the revised curriculum in the 2000s.

We employed critical discourse analysis (CDA) throughout the description, analysis, and interpretation of data[55] in this study. As the name suggests, CDA entails a reading of a discourse in relation to its "broader enveloping contexts"[56] from a liberating and power-conscious perspective.[57] CDA enables researchers to "take into account the insights that discourse is structured by dominance; that every discourse is historically produced and interpreted, that is, it is situated in time and space; and that dominance structures are legitimated by ideologies of powerful groups."[58] Using CDA, we coded the texts and developed them into manageable categories and emerging themes.[59] Our intention is to reveal how the discourses of citizenship conveyed in China's citizenship curriculum have functioned to shape a dulled or misled citizenry and to inform people of places where they can exercise their critical agency. In other words, by making explicit the oftentimes unspoken position on citizenship that reflects a certain political, most likely hegemonic idea about the role of the individual within society, we want educators as well as other stakeholders, such as curriculum writers and policymakers, to be aware of their responsibilities to empower students.

FINDINGS

We arrived at two important findings in response to our research question. In our first finding, we identified each of the discourses in policy documents and curriculum standards. We then discussed the four discourses based on the extent to which each discourse is visible on the discursive field of citizenship education in China. It should be noted that even though one may appear more than another, they are interrelated such that abundance of appearance is less relevant and the interconnectedness is where the greater analytic power lies. For example, the discourse of neoliberalism can interact with nationalism to promote citizenship education that produces self-sufficient, enterprising workers who take responsibility for their own learning in order to strengthen the nation's standing in a global marketplace. This discourse is often apparent in rationales for educating citizen/workers to compete globally in order to strengthen the national economy. In this example, the discourses of neoliberalism and nationalism function with each other to increase the power of both. This can be said with other discourses too. The discourse of Confucianism can also interact with the discourse of nationalism in citizenship education to create subjects with a strong sense of nationalism built upon moral imperatives. These combinations, as well as others, were apparent in our data. In our second finding, we extended our first finding by analyzing the function of each discourse and interpreting how these discourses have been used to reify structures of oppression by the power elite in China.

Order of Discourses

Among the four discourses of nationalism, cosmopolitanism, neoliberalism, and Confucianism, nationalism was the most frequent and dominant discourse on China's citizenship education discursive field, a finding that echoes many other studies.[60] The first strong presence of nationalism in our data set could be found in the curriculum guideline of *liangshi yiqing,* i.e., near-modern and modern Chinese histories and China's national development, promulgated by the State Education Commission in 1991. In the wake of the Tiananmen Square incident in 1989, the CPC launched a nationwide campaign to enhance students' sense of patriotism and reinforce the Party's control based on the perception that the incident was the conspiracy of "the United States and some other Western countries. . . to bring about a peaceful evolution towards capitalism in socialist countries."[61] An important part of this patriotic education campaign was promoting the learning of *liangshi yiqing* by adding them to the primary and secondary school curricula. Specifically, the curriculum guideline of *liangshi yiqing* as incorporated in various content areas including citizenship education consisted of six major parts: (a) China's 5,000-year-old civilization with laudable achievements in various aspects; (b) near-modern Chinese history between 1840–1940s when the country suffered from a century-long foreign invasion and domestic turbulence; (c) modern Chinese history that emphasized New China's achievements under CPC's leadership from 1949 onward; (d) China's population, environment, resources, and fifty-six ethnic groups; (e) Construction of Socialist China with Chinese characteristics which is superior to the Western model of democracy; and (f) the treacherous international environment that China is situated in.[62] The message conveyed in the guideline was clear: by highlighting China's achievements in both ancient and modern times, the CPC-led state was eliciting a proud, uncritical identification with the monolithic and "exceptional" Chinese national culture and history from its students. At the same time, by emphasizing the insult and hostile treatment China received and is receiving from Western countries, the government was evoking strong nationalistic feelings to pursue its own populist goals.[63]

The functioning of the discourse of nationalism is also evident in the revised citizenship curriculum at both elementary and secondary levels in the 2000s. Because citizenship education is traditionally perceived as a Western political construct, ideomoral education (at the elementary levels) and ideopolitical education (at the secondary levels) are used as near equivalents in China's contexts. Currently, China's citizenship education is conducted mainly through the curricula of Moral Character and Life for first and second graders, Moral Character and Society for third to sixth graders, Thought and Moral Character for seventh to ninth graders, and Thought and Politics for high schoolers from the tenth to twelfth grades, which can be further divided into four compulsory courses (i.e., Economic Life, Political Life, Cultural Life, and Life and Philosophy) and six elective courses (i.e., General Knowledge about Scientific Socialism, General Knowledge about Economics, General Knowledge about Countries and International Organizations, General Knowledge about Scientific Thinking, General Knowledge about Laws in Life, and General Knowledge about Citizen Morality and Ethics). When the experimental curriculum standards for citizenship education at elementary schools were issued,[64] the national and sub-national dimensions of citizenship were addressed more than the global dimension.[65] Like the curriculum guideline of *liangshi yiqing,* the revised citizenship curriculum also made efforts to promote a strong sense of affiliation with China as well as reasserting CPC's leadership role. For instance, as a theme with a strong national sentiment, "I am Chinese" runs through the curriculum. Students are asked to know China's time honored history and its contribution to world civilization. Students are also required to learn how CPC has led China to rise from a humiliating past, especially after the adoption of the reform and opening up policy. Moreover, living Chinese personalities who have made extraordinary accomplishments are taken as role models to encourage a sense of pride for being Chinese in students.

In a similar vein, the Ministry of Education also revised and updated the citizenship education curriculum for secondary students in the mid and late 2000s, respectively. The first revision occurred around the year of 2003. For junior high students, learning contents were structured around three curricular themes: My Growth; My Relations to Others; and My Relations to the Collective, the Country and the (Local) Society. Within the last theme, there is a sub-theme entitled Knowing China's Situations and Loving the Chinese Nation.[66] As the names suggest, affinity to and identification with the Chinese nation weighs more heavily than all other themes because it is not only included prominently but addressed twice in the text. Likewise, the revised curriculum for senior high students[67] reflected the same emphasis on fostering national-bound pride and loyalty but at a more conceptual level.[68] The second revision of secondary citizenship curriculum took place in 2007.[69] The new curriculum for both junior high and senior high students made amendments in light of Hu Jintao's version of socialism with Chinese characteristics, a theory that stresses reinforcing an ethnic spirit centering on patriotism and reasserts CPC's leadership roles in guiding China toward a more prosperous future. Clearly, the discursive field of China's citizenship education is marked with a very strong and tenacious grip of nationalism.

Based on our analysis, Confucianism was the second most frequently cited discourse on the discursive field of China's citizenship education. We illustrate this finding with two documents where Confucianism is invoked and emphasized. The first is a document entitled *Gongmin Daode Jianshe Shishi Gangyao* (The Implementation Guidelines to Construct Civic Virtues of Citizens) promulgated by the Central Committee of the CPC in late 2001 right after China became a WTO member. In the document, the Central Committee constructed a collectivistic socialist citizenship model featured with a set of ten virtues as the national code of ethic building. These virtues were conveyed in twenty Chinese characters as follows: *ai guo* (patriotism), *shou fa* (law abiding), *ming li* (courtesy), *cheng xin* (integrity), *tuan jie* (solidarity), *you shan* (friendliness), *qinjian* (diligence and frugality), *zi qiang* (self-strengthening), *jing ye* (dedication to work), and *fengxiang* (contribution and sacrifice). Though there was one element that is more of a Western orientation (i.e., law abiding), the majority of the virtues are with a clear Confucian inscription.

Five years later, the CPC initiated another similar morality drive in response to the prevalence of perceived moral decadence. On October 11, 2006, the 16th Central Committee of the CPC adopted a resolution that specifically addressed "major issues concerning the building of a socialist harmonious society."[70] Within the framework of the socialist harmonious society concept, the government has also developed a set of moral values called "Socialist Concepts on Honors and Disgraces," or "Eight Honors and Eight Shames" in March, 2006. Noticeably, both the concept of harmony and a large part of eight honors and shames embody Confucian ideals and moral virtues. Among the eight pairs of opposing moral codes with rhyming poetic lilt in Chinese, "make no gains at others' expense" and "be honest and trustworthy" are both congruent with the teachings of the Analects, which is the collection of Confucius' sayings and ideas; also "live plainly, work hard; do not wallow in luxuries and pleasures" are what Confucianism advocates. Though termed as "building a socialist harmonious society" and "Socialist Concepts on Honors and Disgraces," both propaganda campaigns are deliberate efforts made on the part of CPC to tackle the problem of the loss of human virtues and morals in today's Chinese society[71] by invoking Confucianism.

Aligned with guidelines of policy documents, citizenship curriculum at all levels also went through some changes by reinstating the Confucian tradition, with an emphasis on its moral code and sense of social responsibility. For example, the revised citizenship curriculum for junior high students in 2003 highlighted the importance of traditional Chinese culture and virtues. The discourse of nationalism, with its appeal to a "timeless and monolithic national culture," and the discourse of Confucianism, with its appeal to virtues, combine to influence the citizenship education curriculum more together than they do separately. The curriculum updated for senior high students in 2007 also made an effort to promote Chinese traditions. Law has argued that the CPC-led government turned to Confucianism also to cope with international challenges under pressures from globalization.[72] He has reasoned that the Chinese traditional culture is "a key foundation of ethnic solidarity and unity in ethnically diverse China" and "a bridge between China and other countries in an ethnically diverse world."[73] The traditional culture and values that Confucianism embodies is thus expected to bolster the Chinese people's confidence and loyalty toward their motherland when they are engaged in dealings with foreign people and cultures. Along this line, it is fair to say that the discourse of Confucianism is interwoven with that of nationalism in China's context. While socialism, China's state orthodoxy, demonstrates decreased appeal and market value,[74] Confucianism and nationalism are upheld together as powerful, countervailing discourses against destabilizing factors at home and abroad that spring up in China's social transition.

Next, we found the discourse of cosmopolitanism is gaining traction in both the official and popular parlance in China's citizenship education discursive field. In almost all of the policy documents and curriculum standards that we analyzed, the government has explicitly and consistently encouraged students to be open to the outside world and develop a correct world outlook. In the revised curricula published in the 2000s, new elements were added that required students to love peace and resist all forms of terrorism.[75]

Though there has been an increased presence of the cosmopolitan citizenship discourse in China's school curriculum since the country's adoption of the opening up policy, we interpreted this discourse as weaker in relation to the discourses of nationalism and Confucianism. For instance, in the curriculum guideline issued in 2002 for the course of Moral Character and Society (Grades 3–6), which is the major site where citizenship education is conducted at upper elementary levels, only eight topics were related with the world whereas 14 topics were devoted to national issues. Likewise, the topic for the global dimension of citizenship education was housed under the topic on the Country in the curriculum for the course of Thought and Moral Character (Grades 7–9) issued in the year of 2003. Four years later, in the directive that guided the curricular amendment for senior high school's Thought and Politics education, the emphasis was still given to China's peaceful rising and increasing participation in international arenas when China's relations with the international community was discussed. We are concerned that the way global issues are approached in China's citizenship education might leave students with the impression that national interest should be the point of departure and return for most topics and issues.

Moreover, sometimes the cosmopolitan discourse that functions in China's citizenship curriculum is tangled with the discourse of neoliberalism. In the curriculum published for junior high students in 2003, the Ministry of Education highlighted the two-pronged approach China takes to accumulate global capital for national development. The sum of these discourses is more powerful than their functioning in isolation. The creation of citizens who compete in global markets is imperative for the strengthening of China. Even more, the discourses of cosmopolitanism and Confucianism function in dyads, such that cosmopolitanism adds a moral legitimacy to neoliberalism and Confucianism adds a moral legitimacy to nationalism. In tandem, this network of discourses operates on the discursive field of citizenship education in China. Although the discourses understood separately might seem in opposition, in tandem they function to increase the power of each other. A close reading of the text suggests that China's interaction with the world is indeed weighted with a nation-bound concern about the country's ability to thrive in a fast-growing and unforgiving global marketplace.

Finally, when it comes to the discourse of neoliberalism, we consider it the least visible but not necessarily the least powerful among the four citizenship discourses in China's context. Earlier in this chapter, we mentioned that China has undergone a series of unprecedented changes since its adoption of the opening up and reform policy in 1978. One remarkable and often the most referenced change is the country's gradual shift from a socialist planned economy to "a socialist market economy" since the early 80s. Despite the "socialist" modification, this market economy is also featured with market-centeredness and underscored by market rationality[76] because Deng Xiaoping, the mastermind of China's economic reform, argued that the market does not belong exclusively to the capitalist economy. China's determination to further marketize its economy was reinforced when it joined WTO in 2001. The implication of this economic change on China's citizenship discursive field is tremendous: neoliberalism has hence become one officially endorsed and commonly recognized citizenship discourse in China's context.

Unlike the previous three discourses, neoliberalism was never referenced in a direct sense. Rather, it was often alluded to in the policy documents and curriculum standards that we analyzed when the CPC-led state expressed its determination to develop a socialist market economy and concern for training a competitive, efficient workforce. We equated the presence of neoliberalism with the times that socialist market economy was emphasized or applauded because the latter is an indication of CPC's subscription to the neoliberal ideology. Basically, neoliberalism had a more frequent presence in the curriculum standards or policy documents issued in the 1990s than in those published in the 2000s because the 1990s appeared to be a critical time for the idea of building a socialist market economy to be disseminated and accepted among the public. The functioning of the discourse of neoliberalism could be found in the amendment made to the junior high school's curriculum in 2007 where prioritizing economic development as the focus of nation building was hailed as one of China's national strategies. What this example also illustrates is that neoliberalism often intertwines with nationalism in China's context to train competitive "economic soldiers"[77] who fight for national security and economic prosperity.

The Oppressive Nature of the Officially Endorsed Citizenship Discourses

Our second finding sheds light on the underlying oppressive nature of the officially endorsed citizenship education discourses in China's context. As discussed earlier, the four discourses of nationalism, cosmopolitanism, neoliberalism, and Confucianism are all officially embraced, though cosmopolitanism is promoted in a limited sense. Referenced in either policy documents or official citizenship curriculum, these discourses, without exception, "communicate national leaders' economic and sociopolitical goals as students' aspirations," and "prepare students for future sociopolitical behaviors"[78] in China. In other words, they function as a hegemonic and normative tool wielded by those in power for social control because these discourses work, either in separation or combination, in the best interest of the most powerful in society. From a critical perspective, it is not hard to see that all the discourses meet the hidden agenda of the power elite in each society, which is to maintain status quo by training an obedient and civically apathetic citizenry. These discourses function to create a citizenry that is: entrepreneurial, flexible, lifelong learners (discourse of neoliberalism), understanding of global markets and culture (discourse of cosmopolitanism), dedicated to the interest of the nation-state (discourse of nationalism), and adhering to a moral code that emphasizes unity over diversity (discourse of Confucianism).

To begin with, the discourse of nationalism works most effectively in China, where a citizenry loyal to the CPC-dominated state is of paramount importance to the ruling party.[79] One effect of the nationalist discourse is to construct and perpetuate a national myth (i.e., a common, monolithic national culture and history that is deemed appropriate by the ruling class). Not only does the myth negate the multiplicity and hybridity of personal identities but it also defies criticism from both inside and outside the national borders, especially in times of national crisis.[80] Through subsuming various individual identities under a national whole and maintaining imagined consensus in the name of national unity and security, nationalism realizes its suppressive function.[81]

Moreover, in this one-party state, CPC claims full ownership toward the nation and state power. Although the Chinese people are rhetorically phrased as the "masters" of the country, CPC is rationalized as their representative and agent to exercise the ruling power.[82] Given that China is considered CPC's property,[83] any threat toward China's solidarity and sovereignty are, in effect, challenges to CPC's legitimacy and leadership. Along this line, the nationalist discourse that the CPC-led government promotes entails loyalty to both the nation and the CPC. To put it another way, nationalism in China's context refers not only to strong patriotic sentiments but also to faithful expressions to the ruling party. Therefore, the nationalist discourse in China functions to deflect any criticism toward the CPC through characterizing such comment making as a betrayal of the nation, which is itself framed as a shameful action.

Besides nationalism, Confucianism is the other powerful official citizenship discourse in China. Law explained well Confucianism's contribution to the making of a submissive citizenry in imperial China since 156

B.C.[84] According to him, the imperial state of different dynasties in the Chinese monarchy upheld Confucianism as the state-supported orthodoxy to "legitimize and consolidate its rulership, and to maintain social stability and harmony, by using it to justify sociopolitically hierarchical relations."[85] Both Confucianism and Confucian education "played important roles in fostering and reproducing a traditional Chinese citizenry that was submissive to the emperor and the ruling class."[86]

Though eradicated as a feudal legacy during Mao's era, Confucianism has been re-invoked by the CPC-led government in recent years. For instance, the harmonious society platform promulgated by the CPC central committee in 2006 is with a clear Confucian inscription. Many have argued that the platform is promoted by the power elite with the intent of ensuring a firm centralized control,[87] because harmony as a key element of Confucianism is just "a veiled reference to assimilation."[88] In Law's (2006) words, the Confucian traditions and virtues function as "an internal, self-impelling force of social conformity,"[89] as they did in the long history of the Chinese monarchy. Though the contingency of the current historical moment has required the infusion of a global outlook and orientation, the traditional repressive nature of Confucianism has not been changed in China's context. Thus, through promoting a submissive, obedient good citizenship imaginary, Confucianism is another important discourse for the ruling party to use to maintain its rule in China.

Neoliberalism also serves the interest of the most powerful in Chinese society. Foucault pioneered the critical analysis of neoliberalism in this regard through coining the term of governmentality. In an interview entitled "truth and power," Foucault (1980) elaborated on the operation of governmentality at times when a market rationality and neoliberal mentality holds sway.

According to Foucault, the neoliberal seed has been planted since the seventeenth and eighteenth centuries when the market became the decisive power in economic and political policymaking.[90] As a result, the new economy of power or the new form of governmentality emerged as an alternative and better mode of regulation because compared with the old controlling technique, the new one seemed more efficient, more economic, more effective, and less provocative. However, Foucault did not see the establishment of this new mode of governance as a signal of the retreat of the state from the role in regulation as it appears. Instead, he argued that it is a deceptive and strategic maneuver of the state, the governing mechanism, to shift its role from "that of directing to one of enabling"[91] and tricks individuals into self-governance while the controlling power is as forceful, if not more, as before. Echoing Foucault's view, Ong confirmed that "in contemporary times, neoliberal rationality informs action by many regimes and furnishes the concepts that inform the government of free individuals who are then induced to self-manage according to market principles of discipline, efficiency, and competitiveness."[92]

The making of a self-governing, market-minded citizenry is indeed in line with the best interest of those with the most power in China because such a citizenry often shows little interest in civic and communal activities that could often pose challenges to the power elite's hegemonic control. Human history is replete with examples of where the government introduced the neoliberal doctrine with a hidden intention to produce a politically apathetic citizenry, a citizenry who, in turn, would facilitate the rule of the existing government. Interestingly, the CPC-led state is resorting to this strategy to reinforce the ruling party's leadership. As Lee and Ho observed, the government's overwhelming focus on economic development is just "a disguise of an apparent reinstatement of political control."[93] In a similar vein, Law noted that the CPC frequently cited China's achievements in a market economy as important evidence to demonstrate its ability to make China strong and thereby bolster its legitimacy of leadership.[94] In light of these remarks, it is fair to say the neoliberal discourse functions to maintain CPC's monopoly of power in China by orienting the focus of citizens exclusively to the making of money for money's sake.

As for cosmopolitanism, there has been a growing recognition that cosmopolitanism is "a floating signifier with a diversity of competing meanings."[95] Depending on the context and location, the discourse of cosmopolitanism often displays different qualities and intents. For instance, in their research, Camicia and Franklin have repeatedly found that themes of neoliberalism and occasionally democracy are central to the understanding of cosmopolitanism in places like the U.S., the U.K., and the Philippines.[96]

In the context of China, the discourse of neoliberalism provides a new lens for understanding the complexity of cosmopolitanism. Like all other brands of cosmopolitanism, the neoliberal cosmopolitan discourse upholds an allegiance to the global community; but unlike others, it emphasizes "a global community that is best related by market rationality."[97] Indeed, under the discourse of neoliberal-cosmopolitanism, Chinese citizens are portrayed as global workers, consumers and entrepreneurs subjected to what Foucault called governmentality.[98] Despite the illusion of freedom and democracy that neoliberalism offers, no one is as free as the market promises them to be. Rather, people are enslaved by the market, which is in effect controlled by those with the most money and power in the Chinese society. Ideally, cosmopolitanism takes equality and freedom of humankind as its ultimate goal and thus serves as a valuable alternative to parochial nationalism. However, once modified by terms such as neoliberal and Confucian, cosmopolitanism loses its ring of nobility. Instead, it is exploited by the power elite in China to be part of the controlling mechanism. The lofty goal of peace and freedom is adulterated by hegemonic economic and political intentions.

We wish to emphasize here that the four discourses also interact with each other to increase their power. For example, the discourse of neoliberalism interacts with that of nationalism to promote China's citizenship education that focuses upon self-sufficient workers and nation-bound economic soldiers who would hardly challenge CPC's leadership. The two discourses together strengthen the power of both. This can be said with other discourses too. The nationalist discourse also interacts with Confucianism to train parochial patriots and obedient citizens in China.

CONCLUSION

> Yes, citizenship—above all in a society like ours, of such authoritarian and racially, sexually, and class-based discriminatory traditions—is really an invention, a political production. . . Citizenship implies freedom. . .citizenship is not obtained by chance: It is a construction that, never finished, demands we fight for it. It demands commitment, political clarity, coherence, decision. For this reason a democratic education cannot be realized apart from an education of and for citizenship.[99]

In the preceding section, we first located the four citizenship discourses (i.e., nationalism, cosmopolitianism, neoliberalism, and Confucianism) on China's discursive field of citizenship education. Among the competing citizenship discourses with some being more powerful than others, however, we scarcely find ones that are "an unambiguously emancipatory, empowering institution."[100] Our findings illustrate the way that discourses of nationalism, cosmopolitanism, neoliberalism, and Confucianism function on the discursive field of China's citizenship education. The effect of these discourses is the production of a citizenship subjectivity that is patriotic and entrepreneurial, bolstered by the morality of cosmopolitanism and Confucianism. This image of a "good citizen" is one of a docile body devoted to markets and the nation, an image that constrains understandings of a good life to those in the service of the nation and power elite.

All of the four discourses espoused in China's citizenship education curriculum standards and policy documents function as technologies of governance. Instead of enabling Chinese citizens to thrive toward emancipation, these conceptions facilitate the society's most powerful group to maintain the status quo and hegemonic control. Thus, more discussion, research, and practice should be encouraged to explore some truly liberating models of citizenship as they relate to the context of China. Freire's perception of citizenship provides an important frame of reference. A desirable citizenship model should, as Freire claimed, "imply freedom." While the discourses of citizenship have been utilized mainly by the rulers to subjugate people in China, it can also be used by the ruled to seek emancipation because power is "a machine in which everyone is caught, those who exercise power just as much as those over whom it is exercised."[101]

Before we conclude, we want to make it clear that although we are talking exclusively about the discursive field of China's citizenship education in this study, we are not indicating China as the only country that advances citizenship discourses for a hidden and repressive purpose. Many nation-states, if not all, are constructing and manipulating citizenship discourses in the best interest of the power elite in society, though their discursive fields of citizenship education may look different from China's. Our hope is that our study serves as a springboard for further discussion and research on empowering citizenship discourses that enable true freedom globally.

NOTES

1. Bryan Turner, (Ed.), *Theories of Modernity and Postmodernity*, Sage, London, England, 1990, p. 190.
2. James Arthur, Ian Davies, and Carole Hahn, (Eds.), *The Sage Handbook of Education for Citizenship and Democracy*, Sage, Los Angeles, CA, 2008, p. 5.
3. For a detailed discussion of China's citizenship throughout its history, see Wing-Wah Law, *Citizenship and Citizenship Education in a Global Age: Politics, Policies and Practices in China*, Peter Lang, New York, NY, 2011.
4. Gregory P. Fairbrother, "Citizenship Education in a Divided China, 1949–1995," *Asia Pacific Journal of Education,* vol. 24(1), 2004, p. 31.
5. Ibid., p. 34.
6. Yangguang Chen and Ivan Reid, "Citizenship Education in Chinese Schools," *Research in Education,* vol. 67, 2002.
7. Ibid.
8. Wing On Lee and Ho Chi-hang, "Citizenship Education in China: Changing Concepts, Approaches and Policies in the Changing Political, Economic and Social Context," In James Arthur, Ian Davies, and Carole Hahn (eds.), *The Sage Handbook of Education for Citizenship and Democracy*, Sage, London, England, 2008, p. 140.
9. Ibid., p.145.
10. Ibid.
11. Richard Franklin, "Intellectuals and the CCP in the Post-Mao Period: A Study in Perceptual Role Conflict," *Journal of Developing Societies,* vol. 5, 1989.
12. Lee and Ho, "Citizenship Education in China."
13. Wing-Wah Law, "The State, Citizenship Education, and International Events in a Global Age: The 2008 Beijing Olympic Games," *Comparative Education Review,* Vol. 54, 2010, p. 343.
14. Ai Guo Han, "Building a Harmonious Society and Achieving Individual Harmony," *Journal of Chinese Political Science,* Vol. 13(2), 2008.
15. Chen Lai, n.d., as quoted in S. Y. Nan, "Zhongnanhai fachu hongtouwenjian Jinagzemin tuidong aiguo jiaoyu [Zhongnanhai document: Jiang Zemin's initiation of patriotic education]," *Guangjiaojing [Wide Angle Monthly],* 272, 1995, p. 36.
16. Han, "Building a Harmonious Society and Achieving Individual Harmony," p. 146.
17. Paul Morris, John J. Cogan, and Meihui Liu, "A Comparative Overview: Civic Education across the Six Societies," In John J. Cogan, Paul Morris, and Murray Print (eds.), *Civic Education in the Asia-Pacific Region: Case Studies across Six Societies*, Routledge Falmer, New York, NY, 2002, p. 185.

18. Sara Mills, *Discourse*, Routledge, London, England, 1997, p. 11.
19. Marc W. Steinberg, "The Talk and Back Talk of Collective Action: A Dialogic Analysis of Repertoires of Discourse among Nineteenth-Century English Cotton Spinners," *American Journal of Sociology*, Vol. 105(3), 1999.
20. Anwei Feng, "Contested Notions of Citizenship and Citizenship Education: The Chinese Case," In Geof Alred, Michael Byram, and Michael P. Fleming (eds.), *Education for Intercultural Citizenship: Concepts and Comparisons*, Multilingual Matters, Clevedon, England, 2006.
21. Minghua Zhong and Wing On Lee, "Citizenship Curriculum in China: A Shifting Discourse towards Chinese Democracy, Law Education and Psychological Health," In David L. Grossman, Wing On Lee, and Kerry J. Kennedy (eds.), *Citizenship Curriculum in Asia and the Pacific*, Comparative Education Research Centre, University of Hong Kong, Hong Kong, China, 2007.
22. Liu Bao-cun, "Education for International Understanding for Cosmopolitan Citizenship in a Globalized World, " *Institute of Education, University of London*, accessed November 19, 2012, http://www.ioe.ac.uk/about/documents/About_Overview/Liu_B.pdf; Chen Yangguang, "Becoming Global Citizens through Bilingualism," *Institute of Education, University of London*, accessed November 19, 2012, http://www.ioe.ac.uk/about/documents/About_Overview/Yangguang_C.pdf
23. Wing-Wah Law, "Globalization, City Development and Citizenship Education in China's Shanghai," *International Journal of Educational Development*, Vol. 27, 2007.
24. Wing-Wah Law, "Citizenship, Citizenship Education, and the State in China in a Global Age," *Cambridge Journal of Education*, Vol. 36, 2006, p. 602.
25. David Harvey, *A Brief History of Neoliberalism*, Oxford University Press Inc., New York, 2007, p. 120.
26. Audrey Osler, and Hugh Starkey, *Teachers and Human Rights Education*, Trentham, Stoke-on-Trent, England, 2010.
27. Homi K. Bhabha, *The Location of Culture*, Routledge, New York, 1994.
28. Benedict Anderson, *Imagined Communities: Reflections on the Origin and Spread of Nationalism*, Verso, London, England, 1991.
29. Adrian Oldfield, *Citizenship and Community: Civic Republicanism and the Modern World*, Routledge, London, England, 1990, p. 73.
30. Pilvi Torsti, "How to Deal with a Difficult Past? History Textbooks Supporting Enemy Images in Post-War Bosnia and Herzegovina," *Journal of Curriculum Studies*, Vol. 39(1), 2007.
31. Steven Vertovec and Robin Cohen, "Introduction: Conceiving Cosmopolitanism," In Steven Vertovec and Robin Cohen (eds.), *Conceiving Cosmopolitanism: Theory, Context & Practice*, Oxford University Press, New York, NY, 2002.
32. Martha Nussbaum, "Patriotism and Cosmopolitanism," In Joshua Cohen (ed.), *For Love of Country: Debating the Limits of Patriotism*, Beacon, Boston, MA, 1996,p. 4.
33. Patricia Bromley, "Cosmopolitanism in Civic Education: Exploring Cross-National Trends, 1970–2008," *Current Issues in Comparative Education*, Vol. 12(1), 2009, Retrieved from http://www.tc.columbia.edu/cice/Issues/12.01/12_01_Bromley.html
34. David Held, 2001 as cited in Audrey Oslerand Hugh Starkey, "Learning for Cosmopolitan Citizenship: Theoretical Debates and Young People's Experiences," *Educational Review*, Vol. 55, 2003.
35. Nel Noddings, "Global Citizenship: Promises and Problems," In Nel Noddings (ed.), *Educating Citizens for Global Awareness*, Teachers College Press, New York, NY, 2005.

36. Michael W. Apple, "Between Neoliberalism and Neoconservatism: Education and Conservatism in a Global Context," In Nicholas C. Burbules and Carlos Alberto Torres (eds.), *Globalization and Education: Critical Perspectives*, Routledge, New York, NY, 2000.
37. Ibid., p. 60.
38. Ibid., p.18.
39. Walter C. Parker and Steven P. Camicia, "Cognitive Praxis in Today's 'International Education' Movement: A Case Study of Intents and Affinities," *Theory & Research in Social Education,* Vol. 37(1), 2009, p. 55.
40. Gilbert Rozman, (ed.), *The East Asian Region: Confucian Heritage and its Modern Adaptation*, Princeton University Press, Princeton, NJ, 1991; Tu Wei-Ming, (ed.), *Confucian Traditions in East Asian Modernity: Moral Education and Economic Culture in Japan and the Four Mini-Dragons*, Harvard University Press, Cambridge, MA, 1996.
41. William Theodore De Bary, *The Liberal Tradition of China,* The Chinese University Press, Hong Kong, China, 1983; Gay Garland Reed, "Multidimensional Citizenship, Confucian Humanism and the Imaged Community: South Korea and China," In Wing On Lee, David L. Grossman, Kerry J. Kennedy, and Gregory P. Fairbrother (eds.), *Citizenship Education in Asia and the Pacific: Concepts and Issues*, Comparative Education Research Centre, University of Hong Kong, Hong Kong, China, 2004.
42. Wing On Lee, "Emerging concepts of citizenship in the Asian context," In Wing On Lee, David L. Grossman, Kerry J. Kennedy and Gregory P. Fairbrother (eds.), *Citizenship Education in Asia and the Pacific: Concepts and Issues*, Comparative Education Research Centre, University of Hong Kong, Hong Kong, China, 2004, p. 27.
43. Ibid.
44. Yao Xinzhong, "Confucianism and Its Modern Values: Confucian Moral, Educational and Spiritual Heritages Revisited," *Journal of Belief & Values,* Vol. 20(1), 1999, p. 37.
45. Rozman, *The East Asian Region: Confucian Heritage and its Modern Adaptation*; Tu, *Confucian Traditions in East Asian Modernity: Moral Education and Economic Culture in Japan and the Four Mini-Dragons.*
46. Rozman, *The East Asian Region: Confucian Heritage and its Modern Adaptation*, p. 30.
47. Tu, *Confucian Traditions in East Asian Modernity: Moral Education and Economic Culture in Japan and the Four Mini-Dragons,* p. 8.
48. Ibid., p. 7.
49. Ibid.
50. Michel Foucault, *The History of Sexuality. Volume I: An Introduction* (R. Hurley, Trans.), Vintage Books, New York, NY, 1990.
51. Michel Foucault, "The Order of Discourse," In Robert Young (ed.), *Untying the Text: A Post-Structuralist Reader*, Routledge & Kegan Paul, Boston, MA, 1981.
52. Vertovec and Cohen, *Conceiving Cosmopolitanism: Theory, Context & Practice.*
53. Kwame Anthony Appiah, *Cosmopolitanism: Ethics in a World of Strangers,* W. W. Norton & Company, New York, NY.
54. Mirka Koro-Ljungberg, Diane Yendol-Hoppey, Jason JudeSmith, and Sharon B. Hayes, "(E)pistemological Awareness, Instantiation of Methods, and Uniformed Methodological Ambiguity in Qualitative Research Projects," *Educational Researcher,* Vol. 38, 2009.
55. Harry F. Wolcott, *Transforming Qualitative Data: Description, Analysis, and Interpretation*, Sage, Thousand Oaks, CA, 1994.

56. David A. Snow, "Framing Processes, Ideology, and Discursive Fields," In David A. Snow, Sarah A. Soule, and Hanspeter Kriesi (eds.), *The Blackwell Companion to Social Movements*, Blackwell, Malden, MA, 2004, p. 402.
57. Parker and Camicia, "Cognitive Praxis in Today's 'International Education' Movement: A Case Study of Intents and Affinities."
58. Ruth Wodak, "The Discourse-Historical Approach," In Ruth Wodak and Michael Meyer (eds.), *Methods of Critical Discourse Analysis*, Sage, London, England,2001, p. 3.
59. Corrine Glesne, *Becoming Qualitative Researchers: An Introduction* (3rd ed.), Pearson Education, Boston, MA, 2006.
60. Zhong and Lee, "Citizenship Curriculum in China: A Shifting Discourse towards Chinese Democracy, Law Education and Psychological Health"; Law, *Citizenship and Citizenship Education in a Global Age: Politics, Policies and Practices in China*.
61. Deng Xiaoping, "Women You Xinxin Ba Zhongguo De Shiqing Zuo De Geng Hao [We Are Confident That We Can Handle China's Affairs Well]," In Central Committee of Communist Party of China Document Editorial Commission (ed.), *Deng Xiaoping Wenxuan, 1983–1992 (Selected Work of Deng Xiaoping, 1983–1992)*, Renmin Publication House, Beijing, 1989, p. 325.
62. State Education Commission, "Guanyu Zai Zhongxiaoxue Jinyibu Kaizan Aiguo Zhuyi Jiaoyu Huodong De Yijian [Circular Concerning Further Implementation of Patriotic Education Activities in Primary and Secondary Schools]," *Renmin Jiaoyu [People's Education]*, 9, 1991.
63. Anatoli Rapoport, "Lonely Business or Mutual Concern: The Role of Comparative Education in the Cosmopolitan Citizenship Debates," *Current Issues in Comparative Education*, Vol. 12(1), 2009.
64. Ministry of Education, *Xiaoxue Sixiang Pinde He Chuzhong Sixiang Zhengzhike Kecheng Biaozhun De Tongzhi [A Circular on the Revision of the Curriculum Standards of Thought and Moral Character in Primary Schools and Thought and Politics in Junior Middle Schools]*, Ministry of Education, Beijing, China, 2001.
65. Law, *Citizenship and Citizenship Education in a Global Age: Politics, Policies and Practices in China*.
66. Ministry of Education, *Sixiang Pinde Kecheng Biaozhen: Shiyangao [Curriculum Standard for Thought and Moral Character: Pilot Version]*, Ministry of Education, Beijing, China, 2003.
67. Ministry of Education, *Putong Gaozhong Sixiang Zhengzhi Kecheng Biaozhun (Shiyan) [Curriculum Standard on Thought and Politics for Senior High Education, Experimental Version]*, People's Education Press, Beijing, China, 2004.
68. Law, *Citizenship and Citizenship Education in a Global Age: Politics, Policies and Practices in China*.
69. Ministry of Education, *Chuzhong Sixiang Pinde Ke, Gaozhong Sixiang Zhengzhi Ke Guanche Dang De Shiqida Jingshen De Zhidao Yijian [Guidelines on the Implementation of the Spirit of the 17th National Congress of the Communist Party of China in Thought and Moral Character in Junior High Schools and Thought and Politics in Senior High Schools]*, Ministry of Education, Bejing, China, 2007.
70. Communist Party of China, "*Communiqué of the sixth plenum of the 16th CPC Central Committee*," accessed October 11, 2006, http://news.xinhuanet.com/english/2006–10/11/content_5191071.htm. (October 11, 2006).
71. Ibid.
72. Law, *Citizenship and Citizenship Education in a Global Age: Politics, Policies and Practices in China*.

73. Ibid., *Citizenship and Citizenship Education in a Global Age: Politics, Policies and Practices in China*, p. 206.
74. Ibid.
75. Ministry of Education, *Sixiang Pinde Kecheng Biaozhen, Chuzhong Sixiang Pinde Ke*.
76. Zhang Wei-Wei, *Transforming China: Economic Reform and Its Political Implications*, St Martin's Press, New York, NY2000.
77. Parker and Camicia, "Cognitive Praxis in Today's 'International Education' Movement: A Case Study of Intents and Affinities," p. 63.
78. Law, *Citizenship and Citizenship Education in a Global Age: Politics, Policies and Practices in China*, p. 205.
79. Ibid.
80. Osler and Starkey, *Teachers and Human Rights Education*.
81. Homi K. Bhabha, *The Location of Culture*, Routledge, New York, NY, 1994.
82. Law, *Citizenship and Citizenship Education in a Global Age: Politics, Policies and Practices in China*.
83. Ibid.
84. Ibid.
85. Ibid., p. 194.
86. Ibid., p. 19.
87. Steven P. Camicia and Zhu Juanjuan, "Citizenship Education under Discourses of Nationalism, Globalization, and Cosmopolitanism: Illustrations from China and the United States," *Frontiers of Education in China*, vol. 6, 2011; John P. Geis II and Blaine Holt, "'Harmonious Society': Rise of the New China," *Strategic Studies Quarterly*, vol. 3(4), 2009.
88. James A. Banks, Foreword, In Wing-Wah Law (ed.), *Citizenship and Citizenship Education in a Global Age: Politics, Policies, and Practices in China*, Lang, New York, NY, 2011, p. xii.
89. Law, "Citizenship, Citizenship Education, and the State in China in a Global Age," p. 604.
90. Michel Foucault, *Security, Territory, Population: Lectures at the College de France, 1977–1978* (G. Burchell, Trans.), Picador, New York, NY, 2007.
91. Steven P. Camicia and Barry Franklin, "Curriculum Reform in A Globalized World: The Discourses of Cosmopolitanism and Community," *London Review of Education*, vol. 8(2), 2010, p. 98.
92. Aihwa Ong, *Neoliberalism as Exception: Mutations in Citizenship and Sovereignty*, Duke University Press, Durham, NC, 2006, p. 4.
93. Lee and Ho, "Citizenship Education in China," p. 144.
94. Law, *Citizenship and Citizenship Education in a Global Age: Politics, Policies and Practices in China*.
95. Camicia and Franklin, "Curriculum Reform in A Globalized World," p. 101.
96. Ibid.; Steven P. Camicia and Barry Franklin, "What Type of Global Community and Citizenship? Tangled Discourses of Neoliberalism and Critical Democracy in Curriculum and Its Reform," *Globalization, Societies and Education*, vol. 9, 2011.
97. Camicia and Franklin, "What Type of Global Community and Citizenship? Tangled Discourses of Neoliberalism and Critical Democracy in Curriculum and Its Reform," p. 314.
98. Michel Foucault, "The Eye of Power," In Colin Gordon (ed.), *Power/Knowledge: Selected Interviews and Other Writings 1972–1977*, Pantheon, New York, NY, 1980, p. 119.

99. Paulo Freire, *Teachers as Cultural Workers: Letters to Those Who Dare Teach* (D. Macedo, D. Koike, and A. Oliverira, Trans.), Westview Press, Boulder, CO, 1998, p. 90.
100. Patricia Wood, "The Impossibility of Global Citizenship," *Brock Education,* vol. 17, 2008, p. 25.
101. Foucault, *Power/Knowledge: Selected Interviews and Other Writings 1972–1977,* p. 156.

4 Creating Citizens in a Capitalistic Democracy

A Struggle for the Soul of American Citizenship Education

Jessica A. Heybach and Eric C. Sheffield

FIELD NOTES FROM SUMMER VACATION: A LESSON IN AMERICAN CITIZENSHIP EDUCATION

> *The Lakota and others say that Mount Rushmore isn't just a piece of art they dislike; it's a piece of art they dislike that, to put it in European terms, has been forcibly installed in their own church.*[1]

This past summer, I found myself driving across the middle of the country to show my children ages 10 and 7 more than the corn fields of the Midwest. We arrived at Badlands National Park to embark on what was to be a week of exploring the Black Hills region of South Dakota: the mud houses of the early settlers on the prairie, the strange and beautiful landscape of the Badlands rock formations, Wall Drug, a safari-like quest to find and see real "buffalo," Mt. Rushmore, Crazy Horse, Custer State Park and the Needles Highway, a live reenactment of a shootout in Deadwood, and Wind Cave National Park. I had landed myself right smack in the middle of "America"—and as someone who associates themselves with the philosophical questions of education, this experience was quite jarring. What were my children learning about who "we" were on this trip? This tour de force of "Americana" was nothing short of a relentless narrative that sought to shape the spectators' aesthetic, patriotic consciousness. As we embarked on the return trip home, we decided to spend one more day in the Badlands in order to see the site of the Wounded Knee Massacre on the Pine Ridge Indian Reservation. The critical teacher in me couldn't resist showing my children a neglected and repressed part of our actual history— rather than the officially narrated version of who we hope to be—found on the placards we read.

Pine Ridge. To many who are reading this, you might already know the story here, or anticipate where I'm going with this narrative, but in that moment I was a naïve tourist. The landscape is desolate and beautiful, sweeping skies that go on forever—then suddenly, up a ridge, we pass an American flag being flown upside down: "Mom, why is the flag upside

down?" "I'm not sure [enter the smartphone], ohhh, it means distress."
Silence. Driving through the small towns that exist on Pine Ridge, the
landscape is riddled with scenes off abject poverty. Silence. These homes
are make-shift at best—why are Native Americans living in mass-pro-
duced trailers? Silence. Suddenly, out of nowhere, a car races past us with
U.S. government issued license plates kicking dust up into the air. Silence.
Turning down what seems like a main street in one of the towns, to the
left is a large sign, so out of place, listing the names of Pine Ridge residents
lost in the wars of Iraq and Afghanistan. Silence. The only thought running
through my head: what have "we" done? What have "we" continued to
do—or not to do—that makes these sights possible?

We made our way to the site of Wounded Knee, and began reading
the sign that tells the story of what happened there in 1890, when the 7ᵗʰ
Calvary armed with the latest advancement in weaponry, the Hotchkiss
gun, opened fire on Lakota men, women, and children. This "battle"
known as a "massacre" to the Lakota, resulted in twenty Medals of
Honor bestowed upon U.S. soldiers. Silence. My daughter immediately
wanted to get out of the car and talk to the people who were selling
bracelets at the base of the hill; my son replied, "No, I'm not getting out
of the car—this is bullshit, Mom!" Silence [now was not the time for
a lecture on appropriate language]. "What's the matter?" "What's the
matter!? This is too sad—I don't get it, Mom. Why is it so bad here, why
is it like this!?" Silence. I usually have a warehouse full of answers as a
teacher-mom, but this moment escaped even my own critical narrative
*of whys. What could possibly be said for **this** to make sense? Should **this***
***ever** make sense? I convinced my son to get out of the car, and we were*
immediately met by a woman who started flipping through a laminated
newspaper telling us the story of Wounded Knee. The old black and
white photos were horrific, the story—her words, were even more tragic:
"You see. . .we need housing, we need jobs, we have so many families in
one house, our water is contaminated, we don't have heat in the winter,
and instead all we get is a new prison for our young people to end up in."
"And, a white man owns the land of Wounded Knee, and he is trying to
*sell it back to **us!**"*

The juxtaposition of the majestic spectacle of Mt. Rushmore along-
side the abject desperation of Wounded Knee was disruptive in unantici-
pated ways. I could have launched into a lecture on broken treaties and
Manifest Destiny for the benefit of my kids, but this moment was about
so much more than history: It was about perpetual, structural violence
and enforced despair at the hands of an occupying aggressor. This desper-
ate scenario seemed more than simply an issue of economic injustice. It
occurred to me that this social reality was ultimately about broken spir-
its at the deepest most visceral level. "Mom, why was everyone at Mt.
Rushmore, and no one is at Wounded Knee?" Phew [My head raced with
reasons, most of them not age appropriate]. "That's a good question. Why

do you think so?" "I don't know . . . maybe because this is so sad and it's not nice here—I'm mad, Mom. This is not right."

Later that night, as we sat in the only restaurant in Badlands National Park eating dinner, far from the sights of unemployment, despair, alcoholism, violence, grief, and wreckage, my son looked up at a row of paintings on the wall. "Mom, I like that one." "Which one?" "That one." He was pointing to a painting of Mt. Rushmore, but the faces of George Washington, Thomas Jefferson, Theodore "Teddy" Roosevelt, and Abraham Lincoln had been changed to Sitting Bull, Crazy Horse, Red Cloud, and Geronimo. I smiled. "Really? Why's that?" "Because they belong here, Mom—they were here first."

INTRODUCTION

When we were invited to write this chapter, we initially had several reactions that came in the form of (mostly) rhetorical questions. The most immediate was, "what citizenship education?" We in the United States find ourselves in the midst of state and nationally mandated "standards," most recently what is known as Common Core; a not-so-creeping corporate appropriation of public schools by none other than Bill and Melinda Gates, the Walton family, and various hedge funders to name a few; the surveillance of teachers and students alike via the development of databases such as *InBloom* that match student standardized test scores with teachers over long periods of time (we in the States call this "accountability"); and, a myriad of national educational policies meant to ensure that the U.S. remains the only economic/military superpower on the planet.[2] Given all of this, we have precious little time or energy to spend on such wasteful studies as critical democratic citizenship. Patriotism? Sure. We pledge allegiance at the start of every school day. Critically active democratic citizenship? Actively addressing questions such as those posed by the young ten-year-old? Surely not.

We also wondered how to capture the state of citizenship education in such a diverse, multifaceted, multiregional, multicultural, and multi-ideological place such as the U.S. (and as seen in our opening vignette). Our editors hint at this regional multiplicity in their brief discussion of Texas in this volume's introduction. While Texas emphasizes curricular matters important to Texans, New Yorkers (Californians, Missourians, etc.) might very well determine that those same matters are regionally less important or not important at all.[3] The result can be very different curricular structures dependent upon state and regional differences. On the other hand, we have, particularly since 1958 when Congress passed and Dwight D. Eisenhower signed the National Defense Education Act, been slowly but surely moving toward a nationalized system of education even while, constitutionally speaking, education is not a stated concern of the federal government. Yet, in utilizing its power of the purse, the federal government is clearly moving toward establishing centralized educational policy as evidenced by increasingly intrusive legislation coupled with moderate increases in funding over the last decade.[4]

Finally, we were struck by our editors' commentary in the Prologue that the authors contained in this volume "make recommendations as to what a humane, intellectually driven citizenship education might look like in the service of democracy." An important matter—what, in practice, might yield what democracy demands: an intellectually curious, knowledgeable, critical, and active citizenry? There are, of course, programs and practices at various schools around the country that seem still to provide a critical education in democratic citizenship; but, they are few and far between and increasingly find themselves in an uphill battle to remain viable given the policy trends just noted. And, not surprisingly, these programs look to be practices suggested in the early part of the twentieth century by social reconstructivists and progressive educators.

One might wonder why we opened a chapter on the contemporary state of citizenship education in the United States with a summer vacation story. We will, in working through our suggestions, use the opening vignette as the foil to the argument that citizenship in America is equated with economic imperatives of the global economy and not indebted to questioning what it means to be a citizen, and how to best address human societal problems. We will return to this narrative to argue that economic imperatives sought by neoliberal and neoconservative forces are viable and desired to them only so long as citizens do not question the very nature and aims of America's domination and socioeconomic hierarchy. As we hope will become clear in reading the chapter, we believe the opening vignette symbolizes much of what is missing currently in American citizenship education.

In what follows, we suggest the following: schooling in the U.S., and particularly citizenship education, has very recently been severely impacted by two contemporary and essential economic, social, political, and moral reconstructions. These two reconstructions—conservatism into neoconservatism and liberalism into neoliberalism—have resulted in the conflation of once vehemently contested positions on the goals of schooling. The source of this conflation, we suggest firstly, can be found in reconstructed ideologies as to the "democratic" relationship that the state "ought" to have with the individual. Though certainly nuanced, these reconstructed understandings of the self in relationship to the state are so similar in their implications that they have paved the way for a move from state and local legislative control of schools increasingly toward centralized federal legislative control of schools and, importantly, reconstruct what citizenship education should entail.

Secondly, citizenship education is increasingly meant to inculcate nothing more nor less than the underlying ("premeditated") understandings of citizen duties to the state that are implied in the neoconservative/neoliberal conflation: patriotic support of free market processes; being good consumers;

accepting that we must control the global economy as a national defense matter (often via military incursions and drone attacks); and, unwavering allegiance to the mantra that the United States is, in fact, the "shining city on the hill."[5] These "premeditated" conceptions of citizenship education, because they have been rationalized to the point of certainty, have resulted (we suggest) in a merely "aesthetic" set of teaching practices meant to engender uncritical patriotic feeling rather than an "intellectually driven" critical version of democratic citizenship.

Finally, we describe one program of study that we believe successfully interrogated—past tense—these conflationary assumptions as well as the shortcomings of patriotism-as-aesthetic-spectacle and in its place adopted an intellectually critical counter-aesthetic of active citizenship education: the Raza Studies program in Tucson, Arizona.[6] We conclude with a final suggestion: social studies scholars themselves at every level might adopt this intellectually critical and active counter-aesthetic as the means to speak truth to power and reinvigorate an "intellectually driven" version of citizenship education.

Before getting to the meat of our suggestions, we want to briefly comment on our use of two oft-contested conceptions that we utilize throughout the chapter: "aesthetics" and "citizenship." The "aesthetics" that we suggest is derived from the Greek verb, *aisthanomai*, meaning to "perceive" or "to [merely] feel." Unlike, for example, John Dewey's construction of an aesthetic that implies critically considered action, this mere aesthetic stops criticality (and any ensuing action) in its tracks. In merely feeling patriotic, our student-citizens will, we believe, increasingly support the notion that the United States is, without question, the shining city on the hill; and, rather than critically question our actions here and abroad, our student-citizens will (and with great patriotic feeling) unquestioningly support those actions. Our use of "citizen," "citizenship," and "citizenship education" is directly connected to our understanding of aesthetic as mere feeling. We want to distinguish "instrumental citizenship" from "emancipatory citizenship." Instrumental citizenship is captured in the simple right to vote; emancipatory citizenship goes well beyond the instrumentality manifested in going to the voting booth and well beyond the paralyzing aesthetic just described. Emancipatory citizenship involves a deep engagement with others of the nation—engagements that include dialogue, debate, public reflection, dissent, protest, and even revolution. We are concerned in this chapter with emancipatory citizenship.

THE POLITICAL CONFLATION OF VALUES IN AMERICAN CITIZENSHIP EDUCATION

In the last thirty-five years or so—particularly since the *Nation at Risk* report was made public—we Americans (as well as, we suppose, citizens in other Western democracies) have witnessed several strange political evolutions that have informed educational reform policies.[7] The first is the muzzling of both the radical left and the radical right. If you pay attention to talk radio or Fox News it certainly seems that the radical right is still alive and well, but beyond some verbal posturing, they have had only a small impact on actual widespread legislation—particularly education legislation. This is not to say that, especially social conservatives, aren't wading into the educational fight; the work done in places such as Texas to revise American history (recently wanting to dump Thomas Jefferson as too radical among other "revisions"), include "intelligent design" in science classes, and provide students "abstinence only" sex education are ongoing. These are issues that traditional social conservatives have and will probably always take up in our schools.[8] All in all, however, radical social conservatism has been marginalized to a talk-only status by a reconstructed conservatism: neoconservatism.

The radical left is, it seems, in the same muzzled position. Aside from some quiet complaining from within academia (and often directed only inwardly, back into the ivory tower), the rhetoric of the left, often seen as incendiary and "communistic," continues to fall on deaf ears. In fact, even the moderate left has begun taking shelter underground to avoid the vicious attacks on public service unions, collective bargaining, social services, and even teaching practices imagined to be Marxist or oriented towards socialism. And, as successful as the right has been in narrating President Obama as a leftist, socialist, un-American communist, his policy record certainly shows none of these characteristics.[9]

So, what happened while the traditional American radicals were fiddling away as Rome burned? The muzzling of the radical right and left is, it seems, either the cause for or the result of (did the chicken or the egg come first?) serious reconstructions of what conservatism and liberalism mean in theory and practice. And these reconstructions have, we believe, brought us to a very strange educational policy place: a conflation of beliefs about the goals of education, most particularly, citizenship education. What we suggest in the following analysis is that this conflation of theory and practice, coming as it does in whole cloth reconstructions of liberalism and conservatism, encourages a morality that is economic; a social perspective that is individualist; a politics that is aesthetically patriotic; and, an economic understanding that is merciless. These values are championed in public schools generally and particularly in an aesthetic, spectacle-oriented, citizenship education.

The Reconstruction of Conservatism

Neoconservatism traces its philosophical roots to Levi Strauss, Michael Oakshotte, and Alan Bloom. More recently it is seen in the work of such communitarians as Amantai Etzioni, Charles Taylor, and Alasdair

MacIntire.[10] Its birth into American politics dates back to Ronald Reagan's concept of America as "the shining city on the hill" and his 1983 speech wherein he described the former Soviet Union as "the evil empire." Neoconservatism's most recent political resurgence came with the election of George W. Bush in 2000. It is not our purpose here to outline the entire history of neoconservatism's development but it is important to distinguish neoconservatism from traditional conservatism to get at the driving ideology behind its educational policy positions.

In a recent article describing the essential political, social, economic, and moral distinctions between traditional conservatism and neoconservatism, Jack Kerwick writes that for neoconservatives,

> First, morality consists primarily of "self-evident" *principles* specifying "natural" or "human *rights*" that belong to *all* human beings just by virtue of their humanity. Second, because these principles are "self-evident," they are rationally or intellectually accessible to *all people* in *all places* and at *all times*. Third, since "liberal democracy" is the only kind of regime that embodies principles of "natural rights," and since the United States is *the* "liberal democracy" extraordinaire, the first society in all of human history erected upon "the proposition that all men are created equal," "liberal democracies" in general, and the United States in particular, have an obligation to advance "the human rights" of people *everywhere*. Finally, the only alternative to the "moral realism" of "natural rights" is "historicism" or "relativism" (emphasis in original).[11]

Neoconservatism's *a priori* rationalism brings a level of certainty that is the cause for a complete reconstruction of traditional conservative thinking on the role of the state, and by extension, citizenship education. As Kerwick implies, this certainty is entailed in the notion that the United States is self-evidently morally exceptional and has the responsibility for spreading our exceptional ideals across the globe—we are, without question, the shining city on the hill. This neoconservative self-evident certainty is based on an important distinction made by Michael Oakshotte (and explained by Kerwick) between an "enterprise notion" of state responsibility and that of a "civil association," championed by traditional conservatives.[12]

Kerwick notes that this neoconservative move away from the traditional conservative notion of the state's role, coming as it does out of a belief in universally understandable and undeniable "premeditated" timeless absolutes, is the source for a radical reconstruction of conservative beliefs regarding the role of government. From "an enterprise association" conception of the state, "citizens are partners or comrades joined together in collective pursuit of a common end . . . The purpose is taken to be a premeditated ideal— like, say, Equality or Virtue—toward the realization of which all citizens must devote (at least) some of their resources."[13] Moral principles, which inform notions of citizenship, are, then, to be handed down having already been established in and by nature, not socially constructed in the milieu of democratic dialogue, debate, and dissent.

This reconstruction results in an ideology quite different from the traditional conservative understanding of "civil association." Kerwick writes that under the civil association conception, "The state has no supreme purpose or common good in the service of which citizens must be enlisted. The citizens of a civil association are united not in terms of a common substantive purpose that demands their devotion but in terms of *law*."[14] The laws enacted by the state under the civil association understanding are *not* to be regarded as prescriptive of specific ideologies, practices, or routines. They are not substantive, but provide the *conditions* under which any citizen is to choose and act. The usurping of the conservative conditional by the neoconservative substantive implies an already established, unquestionable, dogmatic, and obligatory set of "virtues" to be prescribed and spread globally by the shining city on the hill. Charles Taylor has described these as "horizons of belief."[15] These "horizons of belief" imply a particular role for citizenship education—a "merely" aesthetic one.

The Reconstruction of Liberalism

Nearly simultaneous to the advent and growing influence of neoconservatism, liberalism has gone through an equally strange and interesting reconstruction. And much like neoconservatism's connection to classical conservatism, neoliberalism can be traced backwards to classical liberalism. It is also common for political philosophers attempting to define or at least loosely describe neoliberalism to mention its common parlance as a pejorative term for anything and everything deemed "undesirable."[16] Certainly its imprecise pejorative use is very common. But, beyond its pejorative connotations there is much substantive to be said about neoliberalism.

Gavin Kendall suggests that neoliberalism marks the second stage of liberalism's reconstruction, the first being the welfarism shift after WWII.[17] Kendall writes,

> The second phase emerged roughly in the 1970s, and is characterized by "economic rationalism," the disposal of publicly owned national industries to the private sector ("privatization"), the rolling back of the welfare state, the introduction of market-style competition into a range of arenas previously uncontaminated by such an ethos, and enforced state-sponsored inspection of zones such as education and health (which had previously been granted a greater degree of professional autonomy).[18]

Though a bit more difficult to define than neoconservatism, there are clearly common themes contained in these (and other) conceptions of neoliberalism. Those common themes include an essential grounding in economic rationalism; a reduced role for the state; and, a simultaneous shifting of social services to private entities which require, ironically, increased state oversight.

The irony of claiming that the state should only be responsible for safeguarding individual liberty and then legislating for state oversight of services that are deemed important for such liberty is not lost on scholars who have written on this matter. Kendal says it this way:

> The neoliberal turn understands government as the active constitution of the conditions under which civil society might flourish. The conditions include both the introduction of market forces and the attachment of performance targets in social areas such as health, education, and so forth. . .While there is an element of reducing the state, what is fundamental to these efforts is that a more authoritative state must now concentrate on providing the conditions under which individual entrepreneurship, self-government, freedom and responsibility can be possible.[19]

In much the same vein, Dag Einar Thorsen writes that with liberalism's reconstruction "one has moved away from a society marked by a large room for democratic governance and for exercising political authority, to a new type of society in which the 'conditions for politics' have been severely curtailed because of the onslaught of political reforms inspired by neoliberal thought and ideology."[20] These neoliberal political reforms define democratic virtue ("freedom") in economic terms and posit capitalism as an a priori "horizon of belief" similar in its implications to neoconservatism.

On the assertion that democratic virtue is essentially economic and capitalism is an *a priori* "horizon of belief," Kendal writes:

> First, they [neoliberals] establish the artificiality of the social; second, they understand the market as the source of liberty, and a true description (in the case of the Chicago School) of other areas of life, especially the social; third, they stress the importance of the manipulation of the frameworks (*Ordoliberalen*) or the stimuli (Chicago School) that surround the market; finally, they construct a new notion of self, in which actors can be seen as fundamentally economic, while their aptitudes and skills can be understood as human capital. As for the state: it has moved from being "social" to being "enabling."[21]

That is, morality, freedom, and even human selves, are envisioned as economic matters only and, given that, it is the state's role to ensure virtue via the manipulation of market stimuli that provide the optimum in individual market freedom—not by providing (as one example) public space to develop morality, freedom, and autonomous selves socially. Similarly,

Thorsen argues that neoliberal economic rationalism implies that "the virtuous person is one who is able to access the relevant markets and function as a competent actor in these markets. Inequality and glaring social injustice are under this perspective morally acceptable."[22] Given this neoliberal/neoconservative conflation of "indisputable" starting points, it is not surprising that both neoliberal and neoconservative ideologues would champion a version of citizenship education that lacks meaningful criticality, and represses difficult knowledge regarding American identity—one that is instead merely aesthetic in its means and ends. We would here remind the reader of the stark contrasts between the aesthetic spectacle of Mount Rushmore—a massive granite bust of our "founding fathers"—complete with a perpetual narrative of manifest destiny and Western expansion that celebrates the exceptionality of the American experience, versus the utter devastation and isolation of the Wounded Knee Memorial on the Pine Ridge Indian Reservation.

THE TRAITS OF CONFLATION

There is certainly plenty of commentary that might be made here in regard to the conflation we described earlier—volumes might be written. We leave it to our very able readers to connect the myriad nuanced dots and will simply point to a few of the most essential common traits of this neoliberal/neoconservative conflation. The first of these, and the most essential to the topic of citizenship education, is the premeditated nature of each camp's version of rationalism. As noted previously, neoconservatism's understanding of the "enterprise association" relationship between the state and the individual implies that there exists a set of *a priori* "givens" that cannot be questioned and that serve as the enterprise's goals-to-be-achieved. Those givens come out of a naturalistic rationalism that posits the rights of individual humans to act freely with little regard for others—a "freedom from" conception of liberty—and, importantly, to act in ways that spread this premeditated understanding across the globe. This freedom to act as individuals is to be unfettered so long as it supports (or at least, doesn't interfere with) the neoconservative collective pursuit, and is to be spread by way of economic and military power by the shining city on the hill. Implied in this is that any policy, nation, or individual who critically condemns this West-is-best starting point is, by virtue of that critique, immoral and stands against the enterprise of individual economic freedom.

Though neoliberals begin with a slightly different version of rationalism, it implies much the same as the neoconservative position. Neoliberal rationalism asserts that there exists an *a priori* virtue in human beings that can be described and measured via an economic calculus. The virtuous neoliberal can be judged as to her level of "goodness" by evaluating her ability to access markets, take risks in those markets, and understand that any failure on her part is not because of systemic matters but because of a failure on her part to be a moral actor. In both neoliberalism and neoconservatism the "rationalized" morality-defining starting point cannot be questioned as each is accepted as being a manifestation of human nature: acting virtuously is to participate as an individual economic agent or to participate as a supporter of the shining city on the hill; individual freedom is to be made available in the very limited space of the economic system and freedom's goal is to spread neoconservative/neoliberal conflationary ideologies across the globe.

Additionally, schools (public or private) should be provided a level of federal economic support to inculcate these goals into our students via particularly "citizenship education" that champions these beliefs and, in so doing, "teaches" our young citizens how to feel and then act in order to be a successful spreader of Western belief, or a virtuous economic actor, both of which can be judged by individual economic success and/or failure. Educational policy should, then, engender practices that create individuals who champion the American way of life, and support the American economic system as a matter of national defense.

Evidence that the conflation suggested here impacts educational legislation is not difficult to find. The mother of all federal educational policy "mandates," No Child Left Behind (NCLB) was sponsored by none other than Ted Kennedy and John Boehner—strange conflationary bedfellows indeed.[23] Furthermore, NCLB passed both the House and the Senate in landslide fashion: 384–45 in the House and 87–10 (with 3 abstentions) in the Senate.[24] As to NCLB commentary on "citizenship education," (and with no explanation) it lists under its Character Education section simply that "Citizenship and Civic Virtue" be taught.[25] Of course, why would "Civic Virtue" need explaining given the conflation of premeditated beliefs?

Additional legislative evidence can be found in the broadly applauded Race to the Top grant program (requiring states to develop data base teacher-student accountability tracking systems), the omission of state-wide tests on social studies, and contemporary political speech couching schooling's importance as an economic matter only.[26] In fact, as we write this chapter, our "socialist" president is on a town hall meeting tour advocating the value of higher education as the means to ensure America's economic security—not as the means to ensure a democratically critical citizenry, but as a national defense matter.[27] The final evidence of this conflation is in the most recent iteration of centralized control over educational policy and practice: Common Core Standards.

CITIZENSHIP IN SCHOOLS

The Common Core Standards, which were conceived by state Governors and the Council of Chief State School Officers in partnership with the nonprofit organization Achieve, are the most federalized form of curriculum to make its way into American classrooms in the history of schooling in the United States.[28] To date, forty-five states and the District of Columbia have adopted these standards; a surprise holdout: Texas. Texas has repeatedly defended their autonomy—or, state's rights—over curriculum and assessment as the rationale for rejecting Common Core. Recently, the Texas state legislature in a vote of 140–2 banned Common Core standards from being used in public schools as well as the "adopt[tion] or develop[ment] [of] a criterion-referenced assessment instrument . . . based on common core state standards."[29] This law, known as HB 462, was signed into law in on June 14, 2013, by Governor Rick Perry, and stands as a symbolic line in the sand regarding any move towards a federal curriculum in the United States. To be sure, the irony of Texas's position on Common Core is not lost on educational policy observers and educators who often cite Texas as the midwife of standardization and accountability.

The move to Common Core standards follows a decade of educational policy that seeks to dismantle the traditional understanding of public schooling in America, and replace it once and for all with a privatized system that can overtly be tied to the conflationary economic agenda of advanced capitalism. The explicit and ominous mission statement of these standards uncovers this intent by aiming to provide

> . . . a consistent, clear understanding of what students are expected to learn, so teachers and parents know what they need to do to help them. The standards are designed to be robust and relevant to the real world, reflecting the knowledge and skills that our young people need for *success in college and careers*. With American students fully prepared for the future, our communities will be best positioned to *compete successfully in the global economy* (our emphasis).[30]

There exists in these standards no direct discussion of citizenship education, except the unwritten implication that all one must do in society is be "successful" in college, careers, and the global economy. Thus, success in the global economy *is* the defining characteristic and moral obligation of the "good" citizen. This notion has become so prevalent in educational policy that it need no longer be questioned by most educational reformers and school officials—it has become rationalized. Any other educational aim is seen as a diversion at best and anti-American at worst.

The stated economic imperatives of Common Core are echoed elsewhere in the American power hierarchy. In a 2012 report issued by the Council for Foreign Relations, headed up by Joel Klein, former Chancellor of the New York City Department of Education, Condoleezza Rice, former Secretary of State under the Bush administration, and a long list of noteworthy task force members, the rhetoric of economic security vis-à-vis educational preparation was ratcheted up to what appears to be an all new level of hysteria:

> The lack of preparedness poses threats on five national security fronts: economic growth and competitiveness, physical safety, intellectual property, U.S. global awareness, and U.S. unity and cohesion, says the report. Too many young people are not employable in an increasingly high-skilled and global economy, and too many are not qualified to join the military because they are physically unfit, have criminal records, or have an inadequate level of education.[31]

According to this logic, American teachers have become *the* core factor responsible for the state of national and global security.[32] Although we do not want to claim teachers and schooling have no influence in shaping these issues, the list of other significant social factors that aid the production of citizens who are "unfit," possess "criminal records," and suffer from "inadequate level[s] of education" seems to have been omitted from the discussion. Unfortunately, the effects of high-fructose corn syrup in our food supply, minimum sentencing requirements in our courts, and the closure of dozens of public schools and programs in Chicago and elsewhere (to name a few other potential factors) do not rise to the level of national and global security and such questions present difficult challenges to the premeditated conflationary rationalities outlined earlier.

Specific to the topic at hand, the Task Force document addresses "civics" and citizenship education by calling on schools and educators to take seriously the unpreparedness of American students which, "leaves most twelfth graders unable to describe how laws are passed, unfamiliar with landmark Supreme Court decisions, and unsure of the functions of the U.S. Constitution or the Bill of Rights."[33] This aspect of the report was commended by many education scholars and policymakers that served on the Task Force (Linda Darling-Hammond, Randi Weingarten, etc.).[34] However, the report goes on to explain:

> The Task Force does not necessarily believe that every U.S. student should be reading Chinese; indeed, too many are not reading English well enough. However, the group is troubled by the language deficit, and fears that it will prevent U.S. citizens from participating and competing meaningfully, whether in business or diplomatic situations. It will also have a negative impact on government agencies and corporations attempting to hire people knowledgeable about other countries or fluent in foreign languages.[35]

Thus, it becomes clear that "civics" education only matters as it relates to global economic imperatives; certainly not as a matter of developing an "intellectually driven" critical citizenry who might question the *a priori* assumptions of U.S. global domination and security.

Beyond Common Core standards as political rhetoric and economic imperative, these standards have effectively reduced social studies instruction to literacy-only instruction. These standards include no content traditionally thought of as "social studies," and rely on the states to craft or utilize a supplemental set of standards to ensure content is included.[36] Instead, Common Core attends to social studies-as-reading in the following manner:

> The standards. . .begin at grade 6; standards for K–5 reading in history/social studies, science, and technical subjects are integrated into the K–5 Reading standards. The CCR [Common Core Reading] anchor standards and high school standards in literacy work in tandem to define *college and career readiness expectations*—the former providing broad standards, the latter providing additional specificity (our emphasis).[37]

In addition to this general discussion of history/social studies as reading literacy, the Common Core document does make suggestions for the inclusion of certain informational (nonfiction) texts often associated with social studies instruction.

Under the section titled "Texts Illustrating the Complexity, Quality, & Range of Student Reading 6–12," Common Core lists Lincoln's *Gettysburg Address*, Martin Luther King's *Letter From a Birmingham Jail*, Thomas Paine's *Common Sense*, Fredrick Douglas' *Narrative of the Life of Frederick Douglass, an American Slave*, Emerson's *Society and Solitude*, Elie Wiesel's *Hope, Despair, and Memory*, and so forth.[38] Still, such important historical texts are included as a matter of literacy instruction only and not necessarily as part of an interdisciplinary approach to understanding the value these texts have for developing a critical, intellectually driven, active citizenry. Although phrases such as, "analyze," "compare and contrast," "compare points of view," "assess reasoning," and "determine central ideas" are repeated throughout the document, sans a substantive discussion of disciplinary content knowledge and experiential learning opportunities, social studies will surely become only a means for reading and writing instruction and result in an "in-your-seat-only" citizenship experience. Furthermore, aside from the inclusion of the traditional dichotomy of "dead old white guys" and "black civil rights leaders," there are glaring omissions in the Common Core suggested readings—most importantly: the diminution of current events that might result in "global cultural awareness" needed for actively engaged citizens of the world today.

If we return to the opening vignette, we see clearly that experiences based on meaningful interaction and engagement in and with community as a means to develop action-oriented citizenship skills, or a critical consciousness, have been successfully eradicated from the aims of education, and will likely never see the light of day within the walls of a school. Further, given the political conflation of the aims of schooling it is not surprising to see such experientially active educational practices eliminated from schools: such practices are far too dangerous to the premeditated economic enterprise so crucial to maintaining our place as the only superpower on the planet.

CITIZENSHIP OUTSIDE OF SCHOOLS

In this final section, we want to highlight one recent school program that has challenged the status quo of citizenship education, and the citizen-as-economic-actor-only education, by focusing on an action-oriented, inquiry-driven, critically conscious investigation of American society; a program led by teachers and community activists who interrogated what it means to be an educated citizen in a democracy. Tucson, Arizona—ground zero for ethnic studies in America—experimented with a curriculum that infused critical pedagogy, a structural analysis of social problems, indigenous knowledge, and community activism at a deeply intellectual and emotional level to reach students that had been neglected, mis-educated, and forgotten by the larger system.

Mexican American Studies, otherwise known as "Raza Studies," was developed to address the alarming high school drop-out rate among Latino/a youth—a rate higher than any other minority group in America.[39] These classes explicitly used "social justice pedagogy" to develop a critical consciousness in students, and inspire them to act in their communities to solve societal problems. The success of the program in raising graduation rates to 93% among its participants was noted and praised by many in education.[40] According to David Scott, Director of Accountability and Research for the Tucson Unified School District (TUSD), "Juniors taking a MAS course are more likely than their peers to pass the reading and writing AIMS subject tests if they had previously failed those tests in their sophomore year. And, seniors taking a MAS course are more likely to persist to graduation than their peers."[41] Similarly, "ethnic studies" programs generally have been shown to benefit both minority and nonminority students' understandings of what it means to be a citizen of a democracy, or what contemporary researchers call the "outcomes of democracy."[42]

Regardless of such improvements in academic outcomes and its success in developing both minority and nonminority students' inclinations toward actively engaged citizenship (or because of it), the State Superintendent of Public Instruction for Arizona, Tom Horne, issued an *Open Letter to the Citizens of Tucson* in 2007 calling for an end to the Mexican American Studies program.[43] Following the publication of this letter, a fierce debate over ethnic studies ensued, spilling into the streets of Tucson, and in the process inextricably entangled the ethnic studies issue with the strictest immigration bill passed in generations: SB 1070.[44] In 2010, Governor Jan Brewer signed the immigration bill into law as well as HB 2281 which banned any "courses or classes that: (1) promote the overthrow of the United States government; (2) promote resentment toward a race or class of people; (3) are designed primarily for pupils of a particular ethnic group; or (4) advocate ethnic solidarity instead of the treatment of pupils as individuals."[45] We find the language in this bill quite telling: it is clearly indicative of the conflation described previously and came with other public commentary suggesting that Raza studies was "anti-American" and "seditious" in its questioning of systemic oppression—in a word, the Raza studies program was seen as politically, ethically, and economically immoral as understood from within the neoconservative/neoliberal conflationary perspective.

The documentary film, *Precious Knowledge*, produced by a parent of one student enrolled in the classes, uncovers the intense power of this type of citizenship education, and the dangerous nature of engaging youth in the supposed controversial content that is so often neglected and/or repressed in contemporary P–12 classrooms.[46] Ironically, the methods used in these classes clearly adhere to and achieve the aims of Common Core standards. Students "read" and "analyze," "compare and contrast," "evaluate explanations . . . to address a question or solve a problem," "determine the meaning of words," "evaluate different points of view," "cite specific textual evidence to support analysis of primary and secondary sources." Without a doubt, we believe this curriculum produces students that can, "read and comprehend history/social studies text complexity . . . independently and proficiently." Furthermore, these are *the* skills needed to become "successful in the college, careers, and the global economy." So what then is all the controversy about?

It appears the ethnic studies controversy is not about adhering to arbitrarily conceived national standards that are meant to achieve global economic success—on paper, it does this well; but rather, the controversy was driven by the potential disruption of aesthetically generated nationalistic forms of allegiance to the idea of "America"—disruptions that were part and parcel of the Raza studies program. Thus, it is not a matter of *how* students were learning so much as *what* students were learning, namely to question the ideology of America as the shining city on the hill. Clearly, the students who are able to perform better on standardized tests, graduate high school, and enter college are achieving the aims on Common Core by becoming "successful in college, career, and the global economy"—these students can now enter American society as successful economic actors. But this is not all that is desired from within the neoliberal/neoconservative conflationary morality; docility, it seems, must be the final essential trait of American citizenship in the neoconservative/neoliberal worldview. Thus, programs of study need not develop a student's desire to question the social order and disrupt the hegemonic economic life of the United States; rather, a good consumer learns to act within the system that already exists because of their allegiance to American capitalism and market imperatives. The Raza Studies ability to inspire students to become active intellectually critical citizens appears to be what makes this type of pedagogy too dangerous.

Although this curriculum was legally banned in 2010, in 2013 the program was resurrected to meet the requirements of a 1978 federal desegregation court order that found the Tucson school district had historically acted with "segregative intent." As a result, the Tucson school district was required to "undertake a specific task, implement a specific program or adopt a specific policy" to remedy the discriminatory practices of the past.[47] Yet, it remains to be seen if the revised Mexican American Studies program will retain, in spirit or substance, the aims of the original Raza Studies. The new program director, Maria Figueroa stated in a recent interview: "All I know is we have to do what board members say, and we have to be in compliance with the state . . . I do stand firm in knowing and understanding that children need to read literature that is relevant to them and know the contributions they've made to society. I think that's where our teachers were coming from."[48]

CONCLUSION

As we noted at the outset, it is exceedingly difficult to capture the whole of contemporary citizenship education in such a vastly diverse place as the United States. Our suggestions are that the neoconservative/neoliberal conflation on the goals of schooling, with particular attention to citizenship education has landed us in a very precarious position: citizenship education has come to be seen, in increasingly centralized policy and practice, as an exercise of inculcating into our students an uncritical, aesthetically oriented, patriotism—a patriotism that is predicated on the unquestioned belief that America, as the only economic and military superpower on the planet, is indeed the shining city on the hill. And, we will only continue to be that shining city if citizens remain virtuous in freely, yet uncritically, acting within the premeditated confines of a morality that is politically patriotic, socially individualistic, and economically merciless. We must feel this patriotism, not interrogate its meaning.

To conclude, we want to return to the public debate regarding the nature and intent of the Raza Studies programs, and draw from that discourse a profound question regarding this type of citizenship education. During a press conference, one member of the audience responded to Tom Horne's accusations against the Raza Studies with the following: "You mentioned the group in the uniforms there [pointing at a picture of the Tucson Brown Berets], and I spoke to one of them last week and it's a movement in the Barrio. . .it's not militant, but more a matter of unity together, to stay in school and to succeed—is that a threat?"[49] And perhaps, this question brings into sharp focus the underlying "threat" that critical intellectually driven citizenship education presents for neoconservative and neoliberal forces in American culture—what will happen to existing power structures if American citizens are awakened to their civic power rather than their economic potential? Or to put it another way, what if all our children spent a day on Pine Ridge questioning who "we" are? Until social studies scholars themselves become actively engaged in recovering an "intellectually driven," active version of citizenship education based on the question of who "we" are, citizenship education in the United States—and citizenship generally—will remain in deep and abiding distress.

NOTES

1. Indian Country Today Media Network Staff, "A Different View of Mount Rushmore," *Indian Country Today Media Network*, April 14, 2012, http://indiancountrytodaymedianetwork.com/ article/a-different-view-of-mount-rushmore-108274. Mount Rushmore National Memorial is near Keystone, South Dakota, in the United States and features a colossal sculpture carved into the face of a granite mountain. The carvings represent portraitures of George Washington, Thomas Jefferson, Theodore Roosevelt, and Abraham Lincoln. For more on the Memorial's history, see: http://www.nps.gov/moru/historyculture/carving-history.htm.
2. InBloom is a commercial "system" that can be purchased to track student/teacher performance: https://www. inbloom.org/.
3. We write this chapter just after Texas passed a law forbidding the state of Texas from participating in the Common Core.
4. "The Federal Role in Education," U.S. Department of Education, accessed September 5, 2013, http://www2.ed. gov/about/overview/fed/role.html.
5. Ronald Reagan used this phrase often throughout his political career to indicate his neoconservative belief that only the United States could lead the world.
6. For the complete story of the Raza Studies program in Tucson, see Ari Luis Palos, Eren McGinnis, Sally Jo Fifer, Jacob Bricca and Naim Amor, *Precious Knowledge* (2011, Dos Vatos, Mexico, Dos Vatos Productions), DVD.
7. U.S Department of Education, the National Commission on Excellence in Education, *A Nation at Risk: The Imperative for Educational Reform*. Washington, DC: United States Government Printing, 1983, 65 pp. This controversial report suggested "a rising tide of mediocrity" in U.S. education.

8. James C. McKinley, Jr., "Texas Conservatives Win Curriculum Change," *New York Times.com*, (New York, NY), March 12, 2010, http://www.nytimes.com/2010/03/13/education/13texas.html?_r=0.
9. One such bizarre narrative was that the bailout of Wall Street was somehow socialist in that the government would temporarily take some ownership of the banks during the bailout period. But as David Harvey noted soon after the bailout, "The term 'national bailout' is therefore inaccurate, because they're not bailing out the whole of the existing financial system—they're bailing out the banks, the capitalist class, forgiving them their debts, their transgressions, and only theirs. The money goes to the banks but not to the homeowners who've been foreclosed on, which is beginning to create anger. And the banks are using the money not to lend to anybody but to buy other banks. They are consolidating their class power." David Harvey, "Is this Really the End of Neoliberalism?," Counterpunch, March 13, 2009, http://www.counterpunch.org/2009/03/13/is-this-really-the-end-of-neoliberalism/.
10. For a discussion of the communitarian position on liberty, see Eric C. Sheffield, *Community Service Learning: Philosophical Perspectives* (New York: Peter Lange Publishing, 2011), 55–70.
11. Jack Kerwick, "The Neoconservative Conundrum," *Modern Age*, Winter/Spring 2013: 9.
12. Ibid., 11.
13. Ibid.
14. Ibid.
15. Charles Taylor, *The Malaise of Modernity*, Toronto, ON: House of Anansi Press, 1998.
16. Einar Dag Thorsen, "The Neoliberal Challenge: What is Neoliberalism?," *Contemporary Readings in Law and Social Justice 2* (2), 2010: 190.
17. Gavin Kendal, "What is Neoliberalism?," The Australian Sociological Association 2003 Conference Proceedings (Sydney: TASA, 2003): 1.
18. Ibid.
19. Ibid., 2.
20. Thorsen, "The Neoliberal Challenge," 208.
21. Kendal, "What is Neoliberalism?," 5.
22. Thorsen, "The Neoliberal Challenge," 204.
23. No Child Left Behind, commonly referred to as NCLB was a successful reauthorization of the Elementary and Secondary Education Act that increased accountability schemes. The bill was cosponsored by a list of unusual allies: John Boehner (Republican–Ohio), George Miller (Democrat–California), Edward Kennedy (Democrat, Massachusetts), and Judd Gregg (Republican–New Hampshire). Any close observer of American politics would note the unusual consensus that was generated in the passing of this landmark legislation. NCLB was passed with a vote of 91–8 in the U.S. Senate, and signed into law by George W. Bush. No Child Left Behind Act of 2001, Pub. L. No. 107–110, § 115, Stat. 1425 (2002).
24. Ibid.
25. United States House Bill, H.R. 1 (*The No Child Left Behind Act*), 2001, 395.
26. U.S. Department of Education, "Race to the Top Fund," accessed September 7, 2013, http://www2.ed.gov/ programs/racetothetop/index.html.
27. The White House, President Barack Obama, "A Better Bargain for the Middle Class," accessed September 7, 2013, http://www.whitehouse.gov/a-better-bargain.
28. Achieve is a nonprofit organization supporting Common Core and Next Generation Science Standards. The Chairman of Board of Directors for Achieve

is the former CEO of Intel Corporation, Craig R. Barrett. Other board members include a handful of state Governors, former Prudential Financial, Inc. and IBM executives. See www. achieve.org.

29. LegiScan, "Bill Text: TX HB462/2013–2014/83rd Legislature," accessed September 6, 2013, http://legiscan.com/ TX/text/HB462/id/682268.

30. Common Core State Standards Initiative, "Mission Statement," accessed September 5, 2013, http://www. corestandards.org/.

31. Council on Foreign Relations, "U.S. Education Reform and National Security, Accessed September 5, 2013, http://www.cfr.org/united-states/us-education-reform-national-security/p27618, 3.

32. The rhetoric in this document is worthy of much more commentary than space allows for in this chapter. Most importantly, the task force issues three recommendations: "Implement educational expectations in subjects vital to protecting national security. . . Make structural changes to provide students with good choices . . . Launch a "national security readiness audit" to hold schools and policymakers accountable for results and to raise public awareness. At the heart of this recommendation is the creation of more meaningful assessments and simulations of student learning and, then, a coordinated, national effort to create targets and repercussions tied to the Common Core. A high-publicity public awareness campaign linked to the audit will engage the American people." Ibid., 44–45.

33. The report uses 2010 NAEP data from fourth and eighth grade students to support this claim. Ibid., 16.

34. Linda Darling-Hammond and Randi Weingarten, in particular, issued dissenting views to the final Task Force document, attached to the final document as an appendix. Other dissenting views were noted by Stephen M. Walt (Harvard Kennedy School), Jonah M. Edelman (Stand for Children), Shirley Ann Jackson (Rensselaer Polytechnic Institute), Carole Artigiani (Global Kids, Inc.), Ellen V. Futter (American Museum of Natural History). In total, there were thirty participants who were asked to join a consensus signifying that they endorse "the general policy thrust and judgments reached by the group, though not necessarily every finding and recommendation." Ibid., v.

35. Ibid., 16.

36. Social studies is defined by the National Council of Social Studies (NCSS) as "the integrated study of the social sciences and humanities to promote civic competence. Within the school program, social studies provides coordinated, systematic study drawing upon such disciplines as anthropology, archaeology, economics, geography, history, law, philosophy, political science, psychology, religion, and sociology, as well as appropriate content from the humanities, mathematics, and natural sciences. In essence, social studies promotes knowledge of and involvement in civic affairs. And because civic issues—such as health care, crime, and foreign policy—are multidisciplinary in nature, understanding these issues and developing resolutions to them require multidisciplinary education. These characteristics are the key defining aspects of social studies." National Council for the Social Studies, "About National Coucil for the Social Studies, Accessed September 7, 2013, http://www.socialstudies. org/about. We remind the reader that assessments of common core will not include social studies. Thus, we question if social studies will in fact be taught. Since NCLB the amount of time spent on social studies and science has plummeted to all-time lows. In many elementary schools, these two subject areas have been completely extinguished and traded-in for "literacy and math" only instruction. See FairTest, "New Evidence Strngthens Claim that Testing Narrows Curriculum," Accessed September 6, 2013, http://www.fairtest.org/new-evidence-strengthens-claim-testing-narrows-cur.

37. Common Core State Standards Initiative, "English Language Arts Standards—History/Social Studies/Introduction," Accessed September 6, 2013, http://www.corestandards.org/ELA-Literacy/RH/introduction.

38. Ibid.,"English Language Arts Standards/Standard 10: Range, Quality, & Comlexity/Texts Illustrating the Complexity, Quality, & Range of Student Reading 6–12," Accessed September 6, 2013, http://www.corestandards.org/ELA-Literacy/standard-10-range-quality-complexity/texts-illustrating-the-complexity-quality-range-of-student-reading-6–12

39. The actual data on graduation rates is technically difficult to say the least. See: Alliance for Excellent Education, "Understanding High School Graduation Rates in Arizona," Accessed September 6, 2013, http://www.all4ed.org/files/Arizona_wc.pdf.

40. IndependentLens, "Precious Knowledge," Accessed September 6, 2013, http://www.pbs.org/independentlens/ precious-knowledge/film.html.

41. Cambium Learning, Inc. *Curriculum Audit of the Mexican American Studies Department Tucson Unified School District*, Miami Lakes, FL: National Academic Educational Partnership, 2011.

42. Christine Sleeter, *The Academic and Social Value of Ethnic Studies: A Research Review*, Washington, DC: National Education Association,. 2011.

43. The complete text of Horne's letter can be found at Scribd.com: http://www.scribd.com/doc/32001977/An-Open-Letter-to-the-Citizens-of-Tucson.

44. SB 1070, *The Support Our Law Enforcement and Safe Neighborhoods Act*, is meant to help put an end to illegal immigration.

45. State of Arizon House Bill 2281, Accessed September 6, 2013, http://www.azleg.gov/legtext/49leg/2r/bills/hb22 81s.pdf. Subsequently, the 2011 Cambian Learning, Inc. report found that "during the curriculum audit period, no observable evidence was present to indicate that any classroom within Tucson Unified School District is in direct violation of the law . . . In most cases, quite the opposite is true. Consider, if classes promoted resentment or ethnic solidarity, then evidence of an ineffective learning community would exist within each school aligned with the Mexican American Studies Department. That was not the case. Every school and every classroom visited by the auditors affirmed that these learning communities support a climate conducive to student achievement." Cambium Learning, Inc. *Curriculum Audit, 50.*

46. Paulos, et. al., *Precious Knowledge.*

47. Roy Fisher, *et al.*, and Maria Mendoza, *et al.* v. Tucson Unified School District (Nos. 10–15124, 10–15375, 10–15407).

48. Alexis Huicochea, "Mexican American Program Gets New Leader, Name, Focus, *Arizona Daily Star Online*, Accessed September 6, 2013, http://azstarnet.com/news/local/education/precollegiate/mexican-american-program-gets-new-leader-name-focus/article_3ed1cffc-d3f3–5f53-b6bd-bf26a290916c.html, 1.

49. Paulos et. al., *Precious Knowledge.*

5 Citizenship Education in Spain in the Twenty-First Century

Miquel Martínez and Enric Prats

INTRODUCTION

Citizenship education has shown itself to be a decisive factor in the construction of democratic societies, if the declarations of experts and international organizations are anything to go by. But its presence in education is not free from technical controversy and political dispute, as reflected in the case of Spain that we describe in this chapter. Briefly, the effective integration in schools of the task of educating for citizenship requires more than simple curricular and ideological agreements. It also needs actions aimed at teacher training and achieving a school model that facilitates practice of the active and participatory citizenship it proclaims. The matter needs special treatment, quite different from that received by other school areas or subjects, not only because of its marked ideological profile but also due to the ambiguity that surrounds it. In addition to the epistemological requirements necessary in any curricular program, citizenship education demands significant social consensus for its effective integration into the school. Once these requirements have been resolved, the methodological approaches that will most ensure accomplishment of the educational goals they seek to accomplish must be specified.

The first part of this chapter sets out the social and political conditions that explain the situation of citizenship education in primary and secondary schools in Spain. Thus it presents the ideological disputes arising out of introduction in the 2006 Law on Education of a specific subject dedicated to education for citizenship, which has now been eliminated with the recent education reform launched in May 2013 by the current Spanish government. This situation responds to a political climate contaminated by party disputes that hamper fruitful dialogue and the establishment of consensual educational programming. Until recently, European reports on citizenship education had placed Spain at the forefront thanks to the initiatives emanating from the 2006 law, but the newly announced changes could now position the country with its back to Europe. In our argumentation we analyse the difference between civics and citizenship, as an example of this ideological conflict.

In the second part of the chapter, we put forward a proposal for education in citizenship and values that transcends the curricular setting and appeals to the individual's sense of community responsibility. In particular, it contends that the importance of this matter should merit the involvement of all actors in the education process, from teachers to families, with the full participation of students. The proposal outlines a model of learning ethics in which the importance of acquiring social and citizenship competence is underlined through an educational focus that sets situations to facilitate experience in this area. The aim, in short, is to clarify what type of citizenship we want to promote from the school, so that we can design an educational method fit to purpose.

THE SPANISH SOCIOPOLITICAL CONTEXT

In a rapid diagnosis, citizenship education in Spain responds faithfully to the swings from progress to retrogression experienced by the Spanish education system and the general political situation over recent decades. Politically, the setting has been dominated by two tendencies, one axis formed by the right-left dichotomy, crossed with another arising out of the demand for nationalist recognition present in some areas of Spain, such as Catalonia and the Basque Country. Moreover, in order to understand the Spanish education system, it helps to make a brief review of its historical development since emergence from the Franco dictatorship, formally ended in 1975 on the general's death but perhaps still valid decades later in the minds of some.

Democracy arrived in Spain in 1978, with the approval of a constitution which outlines fundamental rights and the current system of political operation. It is a framework text of public freedoms, one of whose outstanding features is a system of administrative decentralization into autonomous territorial communities, an aspect which would have significant relevance in the subsequent shaping of the education system. In the intervening period of almost four decades, the Spanish parliament has maintained a certain stability in terms of its composition, with two majority parties succeeding each other in responsibility for governing, along with other groups that are smaller but highly representative in their respective geographical areas, in addition to a number of minority forces on the national scale. The first democratic elections in 1979 resulted in triumph for a coalition of small groups, many of which were heirs of Francoism, under the name Union of the Democratic Centre (Unión de Centro Democrático [UCD]), whose short life was truncated by the attempted military takeover of 1981. This event had a determining influence both on the future of Spanish politics as well as on how the Spanish constitution would develop.

A Debate between Political Parties: The Citizen in the Middle

Thus the elections of 1982 handed victory to the Spanish Socialist Workers Party (Partido Socialista Obrero Español [PSOE]), which brought together left-wing intellectuals and workers' organizations and obtained an overwhelming majority, enabling them to govern alone. One of the new government's first measures was to develop the right to education, in a law passed in 1985 which recognized not only universal access to a basic education but also families' freedom to choose the schools to which they would send their children. The 1985 law also developed the democratic school model with broad participation by the families in school governance, and recognized the role of private initiative in opening education centers. This law remains in force to this day. The same government would, in 1990, enact legislation which would prove fundamental for Spanish education and which is also still valid today. It describes the structure of education by stages, specifies innovative curricular principles—which we will examine later—and establishes a clear distribution of educational responsibilities between the central government and the governments of the autonomous communities. These aspects are critical to understanding the current education model.

The general elections of 1996 handed partial victory to the Popular Party (Partido Popular [PP]), a political force that had united the former Union of the Democratic Centre and other center-right groups. With support from the small nationalist parties of the Basque Country, the Canaries, Navarre, and above all, Catalonia, the right was able to build a government and launch a policy of reforms in such sensitive areas as healthcare, social services and education, in patent opposition to previous left-wing policies. Furthermore, the absolute majority subsequently gained in the 2000 elections enabled the conservative government to intensify its program of change and embark upon laying the foundations for more radical modification of the educational model, which it would embody in a law in 2002, replacing that of 1990.

This 2002 law was never implemented, however, as an unexpected victory by the left in the 2004 elections and the education community's widespread rejection of the legislation led to its immediate abolition. Despite not holding an absolute majority, the left succeeded in passing a new law in 2006 which maintained the principles of the 1990 measures, though somewhat diluted, and introduced a subject called Education for Citizenship, which would enjoy a timid presence in the curriculum of compulsory education stages, as we will discuss later.

In response to the 2008 economic crisis, the government called early elections in 2011, which once again resulted in victory for the right by an absolute majority. This has enabled them to recover their program for reforms in the social sphere, with the introduction of a new education law in force since January 2014, and whose application is anticipated from the 2014–2015 academic year.

As we have mentioned, in addition to the alternation between right and left the Spanish political panorama is crossed by a nationalist axis which is also present in the social debate. More specifically, nationalist demands in the Basque Country and Catalonia have determined political action throughout the almost four decades of democracy. The secessionist drive for independence from Spain coexists socially and politically with a unionist movement committed to remaining in the same State, which also explains the political toing and froing in Spain, given that the national-ist forces often have major significance in forming parliamentary majori-ties. In concrete terms, the center-right oriented nationalist forces of both regions have dominated the political scene of recent decades with a notable presence in their respective governments, except for a few brief periods in which the local left has managed to prevail over regional parliaments.

The importance of Catalonia and the Basque Country in Spanish soci-ety as a whole cannot be understood solely from the political standpoint for the support their respective parties can offer the Spanish government, because their relevance also extends into the economic plane. According to data from the World Bank, in 2011, Spanish GDP stood at around 1.5 tril-lion dollars, comparable to that of Canada, which produced an income of 31,440 dollars per capita. The Spanish contribution to the European Union is almost 10% and, in comparison to other European countries of the same demographic characteristics, it occupies a middle-to-low position (German GDP, for example, is 3.2 trillion; that of France and the United Kingdom, 2.3; Italy 1.8; Turkey 1.1, and Poland 0.8).

From an internal perspective, Catalonia and the Basque Country con-tribute a quarter of Spain's total GDP, each having a per capita income situated at the high end of that of the country as a whole. This prominent economic position also explains the secessionist unease felt by a good deal of the population of these regions, though the reasons for their separat-ist zeal are rooted in history and culture. Besides Spanish, both regions, together with Galicia (which has less weight in the overall economy), have their own languages, namely Catalan and Euskera, which are deeply established in each community. Prohibited during the recent dictator-ship, these languages have received a significant boost with the demo-cratic progress in education, acquiring the same official status as Spanish in their respective geographical domains. Nonetheless, this co-official ranking has given rise to reticence in certain sectors more determined to maintain a common Spanish identity. This feeling spans the ideological spectrum from left to right and culminates in a legislative seesaw of con-stant centralization-decentralization.

At the same time, mention should also be made of Spain's recent demo-graphic evolution, which has experienced significant growth in the early twenty-first century, reaching 42 million inhabitants and a net increase of 6 million people, a rise of 15% with respect to 2001 data. This was princi-pally caused by the substantial entry of emigrants from North Africa, Latin America, and Eastern Europe, attracted by the 1996–2006 economic boom, an influx which necessarily led to adaptation of the country's social and education policies.[1] The immigration phenomenon and growing cultural diversity in Spain has, of course, been one of the points of confrontation in the party-political debate. This has perhaps been more notable in the local sphere, where the emergence of political groups with a xenophobic and racist agenda has received a good deal of attention. This situation has exercised a certain influence in the general debate and has polarized positions with regard to the social function of education. In particular, and as we will see in the next section, immigration has been one of the main arguments in the formation of curricular proposals that emphasize the Spanish identity as the central core of citizenship, leaving aside or completely ignoring the individual identities present in some regions.

In short, comprehension of the social and political context in conjunction with the economic and demographic evolution is essential to make a proper interpretation of the Spanish education system's current situation. The legacy of Franco's dictatorship has represented a significant burden in the democratic period. The population's levels of education had plummeted to alarming depths, with illiteracy indices of almost 10% in 1970, more pronounced among women and residents in rural zones. But in addition, that legacy obliged the authorities to modernize and democratize educational structures and adapt them to the requirements demanded by Spain's then imminent entry into Europe, a compulsory reference in Spanish educational policies both in the positive sense as well as the negative, as we will see in later paragraphs.

CIVIC EDUCATION VERSUS EDUCATION FOR CITIZENSHIP: TWO OPPOSING MODELS

An almost irreconcilable disparity has emerged in Spanish education policy between two models. These may be reduced to the expressions and concepts of "civic education" and "education for citizenship," and have come to represent deeply divided political positions. What could be considered from the perspective of complementarity has been translated into determined confrontation between supporters of civics, a term and concept which has been hijacked and defended by the political right, and those who advocate the development of citizenship in its broadest sense, endorsed by sectors of the left.

The defense of civic education, understood as a mechanism for connection with the immediate community, encompasses interest in civility, good manners and public virtues. It also reserves for itself other related notions, such as patriotism and national consciousness which, from a political standpoint, have been grouped together under the concept of constitutional patriotism, as conceived by Habermas. The appearance of this term and its adoption among the Spanish political class since 2000 signifies a crucial point in the debate on the development of citizenship education in Spanish legislation. The Habermasian concept of constitutional patriotism[2] was interpreted in divergent ways by the two majority Spanish parties as they incorporated it into their respective discourses. At first and following his election as general secretary of PSOE, the majority party of the left, José Luis Rodríguez Zapatero suggested in 2001 the adoption of this concept to build a State which combined the equality of all individuals before the law and the plurinational reality of Spain, a model conceived more out of "demos" (people) than "etnos" (culture or nation). The intention was to provide an outlet for calls for nationalist recognition, above all from Catalonia and the Basque Country, without prejudicing individual rights viewed through the prism of egalitarianism characteristic of left-wing ideologies.

The idea of constitutional patriotism enlivened the theoretical debate among philosophers of the day, but it especially drove PP, representative party of the Spanish right with an absolute majority in parliament, to rapidly include the notion in the political platform of their 14ᵗʰ Congress in 2002 and in the 2004 election manifesto, signed by the then candidate Mariano Rajoy. The link between patriotism, constitution, and maintaining order was thus well established, especially as regards the political struggle against ETA, the terrorist organization which had since the 1960s been fighting for Basque independence. Moreover, the concept of constitutional patriotism in the right-wing discourse has always been seen from the perspective of Spanish nationalism, and was thus translated in the frustrated education reform of 2002 as civics and constitutionalism.

The pending issue of Spanish constitutionalism, that of achieving a satisfactory structuring of the plurinational reality, is seen in entirely different ways on each side of the parliamentary divide: some timidly attempt to achieve an almost federal structure in which all regions enjoy sufficient autonomy without losing the "unity" of Spain; others, with a more vehement defense, seek the recentralization of powers and relaunching of Spanish patriotic pride as a mechanism to avoid centrifugal tendencies. This dichotomy in the interpretation of constitutional patriotism marks the origin of the ideological distance which later, with the left in power once again as from 2004, would be exacerbated in the 2006 Law, with the inclusion of a specific subject, Citizenship Education, in compulsory education curricula.

This is not the place to reproduce the controversy,[3] in fact more media- and party-based than pedagogical, over the new subject which shook Spanish society from 2005 to 2011. We will instead focus discussion on what the two opposing parties understood constitutional patriotism to be: in the model defended by the left (model 1), it meant adherence to a set of necessary principles that regulate life in common or, to put it more clearly, abstract constitutionalism; in contrast, those on the right (model 2) held that it should mean adhering to the written letter of the constitutional text, which for some would be considered somewhat more like constitutional fundamentalism, sticking indisputably to what is written rather than the spirit of the words, of the 1978 Spanish Constitution, without further abstract considerations.

Naturally, model 1 would appeal to the need to endorse an education system capable of producing citizens committed to constitutional values, not bound by a single national text (the Spanish Constitution, for instance) but guided by a notion of citizenship of a cosmopolitan nature and world-wide scope. This model would be more in harmony with such concepts as democratic education or education for democracy, education in human rights, and education for active and participatory citizenship, from a necessarily critical and transforming perspective. For its part, model 2 would focus on training in those skills deemed essential for good government of the public sphere, from a heavily judicial or institutional point of view, as declared in the manifesto that won the elections in 2011: "We will raise the civic education of pupils, substituting the subject of Citizenship Education for another whose content is based on learning constitutional values and knowledge of the Spanish and European institutions."[4]

As we have mentioned, the timid education reform, initiated by the left-wing government through the 2006 Law on Education in response to the law of 2002 approved by the right but withdrawn when the left entered office, had created a specific subject of Citizenship Education. This represented a major shift with respect to the previous curricular focus, that of the 1990 Law, which included content relating to the development of citizenship as cross-curricular elements, concrete areas of content intended to complement the classic curricular subjects or areas. The 1990 Law had already recognized the importance of values and attitudes of an ethical nature as an inseparable part of educational content together with the concepts that are learnt and the skills and strategies necessary to apply this learning. But the establishment of cross-curricular themes represented a more determined drive to implement educational content related to the development of democratic citizenship.

In fact, this position is somewhat distanced from model 1, given that access to the world's learning and knowledge, the core goal of education, necessarily entails knowing how to question reality from a critical point of view, to activate initiatives capable of transforming the conditions of life. The position is actually closer to model 2, in which only repetition prevails, enhanced by means of mechanisms of ideological inculcation whose sole intention is to maintain the established order or recover lost privileges.

The chronological summary of political ideas about the implementation of citizenship education can therefore be described in the following points:

- Education laws prior to democracy in Spain had emphasized a focus on citizenship limited to adherence to the established political regime. This would begin to change with the social movements of the 1970s, which called for greater degrees of democracy and participation in education.
- With a left-wing government, an education law was passed in 1990 which established the cross-curricular integration of ethics- and citizen-based subjects.

- The education reform of 2002 (an initiative of a right-wing government) eliminated those cross-curricular themes along with the explicit values associated with their content. This law was never applied, due to the victory of the left in 2004, following the Madrid terrorist attack.
- The 2006 Law (once again with a government of the left) followed European guidelines and introduced a curricular model including social and civic competence, and created a specific subject with the name of Education for Citizenship and Human Rights (a dubious and hardly appropriate addition), while at the same time promoting parallel training programs.
- The current Bill, in force since January 2014, returns us to the curricular misery of yesteryear in comparison to Europe, where citizenship education under different names and in varying formats, is enjoying the best of health.

This historical review seeks to demonstrate the ideological drift produced in Spanish education policy. The curriculum design adopted in each law illustrates the alignment with or divergence from the two models suggested. In short, the cross-curricular proposals seem to approach model 1, while the subject-based curriculum corresponds to model 2, closer to indoctrination. This historical development reveals the lack of a wide political consensus, very necessary to adequately resolve the historical gap of nearly eight decades that the political education of young people in the Spanish educational system has suffered.

CITIZENSHIP EDUCATION IN THE CURRENT EDUCATION REFORM IN SPAIN: WITH ITS BACK TO EUROPE

The Maastricht Treaty of 1992, by which the European Union took a giant leap forward in consolidating its common political structures, included the concept of "European citizenship" as one of the fundamental cornerstones in the construction of Europe, together with introduction of the Euro as a single currency and the mechanisms for freedom of internal movement and shared security. In its meeting in 1994, the Conference of Ministers of Education of the EU member states passed a resolution aimed at fostering education for democracy, human rights and tolerance in member states. This call has subsequently been succeeded by others from the European Commission, one of the EU's highest-ranking bodies, and the Council of Europe, which also brings together the remaining European countries that are not members of the EU. Thus, in the last two decades, European recommendations and initiatives have proliferated to encourage the integration of citizenship education into school curricula.

A first study of European policies relating to education for citizenship was published in 2005 by Eurydice, the information network at the EU

Education, Audiovisual, and Culture Executive Agency (EACEA). The text underlined the importance of this matter: "It has become increasingly important to provide young people with an idea of what is meant by responsible citizenship within a democratically based society."[5] Among its findings, the report highlighted the following conclusion:

"All European countries generally agree on the need to include citizenship education in the formal school curriculum in one way or another. However, the way it is developed and provided varies considerably from one country to the next. It would appear that, as yet, there is no single prevailing general approach adopted by most countries."[6]

Thus what the report suggested is that citizenship education does not consist solely in transmitting knowledge about "political culture," but that it is also concerned with developing civic-minded attitudes and values, and in many countries promotes active citizenship through student participation in schools and the wider society. These goals are being sought through three main mechanisms: the inclusion of citizenship education in curricula, the existence of mechanisms for democratic management and participation in schools, and the development of initiatives to engage students in community involvement activities. The Spanish education system received relatively positive reviews in the report, but while it effectively boasted a model of democratic participation in schools and promoted community activities, their curricular presence was scant.

The following edition of the study, published in 2012, revealed a very different situation for Spain however. The model of democratic culture in the school remained, and examples of student involvement in the community were presented, especially those encompassed in the concept of service learning and, moreover, innovative initiatives were proposed for the continuous training of teaching staff. The most significant advance, however, was to be found in the curricular field. As we have analysed in the preceding section, the curriculum established a key competence called "social and civic competences"[7] in line with European guidance, and also introduced it in a specific subject at three levels of compulsory and basic education, in addition to the usual presence of content in related areas, such as social sciences and philosophy.

In this context, the recent education reform in Spain in force since 2014 significantly alters the situation of citizenship education in the Spanish system. Preparation of this reform occurred in two stages: initially and in accordance with the winning party's election manifesto, a reformulation of the subject of Education for Citizenship was proposed; later however, it was completely eliminated and Religion proposed to replace it as a compulsory subject, with the alternative of Civic and Cultural Values as an option.

In his first declaration to the Education Committee of the Spanish parliament and continuing the line of the PP election manifesto, the Spanish Minister of Education set out his intentions. Following an initial assessment he described as "frankly worrying," the Minister went on, surprisingly, to announce a package of five major reforms of the school system that bore little relation to his previous diagnosis: teachers' statute, school autonomy, secondary-school reform, Spanish-English bilingualism, and citizenship education. With regard to the latter, his idea was to replace the subject imparted since 2006 with one of new creation, called Civic and Constitutional Education, "free from controversial issues susceptible to ideological indoctrination. [A subject] which is relevant because [. . .] I think that education has an essential function, that of producing *free and responsible* citizens, with the capacity to be *active subjects* in our democratic society. Without doubt this new Civic and Constitutional Education will meet this goal, and none other"[8] (the italics are ours). That appearance before the Education Committee of the Spanish parliament was plagued with serious contradictions and huge mistakes, and included the presentation of false material.[9]

This change in name required a change in the law, but in the meantime during March and April 2012 the government announced it had revised the content of the subject, leaving the new name to be introduced by coursebook publishers in materials for the 2012–2013 year. These modifications coincided with the line proposed in the Concordat between Spain and The Holy See (signed in 1953 under the dictatorship, and partially modified in 1978),[10] and offered a clear indication of the direction the new subject might take:

- Some of the content set out in the Universal Declaration of Human Rights was eliminated, such as diversity in family models and in sexual orientation. The revision also excluded study of the root causes of human rights abuses, inequality on the planet and gender inequality, and even cut out the situation of women in the analysis of causes of poverty.
- Content was added relating to the private economy's role in society, citizenship was linked to legal adherence to the State, and the debate over biotechnology was submitted to moral guidelines, in a clear allusion to abortion and stem-cell research.

The ideological justification offered by the Minister did very little to ease tension in this area. During that first appearance he had justified the future reforms relating to the teachers' statute, school autonomy and the changes in secondary by providing data (questionable, but data nonetheless) of school failure, early school leaving and poor performance in PISA studies, all topped off with the soaring youth unemployment figures in Spain and excessive per-student expenditure in comparison with the OECD average (but distanced from the most advanced countries in Europe). But all of this more or less empirical and objective basis disappeared when it came to defending the proposal to replace the subject of Education for Citizenship. In other words, reform of the subject and its subsequent elimination were not based on a rigorous assessment of empirical data about the extent to which objectives set in their day had been met, but rather the issue was laid to rest with a couple of ideological arguments, as might have been expected.

Later, with the first formal drafts presented in May 2012, the name proposed for the subject would be that of Civic Education and Entrepreneurship. The change was not trivial: the "constitutional" reference was dropped and for the first time the concept of entrepreneurship appeared, relating to the capacity of personal initiative to develop business ventures. This decision must inevitably be linked to the initial text of the law, subsequently withdrawn, in which it was possible to read a truly devastating phrase: "Education is the engine that drives the competitiveness of the economy and a country's levels of prosperity; its [a country's] educational level determines its capacity to compete with success in the international arena and to confront the challenges of the future."[11] The repeated call for competitiveness, twice in three lines, revealed the evident market orientation of the Bill.

The draft law presented in early December 2012 to ministers at the Sectorial Conference of Regional Ministries with powers in education matters introduced even more far-reaching changes in this area: it eliminated once and for all the subject in primary (ISCED1) and installed as compulsory that of Religion or Ethical Values, to be chosen by the families; the same occurred in basic secondary (ISCED2), given that the subject was also eliminated, religion or ethical values became compulsory, and an optional subject appeared with the name of Introduction to Entrepreneurial and Business Activity, which summed up the true spirit of the reform. As a final offering, it established that civic and constitutional education would have to be worked in all subjects, specifying neither times nor specific content, and not even establishing the need for it to be assessed. Thus all reference to citizenship education was now completely removed, but so was the subject on civic and constitutional education, breaking one of the promises in the PP election manifesto.

This being the situation, it seems obvious that two completely opposing models had been followed in addressing the educational treatment of social and civic competences. On the one hand, Spanish education legislation prior to 2012 reflected the introduction of model 1 set out above, with a good number of social and educational initiatives; the cosmopolitan constitutionalism model which, as shown in the report entitled *Citizenship Education in Europe* de 2012,[12] is predominant throughout Europe. On the other hand, the reform proposed by PP poses radical changes once again that draw us closer to model 2, that of constitutional fundamentalism.

The reform process will situate Spain at the tail end of Europe. If the articles of the 2006 Law seemed to bring Spain timidly in line with European thinking on the subject of education for citizenship, the decision of the country's current conservative leaders will take it in completely the opposite direction. The subsequent legislative provisions of the 2006 Law established that compulsory education should pursue development of students' social and citizenship competence. As we have seen, this competence goes beyond what we know as civics (knowledge of the rules of courtesy) and constitutionalism (knowledge of the democratic mechanisms and institutions established in the Spanish "Magna Carta"), expressions which initially abounded in the ministerial proposals. Of course, the substance of the matter is not resolved by a change of name or curriculum. It requires a comprehensive approach through a set of measures running in parallel to the strictly curricular implementation: teacher training, the fostering of student and family participation, community outreach activities, and so on. It should also be mentioned that the funding cuts in place since 2009 have obviously played their part in the elimination of these initiatives.

The Minister's intentions place Spain in a complicated international position. The general trend in Europe is for a model of cosmopolitan constitutionalism which, above all, addresses the development of critical capacity and knowledge of human rights, from the perspective of the promotion of tolerance and the elimination of all kinds of discrimination (including homophobia, xenophobia, and misogyny). In clear contrast, what the education reform proposes is a shift towards narrow-minded constitutionalism, centered on a highly patriotic Spanish vision, limiting the horizon of rights to that laid down in the letter of the 1978 Spanish Constitution. The new Spanish reform based in fundamentalist constitutionalism distances Spain from the goal of a shared European citizenship. It is likely that no intervention of either an economic or a financial nature will rescue Spain from the intellectual quagmire into which we will be dragged if these neoconservative proposals are imposed.

BEYOND THE CURRICULUM AND THE SUBJECT: AN INTEGRATING MODEL

To close this chapter, we present our vision of education for citizenship and in democratic values from a cross-curriculum perspective, but one which also acknowledges the importance of curricular activity, treating the concept as a subject or timetable space to be worked systematically and formally. We are particularly interested in identifying the ideal conditions for learning in the classroom and school (as well as in the spaces of participation and coexistence it generates) to ensure the practice of active citizenship from the cradle to the grave. But what kind of citizenship are we talking about? How do we learn ethically the values, knowledge and competences that guarantee the best citizen training in diverse societies seeking to be pluralist? How can we gain an in-depth understanding of democracy? By what means? What is the role of the school, its spaces and moments, in providing an adequate education for citizenship?

Educating for What Kind of Citizenship?

The crisis in the economy and in trust among citizens brought about by the actions of leaders of political and economic organizations and institutions is having a profound effect in Spain as well as in the rest of the EU. It is attacking the basic pillars of the welfare state and enjoyment of the second and even the first generation of human rights in the population. This factor must be added to the distortion and lack of efficiency and effectiveness of the representative democratic model in failing to achieve the levels of transparency and deliberation which could be expected of it. Moreover, the continuing inequalities and perpetuation of privilege, together with the indignation felt by a population powerless to transform society, cry out more than ever for a citizenship which is educated, active and hopeful. Representative democracy, which should be conserved and improved, has not fulfilled expectations. It has limited itself to exercising a parliamentary democracy, which is now viewed with a mixture of scepticism and cynicism, when not as a simple fraud. However, despite this not being the best of times, a good number of young and not-so-young people using traditional mediums and other technologies have created networks for critical reflection on and construction of the collective conscience. They have promoted transforming actions which have had positive effects and should be assessed in the hope that change is possible. It is therefore essential to build a citizenship that reinforces the values of real democracy: an active and participatory citizenship prepared to explore radical democracy. Of course, basic levels of education are required that enable the acquisition and development of elementary competences. Such competences serve the exercise of the rights all citizens have and the effective demand for those rights when they are found lacking. Also required are levels that encompass the acceptance of rules and fulfilment of obligations as a guarantee of active trust among citizens in societies that have assumed systems of regulating coexistence through the participation of all those involved.

Nonetheless, and despite general consensus on the importance of forming good citizens, "education for citizenship" is a controversial topic. The issue is further complicated when we propose its introduction into the school curricula of compulsory education systems. In this case, for some people, citizenship education becomes undesirable and inacceptable; for others, desirable and necessary. The former take up opposition because they consider the educational proposal has indoctrinating effects and reproduces the dominant ideology of the government that regulates it. The latter are in favour of the subject because, irrespective of the education in values that every family can offer their children, through citizenship education offered by the State society ensures that, especially in school, all citizens receive such training. The discussion around civic-mindedness and citizenship opened on previous pages is thus reproduced.

In the following paragraphs we briefly re-examine three considerations regarding where and how we learn citizenship, after which we analyse how we learn ethically, by which means, and the school's role in this task.[13] The first consideration is that education for citizenship and coexistence requires actions that affect the entire population. Citizenship education cannot be an objective aimed solely at the younger generations, at children and adolescents. One of the dimensions of good citizenship is living together in harmony, and this is a matter that also concerns older generations. Appreciating coexistence as something worthwhile depends to a large extent on whether one has been brought up in a context in which it was successfully practiced. Since children are educated or miseducated both formally and informally, the formation of citizens entails undertaking actions that affect the population as a whole.

The second consideration is that educating for citizenship which holds justice and equity in high regard requires leaders that put those principles into practice. A good citizenry also safeguards such values. The struggle to ensure that our societies are increasingly more just and democratic communities and that society in general enjoys greater equity concerns us all, but especially those who exercise decision-making powers, from whom we can demand greater social and ethical responsibility. The behavior of leaders in governments, business and trades unions, of directors in companies and the mass media, generates models and ways of doing things and thinking which are prone to imitation on a small scale, but which have a multiplier effect. So their conduct can contribute to society being more equitable and inclusive or, in contrast, can increase inequalities and give rise to more vulnerability and social exclusion. In short, we would say they create a social climate that affects the worlds of work and family and can contribute to younger citizens perceiving justice and equity as something of value. Or on the contrary, that the young at least acknowledge these elements as values, though distanced from this world and thus unattainable.

The third consideration is that alliances should be established between the different agents of socialization who are potentially educators, such as the family, the media and the local community or town, among others, with a view to generating enhanced active trust and social capital. There are factors that have strong influence in the development of values in the young, as well as in their training as citizens, which should be borne in mind. Among these we find the family; friends and classmates; leisure and entertainment spaces; and the way the media reflects values, worldviews and the models and lifestyles of leaders in the worlds of culture, sport, show business and politics. The fabric of different personal identities as a member of a community or country, or citizen of the world, is woven in social networks, today highly extended thanks to technological developments and the globalization of information, and is consolidated through social and communicative practice in the community we live in and feel part of.

The social learning processes that occur in informal education contexts can be as powerful as the educational processes that we propose in the formal or school settings, or more so. If there exists an educational continuity between these contexts and they share the same expectations and values it will be easier to educate for citizenship in the school. Bonds of trust will be established between members of a community, the acceptance of rules will be fostered and greater social capital will be created. With these ingredients it is easier for community members to become interested in being good citizens and for younger generations to understand the need for and real sense of training in citizenship. The more social capital and alliances between actors in formal education we create, the more possibilities we have of developing and generating combined capabilities for the practice of active citizenship.[14]

We cannot therefore treat citizenship education solely as a curricular item, in which the only concern is to define a specific range of subjects and establish a timetable. It should be approached as a set of systematically organized cross-curricular activities undertaken in the different subjects that make up the curriculum, as well as from a more transversal and global perspective, integrating the formal and the informal aspects of education, assimilating what happens in school and what happens outside it. We should not ignore either the specific curricular approach or study of the subject across all areas of the curriculum. We must conserve and cultivate reserved spaces for this purpose in schools, but we cannot afford to limit our efforts to this and nothing else.

How Do We Learn Values? And When Do We Learn Them?

Educating is, to a large extent, a logistical task, and educating for citizenship consists essentially in creating conditions which lead to learning that allows us to understand our world better. Such knowledge comes from developing capabilities to construct our own model of a good and fair life, appreciating values and condemning their absence, and shaping our own model of personal values matrix. But how can we learn ethically? The learning process takes place in the world of feelings, in our most primary educational upbringing contexts, and we progress by means of language towards the construction of values and principles that we would like to be universalizable.[15] That is why educating in values and for citizenship consists, first, in creating conditions that foster moral sensitivity in those who are learning, with a view to their discovering and living the conflicts of our world. Second, and based on having and analysing experiences which as participants, patients or observers, can generate the conflicts in our context, educating in values and for citizenship has to enable the subjective level of feelings to be overcome and thus, through dialogue, allow us to construct together a set of shared, potentially universal moral principles. Third, diverse societies such as ours should promote the conditions that help us recognize those differences, values and traditions of each culture that foster the building of consensus around the minimum basic principles of a civil ethic or active citizenship based on coexistence in plural societies.

Individuals are subject to rights, responsibilities and feelings, and education should offer them resources to enable them to demand their rights, reject the silences of those who are accountable, assume their responsibilities, and feel morally. It should equip them to participate actively in the community of which they form part, acknowledge the other as a valid interlocutor in the quest for what is fair and build a life seeking happiness in their immediate society. Educating for citizenship is a matter of training people to develop the sense of belonging to their community and to prioritize their actions on the basis of criteria of justice. As Adela Cortina[16] points out, each community has traditions of good life which citizens have to assume; but a good citizen must also get on with others in a shared project of justice and be able to deliberate along with others on what is just and what is not.

Consequently, in democratic societies the fundamental value to be promoted is pluralism. This concept implies something more than simply respect and tolerance, or even active tolerance. Pluralism is the value that will enable us to gain a deeper understanding of democratic ways of life, at the family, social, work and community levels, and to build a more just and equitable society. Focusing on pluralism as a fundamental value[17] and basis of democracy means focusing on a model of citizenship building and education that understands citizenship as a notion which is open and under construction. Such education sets out, not only to produce a citizenship which guarantees rights and demands responsibilities of each in their respective sphere, but also to develop a citizenship—a new citizenship—prepared to build, together, the sense of belonging. It is an education for citizenship that highlights respect for the autonomy of the person, the practice of dialogue to settle differences, reach agreements and make progress in disputes, and the acknowledgement of diversity as a value, as inseparable qualities that should be promoted jointly because they make everyone's life more dignified, because they are moral values associated with the value of pluralism.

In Which Ways?

Human learning takes place in different ways, and to learn to appreciate these values we also use different learning pathways. The three most important of these are practice, observation, and personal reflection and construction.[18] They are elements we employ at the same time but with varying intensity, depending on whether the situation is one of formal or informal learning. The ethical development we achieve through these pathways entails relatively stable changes in the person's behavior that influence their knowledge and capabilities in a way that enables them to be more competent at the social level, in their socio-moral reflection and in the construction of the "self." Citizenship education can serve these three pathways and exert influence in these three areas of students' moral personality by means of different learning strategies and content.

We propose four areas related to learning practices and school life likely to be good spaces for educating in values and training in citizenship[19]: curricular content, student-teacher relationships, practices associated with learning activities and participation, and social and community involvement of the learning at school. These are four areas which in practice are interrelated and exert influence mutually, but which we will differentiate here solely for the sake of explanation. In all of them we can identify processes of learning in an ethical way by exercise or practice, by observation, and by reflection and personal construction. However and despite the cross-curricular and comprehensive characteristics they bring to education in values and for an active citizenship, when referring to the school we should differentiate them because the pedagogical power of each of them is different and requires actions that can and should be analysed separately.

What is the School's Role in this Field?

Curricular content

The school and its teaching staff have the real capability to choose one set of content or another, providing this content offers what is required to achieve the established learning objectives. When making their choice they can opt to situate issues that generate social, citizen-based and ethical discussion in the center of an activity, or to ignore or avoid them. The selection of curricular content is not exempt from ethical considerations. The perspective of education for citizenship should be incorporated not only through subject-specific content, but also through that of other areas of study.

Citizenship education proposals should include the promotion of learning two types of competences: some of a specific nature and others that are more generic. We will call the former competences for the exercise of citizenship and the latter ethical competences. The former can be developed through a specific subject or in specific learning contexts; they can also coherently structure a set of knowledge, aptitudes, values and attitudes and mobilize them for application in the everyday exercise of citizenship. Ethical competences on the other hand are developed by being exercised in different subjects and learning contexts, and aim to structure a personal life model, created autonomously in a situation of social interaction, which enjoys the characteristics necessary to be good and, at the same time, just.

With regard to the first, specific type of competences, we propose identifying the informative and conceptual learning content that can lead to an understanding of our world from a political and ethical point of view, that relates scientific and technological developments to the social and ethical impact they bring about and facilitates the understanding of our society in economic terms. It is also important to take full advantage of the learning contexts in which this content is taught in order to put procedures and attitudes into practice, and to enable students to construct their value systems by developing the critical comprehension to understand controversy.[20] To do this, teachers must conduct themselves with precision, impartiality, responsibility, modesty and sincerity, and at the same time specify when their opinion is being offered as an expert because of the curricular relevance of the subject in controversy, or when it is given as a simple citizen. In both cases, the teacher should know how to demonstrate authenticity and sincerity in his or her opinions, and be respectful and proactive in the promotion of autonomous thinking on the part of the student. With respect to the generic competences, we propose their development in the different areas that we have been considering, such as those referred to above regarding exploitation of the informative content for the practice of procedures, attitudes, and values.

Relationships with teachers

The school is a space of coexistence in which we learn from infancy to be a member of a community who has rights and responsibilities. But it is also a space where one can learn to be excluded and unrecognized. Relationships with peers and teaching staff are crucial. But in the area of relationships with teachers, two types of situation must be identified: that of students and teachers in the strictest sense of these terms, and the interpersonal relationship they establish as people. In the first category, there is little symmetry. The teacher's role as expert in a subject or field of knowledge in which the student is a learner, his or her function as a guide or tutor and, of course, that associated with the task of assessment, make it difficult for the teaching relationship to be symmetric, and it probably should not be so. In the second situation, however, symmetry is not only possible, it is also necessary. The set of relationships generated in this area is an excellent setting for learning competences that help students advance towards progressive levels of autonomy, not only in learning but also in knowledge building in general, as well as in the manner of designing and organizing their own personal life projects.

In the first type of situations, we would highlight the importance of two relationships: the teacher as tutor, and as the person responsible for assessing the student's learning. The educational potential of relationships established by the teacher in the tutorial situation should be emphasized. By acknowledging the student's communicative competence and despite the relationship not being symmetrical, teaching staff can and should reassure the student that he or she is recognized as a person and respected. Likewise, periods when students are being assessed or called upon to deliver project work are effective settings for them to learn whether the values of justice and equity, or the right to protest and the responsibility to fulfil a task or commitment, form part of the real world, or are in fact merely the content of a subject. Teachers should be aware of the influence these times have on developing citizenship and allow their behavior to be guided by the values of respect and responsibility.

Practices associated with learning and participation activities

A model of citizenship and democratic society based on cooperation, mutual support and participation demands a model of citizenship education based on situations of collaborative and participatory socialization and learning. Developments in the field of human learning, especially those of the last decade,[21] show that knowledge is not only constructed in interaction (between the subject who learns and the medium, or among subjects who learn), but that it is also built thanks to the social participation of the learner, through actions and practices in the learning context.

Activity and context are essential factors in learning in general, and the case of citizenship education is no exception. The learning that "sticks" will be less related to the acquisition of knowledge and more the result of participation in the contexts and practices of coexistence, life and learning at school. When practices associated with such activities foster cooperation and participation they generate learning which facilitates active and participatory citizenship.

It is the actions and practices experienced in our day-to-day activity (social participation, irrespective of the level) that lead to learning and to that learning being retained, not the knowledge acquired in the process. So citizenship education proposals should pay more attention to the conditions that make up practice and its structure than to the strategy, technique or methodology to be employed. Following the line of Dewey,[22] our proposal on education and learning understands that learning and doing are inseparable actions, and that the relevance of the context is a key factor in effective learning. That is why the contexts that promote the collaborative construction of knowledge, irrespective of the type of knowledge involved—school-based, academic, social or any other—are excellent spaces for the construction of a citizenship built on mutual support, active trust and coexistence.

The recovery of Dewey's pedagogical principles in the framework of approaches derived from the study of learning and cognition entails highlighting once again the fact that human learning, in its different dimensions, is a process of engagement in a community—of real participation—and that such engagement necessarily means learning to communicate and act in accordance with the group's rules. If these are based on criteria of justice and freedom it is more likely that newly arrived learners will accept and appreciate those values as a guide in their actions and behaviors. Likewise, if dialogue, discussion and communicative competence are considered valuable and useful for group life, they will also be elements established as valuable for life in the community. Thus, proposals of education for an active and participatory citizenship should bring together the conditions necessary and turn them into learning and authentic participation practices based on collaborative knowledge building.[23]

Relationships with the community

An interesting and powerful way to explore some of these considerations in greater depth consists in establishing bonds with the community and the district in which the school is located. The practices of service learning are an excellent resource for this purpose, and should be integrated into proposals for citizenship education.[24] They are practices that enable school learning to be combined with offering service to the community, and they work with dense learning content from the ethical and social point of view, addressing issues of interest for the district related to the needs of the population and the community. Service learning facilitates collaborative learning, develops moral and citizen sensitivity and educates in the will and perseverance to achieve a shared project that commits all its participants. It also fosters initiative and entrepreneurship, and above all creates humanity and active citizenship through participation, transformation and improvement of the local environment.[25]

CONCLUSION

To conclude the chapter, political conditions in Spain over the last two decades have not enabled profound, enlightened debate on the appropriateness and characteristics of values and citizenship education in this country. We have explained that there are two models that respond to different political trends, represented by the principal parties in Spain, with sharply conflicting ideological positions. In brief, the conservative proposal seeks a blind allegiance to the state, while the socialist approach pursues critical engagement with the community. The first model means a homogeneous perspective in education and includes a narrow view of the Spanish nation, with uniform orientation under a single language and culture. In contrast to this, the socialist option presents an educational model based on social and cultural diversity, where all languages and national sensibilities can be better accommodated.

In our opinion, it would be highly desirable for both lines to find points of intersection and common ground in order to establish a dialogue that brings values and citizenship education under the settings we have outlined in the second part of this chapter. A school-based model is absolutely essential in this issue. The conservative option must revise its tendency to block content in the syllabus, but the other party should bear in mind that there are parents, principals and teachers who specifically want (and probably need) this: linking the syllabus to their beliefs and sensitivities. Teachers are a central point in both models, but we think that they could engage more purposefully. Politicians must change the relationship they have with educational movements and unions in order to meet both positions. The conservative party has a long tradition of disagreement with these agents, usually of left-wing ideology, but so does the socialist party. One fact remains, however: without the teachers, it will not be possible to change either the education system or the schools. Finally, learning democracy means improving participation in activities that concern the community. We think that it is absolutely necessary to emphasize the role of the school within its context, as a core agent to change the life conditions of children and adolescents and improve social relationships in the community. In this sense, we advocate an educational space where autonomy of the subject prevails, alongside respect for differences and the right to disagree. As we have said, we believe that citizenship and values education is not solely a curricular item, but rather is a common concern for the community as a whole, and it must, therefore, to be worked in the community.

NOTES

1. The data may be consulted on the World Bank website: http://databank. worldbank.org/data/views/reports/tableview.aspx.
2. German political scientist Dolf Sternberger used "constitutional patriotism" for the first time in the title of an article in the press (cf. Dolf Sternberger: "Verfassungspatriotismus," *Frankfurter Allgemeine Zeitung,* 23 May 1979; he also used it in his book, Dolf Sternberger: *Verfassungspatriotismus.* Insel Verlag, Frankfurt an Main, 1990). Later, in the 1990s, philosopher Jürgen Habermas helped to spread the concept to reinforce the process of the European Union. (cf. Jürgen Habermas, *Staatsbürgerschaft und nationale Identität. Überlegungen zur europäischen Zukunft* [Citizenship and national identity. Considerations for the future of Europe]. Erker, St. Gallen, 1991). In brief, the term is the opposite of "civic nationalism" and reflects the debate between universalism versus communitarian paradigms. See further discussion in Dietmar Schirmer "Closing the Nation: Nationalism and Statism in Nineteenth- and Twentieth-Century Germany," in Sima Godfrey and Frank Unger (eds.), *The Shifting Foundations of Modern Nation-states,* University of Toronto Press, Toronto, 2004.
3. For a discussion of these issues see (in Spanish): Juan Manuel Fernandez-Soria "Educación para la ciudadanía y los derechos humanos: controversias en torno a una asignatura (o entre ética pública y ética privada) [Citizenship education and human rights: controversies around a subject (or between public and private ethics)]. *Trasatlántica de Educación,* vol. IV, 2008, pp. 45–64 (available at http://dialnet.unirioja.es/descarga/articulo/2690398.pdf, accessed: 11 September 2013).
4. Partido Popular (2011) *Lo que España necesita. Manifesto for the 2011 general elections.* accessed June 1, 2013, http://bit.ly/tT7PSt, p. 85.

5. EACEA, *Citizenship education at school in Europe*. Eurydice (Education, Audiovisual and Culture Executive Agency), Brussels, 2005, p. 7.

6. Ibid., p. 59

7. EACEA *Developing Key Competences at School in Europe: Challenges and Opportunities for Policy, 2011/12. Eurydice Report*. Publications Office of the European Union, Luxembourg, 2012.

8. "Appearence in Congress of the Minister of Education, Culture and Sport, on general lines in education and sport." *Gobierno de España. Ministerio de Educación, Cultura y Deporte*. (in Spanish), publication date: January 31, 2012; accessed June 10, 2103, http://www.mecd.gob.es/prensa-mecd/discursos/2012/01/20120131-comparecencia-edu-dep-congreso.html

9. "Wert lies to justify the elimination of Citizenship." *Público*, February 2, 2012. Available (in Spanish) at http://www.publico.es/espana/419918/wert-miente-para-justifcar-la-eliminacion-de-ciudadania http://www.publico.es/espana/419918/wert-miente-para-justifcar-la-eliminacion-de-ciudadania(accessed June 12, 2013).

10. See an interesting review about the relationship between the Catholic Church and the Spanish state in José Antonio Souto Paz "Perspectives on Religious Freedom in Spain," *Brigham Young Law Review*, vol. 2001_2, pp. 669–710 (available at http://lawreview.byu.edu/archives/2001/2/sou13.pdf; accessed September 11, 2013).

11. The text, since withdrawn, can still be found on some websites: http://www.feteugt.es/data/images/2012/lomce/comanteproyecto_lomce_25_9.pdf (accessed June 12, 2012).

12. EACEA, *Citizenship education in Europe*. Eurydice & Education, Audiovisual and Culture Executive Agency, Brussels, 2012. Available also on line at http://eacea.ec.europa.eu/education/eurydice/documents/thematic_reports/139EN.pdf (accessed June 1, 2013).

13. Miquel Martinez, Francisco Esteban, and Maria R. Buxarrais, "Escuela, profesorado y valores." *Revista de Educación*. Extra 2011, pp. 95–114. Enric Prats, Amelia Tey, and Miquel Martinez (eds.), *Educar per una ciutadania activa a l'escola*. Institut d'Educació, Ajuntament de Barcelona, Barcelona, 2011.

14. Martha Nussbaum, *Creating Capabilities*, The Belknap Press of Harvard University Press, Cambridge, MA, 2011.

15. Miquel Martinez and Guillermo Hoyos, "Educación para la ciudadanía en tiempos de globalización," in Miquel Martinez and Guillermo Hoyos (eds.), *La formación en valores en sociedades democráticas*. Octaedro, Barcelona, 2006, pp. 15–48.

16. Adela Cortina, *Ética de la razón cordial*, Ediciones Nobel, Oviedo (Spain), 2007.

17. The debate about the fit of pluralism in the context of universal values has been widely debated since the publication of *Theory of Justice* by John Rawls (1971). Canadian philosopher Will Kymlicka, in particular, demonstrates the need to establish that bond with his notion of "citizenship" (Will Kymlicka, *Multicultural Citizenship: A Liberal Theory of Minority Rights*, Clarendon Press, Oxford, 1995). In Spanish, you can see more about this field in Guillermo Hoyos "Ética, interculturalidad y pluralismo" [Ethics, interculturality and pluralism], in B. Toro and A. Tallone (Eds.) *Educación, valores y ciudadanía*. Fundación SM, OEI, Madrid, 2010, pp. 29–40.

18. Miquel Martínez, Maria R. Buxarrais, and Francisco Esteban, "La universidad como espacio de aprendizaje ético," *Revista Iberoamericana de Educación*, Vol. 29, 2002, pp. 17–44.

19. Initially we referred to five areas, which here we have adapted into four. See Miquel Martínez, Josep M. Puig, and Jaume Trilla, "Escuela, profesorado y

educación moral" in *Teoría de la Educación, Revista Interuniversitaria*, vol. 15, 2003, pp. 57–94, 2003.

20. Jaume Trilla, *El profesor y los valores controvertidos: neutralidad y beligerancia en educación*. Editorial Paidos, Barcelona, 1992.

21. Begoña Gros, *Aprendizajes, conexiones y artefactos. La producción colaborativa del conocimiento*. Gedisa Editorial, Barcelona, 2008.

22. John Dewey, *Ensayos de Educación*, (Obras de Dewey, vol. II). La Lectura, Madrid, 1926.

23. Jaume Trilla and Ana Novella, "Educación y participación social de la infancia," *Revista Iberoamericana de Educación*, vol. 26, 2001, pp. 137–164. Roger Hart, *La participación de los niños: de la participación simbólica a la participación autentica*, UNICEF. Regional Office in Latin America and the *Caribbean*, Bogota, 1993.

24. Miquel Martinez and Josep M. Puig, "Aprenentatge servei: de l'Escola Nova a l'educació d'avui," *Temps d'Educació*, vol. 41, 2011, pp. 11–24. Josep M. Puig (ed.) *Aprendizaje servicio: Educación y compromiso cívico*. Graó, Barcelona, 2009.

25. Miquel Martinez and Josep M. Puig, Ibid.

6   Lost in Citizenship Education
Questions Faced by Amerasians in Japan[1]

Kanako Ide

INTRODUCTION

This chapter is an attempt to contribute to a theoretical development of citizenship education by exploring a more inclusive view about Japanese citizenry. The chapter specifically demonstrates a potential compatibility between two different educational approaches to citizenship education in Japan: citizenship education for a global age and citizenship education for a multicultural age. In this article, citizenship education for a global age is represented by the Project for Promotion of Global Human Resource Development. This is a national educational policy designed to foster "globalized" Japanese citizens, proposed by the Ministry of Education, Culture, Sports, Science, and Technology Japan (MEXT). This educational policy represents the mainstream discourse and approach to educated Japanese citizenry in the global age. The other educational approach, which represents citizenship education for a multicultural age, is Double Education. In this approach, a designated nonprofit school aims to meet specific educational needs for Amerasians[2] in Okinawa[3] who are children of "Japanese mothers and American fathers who are currently or were formerly U.S. servicemen or civilian personnel."[4] These are almost voiceless minorities in Japan.

As represented by the Project for Promotion of Global Human Resource Development, the trend of contemporary Japanese educational policy is to energetically globalize its system and curriculum. According to Ryoko Tsuneyoshi, the national educational goal of fostering globalized Japanese citizens is so widely accepted that there seems to be no noticeable counterargument being made against it in contemporary Japan.[5] She is also concerned that its tendency promotes a misperception of Japan as an ethnically homogeneous country.[6] Japan is a historically multicultural society. In addition to *Wajin* (Japanese), there are first nations in Japan such as *Ainu* and *Okinawan*. There are also various ethnic minorities such as *oldcomers* (Koreans in Japan and Japanese orphans coming back from China) and *newcomers* (South Americans of Japanese descent, and refugees) in contemporary Japanese society. If Japan is misperceived by its policymakers to be a racially homogeneous country, this mistake would affect any educational policy that has the purpose of fostering good Japanese citizens.

Educational claims made by Amerasians in Okinawa show that Japan is advanced in some forms of multicultural identity education, but fails to address multicultural issues on its own shores. The case of Amerasians allows us to examine a possible reconciliation of the global-citizen approach and the multicultural-citizen approach, for the following two reasons. First, the ultimate goal for Double Education is not secessional. Unlike some communitarian thinkers such as David Miller and Michael Walzer, secessionism is not a choice for reconciliation.[7] For Double Education, Japan is perceived as the relevant society to which Amerasians may make educational claims. However, addressing Amerasians' educational rights is *not* to demand that Amerasians take either their mother's side or their father's side. Second, Double Education does not accept indifference or benign neglect toward Amerasians within Japanese society. Will Kymlicka points out that the worst racism ". . . is the racist denial that [groups under discussion] are distinct peoples with their own cultures and communities."[8] Mainstream Japanese society has treated Amerasians as if they do not exist. But benign neglect is not even acceptable for Amerasians. Double Education aims to develop Amerasians' self-esteem, and demands social participation and social respect in society, not by the path of interference, but dialogue.[9]

By unpacking the incorrect belief that Japan is a simple homogeneous society in the Project for Promotion of Global Human Resource Development, Double Education clarifies the fundamental problem with which mainstream Japanese citizenship education is currently faced. This demands the reexamination of whether or not the Project for Promotion of Global Human Resource Development is an *educational* policy or a policy for some other purpose.The foundational problem of the issue of citizenship education is whether educational questions are answered by a distinctively educational mode of enquiry. The last part of this chapter seeks a way to reform the concept of citizenship education to combine characteristically educational thinking with the idea of interdependency.

JAPANESE IDENTITY: GLOBAL-MULTICULTURAL

The Project for Promotion of Global Human Resource Development, initially proposed in 2012, is a nationwide policy to globalize Japanese education. According to MEXT, the policy,

> . . . aims to overcome the Japanese younger generation's "inward tendency" and to foster human resources who can positively meet the challenges and succeed in the global field, as the basis for improving Japan's global competitiveness and enhancing the ties between nations.[10]

According to MEXT, development of language skills and establishment of Japanese identity are needed to overcome a Japanese "inward tendency" and to survive in global society. Therefore, the Global Human Resource project consists of three features: (1) language and communication skills, (2) subjectivity, positive attitude, high aspiration, cooperative attitude and flexibility, responsibility, and sense of mission, and (3) understanding different cultures and acquisition of Japanese identity.[11]

Detailed educational policies for the Global Human Resource project were proposed by the Liberal Democratic Party (LDP) after they came into power in December 2012 with a manifesto that promised to promote them as an educational policy. "Communication skills," one of the features of the Global Human Resource project, means English proficiency. To be familiar with English from an early age, LDP proposes an early education plan that incorporates English lessons from the middle years of elementary school. In addition, LDP proposes to adapt TOEFL as a university entrance examination to achieve a global standard of English skills. Robert W. Aspinall reports that the enthusiasm for acquisition of English language skills in Japan is caused by the social assumption that English learning has failed over the past 30 years in Japanese junior and high school.[12]

The establishment of Japanese identity associated with the other features of the Global Human Resource project also suggests the curriculum reform of moral education and social studies. In the general provisions of curriculum guidelines for Japanese elementary schools, renewed in 2013, MEXT emphasizes the importance of moral education to develop Japanese identity in a global age:

> Moral Education is aimed at cultivating morality as a foundation for developing Japanese citizens with a proactive attitude who would apply a spirit of respect for human dignity and reverence for life in specific activities at home, school and other social situations, have a generous spirit, respect traditions and culture, love one's country and hometown which have fostered such traditions and culture, create culture with a distinctive character, honor the public spirit, make an effort to develop the democratic society and state, respect other countries, contributing to world peace and the development of the international community and the preservation of the environment, and have interest in exploring possibilities for the future.[13]

To support the MEXT curriculum guidelines, LDP proposes to set up moral education as an official subject. In addition to moral education, the teaching of social studies is identified as important for the development of Japanese identity. LDP believes that since history and geography teach "our" history and culture,[14] students can also nurture their pride as Japanese by studying them. Thus, the new curriculum guideline claims that the study of history and geography especially helps to foster the literacy necessary to live in an international society.[15] Moreover, LDP proposes further enrichment of Japanese identity in a global society by establishing a new subject in high school called *Kokyo*, whose direct English translation is "public." It is proposed that this subject cover issues such as job hunting, marriage, divorce, annuity, health insurance, political participation, disaster prevention, lawsuits, investments, consumerism, and education.[16] LDP explains that *Kokyo* is derived from the citizenship education adopted in Britain from 2002, and is different from a traditional subject in high school called *Koumin*, whose direct English translation is "civics." According to curriculum guidelines, *Koumin* teaches students the role of Japan in world society,[17] by introducing the principles of the Constitution of Japan: foundational human rights, sovereign power of the people, and renunciation of the right to wage war. LDP explains that while *Koumin* helps students acquire the knowledge to understand social structure, *Kokyo* emphasizes experiences that develop practical skills for living well in society. LDP claims that both subjects, however, promote the development of a Global Human Resource which will participate in Japanese society as well as in a globalized world.

To summarize, the Global Human Resource project is a policy expecting to foster Japanese citizens who can actively contribute to world peace, human welfare, and the economy by communicating in English and respecting other cultures while retaining Japanese pride in the global world.[18]

MULTICULTURALISM AND CITIZENSHIP EDUCATION

In contrast to the mainstream educational policy, Double Education for Amerasians in Okinawa[19] suggests the need for a discussion of Japanese citizenship education in a multicultural context. As explained earlier, Double Education is a limited educational approach in Japan as it is prepared only for specific minority students. However, David Janes and Naomi Noiri, advocators of Amerasians' rights on education, claim that Double Education is a process that ". . .develop[s] students who can be effective citizens of both the U.S. and Japan and attempts to enable students to value and become part of both cultures/countries,"[20] while also being ". . . a model for thinking about international education in a time of globalization and increased diversity in the world's school system."[21] Since Double Education addresses Amerasians' dual citizenry,[22] its notion of citizenship education is not framed by national borders.

Midori Thayer, a founding leader of the school for Double Education, explains the legal and social reasons why the school for Amerasians in Japan is necessary. She claims that even though the Japanese Nationality Law allows people to have dual citizenship until the age of 22, there is no consideration about educational needs for those school-age children who have dual citizenship.[23] Thayer also explains the social reasons for this. Until the AmerAsian School in Okinawa was established in 1998, Amer-asians in Okinawa had three school choices: Japanese public schools, the Department of Defense Dependent's schools (DoDDs), or a private school run by a Christian organization. Japanese public schools and DoDDs were not sufficient for Amerasians because these schools only provide either Japanese education or American education. In addition to the curriculum mismatch, Amerasians were at risk of mistreatment in these schools. In Japanese public schools, for mainstream Okinawan/Japanese, Amerasian children are sometimes an object of the hatred against the U.S. forces in Okinawa, which takes the form of abusive speech such as "Yankee Go Home,"[24] indicating that Amerasians do not belong to Okinawa or Japan. Another abusive phrase used is "dirty,"[25] associated with a stereotype of Amerasians as an outcome of the sex trade. On the other hand, DoDDs—which an Amerasian could attend if the father acknowledges the child or if the mother's family is wealthy—are not safe "homes" for Amerasians either. Within American society in Okinawa, hate speech against Amerasians takes the form of phrases such as "Japanese trash!"[26] indicating that Amerasians are not considered to be American. The hate speech from both sides shows the social situation Amerasians are faced with in Okinawa. Another educational choice, the private school, was recognized as the most preferred choice among Amerasians. However, it was a difficult option for Amerasians to choose, due to its high tuition.

The detailed educational approach of Double Education is to learn communication skills in both Japanese and English and to develop one's identity as an Amerasian. Acquisition of both English and Japanese languages is understood as a serious educational need for Amerasians. This is because it facilitates family communication, develops identity as an Amerasian, and provides some of the conditions of access to both American and Japanese society. Double Education also emphasizes teaching both American social studies and Japanese social studies,[27] and understands the importance of acquiring social and historical knowledge of both countries. Janes and Noiri explain how important it is for Amerasians to learn American social studies even though they are not living in the United States:

> AmerAsian students are looking for the tie which connects them with American culture. Some of them were raised by single mothers and the American culture that is available in Okinawa is very specific since its source is primarily from the U.S. military bases. Although AmerAsian children are part-American and most of them have U.S. citizenship, they sometimes feel that they are isolated from the US.[28]

In order to teach the sense of "Double" by fostering ethnicity as Amerasians, Double Education is even sensitive to spell out the word as "AmerAsians." Janes and Noiri explains that

> The word is usually spelled "Amerasian" in the US; however, when the term was used in Okinawa by mothers who founded a school for their children, they spelled their school title "AmerAsian School," capitalizing both As. This was done to make the point that both of American and Japanese culture is treated with equal significance in the school. This bi-lingual bi-cultural education . . . is called "education for doubles.[29]

The goal of Double Education is to provide communication skills and appropriate identity as AmerAsians which include a sense of American citizenship as well as a sense of Japanese citizenship. Double Education is, therefore, a unique citizenship education. It tries to provide an educational opportunity for Amerasians to foster their sense of citizenship without putting national frameworks as its first priority.

ISSUES WITH AMERASIANS

Both the idea of Double Education and the Global Human Resource project consider international society, though in different ways. The development of Double Education has been prompted by the deficiency of legal protection and social discrimination against Amerasians in Okinawa. Amerasians' historical and social backgrounds reflect triplicate colonial relationships: the United States and Japan, Japan and Okinawa, and Okinawan and Amerasians. The relationship between Japan and Okinawa has been colonial since the Japanese government established the Okinawa prefecture in 1879.[30] During World War II, school education was imperialistic everywhere in Japan. However, Okinawans had additional burdens. Okinawans were identified as "inferior" Japanese by main-island Japanese because of their unique cultures. In order to become "Japanese citizens," schools required students in Okinawa to use standard Japanese language and to practice main-island Japanese culture. Okinawan students were punished when they spoke in dialect at school. They were also forced to change their family names by the Japanese government. According to Kenichi Fujisawa, these colonial assimilation policies were justified as a way to modernize Okinawa.[31]

After the war, Japan was occupied by the United States, but most Japanese islands except the Okinawa area recovered their sovereignty in 1951 by the San Francisco Treaty. However, Okinawa remained occupied as part of the United States until 1972.[32] Even after reintegration as part of

"Japan," 20 percent of Okinawa's main island is still occupied by U.S. military bases. As a reward for this "severe burden," the Japanese government gives large-scale subsidies to the Okinawa prefecture.

The relationship between the United States and Japan is also hierarchical even though these two countries are currently forming an alliance. As already described, the United States occupied Japan after World War II. Since then, the U.S. military has been stationed at various locations throughout Japan, including the Okinawa islands. In addition to the unfairness of the Japan-US Status of Forces Agreement and the Japan-US Security Treaty, Japan pays U.S. military bases a tremendous amount of Host Nation Support every year compared to any other host nations. For example, Japan's total budget for hosting U.S. military bases in 2012 was estimated about 4,600,000,000 dollars.[33] It is approximately 5 times bigger than Germany, who pays the second biggest Host Nation Support (about 860,000,000 dollars).[34] This outstanding "hospitality" makes U.S. military bases in Okinawa a very "comfortable" station and brings the length of the U.S. military presence in Japan to about seventy years.[35] Thus, Okinawa is placed in a double-colonial position by the United States and Japanese main islands.

Anti-U.S. base movements by Okinawans have been continuous in Okinawa due to the perception that the U.S. military disturbs the peace of the community. Major claims made against American soldiers are for committing rapes against locals, various accidents during military training, traffic accidents, intrusions, robberies, and murders. Protests against U.S. bases among local people are doubling because these American soldiers are almost never charged with crimes in Okinawa under the US-Japan "Status of Forces" Agreement.[36] Janes and Noiri explain that Okinawan's frustration against the dual-colonial domination promotes a negative image of Amerasians in Okinawa; AmerAsian children were seen less as a product of love and respectful interaction between two people than as the result of an imposing occupying power taking advantage of the local population. In addition, some viewed those Japanese women who fraternized with American men as being somehow socially abnormal and engaging in activity that was not considered respectable.[37]

This negative image of Amerasians' mothers (and Amerasians themselves) sustains further multi-colonialism against Amerasians in Okinawa. This is the background of the need for Double Education.

Unlike Double Education, which was motivated by social discrimination, the Global Human Resource project is consistent with a feature of Japanese educational policy—namely, Westernization—since the opening up of Japan to western countries in the nineteenth century. Lynne Parmenter points out that "globalization is used as a rationale for cultural nationalism"[38] in Japanese education because it is missing a sense of Asia in the context. Parmenter argues that Japanese education policy-makers constrain "students to the aim of being 'Japanese people who can live in international society'"[39] but they neglect developing a sense of being Japanese as Asians. In particular, the Global Human Resource project is designed to unify the Japanese people by maintaining Japan's predominant status in the global economy and in international politics lead by western countries. In the 1980s, at the height of the Japanese economy, Japanese education was internationally celebrated by much Western educational research which purported to demonstrate that Japan's economic success was the result of Japanese educational accomplishments. However, in the 1990s, the Japanese economy experienced a "burst bubble" and the economic decline continued for decades. In 2010, China took the place of the second biggest economy over Japan. In addition, the Program for International Student Assessment (PISA) showed that the educational achievement of Japanese students was no longer at the top. Japan had lost the status of "Lessons for the West"[40] both at the economic level and educational level. Recently, Drew Faust, President of Harvard University, informed a Japanese newspaper that there were only five Japanese students who enrolled in undergraduate programs at Harvard in 2009. Faust commented that Japanese students in Harvard are fewer in number compared to other Asian countries such as Korea and China.[41] Faust's comment is supported by statistics showing that the number of Japanese students who go abroad to study has been declining for six years.[42] This "bad news" fans Japanese society's fear of inferiority: that Japan might be left behind in the stream of "western" version of globalization. It plays the role of a justification of energetic educational reforms to globalize Japanese citizens.

David Blake Willis and Jeremy Rappleye contend that recent educational policies to globalize Japanese education are aimed at prospective Japanese elites. For example, another MEXT policy for globalizing Japanese education, the Global 30 Project, aims to globalize thirteen elite Japanese universities and transform them "into 'world-class' institutions."[43] Junichi Hamada, President of the University of Tokyo, affirms the goal of internationalizing the University of Tokyo and nurturing tough students who can be actively involved in the front lines of globalized society.[44] The national educational policy toward globalizing Japanese citizens is shaped by the national economic strategy toward the global market. In fact, both the Global 30 Project and the Project for Promotion of Global Human Resource Development are actually strands of another policy—the Promotion of Industry-Academia Collaboration. This educational policy clearly states that education should meet economic demands to survive in the global market. It indicates that the Global Human Resource project is beneficial for industry because it cuts the cost and time of training workers.

These differences are also reflective of contrasting motivations for developing English language skills in the two approaches. For the Japanese imagined in the Global Human Resource guidelines, English is to be recognized as a second, not a first language. English language skills are for the purpose of communicating with "other" people in international society. Thus, learning English does not have a connection to the development of national identity as Japanese. In contrast, for Amerasians in Okinawa, English is recognized as one of their native languages. For Amerasians, it is impossible to rank English and Japanese, because one is their father's language and the other is their mother's language. In this way, English is not just a public language to access the labor market, but a private language to communicate with family at home as well as a form of cultural capital to develop their own identity.[45]

Furthermore, even though the development of Japanese identity is another common goal for both educational approaches, they understand "Japanese identity" in different ways, and have different reasons for promoting it. Within the conceptual framework of Global Human Resources, "Japanese identity" means national identity, and also ethnic identity. Here, "Japanese identity" is understood as a skill to compete and cooperate with "other people." Therefore, this approach to citizenship education incorporates a process of standardization, simplification of the image of the Japanese, and a top-down educational system at the national level. In contrast, Double Education is designed to meet educational needs in a multicultural society. In this context, "Japanese identity" means a national identity and a part of cultural identity. However, "Japanese identity" is not taught as the ultimate identity and is separated from ethnic identity because the relevant ethnicity is AmerAsian. Since Double Education puts weight on the development of ethnicity as Amerasians, a bottom-up educational system is understood as a more suitable style for citizenship education.

Kymlicka provides a theoretical framework to organize these differences between the two educational approaches. According to him, there are two types of group claims. One is *external protection*: these are ". . . intended to protect the group from destabilizing impact of *internal dissent*"[46] and the other is *internal restriction*: these are ". . . intended to protect the group from the impact of external decisions."[47] The framework of Global Human Resources justifies fostering "Japanese identity" as an "external protection." This means that since Japan is presumed the smallest unit in global society, fostering national identity is a way to maintain Japan's relevance as a country. However, this view is not an "external protection" in the context of Double Education, because Japan is not identified as the smallest unit in this context. For Amerasians, "Japanese identity" as interpreted in the framework of Global Human Resources is instead an "internal restriction" because it includes the neglect of Amerasian ethnicity. For Amerasians, Double Education is an "external protection" because it maintains their uniqueness in Japanese society.

Kymlicka contends that "in so far as internal restrictions are present, they are often defended in this way as unavoidable by-products of external protections, rather than as desirable in and of themselves."[48] The contradictory evaluations as described, concerning whether "Japanese identity"

proposed by the Global Human Resource project is an external protection or internal restriction, reflect on the gap between the primary objects
between the two educational approaches. The advocates of Double Education criticize the existing Japanese education system because it does not
adjust to "the reality" of multicultural Japanese society.[49] However, to the
advocates of the Global Human Resource project, Double Education has
rather failed to adjust to "the reality" of urgent national unification in our
global age. The most important issue is *not* that the voice of the Global
Human Resource project takes over the voice of Amerasians' educational
needs by political power. Nor is it to make an assessment concerning which
educational approach is the more valuable. The point at issue is that both
educational approaches *correctly* perceive "the realities" but dismiss each
other. Therefore, a theory of citizenship education which accommodates
these two educational approaches has to be explored.

In the next section, I propose the idea of interdependency as a way to
reconcile the Global Human Resource framework and Double Education. I
defend the idea of interdependency from three different levels of objection:
the internal level, the external level, and the disciplinary level.

Through this analysis, I transform the relationship of these educational
approaches from being separate to being interconnected. First, I note the
distinction between interdependency and dependency. Since dependency
is subordination, such a relationship constitutes interference with one by
another. On the other hand, "interdependency" connotes a sense of independence within the connection. Thus the path between two ideas becomes
more dialogical.[50]

INTERDEPENDENCY: THREE SEGMENTS

Internal Interdependency

First, Double Education must examine the question of whether it is reasonable for Japan to expect both mainstream Japanese and Amerasians
to have the same educational needs in citizenship education just because
they live in the same national framework. Kymlicka is sympathetic to
Amerasians' educational claims by saying that citizenship education
should not offer ". . . identical treatment, but rather differential treatment
in order to accommodate differential needs."[51] There are two different
principles to discuss citizenship education: equality-based argument and
equity-based argument. The equality-based argument is the principle
of citizenship education in the framework of Global Human Resources
because it provides the same educational content with the same expected
educational outcomes. However, the equity-based argument is the principle of citizenship education in Double Education because it treats
Amerasians differently from mainstream Japanese culture. Kymlicka

claims that "people from different national groups will only share an allegiance to the larger polity if they see it as the context within which their national identity is nurtured, rather than subordinated."[52] In his argument, the fostering of civic virtue and public-spiritedness as national identity is possible when ethnic and cultural identity is well-treated in the national framework.

Kymlicka points out that two implicit assumptions in the tradition of political philosophy are the major causes of why there is little to be discussed in citizenship education regarding the assumption that people have various needs in multicultural society. First, traditional political philosophy operates with the misperception that a multination-state is a nation-state. Kymlicka contends that:

> . . . contemporary liberal theorists implicitly assume that countries contain only one nation. They are well aware that modern states are culturally diverse . . . But they implicitly assume that this diversity is the sort that comes either from variations in people's conceptions of the good or from immigration—that is, they focus on philosophical, religious, and ethnic diversity within a single culture based on a shared language . . . They do not recognize or discuss the existence of states that are multinational, with a diversity of societal cultures, languages, and national groups.[53]

Even though historical facts demonstrate that most organized political communities have been heterogeneous, political theories have been developed on the assumption of the reverse. As a result, the traditional theory of citizenship education gives no answer to the demands of disadvantaged minority groups in the society.

Second, Kymlicka points out the roots of the traditional belief in the national framework in political philosophy. According to him, most political theorists assume that ". . .the world is, and will remain, composed of separate sates, each of which is assumed to have the right to determine who can enter its borders and acquire citizenship."[54] He points out that the traditional political theories are developed by fixing a hierarchical relationship between states and minority groups. As a result, the equity-based argument in citizenship education has been inhibited.

In order to develop a discussion about citizenship education to include the equity-based argument, Kymlicka proposes to alter the question at hand. He claims that "the question is not how should the state act fairly in governing its minorities, but what are the limits to the state's right to govern them?"[55] In order to realize the coexistence of Double Education with the Global Human Resource project, first of all, the hierarchical relationship between the Global Human Resource project and Double Education should be reformed to bring about a more democratic relationship at the theoretical level.

External Interdependency

Kymlicka's argument seeks for an interdependent relationship between Double Education and the Global Human Resource project at the level of intranational society. The claims of the Global Human Resource project should be taken seriously. It means that, in order to accommodate the equity-based argument into the conceptual framework of Global Human Resources, a theoretical transformation is also demanded at the international level. It is problematic that the framework of Global Human Resources standardizes the image of the Japanese citizen by excluding Amerasians. However, ignoring Amerasians' educational rights is not the purpose of the educational policy but a by-product of it. The standardization of Japanese identity is caused by international pressures in our global age. Thus, it is necessary to examine a way to understand the international climate in a global age, in order to reform the idea of Global Human Resources to fit the multicultural reality of society.

Victoria Tin-bor Hui provides an argument to transform the way we view the international community. She argues that the concept of a national framework, especially the notion of sovereignty, should be reformed to meet the conditions of contemporary world society. She points out that sovereignty should not be identified as isolation of the country, but understood in relationship to other national communities: "Sovereignty is relative to interstate relations as it involves mutual recognition with other states and distribution of relative capabilities."[56] Because national units are related to each other, the notion of sovereignty should be discussed both in relation to and in recognition of other national units. The transformation of the idea of sovereignty helps to reform the view of globalization. In the conceptual framework of Global Human Resources, the international community is presumed the "other" place, separated from Japan. Hui's argument, however, points out that if the idea of sovereignty is understood in the interdependent-base, the international community is not recognized where it is an isolated area from Japan. Hui's proposal is consistent with Amerasians' geographical perception and educational needs because Amerasians perceive themselves placed in between national boundaries.

Melissa Williams proposes a prior concept to transform Hui's idea of sovereignty. Williams claims that interdependency should be the underlying concept in understanding international society. She especially proposes to foster the sense of citizenship with the idea of a shared fate: citizenship as shared fate requires of individuals that they develop a capacity to see themselves as participants in a project of cooperation that includes others who are different and distant from them, and to participate in a manner consistent with the ethical norms that sustain legitimacy, including norms of egalitarian reciprocity and respect for individual freedom.[57] If the idea that each individual is already interconnected becomes the basic assumption, people care about the impacts on each other not only at the community level, but also at the individual level. A community of shared fate is not an ethical community as such. Its members are not bound to each other by shared values or moral commitments, but by relations of interdependence, which may or may not be positively valued by its members. Our futures are bound to each other, whether we like it or not.[58] Regardless of the varieties of identities, such as ethnic identity and sexual identity, people are mutually connected to each other. For Williams, the infiltration of the idea of interdependency is the first step to fostering a sense of citizenship. If the perception of the international community is transformed from one of isolation to one of interdependency, it gives more flexibility in the Global Human Resource framework for understanding Japanese citizens.

Interdependency: Educational Theory

The idea of interdependency fulfills both external needs and internal requirements to reconcile two different citizenship educations. However, it was not intended to conclude the final agreement between two different citizenship educations, but rather to continue the discussion about citizenship education. Kymlicka describes his ideal citizenship education as follows,

> There undoubtedly are limits to the extent to which people are able and willing to 'jump the barriers of experience'. But the solution is not to accept these limitations. Rather we should fight against them, in order to create a political culture in which people are more able and more willing to put themselves in other people's shoes, and truly understand. . .their needs and interests. This is not easy task-it may require changes to our education system. . .[59]

Kymlicka claims that it is important to develop the attitude, passion, and skills to understand other people, but it is also important to recognize that in citizenship education there is a limitation to understanding other people. It is important to create the "political culture" which sustains these two directions continuously through "education." His argument is understandable, as a political theorist. However, his claim should be reexamined in terms of educational theory, because education is not subordinate to political theory in the idea of interdependency. Again, Kymlicka points out that the healthy multicultural society needs not only "the justice of its basic institutions, but also on the qualities and attitudes of its citizens."[60] It is a political task to organize the procedural-institutional mechanisms and information, but it is an educational task to foster civic virtue and public-spiritedness.[61] Since these tasks are interdependent, "The Ties That Bind"[62] is incomplete if citizenship education is discussed only from the political perspective. This is also an important point in addressing the character of Double Education. Due to the highly political background of their own birth, for Amerasians, the problem is one of how to consider educational issues solely within a political framework. Even though Kymlicka's argument supports the idea of Double Education, his argument is only for a "political improvement." The fundamental claim in Double Education is, however, for "educational improvement."

Minoru Murai provides a crucial point on this issue by considering the relations between academic disciplines.[63] Murai claims that many "educational issues" have been distorted into political arguments because educational studies have been held to be parasitic upon other disciplines. As a result, the role of education is misidentified as being merely to fulfill economic and political needs. For example, the topic of studying the existence of U.S. bases in Okinawa (both in American schools and Japanese public schools) has been political, because it has been understood simply as a debate about whether the existence of U.S. forces in Okinawa is just or unjust. This version of such an educational approach does not take account of the existence of groups such as Amerasians who are unlikely (for various reasons) to take either position in the debate. This is how this educational approach is (mis)understood to be *merely* part of a political debate.

Walter Feinberg claims that it is important to differentiate the idea of democracy in politics from that of democracy in education:

> I believe that there is an important distinction between political democracy and educational democracy that can help us to sort out different kinds of claims regarding the responsibility of schools in promoting certain identities. This distinction is frequently overlooked by educators who wish to use education to advance a certain form of enlightened, democratic understanding and who believe that one can determine the right thing to do politically on the basis of deciding what the right thing to do is educationally. It is also overlooked by political theorists who hold that the right thing to do educationally can be deduced by determining what the right thing to do is politically.[64]

Here, Feinberg does not claim that educational issues can be isolated from politics. He claims, rather, that it is important to maintain a distinctively educational way of thinking even if actual educational issues are always influenced by economic, social, and political environment. For Feinberg, an educational perspective is also an important way to evaluate various educational activities and debates in politics.

This entails that educational studies of citizenship education have a double role. First, they may have a role as a specialized area of another field such as political science and economics. Second, they may be for the purpose of engaging educational thought itself. It seems correct to say that a discussion of citizenship education should be examined on the basis of how it contributes to the development of the educational way of thinking.

Paul Standish offers a way to explore a solution by applying a viewpoint of Stanley Cavell: "I do not seek to shore up my own identity but rather am ready for new possibilities—that is, ready to become."[65] This acceptance of ambiguity is also analogous to Murai's argument concerning educational thought. Murai claims that the idea that good education creates anxiety is not part of mainstream discussion about citizenship education. For Murai, to understand education as simply "beautifully solving problems" is to misunderstand the educational way of thinking. Rather, according to a distinctively educational way of thinking, education always carries uncertainty and anxiety.[66] Thus, Double Education and the Global Human Resource project should be perceived as continuous conversational partners to improve the idea of citizenship education itself. This conversation sustains the discussion of citizenship education as an educational theory.

CONCLUSION

This chapter described characteristics of Japanese educational policy and its problems, within a discussion of citizenship education. By contrasting this with Amerasians' educational needs, it was shown that it is important to have two aspects of citizenship education in Japan—recognizing cultural identity through a unique curriculum and teaching the mainstream to show respect for that identity. Also, it is important to be aware of whether the discussion of citizenship education contributes to the development of educational theory itself. An educational perspective is fundamental to the development of citizenship education because it is the mainspring of continuous improvement. The case of Japan pulls us to back to the very basics of educational studies.

I should now address the title of this chapter: "Lost in Citizenship Education." This chapter hopefully demonstrated that what is missing in the discussion of citizenship education is not only the attitude of reconciliation between the frameworks of Global Human Resources and Double Education, but also a readiness to connect discussions of citizenship education with a distinctively educational way of thinking. At the same time, it is important to know that there is no panacea to remove such problems or to realize the perfect peace. This is not only because society is complex; it is also because the character of an educational way of thinking is that *we are already/ready to become*. It is distinctive of citizenship education to seek for the improvement of citizenship education itself continuously.[67]

NOTES

1. This work was supported by JSPS KAKENHI Grant Number 23730770.
2. Amerasians are born in Asian countries such as Cambodia, Japan, Korea, Laos, Philippine, Thailand, and Vietnam where there is U.S. military stationing.
3. Okinawa is the southernmost prefecture of Japan.

4. Naomi Noiri and David Janes, "Preparing for Double Citizenship: Educational Innovation at the AmerAsian School in Okinawa," In *The 10ᵗʰ Anniversaryof the AmerAsian School in Okinawa, Okinawa*, 2008, p. 161.
5. Ryoko Tsuneyoshi, "The 'Internationalization' of Japanese Education and the Newcomers: uncovering the paradoxes," In D. B. Willis and J. Rappleye (eds.), *Reimagining Japanese Education: vorders, transfers, circulations, and the comparative*, Symposium Books, Oxford, 2011, p. 108.
6. Ibid., p. 107.
7. David Miller, *Market, State and Community: The Foundations of Market Socialism*, Oxford University Press, Oxford, 1989. And Michael Walzer, *Shperes of Justice: A Defence of Pluralism and Equality*, Blackwell, Oxford, 1983.
8. Will Kymlicka, *Multicultural Citizenship: A Liberal Theory of Minority Rights*, Oxford University Press, New York, 1995, p. 65.
9. Ibid., p. 171.
10. "Selection for the FY2012 Project for Promotion of Global Human Resource Development," MEXT. accessed September 24, 2013, http://www.mext.go.jp/english/highered/1326713.htm.
11. Ibid.
12. Robert W. Aspinall, "Globalization and English Language Education Policy in Japan: external risk and internal inertia," in D. B. Williams and J. Rapplete (eds.), *Reimagining Japanese Education: borders, transfers, circulations, and the comparative*, Symposium Books, Oxford, 2011, p. 127.
13. MEXT. accessed September 24, 2013, http://www.mext.go.jp/component/a_menu/education/micro_detail/__icsFiles/afieldfile/2011/04/11/1261037_1.pdf.
14. "Shin Gakushu Shido Yoryo," MEXT. accessed September 24, 2013, http://www.mext.go.jp/a_menu/shotou/new-cs/youryou/chu/sya.htm#chiri.
15. Ibid.
16. "Shinkamoku: Jiminbukai ga 'kokyo' Teigene," *Mainichi Newspaper* (Tokyo), June 18, 2013.
17. "Shin Gakushu Shido Yoryo," MEXT. accessed September 24, 2013, http://www.mext.go.jp/a_menu/shotou/new-cs/youryou/syo/sya.htm.
18. "Shin Gakushu Shido Yoryo," MEXT. accessed September 24, 2013, http://www.mext.go.jp/a_menu/shotou/new-cs/youryou/chu/sya.htm.
19. Approximately 250 Amerasians are born every year; thousands of children are of school age in Okinawa.
20. Noiri and Janes, "Preparing for Double Citizenship," p. 172.
21. Ibid., p. 175.
22. Amerasians only have dual citizenship if their fathers acknowledge the child.
23. Kazumi Uezato, *AmerAsian: Mouhitotsu no Okinawa,* Kamogawa Shuppan, Kyoto, 1998, p. 112.
24. Ibid., p.28.
25. Ibid.
26. Ibid., p. 116.
27. Noiri and Janes, "Preparing for Double Citizenship," p. 166.
28. Ibid., p. 175.
29. Ibid., p. 170.
30. Kenichi Fujisawa, *Okinawa/Kyouiku Kenryoku no Gendaishi*, Shakai Hyoron Sha, Tokyo, 2005.
31. Ibid.
32. Until 1972, American dollars were currency and driving in the right hand lane was the traffic rule in Okinawa.

33. "Zainichi Beigun Churyu Keihi Futan," Ministry of Defence, accessed September 24, 2013, http://www.mod.go.jp/j/approach/zaibeigun/us_keihi/suii_img.html.
34. Gaven McCormack & Satoko Oka Norimatsu, *Okinawa no Ikari: Nitibei henoTeiko*, Houritsubunkasha, Kyoto, 2013, p. 193.
35. For example, the U.S. military was stationed in Iraq for just eight and a half years.
36. Some Okinawans, however, accept coexistence with U.S. bases for economic reasons.
37. Noiri and Janes, "Preparing for Double Citizenship," p. 167.
38. Lynne Parmenter, "Asian (?) Citizenship and Identity in Japanese Education," In *Citizenship teaching and Learning*, 2(2), 2006, p. 14.
39. Ibid., 18.
40. Willis David Blake Willis and Jeremy Rappleye, "Reimaging Japanese Education in the Global Conversation: borders, transfers, circulations, and the comparative," In D. B. Willis and J. Rappleye (eds.), *Reimagining Japanese Education: vorders, transfers, circulations, and the comparative*, Symposium Books, Oxford, 2011, p. 23.
41. "'Nihonjin Gakusei Sonzaikai Usui' Harvard Daigakucho Kaiken Funki Unagasu," *Yomiuri Newspaper* (Tokyo), Mar. 11, 2010.
42. "Kaigai Ryugaku 6nen Renzokugen," *Yomiuri Newspaper* (Tokyo), February 9, 2013.
43. Willis and Rappleye, "Reimagining Japanese Education in the Global Conversation," pp.25–26.
44. Mayumi Ishikawa, "Redefining Internationalization in Higher Education: Global 30 and the making of global universities in Japan," In D. B. Willis and J. Rappleye (eds.), *Reimagining Japanese Education: vorders, transfers, circulations, and the comparative*, Symposium Books, Oxford, 2011, p. 194.
45. Noiri and Janes, "Preparing for Double Citizenship," p. 171.
46. Kymlicka, *Multicultural Citizenship*, p. 35.
47. Ibid.
48. Ibid., p. 44.
49. Noiri and Janes, "Preparing for Double Citizenship," p. 174.
50. Kymlicka, *Multicultural Citizenship*, p. 171.
51. Ibid., p. 113.
52. Ibid., p. 189.
53. Ibid., p. 128.
54. Ibid., p. 124.
55. Ibid., p. 118.
56. Victoria Tin-bor Hui, "Problematizing Sovereignty: Relative Sovereignty in the Historical Transformation of Interstate and State-Society Relations." In Michael Davis, Wolfgand Dietrich, Bettina Scholdan and Dieter Sepp (eds.), *International Intervention in the Post-Cold War World : Moral Responsibility and Power Politics*, Armonk, M.E. Sharpe, New York, 2004, p. 88.
57. Melissa Williams, "Citizenship as Identity, Citizenship as Shared Fate, and the Functions of Multicultural Education," In Walter Feinberg and Kevin McDonough (eds.), *Liberalism and the Dilemma of Public Education in Multicultural Societies*, Oxford University Press, New York, 2003, p. 233.
58. Ibid., p. 229.
59. Kymlicka, *Multicultural Citizenship*, pp. 140–141.
60. Ibid., p. 175.
61. Ibid., p. 176
62. Ibid., p. 172.

63. Minoru Murai, *Kyouikukara no Minaoshi: Seiji, Keizai, Housei, Shinkaron,* Toyokan, Tokyo, 1996.

64. Walter Feinberg, *Common Schools / Uncommon Identities : National Unity and Cultural Difference*, Yale University, New Haven, 1998, p. 27.

65. Paul Standish, "Social Justice and the Occident," In *Proceedings of the 5th International Symposium between the Graduate School of Education, Kyoto University (Japan), and the Institute of Education, University of London (UK)*, 2012, p. 26.

66. Murai, *Shin Kyouikugaku no Susume,* p. 78.

67. The author thanks Dr. Walter Feinberg for his generous support and encouragement throughout the writing of this chapter.

7 Citizenship Education and the Construction of Identity in Canada

Dianne Gereluk and David Scott

INTRODUCTION

One of the key challenges in how educators and policymakers foster citizenship rests on the philosophical tension between recognizing and accommodating cultural differences within a society while also ensuring unity and social cohesion. The willingness of most states to acknowledge and respond to this tension, however, is a fairly recent phenomenon. Historically, one of the defining features of almost all states was the presence of a dominant national group who used various mechanisms at their disposal, including control over public schooling, as a means to assimilate minority peoples into its own language, history, and culture. This is true in Canada where elite descendants of settlers from the British Isles (i.e., England, Scotland, Ireland) have sought to impose upon the larger population their own language and cultural traditions. However, these efforts were never fully successful due, in large part, to an already established French-speaking community (the Québécois), who vigorously contested the imposition of British values on their society. As a result of this reality, very early on the Québécois have retained the right and governmental means to preserve and protect their distinct Francophone identity within the provincial jurisdiction of Québec. Although this accommodation was made to Québec, within the rest of Canada, provincial and federal levels of government sought to assimilate minority communities including Aboriginal peoples and various immigrant groups into the dominant English language and Anglo culture. Beginning in the post-World War II era, however, this drive to forge a unitary and homogenous national community outside of Québec has given way to forms of citizenship guided by the theory and practice of "multiculturalism."

In Canada, the term multiculturalism is contested and carries with it differing meanings informed by a variety of ideological and conceptual positions.[1] However, most prominent among these are the ideals and principles of "liberal multiculturalism," which starts with the premise that the state should recognize and accommodate the distinct identities and aspirations of various minority peoples while also promoting equalization opportunities to remedy historical injustices against marginalized populations.[2] Although many Canadians have embraced ideals and principles of liberal multiculturalism, both within the sphere of education and within the greater public space, this model of citizenship has not been without its detractors. Some critics, informed by the rhetoric of neoliberalism, see its emphasis on reducing inequalities within society as a threat to social cohesion as well as a distraction from preparing young people for the competitive realities of the global marketplace. In its place, advocates of this view have called for a "notion of citizenship supportive of a free market."[3] Additionally, some critics, especially in Québec, argue that policies informed by multiculturalism encourage social isolation among and between people and creates impediments for immigrants to integrate into the already established culture of their host society. To counter these and other perceived shortcomings of multiculturalism, the concept of interculturalism has emerged in Québec as a viable framework for balancing the requirements of integration against the imperatives of respecting diversity. Seeing "the integration of new citizens as part of a dynamic, open-ended process of transforming a common societal culture through dialogue, mutual understanding, and intercultural contact,"[4] those advocating interculturalism believe it is uniquely suited for ensuring social cohesion while not falling back into the trap of assimilationist nationalism.

In this chapter, we examine how educational jurisdictions in Canada, both past and present, have responded to the tension between accommodating cultural difference while also ensuring social cohesion along the lines the dominant group has established. In order to do this, we have divided the chapter into three parts. In the first section, we begin by exploring the ways citizenship education in Canada, particularly during the pre-World War II era, was organized around the principles of forging a unitary nation-state. In the second section, we explore how two strands within the theory and practice of multiculturalism in Canada, including a recognition of diversity dimension and a social justice dimension, reject this model of attempting to assimilate minority peoples into a homogenous national culture. As part of this discussion, we explore how the ideals and principles of liberal multiculturalism in particular have become an important organizing framework for guiding educational policy and citizenship education in English-speaking Canada.[5] In the third section, we outline the ways interculturalism in Québec and a movement toward a more unitary vision of Canadian identity and citizenship within the rest of Canada are challenging particular aspects of multicultural theory and practice. As part of this discussion, acknowledging the strengths of interculturalism, we identify shortcomings with this approach including its tendency to disallow what we deem as reasonable and necessary accommodations for minority groups. Ultimately, we argue that liberal multiculturalism, when tied to an emphasis on social justice, provides the most compelling framework to guide citizenship education in Canada.

CITIZENSHIP EDUCATION AS ASSIMILATION

Citizenship education in Canada, like in other countries, is intimately tied up with attempts to construct a particular kind of national identity. Unsurprisingly, early conceptions of citizenship education in Canada were focused primarily on a unitary vision of the "nation- state." Within this model, a dominant national group has used its power over the state to privilege its own language, culture, history, and even in some cases, religion.[6] In trying to create this ideal of national homogeneity, anyone who did not belong to the dominant national group was subject to a range of nation building policies meant to either assimilate or exclude them. Within the sphere of education, nation-building policies included the creation of a national system of education accompanied by a standardized curriculum, whereby the dominants group's language, culture, and history become the national language, culture, and history.[7]

In the past, the Canadian government and provincial jurisdictions of education have followed this model of citizenship by attempting to assimilate minority peoples into the ethos of the dominant Anglo culture and English language. However, Canada has deviated from this model in one important respect. Historically, the Québécois––Canada's French-speaking population––were afforded a degree of autonomy to protect their distinct Francophone heritage and identity within their traditional territory of Québec. This deviation from the unitary nation-state mold can be attributed to a series of historical and political developments in Canada, the most important of which can be traced back to a decisive British military victory over the French near Québec City in 1759. After this defeat, France ceded most of its possessions in eastern North America, including New France, to Great Britain. Wanting to avoid rebellion on the part of the French habitants and greatly outnumbered, the British government enacted the Québec Act of 1774. This act was unique for its time in that it gave significant authority and autonomy to the Québécois such as guarantees that they could practice the Roman Catholic faith, use the French language in public institutions, and retain French civil law in private matters within Québec. Later, these accommodations were expanded in the British North America Act of 1867, where authority over language and education were devolved to Québec at the provincial level. As a result of this de-evolution of responsibility to Québec, each individual province in Canada was also granted exclusive jurisdiction over education. Accordingly, the nine provinces and three territories that make up English-speaking Canada each have their own ministries of education and are not beholden to any federal department of education.

Although concessions to Québec were a notable part of the British North America Act (1867), it provided no parallel constitutional concessions to Canada's Aboriginal peoples and their diverse languages, cultures, and traditions. [8] Instead, in 1876, the federal government created the Indian Act designating Aboriginal peoples as "Status Indians" and wards of the state. As a result of this legislation, the Canadian government dictated how Aboriginal children would be educated.[9] In many cases, government agents forcibly took Aboriginal children from their families and communities to be educated in off-reserve state funded industrial schools (later called residential schools) often run by the Roman Catholic Church or Protestant denominations.[10] Built on the assumption that Aboriginal culture and traditions were inferior and unequal with European culture and traditions, the primary objective of residential schools was to, as Duncan Campbell Scott, the Deputy Superintendent General of Indian Affairs stated, "kill the Indian in the child."[11] This belief was supported by the Indian Act, which sought to:

> . . . provide the legal basis for the internment of Aboriginal children and to establish government control as a means of pursuing assimilation of these children into majority white euro-centric culture, and effectively eliminate the influence of aboriginal traditional knowledge or culture on the development of these children.[12]

An amendment to the Indian Act in 1920 made attendance at residential schools compulsory for all Aboriginal children. When the last residential school was closed in 1996, it is estimated that as many as 150,000 Aboriginal children went through the residential school system.[13]

The desire to assimilate minority peoples into the dominant Anglo community was not only directed toward Aboriginal people; this policy was directed at immigrant populations as well. At the expense of the original Aboriginal inhabitants (including the Blackfoot and the Plains Cree), from 1896 to 1914, the Canadian government encouraged European immigration to populate and farm western Canada.[14] Of the three million people who immigrated to Canada from 1896 to 1914, more than 800,000 were neither of French nor British origin.[15] In response to the growing ethnic diversity of the country, largely due to immigration from Eastern and Northern Europe, provincial jurisdictions of education in Canada sought a vision of Canadian identity that could subsume minority cultural traditions that might challenge the values of the Anglo-Saxon Protestant elite that dominated Canada outside of Québec.[16]

As part of this process, the primary aim of public schools in English-speaking Canada was to create a homogenous nation built on a common English language and shared cultural values realized through promoting identification with British institutions and practices.[17] A school superintendent in Canada West speaking in 1896, for example, warned: "If these [immigrants] children are to grow up as Canadian citizens they must be led to adopt our viewpoint and speak our speech. . .A common school and common tongue are necessary if we are to have a homogenous citizenship."[18] In attempting to ensure that minority communities adopted "our viewpoint," this unitary understanding of Canadian identity led to the creation of text-books such as *We are Canadian Citizens* (1937) where students learned that "Canadians form but a small part of the British Empire, yet for other reasons our country is one of the most important units of the Empire."[19]

The model of nation building that emerged in Québec differed from the English Canadian model largely due to the relatively small number of immigrants who integrated into French-speaking society during this period. Further, during this time, political elites in Québec did not see immigration as a tool for nation building.[20] Schools in Québec, which were controlled by the Catholic Church and largely a local concern, however, similarly became a space to promote a unified French Canadian national identity. Lévesque writes, for example, that the general purpose of history and geography up into the 1920s involved "the rigid inculcation of religious, moral, and patriotic beliefs in French Canadians, with particular focus on the 'heroic' character of their French ancestors."[21] In promoting these values, the religious and political elite in the province sought to ensure *la surviance* or the survival of French Canadian nationality, language, and culture.[22] Within this frame of reference, the 1759 British conquest of New France marked the beginning of a long and painful struggle by the Francophone peoples in Québec to resist the continued threat of assimilation posed by the surrounding Anglophone majority in Canada and the United States.

THE SHIFT TOWARD LIBERAL MULTICULTURALISM IN CANADA

Following WWII, changing demographics due to increased immigration from outside of Europe led to a rethinking of citizenship education in English Canada. Additionally, since the 1960s, minority groups became increasingly vocal in contesting exclusionary and assimilatory nation-building policies and, in their place, advocated for new "multicultural" policies and political frameworks. Although there are many policies and frameworks that reflect this shift in thinking, Kymlicka argues that "repudiating the idea of the state as belonging to the dominant group; replacing assimilationist and exclusionary nation-building policies with policies of recognition and accommodation; acknowledging historic injustices and offering amends for it, are common to all real-world struggles for multiculturalism."[23] With the explicit goal of promoting social inclusion and educational equity for all students, two dimensions of multicultural theory and practice in particular became central in the ways citizenship education was conceptualized in Canada.[24]

The first of these, informed by more critical discourses in the field of multicultural education, is a social justice dimension that seeks to engage and overcome various forms of discrimination in society. Within the sphere of the classroom, this would involve helping young people critically examine and constructively engage forms of prejudice in society including racism, ethnocentrism, sexism, and other forms of discrimination.[25] In highlighting historical injustices perpetrated against minority groups within the Canadian context, a social justice orientation would specifically examine, for example, the ways:

> official government policies, formulated and implemented with popular public support, served to entrench, among other examples, racial segregation in schools, forced assimilation of First Nations Canadians, racialized immigration restrictions, anti-Semitism, the mistreatment of Chinese immigrant railway workers, and the displacement and internment of Japanese Canadians.[26]

Exploring Canada's long history of discrimination and racism would also implicate the racist ideologies and ethnocentric views that supported these official policies, predicated on the belief that British cultural norms were superior.

Related to the social justice dimension of multiculturalism, is a "recognition of diversity" strand, informed by the principles of "liberal multiculturalism, concerned with recognizing and accommodating cultural difference and fostering intergroup harmony."[27] While the social justice strand of multiculturalism offers a more critical stance for addressing diversity in schools, those working in a "liberal multicultural" conceptual frame also focus on addressing ethno-cultural concerns.[28] At the classroom level, this involves opening up curricula to encompass a wider range of materials from the perspectives of people who have been historically silenced in schools so as to cause attitudinal changes in both students and teachers. In Canada, this would include incorporating materials from Aboriginal perspectives as well as the perspective of other marginalized groups like Canadians of Asian and African descent. For the most part, demands for recognition at the educational policy level have been generally directed toward creating accommodations so that minorities are accepted as full and equal citizens of the country. Policy leaders responding to these concerns have taken various measures to ensure that all public institutions, including schools "accommodate diversity, promote integration, and present a more open and inclusive image of the nation."[29]

Within a "liberal multicultural" framework the kinds of recognition or accommodations different minority groups should be given varies greatly based on the nature and history of the group. In this regard, Kymlicka argues national minorities such as Indigenous peoples and Canada's French-speaking population—the Québécois—demand greater accommodations than other minority groups such as newly arrived immigrant peoples due to their existence as distinct national communities long before the formation of the state.[30] By rejecting models of citizenship tied to assimilatory nation-building policies, under the principles of liberal multiculturalism the state confers greater territorial autonomy and forms of self-government to national minorities to ensure their distinct identities will be preserved into perpetuity. This tenet was reflected in early accommodations to the Québécois who were granted control over language and education. Over the last two decades, Aboriginal leaders in Canada have similarly demanded control and autonomy in crafting educational policies. As we will discuss, at this time, however, control over education continues to rest with the federal government. As a result, the principles of liberal multiculturalism have yet to be lived out with Aboriginal peoples in the same way they have with the Québécois.

Given this, the principles and organizing framework of liberal multiculturalism has greatly influenced citizenship education in Canada in terms of educational policy and practice. This shift can be traced back to the decision in 1971 by the Liberal government of Prime Minister Trudeau to introduce "Bilingualism within a Multicultural Framework" as a new organizing idea for Canadian citizenship. This policy framework provided a response to both a growing separatist movement in Quebec and the increasing ethnic diversity of the country. In a speech to the House of Commons in 1971, Trudeau articulated the rationale for this new federal policy:

> There cannot be one cultural policy for Canadians of British and French origin, another for the original peoples and yet another for all others. For although there are two official languages, there is no official culture, nor does any ethnic group take precedence over any other . . . We are free to be ourselves . . . It is the policy of this government . . . to 'safeguard' this freedom . . . A policy of multiculturalism within a bilingual framework commends itself to the government as the most suitable means of assuring the cultural freedom of Canadians.[31]

Following this initial policy framework, through the Canadian Charter of Rights and Freedoms in 1982, and the subsequent passing of the Canadian Multiculturalism Act in 1988, the federal government enshrined these sentiments into law. Canada thus became the first country in the world to have an official policy of multiculturalism at the federal level.[32] Through these policies, minority communities were encouraged to retain and practice their culture, French and English were recognized as the two official languages of Canada, and various equality rights were conferred onto all citizens including freedom from discrimination based on sex, age, or ethnic origin. The Canadian Charter of Rights and Freedoms also recognized rights of Aboriginal communities gained through previous treaty agreements and required the government to negotiate the meaning and nature of these rights with Aboriginal peoples themselves.

Unlike other rights legislation in countries such as the United States and Britain, the Canadian Charter is unique in that it confers not just individual rights, but also collective rights. In this regard, Aboriginal peoples,

Canada's Francophone population, and Anglophones are all guaranteed collective rights to assist in protecting their unique identities. As part of these collective rights, Anglophones in Quebec are guaranteed the ability to enroll their children in an English school. Likewise, Francophone peoples, regardless of where they live in Canada have the right to enroll their children in a Francophone school as long as the number of Francophone children in the area warrants having a school. Although the specific rights Aboriginal groups are afforded vary depending on the specific community, in general they include rights to self-government, and the right to practice their own culture and customs including language and spiritual practices.

Provincial jurisdictions of education across Canada responded to the new bilingualism within multicultural political framework along with the Canadian Charter of Rights and Freedoms in a variety of ways. Within the sphere of educational policy, Francophone school boards were introduced in every province in English-speaking Canada. This multicultural framework also impacted the teaching of other non-official languages as well. In 1971, the Alberta government, for example, enacted section 150 of the School Act, which stipulated: "a board may authorize that any other language be used as a language of instruction in addition to the English language, in all or any of its schools."[33]The resulting proliferation of so-called heritage languages in schools reflected a larger federal directive to recognize the language and culture of minority groups in society.

IMPACT OF FEDERAL POLICY ON CURRICULUM

Trudeau's Bilingualism within a Multicultural Framework began to impact social studies and related subjects that had, by this point, become the home of citizenship education in Canada. However, the impact of this policy on social studies curricula was not immediate. Perhaps surprisingly, throughout the 1970s, the concept of multiculturalism was not necessarily seen as an important organizing idea for the study of Canadian society.[34] For example, one study examining the extent to which social studies programs were adopting the language and principles of multiculturalism concluded:

> Some socials studies programs neither have explicitly stated rationales on multiculturalism (whether for integration, diversity, or awareness) nor display much evidence in the prescribed content and goals of even an implicit rationale. In such cases, the notion of multiculturalism does not appear to be an important organizing idea for the study of Canadian society.[35]

However, later in the decade and into the 1980s, the language of multiculturalism did find its way into many provincial social studies program documents in English-speaking Canada. Illustrative of this emphasis, a 1985

Manitoba social studies program states that before leaving high school students should appreciate the idea that Canada:

> . . . is a country in which national unity cannot be taken for granted. It is multicultural, with many of its various cultural groups experiencing a new sense of identity. It is geographically diverse, officially bilingual, and often subject to severe divergent forces.[36]

This more inclusive idea of whom "Canadian citizenship" encompasses was often accompanied by a move from primarily passive to more activist forms of civic engagement. Students needed to not only know about issues facing the country, but also be able to, as stated in the same Manitoba social studies document, "frame defensible viewpoints on them and be aware of possible courses of citizen action."[37] Curricular directives like these reflected an increasing movement toward values education and making social studies classrooms a space in which to engage social justice concerns. Programs of studies and textbooks began to emphasize helping students become active decision makers by working through social issues such as poverty and racism. For example, a textbook entitled *Human Rights: Respecting our Differences* published in 1978, and used in multiple jurisdictions across Canada, called on teachers to help students gain empathy toward victims of discrimination and prejudice. As a result of examining their own prejudices, students were encouraged to take social action whereby they could "apply what they have learned in the classroom to various facets of their daily life."[38]

Although the 1970s and early 1980s were notable for increasingly more open, inclusive, and multicultural forms of citizenship along with a shift toward issues-based and activist forms of civic education, the rise of the neoliberal agenda in the 1980s stymied this trajectory. Specifically, a larger international discussion concerning the need for economic competitiveness in a rapidly globalizing world led to the prioritization of market-based principles to determine education policy and practice. Reflective of this trend, the United States' *A Nation at Risk* (1983) report and England's Education Reform Act (1988)––outlining the ways schools were allegedly failing the students and parents they were meant to serve––had significant ramifications for educational policy in Canada. Specifically, there was a sense from the many educational jurisdictions in Canada that schools were not meeting the need for a more globally competitive workforce. As a result, the term "citizen" increasingly became associated within policy documents with one who is economically innovative and able to contribute to a prosperous and competitive nation.[39] This was particularly apparent in Ontario, Manitoba, and Alberta, whose conservative governments began to adopt the corporatist language of serving educational *stakeholders* and developing *human capital resources*. In 1991, the Manitoba Department of Education and Training, for instance, outlined a new educational policy meant to meet the needs of a future where:

> The workforce will demand highly skilled and adaptable workers who have the ability to upgrade existing skills and develop new skills, who can help and participate in a climate that encourages entrepreneurship, innovation and economic growth, and who can understand the complex dynamics of a competitive global environment. [40]

The election of Premier Ralph Klein in Alberta in 1994 furthered the trends toward neoliberal market ideals in education policy. Ralph Klein summed up his vision for education reform as follows: "we are building an education system that will make our kids better prepared, to be more competitive, in a world that demands excellence."[41] This shift in policy documents ironically became increasingly prevalent, at a time when localized curricular practices were beginning to address larger contemporary debates about the environment, global social injustices, and intercultural awareness.

The influence of neoliberal principles had interesting implications for how citizenship education would be conceived and developed. On the one hand, the principles of liberal multiculturalism were still apparent within curriculum documents with a continued emphasis on the recognition and value of diversity in Canadian society. On the other hand, there was a palpable lessening of the activist social justice dimension of multicultural theory and practice within curricula in confronting and challenging past and current inequalities in society. In essence, this meant an increased prominence on tolerance and recognition of ethno-cultural diversity but with little commitment to reducing economic and social inequalities.[42] Some theorists assert that it is no accident that multiculturalism became popular in an era dominated by a neoliberal agenda that was partially intended to dismantle the welfare state.[43] Specifically, without a commitment toward social justice, including attempts to reduce economic inequality, "multiculturalism offers a 'minority-friendly' smokescreen or distraction behind which state reforms that disproportionately harm minority groups are hidden."[44]

Reflecting this shift toward an emphasis on recognizing the diverse nature of Canadian society, while downplaying any social justice analysis of inequalities that exist, by the mid-1990s fostering pluralism became a central objective in developing citizenship dispositions within Canadian social studies curricula. For instance, the Foundation for the Atlantic Provinces Canada Social Studies Curriculum states that students should be able to "demonstrate understanding of their own and others' cultural heritage and cultural identity."[45] Similarly, the Alberta Social Studies Program states that social studies, "fosters the building of a society that is pluralistic, bilingual, multicultural, inclusive and democratic."[46]

More recently, social studies program documents have moved beyond the recognition of cultural diversity in general toward additionally emphasizing the collective rights and unique status of Aboriginal and Francophone peoples as outlined in the Canadian Charter of Rights and Freedoms. This is in part to provide recognition and awareness of Aboriginal and Francophone peoples and communities' rightful place as two of the three founding nations of Canada. In relation to Aboriginal perspectives, this curricular movement also reflects the need to ensure that a rapidly growing Aboriginal youth population, particularly in western Canada, recognizes themselves in the curriculum. The shift in thinking toward engaging Aboriginal and Francophone perspectives is especially apparent within the Western Canadian Protocol, which sought to create a common social studies curriculum framework for all the western provinces. The document states:

> Social studies supports active and responsible citizenship by enabling students to appreciate and respect diverse Canadian cultural perspectives, including Aboriginal and francophone, and understand how these perspectives have shaped Canada's political and cultural realities.[47]

This curriculum framework, adopted particularly in Alberta, is notable for the way it departs from traditional approaches to social studies that seek to create a unitary national identity. In contrast, programs of study across western Canada have restored Aboriginal and Francophone people, communities, and their diverse perspectives to a permanent seat of multi-national deliberations around the future of the country. As can be seen, through affirming the distinct status of Aboriginal and Francophone peoples, while also recognizing the inherently diverse nature of the Canadian federation, social studies program documents reflect the belief inherent with liberal multiculturalism that differing minority communities can possess differing levels of recognition. However, notably, in recognizing the unique place of Aboriginal and Francophone peoples within the Canadian federation, in line with a neoliberal ethos, there has been no accompanying call within these documents for a social justice analysis as to why, for example, half of all Aboriginal children designated as status First Nations in Canada live in poverty.[48] In this way, recent social studies curricular frameworks are willing to speak the language of recognition for Canada's founding nations, but this has not involved any significant emphasis on helping young people interrogate current unequal social and economic arrangements.

In relation to accommodations that would afford Aboriginal communities increased levels of control and autonomy over education, the relationship between Canada's indigenous peoples and the federal government continues to evolve. Although funding of Aboriginal education has been capped at a two percent increase per year, from 2006–2011 the overall Aboriginal population has grown by 20 percent.[49] Consequently, Aboriginal leaders are becoming increasingly vocal about the need to ensure that federal funding for Aboriginal students is equal to the per-student funding for non-Aboriginal students. Aboriginal leaders have also expressed the need to gain greater control over curriculum to better promote and protect their distinct languages and cultures. While many Aboriginal communities do have their own band schools, which gives them the ability to adapt provincially mandated programs of study to reflect their particular culture and language; constitutional authority over elementary and secondary education continues to rest with the federal government. Recently, the Assembly of First Nations has asked the federal government to work with them to pass legislation allowing Aboriginal peoples control over education.[50] As outlined earlier, the principles of liberal multiculturalism would clearly seek to accommodate these demands, thereby seeking to rectify a long history of assimilatory nation-building policies that sought to eradicate the unique identities of Aboriginal peoples. However, the current Conservative government of Prime Minister Harper, greatly inspired by a neoliberal agenda that seeks to minimize government funding where possible, has yet to embrace these principles. Currently, federal funding for Aboriginal education has remained largely static and there has been little indication that the Conservative government is willing to devolve greater control over education to educational authorities controlled by Aboriginal people.

CRITICS OF LIBERAL MULTICULTURALISM

During the early 2000s, a number of scholars have noted an increased interest in citizenship education in Canada over the last decade.[51] However, this interest in citizenship education has not been accompanied by a stronger commitment to the principles of multiculturalism in terms of recognizing and accommodating diversity and promoting social equality.[52] In fact, emerging approaches in the field of citizenship education in Canada, to varying degrees, have openly criticized using principles and ideals of multiculturalism as an organizing framework to guide educational policy into the future. The first set of criticisms has surfaced in Québec where an alternative framework of interculturalism has been proposed. The second set of criticisms has been the result of an initiative led by the Conservative government of Prime Minister Harper seeking to create a more unitary notion of Canadian civic identity. In common, both approaches place greater emphasis on social cohesion at the expense of acknowledging, recognizing, and accommodating cultural diversity. We first turn to the rise of interculturalism in Québec that must be understood within its historical context before we can explain what this concept entails as a framework to guide citizenship education.

Multiculturalism as defined by Trudeau and enshrined in the Canadian Charter of Rights and Freedoms (which was never signed by Québec) continues to be poorly received in Québec. One major reason for the pushback against multiculturalism is that many Québécois believed that this policy framework eroded Québec's special status as one of the founding nations of Canada. Specifically, many people in Quebec believe that "the policy of multiculturalism, in effect, reduced Québec's status from that of one of the three founding nations of Canada to just one of countless ethnic minorities under the domination of a centralized, largely English-speaking Canada."[53] Further, as we will explore next, many people in Québec asserted that multiculturalism discourages new arrivals from integrating into the host community.

A generalized distrust of multiculturalism in Québec was heightened following the outcome of a court challenge examining whether an Orthodox Sikh boy in Québec should be permitted to wear his ceremonial Sikh dagger—the *kirpan*—to school.[54] Although the Québec court ruled in favor of the school's decision not allowing him to do so, when the case went to the Supreme Court of Canada, it was decided in a unanimous 8-0 decision, that this should be permitted but with strict guidelines (i.e., the *kirpan* had to be wrapped and sown in a sturdy cloth envelope and worn under clothing).[55] This case brought to light the principles of "reasonable accommodation" that minority cultural practices are afforded under a liberal multicultural framework. Specifically, within a liberal multicultural framework, until the point of undue hardship for other parties, the state has a duty to adjust, accommodate, and make alternative arrangements with particular individuals or groups in order to reduce discriminatory practices. The rationale is that identical treatment for all people often does not reduce the level of discrimination that is commonly felt by minority groups. Based on these principles, the Supreme Court stated that "unless the school could show that the *kirpan* would cause undue hardship to others, then reasonable accommodation should be applied to protect the boy's religious freedom."[56] In safeguarding and maintaining the multicultural values that Canada purports to have, the Supreme Court felt that providing a "total prohibition" of the *kirpan* would send the wrong message, suggesting that some religious symbols held more weight and privilege over others.[57]

This Supreme Court decision intensified the hostility many people held toward multiculturalism in Québec as they felt federal multicultural policies, as reflected in this Supreme Court decision, went too far in allowing accommodations toward minority groups. Specifically, there was a sense that allowing these kinds of accommodations left the door open for dangerous and illiberal practices—such as coerced arranged marriages, honor killings, or female genital mutilation—that threatened the established liberal democratic nature of the society. In a highly visible response challenging the principles of multiculturalism, the municipality of Hérouxville published an official list of unacceptable practices in their community. The declaration states, for instance:

- Our Education: in our schools, the children cannot carry any weapons real or fake, symbolic or not.
- Our Security: you may not hide your face as to be unable to identify you while you are in public. The only time you may mask or cover your face is during Halloween.[58]

The inconsistency and contradictions in the declaration are noteworthy. For example, the declaration makes the assumption that individuals who cover their faces for religious reasons pose a public safety risk to the public, while those that mask their faces during their Halloween festivities automatically do not pose any risk. However, it is important to put this declaration in context. Commentators have noted that resistances toward multiculturalism have been less apparent in English Canada due to "the hegemonic position the English language holds in world affairs."[59] Specifically, ethnic newcomers do not pose a great threat within a society where the preeminence of the English language and Anglo culture is secure. Thus, the xenophobic undertones of this declaration should be understood within a context of a society engaged in a long struggle for linguistic and cultural survival. These challenges to multiculturalism are emblematic of a wide spread societal concern among many Québécois that newly arrived minority groups were failing, or unwilling, to learn French or integrate into the cultural value system of the majority Francophone culture.

While the Hérouxville municipal declaration was in response to the Supreme Court decision regarding the accommodations made to the Sikh faith, such discussions around the limits of reasonable accommodation continued to gain widespread traction in Québec. In response to these concerns, the Québec government established the "Consultation Commission on Accommodation Practices Related to Cultural Differences" (herewith known as the Bouchard-Taylor Commission) to specifically address the "public discontent concerning reasonable accommodation."[60] As an alternative to multiculturalism, the report outlined the principles of interculturalism as a viable framework for accommodating and acknowledging the reality that Quebec was a diverse society, while also laying out the limits of how much a host society should be willing to accommodate cultural and religious differences. The Bouchard-Taylor report define interculturalism as follows:

> ... we could say that Québec Interculturalism a) institutes French as the common language of intercultural relations; b) cultivates a pluralist orientation that is highly sensitive to the protections of rights; c) preserves the creative tension between diversity and the continuity of the French-speaking core and the social link; d) places special emphasis on integration; and e) advocates interaction.[61]

In advancing these principles, new arrivals to the community are asked to enter into a moral contract with the host community "to further the basic societal values of individual rights and freedoms, democratic participation, the promotion of a common public language, openness to plurality, and intercultural dialogue."[62] In shifting the focus away from an exclusive emphasis on the responsibility of established citizens of welcoming and accepting newcomers, interculturalism also places an emphasis on the newcomers' responsibility to adapt and integrate into the dominant social, linguistic, and cultural reality of the society they are entering. Notably, this approach is asymmetrical in the sense that values and practices of newly arrived immigrant peoples do not carry the same weight as the already established community. In this way, the "ideal is of a balanced but asymmetrical give-and-take of adjustment, exchanges, and compromise between the home society and those of new arrivals."[63]

These principles, thus contrast with multicultural principles in important ways. While the guiding metaphor of multiculturalism is one of a cultural mosaic, the guiding metaphor of interculturalism involves becoming part of a story.[64] The Bouchard-Taylor report explores what this entails:

> The society to which one is deeply attached is this collective enterprise that has taken shape over the centuries, centered on certain values or ideals, which, of course, have continued to change. It belongs to the past but perpetuates itself as a heritage as the future. In this way, everyone can grasp this past in order to prolong the thread that wove it, without there necessarily being agreement on everything that composes it. Some individuals have direct ancestors in this past and others do not, but everyone can adopt the project that this society proposes. The path has been shaped but one can enter it, at any time, which means that one has the right, therefore, to contribute to mapping out the rest of the itinerary, in a word to codetermine it. . . It is the dreams, decisions and common projects, in short everything we have achieved together, that will give substances to this new and perhaps fragile identity.[65]

The emphasis is thus one of shared dialogue toward creating a larger collective civic project. By taking part in a shared dialogue, proponents of interculturalism see the ways diverse peoples and perspectives can work to enrich and jointly build a common societal culture. By seeking to foster stronger social cohesion between old stock Québécois and new immigrants, the three core principles of dialogue, cultural asymmetry, and a basic moral contract are thus advanced to address the perceived gaps found in multiculturalism.

In light of this competing conceptual framework of interculturalism, educational policy leaders in Québec have taken a markedly different approach in addressing the tensions between unity and diversity. This can be seen in the introduction of Québec's Ethics and Religious Culture Curriculum (ERC) that in 2008 became mandatory from kindergarten to grade twelve for all students in Québec. As reflected in the key principles of interculturalism, the ERC focuses on mutual recognition and respect, and the pursuit of the common good. Within this framework, the program highlights, "three main actions: the search, along with others, for common values, the promotion of projects that foster community life; and respect for democratic principles and ideals specific to Québec society."[66] In fore-fronting these actions, the ERC program places greater emphasis on the dispositions required to address competing values within a pluralist society, with particular attention on "ethical reflection, knowledge of religious culture, and the capacity for dialogue."[67] But as part of the explicit asymmetrical stance inherent to the principles of interculturalism, special status is afforded to the historical influence and legacy of Catholicism and Protestantism in shaping Québec's contemporary society. Reflecting the idea of accepting a moral contract, the ERC also emphasizes the obligation of all people to accept the basic norms and regulations that reflect the liberal democratic principles of mutual respect and individual rights and liberties.

In considering to what extent interculturalism provides a viable framework to guide citizenship education in Canada, it is important to highlight some of what we believe are misplaced claims it makes against liberal multiculturalism. The first of these is a belief that interculturalism is better able to overcome the perceived deficiencies of multiculturalism including the need to make more explicate the limits to which a society should be willing to recognize and accommodate difference. In this regard, there has been a belief that policies informed by liberal multiculturalism leave the door open to illiberal cultural and religious practices that no liberal democratic society can tolerate. However, this criticism is unwarranted within the Canadian context as the principles of multiculturalism are framed within the greater parameters of the Canadian Charter of Rights and Freedoms. Kymlicka writes,

> Wherever multiculturalism has been adopted it has been tied to larger human-rights norms and has been subject to the overarching principles of the liberal-democratic constitutional order. No Western democracy has exempted immigrant groups from constitutional norms of human rights in order to maintain practices such as forced marriage, criminalization of apostasy, or cliterodectomy.[68]

The second charge that multiculturalism does not attend to intercultural dialogue seems equally unwarranted given that one of the central concerns of multiculturalism is to promote intergroup harmony by fostering shared understanding and mutual respect.

While the intercultural focus on social cohesion provides a framework to ensure the cultural survival of Québécois identity, recent developments in the province have exposed other limitations to this approach. Recently, the government of Québec, led by the separatist Parti Québécois, has introduced a Values Charter that involves banning "overt and conspicuous" religious symbols and clothing by government employees throughout the province.[69] If passed, this legislation would mean that Muslim women who work in the public sector, including as day care workers, could be fired from their jobs if they refuse to comply. Further, the Parti Québécois government has recommended that a similar ban on religious clothing should be considered and adopted in the private sector as well.[70] It can be debated to what extent interculturalism has informed this proposed policy directive. However, in advocating a moral contract among its citizens along with asserting the asymmetrical relationship between immigrants and the host society, it seems that principles of interculturalism can lead to policy decisions that clearly fail to attend to issues of prejudice, discrimination, and marginalization of minority groups in Québec.

While interculturalism has gained prominence in Québec as a viable alternative to multiculturalism, it has not received the same level of attention in English Canada. However, initial indicators suggest that a pendulum shift might also be occurring across English Canada in terms of a weakening endorsement of multicultural ideals. Recently, the Conservative government of Prime Minister Stephen Harper has similarly tried to outline the limits of multiculturalism as one of the primary means by which people in English Canada have constructed their identity.[71] In particular, he has introduced measures, both concrete and symbolic, to promote a new Canadian identity more closely aligned with Canada's British heritage. To promote this connection within the public sphere, the Conservative government has, for example, restored royal symbols in the military. Harper has also promoted Canada's position as an independent and sovereign nation by moving to strengthen the military while also promoting Canada's history as a warrior nation.[72] As part of this process, the Conservative Government has introduced a $28 million fund to support re-enactments and other remembrances of the War of 1812. In promoting the War of 1812, the government emphasizes a pivotal historical moment of resistance against the Americans whereby the Canadian nation became a separate and distinct political community.[73]

The attempt by the federal government to once again create a more unitary understanding of Canadian identity has some interesting parallels to developments among a number of Western European countries. For instance, European leaders Merkel, Cameron, and Sarkozy have all denounced multiculturalism for the downfall of social cohesion and integration.[74] Similarly, within Canada multiculturalism is increasingly seen by some as the culprit in the breakdown of a stable and cohesive society. A subtle shift in the public discourse in Canada at the federal level suggests that a narrowing of citizenship education might be on the horizon with a greater emphasis toward unity and solidarity, patriotism over diversity, and an "emphasis. . . on one's civic duty to one's nation, rather than on civic engagement and deliberation."[75] Within this frame, public displays of one's love of country are aimed to build a "narrow, unifying and exclusive conceptualizations of national group membership."[76] While the public discourse toward social cohesion and, arguably, a narrowing conception of citizenship has not yet reached provincial educational jurisdictions, these sentiments might push provincial policy leaders to rethink their commitments toward multiculturalism. However, the fact that Canada has never been a unitary nation-state in the traditional sense, has enshrined collective rights for national minority peoples in the Canadian Charter of Rights and Freedoms, makes this possibility seem unlikely. However, in line with a neoliberal ethos that continues to greatly inform much educational policy, it may mean that we will continue to see a lessening emphasis within the domain of citizenship education on attending to social and economic inequalities and discrimination in Canadian society.

CONCLUSION

As can be seen, the state of citizenship education in Canada, as it has always been, is varied, contested, and continues to evolve. At the center of this shifting terrain lies a broader philosophical debate of how to balance the tension between unity and diversity. As policymakers wrestle with this question across the country, it has become clear that they have recognized the need to attend and acknowledge the pluralistic reality of Canadian society. Yet, how this should be achieved continues to be a matter of significant debate. Informed by differing organizing problems and conceptual viewpoints, a range of responses to this central tension has been proposed. Ultimately, when tied to a robust emphasis on lessening cultural discrimination and prejudice, we see a liberal multicultural framework as the most viable means to foster pluralism, social equality, and inclusion for all people while attending to the needs of social cohesion through the promotion of two official languages and a shared set of liberal-democratic values. In addition, the willingness for liberal multiculturalism to confer greater recognition and accommodations to minority national communities make it uniquely suited to the multi-national reality of the Canadian context. Moreover, we argue that the principles of liberal multiculturalism, as compared to the other competing approaches to citizenship in Canada, better attends to the unequal relationships between dominant and minority groups. However, recent debates regarding citizenship in Canada seem to be moving away from a liberal multicultural framework. In order to counter this trend, it is beholden on those of us advocating this approach to better defend it against its detractors and initiate ways to more vocally influence this educational policy debate.

NOTES

1. Darren Lund, "Multicultural education in Canada," in Encyclopedia of Diversity in Education, ed. James Banks (Thousand Oaks, CA: Sage, 2012), 295.
2. Will Kymlicka, *Multicultural Odyssey: Navigating the New International Politics of Diversity* (Oxford, Oxford University Press, 2007) p. 61.
3. Reva Joshee, "Citizenship and Multicultural Education in Canada: From Assimilation to Social Cohesion," in Diversity and Citizenship Education:

Global Perspectives, ed. James Banks (San Francisco, CA: Jossey-Bass, 2004).

4. Bruce Maxwell, David Waddington, Kevin McDonough, Andrée-Anne Cormier, and Marina Schwimmer "Interculturalism, Multiculturalism, and the State Funding of Conservative Religious Schools," *Educational Theory* 62, no. 4 (2012): 432.

5. Throughout this chapter we use the terms "English-speaking Canada" and "English Canada" interchangeably to refer to provinces other than Québec where English is the language of provincial public institutions and the primary language of public and commercial life.

6. Will Kymlicka, *Multicultural Odyssey: Navigating the New International Politics of Diversity* (Oxford, Oxford University Press, 2007), 62–63.

7. Ibid p. 62.

8. We use the term Aboriginal to be inclusive to all indigenous peoples of Canada. We do not use the term "First Nations" because it is a government definition of ethnicity that is not recognized by some Aboriginal people who prefer to not have classifications of ethnicity imposed upon them.

9. The rights of Inuit, Métis, and non-status "Indians" were relegated to provincial or territorial responsibility.

10. For a fuller explanation of the formation of residential schools see: John Miller, *Shingwauk's Vision: a history of native residential schools* (Toronto: University of Toronto Press, 1996).

11. Aboriginal Affairs and Northern Development Canada "Prime Minister Stephen Harper's Statement of Apology," June 11, 2008, http://www.aadnc-aandc.gc.ca/eng/1100100015644/1100100015649

12. Michael Mendelson, *Improving Education on Reserves: A First Nations Education Authority Act.* (Ottawa: Caledon Institute of Public Policy, 2008), 3, http://www.caledoninst.org/publications/pdf/684eng.pdf

13. Aboriginal Affairs and Northern Development Canada, "Prime Minister Stephen Harper's Statement of Apology."

14. To "prepare" the land for European settlement, the buffalo were massacred and indigenous communities were forcibly removed from their traditional territories and put in reserves.

15. George Richardson, *The Death of the Good Canadian* (New York: Peter Lang Publishing, 2002), 59.

16. It should be remembered that the territory we now know as Canada has always been heterogeneous including before European settlement when hundreds of Aboriginal communities inhabited the land.

17. For a more robust explication of the early conceptions of civic education in Canada, see: A.B. Hodgetts, *What culture? What heritage?: A study of civic education in Canada report of the national history project* (Toronto: The Ontario Institute for Studies in Education Press, 1968).

18. Brian Titley and Patrick Miller, *Education in Canada: An Interpretation* (Calgary: Destselig Enterprises, 1982), 132.

19. W. Goldring, *We are Canadian citizens* (Toronto: Dent, 1937), 222.

20. Keith Banting and Will Kymlicka, "Canadian multiculturalism: Global anxieties and local debates 23, no. 1 (2010), 65. Notably, leaders in Québec were far more concerned about out migration where, from the late 1800s to the early 1900s, an estimated one million French Canadians emigrated south of the border to take jobs in New England textile mills.

21. Stephan Léveque, "History and Social Studies in Québec: An Historical Perspective," in Challenges and Prospects for Canadian Social Studies, ed. Alan Sears and Ian Wright (Vancouver: Pacific Educational Press, 2004), 57.

22. For a more detailed explanation of the nature of *la surviance* see: Stephan Lévesque, Jocelyn Létourneau, and Raphial Gani, "Québec Students Historical Consciousness of the Nation," Canadian Issues, spring (2012): 55–60.
23. Will Kymlicka, *Multicultural Odyssey: Navigating the New International Politics of Diversity,* 66.
24. Here we draw on Will Kymlicka's key distinction in the forward of: "Citizenship and Multicultural Education in Canada: From Assimilation to Social Cohesion," in Diversity and Citizenship Education: Global Perspectives, ed. James Banks (San Francisco, CA: Jossey-Bass, 2004), xiv.
25. Darren Lund, "Multicultural education in Canada," in Encyclopedia of Diversity in Education, ed. James Banks, 295.
26. Darren Lund, "Waking Up the Neighbors: Surveying Multicultural and Antiracist Education in Canada, the United Kingdom, and the United States," *Multicultural Perspectives: The Official Journal of the National Association for Multicultural Education* 8, no. 1 (2006): 38.
27. Ibid, 39.
28. There is an ongoing debate as to whether liberal multiculturalism includes a strong social justice element. While the work of Kymlicka, for example, does include a commitment to reducing inequality, these concerns can sometimes become peripheral to a focus on issues of accommodation and recognition.
29. Will Kymlicka, "Multicultural States and Intercultural Citizens," *Theory and Research in Education* 1, no. 147 (2003): 152.
30. Will Kymlicka, *Multicultural Odyssey: Navigating the New International Politics of Diversity,* 66–76.
31. Canada History, "Prime Minister Pierre Elliot Trudeau Announcing Canada's Multiculturalism Policy in the Commons: October 8, *1971,* http://www.canadahistory.com/sections/documents/Primeministers/trudeau/docsonmulticulturalism.htm (accessed July 21, 2013).
32. Will Kymlicka, *Finding Our Way: Rethinking Ethnocultural Relations in Canada.* (Toronto, Oxford University Press, 1998). p. 1.
33. 11.1, *Alberta School Act* R.S.A. 2000.
34. Alan Sears and Andrew Hughes, "Citizenship Education and Current Educational Reform," *Canadian Journal of Education* 21, no. 2 (1996): 137.
35. W. Werner, B. Connors, T. Aoki, and J. Dahlie. (1977), *Whose culture? Whose heritage? Ethnicity within Canadian social studies curricula,* (Vancouver: University of British Columbia, Centre for the Study of Curriculum and Instruction. 1977), 46.
36. Manitoba Education, *Social studies: K–12 overview* (Winnipeg: Manitoba Education, 1985), 1–2.
37. Ibid, 3.
38. Elizabeth McCardle, *Human rights: Respecting our differences, students' manual,* (Edmonton: Department of Education, 1978), 21.
39. Bruce Curtis, *Building the educational state: Canada West 1836–1871* (London: The Althouse Press, 1988).
40. Manitoba Education and Training, "Building a Solid Foundation for Our Future: A Strategy Plan 1991–1996" (Winnipeg: Manitoba Education and Training, 1991), 1.
41. Alison Taylor, *The Politics of Educational Reform in Alberta* (Toronto: The University of Toronto Press, 2001), 73.
42. Reva Joshee, "Citizenship and Multicultural Education in Canada: From Assimilation to Social Cohesion," in Diversity and Citizenship Education: Global Perspectives, ed. James Banks (San Francisco, CA: Jossey-Bass, 2004).

43. X. Albo, "And From Kataristas to MNRistas? The Surprising and Bold Alliance Between Aymaras and Neoliberals in Bolivia," in Indigenous Peoples and Democracy in Latin America, ed. D. Van Cott (New York: St. Martin's Press, 1994).

44. Will Kymlicka "Citizenship and Multicultural Education in Canada: From Assimilation to Social Cohesion," in Diversity and Citizenship Education: Global Perspectives, ed. James Banks (San Francisco, CA: Jossey-Bass, 2004), xv.

45. Newfounland/Labrador, New Brunswick, Nova Scotia, and Prince Edward Island, *Atlantic Provinces Education Foundation Protocol Foundations in Atlantic Studies*, 1.

46. Alberta Education, *Program of studies: Social Studies, Kindergarten to Grade 12*, 1.

47. Manitoba Education, Training, and Youth, *The Common Curriculum Framework for Social Studies, Kindergarten to Grade 9* (Winnipeg: Author, 2002), 4. This initiative involved a cooperative effort by ministries of education in British Columbia, Alberta, Saskatchewan, Manitoba, Northwest Territories, Nunavut, and Yukon Territory under the Western Canadian Protocol for Collaboration in Basic Education.

48. Amber Hildebrandt. "Half of First Nations children live in poverty," CBC news. June, 19, 2013. http://www.cbc.ca/news/canada/half-of-first-nations-children-live-in-poverty-1.1324232. According to this article the rate is over 60% in the provinces of Saskatchewan and Manitoba.

49. CBC News. "Past abuses linger over First Nations education debate," CBC News, http://www.cbc.ca/news/canada/story/2013/07/21/canada-first-nations.html (accessed July 23, 2013).

50. Chiefs Assembly on Education. "A First Nations Education Timeline." October, 2012. http://www.afn.ca/uploads/files/events/fact_sheet-ccoe-2.pdf.

51. Reva Joshee, "Citizenship and Multicultural Education in Canada: From Assimilation to Social Cohesion," in Diversity and Citizenship Education: Global Perspectives, ed. James Banks, 146. See also: D. Wall, M. Moll, B. Froese-Germain, *Contemporary Approaches to Citizenship Education* (Ottawa, Ontario: Council of Ministers of Education.

52. Reva Joshee, "Citizenship and Multicultural Education in Canada: From Assimilation to Social Cohesion," in Diversity and Citizenship Education: Global Perspectives, ed. James Banks.

53. D. Waddington, B. Maxwell, K. McDonough, and A.A. Cormier, and M. Schwimmer, "Interculturalism in Practice: Québec's Ethics and Religious Culture Curriculum and the Bouchard-Taylor Report on Reasonable Accommodation," in Interculturalism, Education and Dialogue, ed. T. Besley and M.A. Peters (New York: Peter Lang, 2012), 314.

54. *Multani v. Commission scolaire Marguerite-Bourgeoys*, [2006] 1 S.C.R. 256, 2006 SCC 6.

55. Dianne Gereluk, *Symbolic Clothing in Schools: What Should Be Worn and Why* (London, England: Continuum International Publishing Group, 2008).

56. Ibid., 66.

57. Ibid., 68–69.

58. Municipalité Hérouxville, "Publication of Standards, English Version of Standards" Author, http://municipalite.herouxville.qc.ca/Standards.pdf (accessed March 26, 2007).

59. Robert Fowler, "Intecultural Education in Canada: Glimpses from the Past, Hopes for the Future," in International Perspectives on Intercultural Education, ed. Kenneth Cushner (Mahwah, NJ: Lawrence Erlbaum Associates, 1998), 309.

60. Gerard Bouchard and Charles Taylor, *Building The Future: A Time for Reconciliation* (Québec City: Gouvernement du Québec, 2008), 17.
61. D. Waddington, B. Maxwell, K. McDonough, A.A. Cormier, and M. Schwimmer, "Interculturalism in Practice: Québec's Ethics and Religious Culture Curriculum and the Bouchard-Taylor Report on Reasonable Accommodation," in Interculturalism, Education and Dialogue, ed. T. Besley and M.A. Peters (New York: Peter Lang, 2012), 314.
62. Waddington, D., Maxwell, B., McDonough, K, and Cormier, A. Interculturalism in Practice: Québec's new ethics and Religious Culture Curriculum and the Bouchard-Taylor report on Reasonable Accommodation in Tina Besley and Michael Peters (eds.) *Interculturalism, Education and Dialogue* (New York: Peter Lang, 2012), 320.
63. Bruce Maxwell, David Waddington, Kevin McDonough, Andrée-Anne Cormier, and Marina Schwimmer "Interculturalism, Multiculturalism, and the State Funding of Conservative Religious Schools," *Educational Theory* 62, no. 4 (2012): p. 434.
64. Ibid., 434.
65. Bouchard and Taylor, *Building The Future A Time for Reconciliation*, 125.
66. Ministère de l'Éducation, du Loisir et du Sport, (MELS), *Quebec Education Program: Ethics and Religious Culture* (Government du Québec, 2008), 2.
67. Waddington, D., Maxwell, B., McDonough, K, and Cormier, A. Interculturalism in Practice: Québec's new ethics and Religious Culture Curriculum and the Bouchard-Taylor report on Reasonable Accommodation in Tina Besley and Michael Peters (eds.) *Interculturalism, Education and Dialogue*, 323.
68. Will Kymlicka, *Multiculturalism: Success, Failure, and the Future*, (Washington, DC: Migration Policy Institute), 8.
69. Giuseppe Valiante. "Québec's proposed ban of religious symbols in public buildings. Toronto Sun, August 21, 2013. http://www.torontosun.com/2013/08/21/Québecs-proposed-ban-of-religious-symbols-in-public-buildings-provokes-defiant-reaction
70. James Fitz-Morris. "Quebec's values charter sends politicians scrambling. CBC news. September 11, 2013. http://www.cbc.ca/news/politics/story/2013/09/11/f-vp-fitz-morris-quebec-charter.html.
71. Jocelyn Létourneau, "Multiculturalism died, and Harper replaced it with 'royalization'" The Globe and Mail, July 1, 2013, http://www.theglobeandmail.com/commentary/reconstructing-the-canadian-identity/article12892670/%23dashboard/follows/.
72. Ian McKay and Jamie Swift, *Warrior Nation: Rebranding Canada in an Age of Anxiety* (Toronto: Between the Lines, 2012).
73. Létourneau, *Multiculturalism died, and Harper replaced it with 'royalization.'*
74. For instance, in a 2005 speech, Trevor Phillips, the then chairman of Britain's Commission for Racial Equality, argued that Britain has "focused far too much on the "multi" and not enough on the common culture. We have allowed tolerance of diversity to harden into the effective isolation of communities, in which some people think special separate values ought to apply" Trevor Phillips, *After 7/7: Sleepwalking to Segregation,* speech given at the Commission for Racial Equality, September 22, 2005. (London: Commission for Racial Equality).
75. Signal Ben-Porath, *Citizenship under Fire: Democratic Education in Times of Conflict* (Princeton, NJ: Princeton University Press, 2006), 13.
76. Ibid., 25.

8   Civic Education in Israel
Between National-Ethnocentricity and Universalism

Zehavit Gross

THE ISRAELI CONTEXT IN WHICH CIVICS IS TAUGHT

The state of Israel was established against a Jewish and Zionist-Jewish background and with ideological underpinnings. For centuries, the Jewish people had existed as a religious and ethnic minority and a people without a political center.[1] The growth of nationalism throughout the world led Theodore Herzl to found in 1897—in Basel, Switzerland—a national Jewish movement known as Zionism. Its overarching aim was to find a national solution for the Jewish people according to "the law of nations" and in 1948 a formal declaration was made, establishing the state following authorization from the United Nations. Zionist ideology, namely the Jewish national ideology, advocated for a Jewish state in the historic homeland of the Jewish people, the Land of Israel. Modern Jewish nationalism developed at the end of the nineteenth century as a response to anti-Semitism, discrimination, and persecutions on the one hand and assimilation on the other hand. While the central motivation was a uniting force within the Zionist movement, at the same time, different and conflicting ideologies emerged in terms of implementation of the concept. There were also groups in the Jewish world that strongly opposed the whole concept. To overcome that difficulty, Theodore Herzl decided to postpone the debate over the question of how the cultural public arena of the state should appear ("the question of culture") and an in-depth internal discussion has still not been conducted or finally settled. Israel has a democratic government subject to pressuring conditions that originate in the external continuing dispute between the Jewish and Arab populations, and with demographic changes resulting from massive immigration from across the world, further compounded by societal and political rifts. Horowitz and Lissak (1990)[2] list five principal rifts in the State of Israel: the religious rift (secular and religious citizens); the political (left and right); class (rich and poor); ethnic (Ashkenazim and Sephardim); and the national rift (between Arabs and Jews).

The national rift is considered one of the most difficult that must be coped with. Beyond the complex rift itself, a unique problem of Israeli society is that it does not maintain within it "an overlap between territory, citizenship, and national identity."³ For example, for French citizens (apart from its migrant citizens—which is a separate question) France is their birthplace, their citizenship is French, and they are part of the French nation. Like in many other diverse nation-states, there are still many Jews with a Jewish national identity who live outside Israeli territory and one can find within Israeli territory citizens with an Arab or Palestinian national definition—some of them have Israeli citizenship, others hold Jordanian citizenship, or are stateless. The lack of such an overlap between the three contributing factors is not a technical matter but encompasses within it complex ideological and political questions that have direct implications for studying civics, as I will describe here.

Ever since its establishment in 1948, the State of Israel—unlike the USA or European nations—has not maintained a separation between state and religion. This stems from the fact that the Jewish people had long considered nationhood and religiosity to be one historical entity.⁴ The phenomenon of non-separation of state and religion affects the public sphere. For example, the national symbols of the state are religious in essence and the state is governed according to the Jewish calendar, and furthermore it strongly impacts on the schooling system. Its schooling system contains religious Jewish education, secular Jewish education, and Arab education—which takes in Muslim and Christian Arab students, Bedouin, Druze, and Circassian students—all of whom study the same curriculum in civics, with a uniform textbook written in Hebrew and translated into Arabic.

Given this sociopolitical context, in this chapter, I will analyze the situation of civics studies in the framework of the official study curriculum of the State of Israel. The subject of civics is taught in Israel in junior high school and high school, and its focus is on characteristics of governance in Israel. The subject frequently foments public disputes and arguments with a significantly political character. I first address the historical milestones of civics education in Israel. Then I analyze the ideological aspect of teaching civics. Specifically, I focus on two primary ways that Civics has been framed: teaching about Israel as a Jewish or democratic state. These framings should be understood within the ideological debates around civics education that approach it, as I will review, as an apolitical, ideological, and/or political enterprise. I then present teaching styles that might inform a more robust conceptualization of civics education. Finally, I present some progressive changes to civics education that have occurred and offer a conceptualization of civics education that should be pursued in Israel.

HISTORICAL MILESTONES IN EDUCATION ABOUT CITIZENSHIP IN ISRAEL

Several milestones can be indicated in the historical development of the subject of civics in Israel. Ichilov (2003)⁵ notes that until 1976 the subject of civics was not taught as an official subject, though various aspects of it were taught as part of history and geography classes (political questions concerning the country's borders) and also as extracurricular school activities (in the form of school trips, ceremonies, and special parties celebrating independence, for example). From 1976 onward, the subject of civics was introduced into the official curriculum and civics classes chiefly focused on the procedural aspects of governance (electoral methods, the ways in which official civil institutions and entities operate, etc.). The program was aimed at Jewish students only, and was taught as part of a learning-unit.[6]

In the late 1990s, a new uniform curriculum was written, intended for use in all schools. It was submitted to the Guttmann Commission and was tested and ultimately approved as a compulsory program for the whole population, including Arab students. During the 2001–2002 school years, the program was taught for three hours throughout a single school year (either in the 11th grade or 12th grade) as a single credit unit (i.e., three weekly hours throughout one school year). Schools had to decide whether to teach the subject in 11th or 12th grade—a decision that indicates the importance which schools ascribe to teaching the subject.

When civics was taught in the 12th grade, there was very little time to study it in depth, since it is the final year of high school, and is thus crammed with matriculation exams. On the other hand, when learning is split between two grades—the 11th and 12th—it becomes possible to study it more thoroughly. Following a government resolution, since 2008, civics studies have had the scope of two credit-units (i.e., six hours over a two-year period). Both the scope of hours and the decision in which year to teach the subject are highly important, and attest to the significance that schools devote to the subject as part of their entire curricular array.

Another structural question is whether to teach civics as a separate subject, or as a part of interdisciplinary studies. Prior to 1976, civics was taught in an interdisciplinary manner, as part of history and geography studies, but lost its uniqueness in that framework because the learning involved was ostensibly interdisciplinary, and civics was only mentioned parenthetically during classes on history and geography. Interdisciplinary teaching is recommended when civics studies provide the center of gravity of studies, and the other spheres of knowledge constitute ancillary topics to help obtain a better understanding of civics. The schooling system also pondered the question of whether to offer a uniform curriculum for the entire schooling system, or a discrete curriculum for each group in the population. It is a question that every so often enters the public agenda in Israel, and later disappears from it. The decision to teach a uniform program stems from the basic melting-pot perception and the desire to create a common statist-civil discourse. Such a decision is liable, however, to have a discriminatory nature and to disadvantage certain groups, since it tends to present in a one-dimensional manner what is a multifaceted complex civil reality: this is what happened in the Israeli case, according to various researchers,[7] when the curriculum was implemented in 1994 and approved officially in 2001. In 1976, the curriculum was named the Curriculum in Civics for State and State-Religious High Schools, and in 2001 its name was the Civics Curriculum for Jewish Schools (Regular and Religious), and Arab and Druze Schools.[8] This is not a merely semantic name change, for it mirrors a substantive change in the inclusion of Arab students in the state's official curricular space. And yet, as other researchers have asserted, such an approach might create hegemonic solutions for shaping the official state narrative, in a way that excludes minority groups. In 2001, for the first time, a citizenship textbook was published by the Ministry of Education, for use in most schools in Israel, and in 2004 the Ministry published the official teachers' guide.

There is a discernible transition from a particularistic approach (that teaches the subject in a voluntary, fragmented manner, particularly among Jewish students, and in a relatively small scope that focuses on theoretical aspects only) to an approach of a universalist-statist character (teaching the subject through a uniform program that by law must be studied in a relatively broad scope by all Israeli citizens—including Arab citizens—and furthermore applying an approach that requires practical tasks and projects). In fact, in view of the schematic description of periodization it is obvious that any exploration of teaching the subject of citizenship as a curricular component has structural, pedagogic, and content-based aspects—as discussed next.

THE IDEOLOGICAL ASPECT OF TEACHING CIVICS

The objectives of civics education in Israel are

> inculcating knowledge, understanding and analytical abilities, judging and deciding on societal and political questions, internalizing the state's values, creating commitment to a democratic regime and willingness to defend it, and the capacity and desire to be active, involved, and responsible citizens.[9]

Thus civics education is a sphere of teaching with a holistic nature that integrates cognitive, emotional, and behavioral aspects: it includes education aimed at preserving procedures and the game rules of democracy, value-based aspects of teaching democracy, and liberal values—supreme and fundamental values. In tandem with developing citizenship skills by providing basic theoretical information and applying it in civil endeavors, the school also works to develop mental intellectual positions regarding questions of citizenship, in order to develop identification and critical engagement with the subject being taught.

Some of the general themes in civics studies in Israel are the Declaration of Independence and its content and status; the laws of the state of Israel; its institutions and emblems; democracy and the forms of governance that implement them; the State of Israel as a Jewish democratic state; the Law of Return;[10] the lack of a constitution; the Basic Laws and legislative resolutions; and the separation of authorities in Israel into the legislative, the executive, and the judicial.

Despite the enunciation of these general themes, one can see a differentiation between Jewish, Arab, and Druze students as regards certain subjects. Jewish students study the connection between the State of Israel and the Jewish people in the diaspora, the Status Quo arrangement,[11] and the religious division among Israeli Jews, while Arab and Druze students learn about local government in Israel, human rights, minority rights and mass communication. Whereas the Jewish curriculum focus on particularistic Jewish ethnocentric issues which intend to enhance a discourse of identity, the curriculum for Arab students focuses on universalistic issues which intend to foster a discourse of rights. Any education about citizenship engages first of all in describing and analyzing the political machine that governs the state where the education is being offered. A close reading of the contents of the civics curriculum and textbook studied by the majority of students in Israel shows that the deep patterns and central trajectory of content that they deal with are a description of the political regime and its definition of the Israeli state as being Jewish and democratic.

At this point, I will explain the significance of that trajectory and the debate that it encompasses, and will then show how that definition finds practical expression in the curriculum. As previously noted, the State of Israel was founded on ideological underpinnings (e.g., Jews have the right to a Jewish state in the Land of Israel, the reconstitution of the Jews as an independent nation in their own state where they have the right to develop and maintain a Jewish majority, while respecting and protecting the individual civil rights of all its citizens). The central question that has engaged the state since its foundation is whether Israel will be a Jewish state, or a state of all its citizens.

Teaching about Israel as a Jewish State

The State of Israel was already defined in its Declaration of Independence as a Jewish national state where the Jewish people would realize its right to self-determination in the Land of Israel. The word "democracy" does not appear in the Declaration of Independence though it is indirectly cited in the undertaking by the state to grant full and equal rights without difference of religion, race, and sex. Since the state's foundation, however, an argument has raged in Israeli society over how its identity and character should be defined. In 1992, in the Twelfth Knesset, two Basic Laws were legislated (and amended in 1994): Human Dignity and Liberty and Freedom of Occupation. Both laws contain an explicit and general definition of a "Jewish and democratic state." That general and opaque expression was the outcome of a compromise between various political parties and it concealed the harsh disagreements over the self-definition of the state and its values, and sparked off numerous public debates within Israeli society.

The first question is what is meant by a Jewish state? Is it a state that functions in compliance with Jewish religious law or Jewish culture? In other words, is it a state whose origins lie in a set of heteronymous laws with a particularistic national tendency aimed at preserving historical continuity, and that is likely on occasion to stand in conflict with democratic values which have an autonomous orientation and universal tones, with an affinity to the Western liberal tradition? Another question is whether the definition of "a Jewish state" implies the state of the Jewish people. Or a state for Jews? Each option embodies a different interpretation of the Jewish elements of the state, and places in doubt the feasibility of a democratic regime with a civil character that is intended to include all citizens of the state, including those who are not Jews. Another question concerns the nature of the link between the two contradictory concepts: is a synthesis between those two components feasible at all? Is there a dialectic between them and, if so, what is its nature and character and how does it unfold in practice? What are the costs that democracy must pay in order to coexist with the world of Judaism, and what costs does Judaism face in order to live in peace with the values of democracy? And most of all how can the schooling systems—composed of a heterogeneous variety of students with different worldviews—cope with that complexity in the framework of civics education?

Such philosophical questions inform very practical considerations. For example, should it be permissible to import and sell pork in the public sphere in a Jewish state (which is prohibited under Jewish law and has negative historical-symbolic connotations)? Is it permissible to sell bread in the public sphere of the Jewish state during Passover, which is also forbidden under Jewish law? A more complex question concerns whether it is permitted in the Jewish state to sell a home to an Arab: the Torah forbids the sale of a house or a field in the Land of Israel to a non-Jew. Such questions reveal how Zionist ideology impinges on the democratic aspect of a state.

When the state was founded, it adopted symbols with a Jewish nature as its official symbols. The Jewish menorah (the seven-branched candlestick) is a significant religious symbol chosen to be the centre of the state emblem. Israel also adopted the Jewish calendar and Jewish holidays as state holidays and official holidays and the Sabbath as the official day of rest. The symbolic aspects were aimed at bolstering Jewish aspects of the state's public arena. In Israeli society in general and in the civics curriculum particularly there have been stringent discussions on this issue. Wahrman[12] maintains that students are presented with several options regarding the interpretation of a "Jewish state" and the connections possible between

Judaism and the state. According to the Religious-Zionist outlook, Israel is a Jewish state because it is an expression of the period of *athalta da'geula* (the beginning of Redemption). Under the ultra-Orthodox approach, Israel is Jewish only if it is conducted as a state based on the Torah, the body of Jewish law—that is, the law of the state is the Jewish law. According to the national cultural approach, Israel is a Jewish state since its public policy allows a range of interpretations of Jewish culture (including a secular Jewish interpretation). Yet another approach argues that the state of Israel is a Jewish state because it acts to protect Jews anywhere in the world. The fact that the state tries to preserve a special relationship toward those who define themselves as Jews creates a triple tension: toward the external non-Jewish group; toward some Jews in the inner Jewish group; and toward Jews in the Diaspora who constitute an inner group that's located outside the inner group.

The concept of a democratic state appears in the civics curriculum in two senses: democracy as a governmental procedure and democracy as a value.[13] The majority of schools focus on the procedural aspects, while a minority focus more on frameworks of studying and discussing the aspect of the values of democracy while addressing values such as justice, liberty and equality, pluralism, tolerance, and human dignity. The procedural aspect focuses on citizens' participation in government, the principle of majority rule, and the separation of authorities, ways of replacing the government, how elections are held, and so forth.

Teaching Israel as a Democratic State

Wahrman indicates four types of concrete knowledge that are transmitted through the concept of a "democratic state" in the curriculum.[14] First, the type deals with information dealing with infringement by the government on individual rights. Wahrman[15] quotes from the curriculum, which states that "the state must safeguard its citizens, ensure that their rights are not violated, provide all citizens of the state with their fundamental rights without connection to their attribution to a specific group, and develop the state for the benefit and well-being of all its citizens."[16] The second type of information deals with concern over violence and lawlessness in Israel by political ideological groups: the goal of that information is to insure that political activity is performed in compliance with the democratic game rules. The third type of information engages with clarifying the question of the population's representation in the government of Israel, and how it actually takes place in the context of the electoral method applied in Israel. The fourth type of information deals with the way in which democratic values are reflected in the definition of formal authority of government mechanisms in Israel; for example, the values reflected in the Basic Law: the Knesset. This Basic Law defines the nature and forms of activity of the Knesset (the House of Representatives of the people). The very legislation of the law mirrors the great value that the state attributes to the principle of rule by the people. The structure of the Knesset as it appears in the Law reflects the great importance that the state attributes to having a House of Representatives of the people, representation with a pluralistic nature, and so on.

We need to ask whether to award greater emphasis in education to the Jewish component or to the democratic component. It is not a technical or procedural question, but reflects the system's clear priorities.[17] Indeed, the introduction to the curriculum states that "as part of civic studies, you will be introduced to different and complex aspects of the Jewish and democratic State of Israel." Later, the curriculum's authors specify how it was designed: first there was a discussion on what constitutes a Jewish state, then what constitutes a democratic state, followed by a discussion on the law and politics in Israel, which is where those two foundations—the Jewish and the democratic, find palpable expression.

The curriculum, according to its authors, is grounded "on the degree of reconciliation and the intensity of the tension between the democratic foundations and Jewish foundations of the State of Israel" (p. 6). However, because of the debate between the authors of the curriculum regarding the location of those contents, the authors of the new curriculum added that "the order in which the matters are to be presented in this curriculum is not binding, neither in the written instructions nor in writing the textbooks, and during the teaching process, the tension between the two themes should also be mentioned."[18] According to some scholars,[19] the curriculum does not engage sufficiently with the concept "Jewish state," though it presents the concept of a democratic state at length. Wahrman (2013)[20] contends that the definitions in the curriculum of the concept "democracy" are biased and strongly emphasize the "liberal logic" (p. 177). He believes that "the rhetorical mechanism revealed in the textbook paradoxically serves the liberal ideology, at the expense of competing ideologies" (such as conservative or radical ideologies). [21]

PATTERNS OF APOLITICAL, IDEOLOGICAL, AND POLITICAL EDUCATION IN ISRAEL

Lamm (1991)[22] asserts that one of the severest problems of education in Israel is that it pretends to be apolitical and neutral, and he differentiates between three types of education—apolitical, ideological, and political. Since its earliest days, the Israeli schooling system has absolutely prohibited any official discussion of political matters. The fundamental assumption of apolitical education holds that there is no room in general education that functions on behalf of society or the state for endeavors that deal with politics: education must be apolitical. Education's role is to transmit the social consensus, since there is an assumption that students are not mature enough to cope with nonconsensual issues, and therefore apolitical education officially ignores ideology or political perception of any kind. Ideological education implies using contents from current political affairs and curriculum content to mobilize the students' support for the political position preferred by their teachers or by the institute they attend. Therefore, in ideological education, one sees education and activity guided toward imparting to the younger generation the ideological outlook that is acceptable to the educators or their managers. In other words, the school is a mechanism for enforcing ideological control of the ruling class on the consciousness of all classes in society. Education is perceived as a mechanism of oppression and its role is to serve the prevailing ideology.

Political education, according to Lamm, is an activity that takes place by means of the curriculum's contents or events in national and international politics, guided at fostering intellectual skills and positions, and moral sensitivity among the students, so they can apply them in situations that require taking a stand in political matters—but not activity guided toward imparting political opinions or outlooks. The principal objective of the school, from the political perspective, is implanting a political experience: the students must be informed and taught that the political experience entails deciding among alternative ideologies, and so first one must encourage in them awareness of how ideology functions. Lamm contends that while political education uses ideology as a means of fostering intellectual ties so that students will be capable of reaching their own conclusions on political questions, ideological education and political contents serve as a goal for their students to acquire a political position acceptable to them.

Lamm argues that neutral, apolitical education is the most dangerous kind of education—he defines it as "absolutely bad"—and he believes that this is the education method employed in the majority of schools in Israel. It is, in his opinion, disguised ideological education by conservative, right-wing and centrist circles in Israeli society, a hypermoral education that is conducted according to the interests that control society. Lamm defines the ideological education applied in religious schools and in kibbutzim, as "the lesser evil" here because, unlike apolitical education, indoctrination is overt and intended.

In the end, political education that is offered in a few schools in Israel is recommendable and appropriate even though Lamm also criticizes it for not providing a direction: a specific distinction implying that it is not education at all—because in his definition, education is intended to provide a direction. Despite that disadvantage, the basic approach offered by political education seems suitable for effective civic education. One of the principal goals of education of that kind is identifying the key interests underlying declarations by politicians and policy setters, and also those underlying political activity performed as part of a democratic regime.

TEACHING STYLE IN CIVICS EDUCATION:
INSTRUMENTAL OR REFLECTIVE?

Among the substantive questions that should be posed to inform a robust reconceptualization of civics education concerns the pedagogic method that should be employed. Examining civic education in religious schools, Gross[23] differentiates between instrumental and reflective education. Under the instrumental approach, the school curriculum is a finished product that includes a structured collection of educational activities. It is the teacher's task to develop a variety of teaching methods and skills with the objective of enhancing the quantity and quality of the civic "product" (i.e., the extent of civic knowledge) and their "civic consumption" (after Willis, 2003,[24] who coined the term "cultural consumption"). Teachers who employ the instrumental approach function according to the basic assumption that the corpus of civic knowledge they are charged with imparting to their students is objective, structured, and organized. Consequently, the learning process involves the passive reception of messages, and the teacher's role is the systematic transmission of the requisite knowledge.

The reflective approach, in contrast, maintains that the civic education curriculum is neither fixed nor predictable but is part of a dynamic process of interaction between the learner and knowledge. It perceives the goal of teaching as the structuring of civic socialization to yield proactive learners whose civic commitment is part of their personal structuring and the result of the internalization of civic knowledge. Such knowledge emerges and evolves as a result of interaction with the environment and constitutes an integral part of cognition. Accordingly, the learning process entails the active structuring of civic knowledge and its implications on civic praxis. The teacher's role is to foster students' development as independent learners who structure and "own" their civic knowledge, in keeping with their individual intellectual tendencies, diverse motivations and styles of learning, and other personal traits.[25] Reflective teachers learn to respond to students' differential learning needs, account for the variance in their individual points of entry into the learning process, and design teaching methods to supply anchors and mediation that ensure their progress[26]

The forms of reflection within the context of civic education translate into differential emphases on the teaching of civic skills (technical); the decision to adopt civic lifestyle under the inspiration of assorted civic ideologies and schools of thought, such as the Jewish ultra-Orthodox, Modern Orthodox, Reform, and Conservative streams (practical); and criticism of religious theory and practice from an ethical-social standpoint (critical). The first two types of reflection relate to the instrumental teaching method and the third to reflective-constructivist teaching. Under certain circumstances, practical reflection may also involve a critical approach.

It therefore seems that the reflective approach is preferable if the objective is inculcating civic understanding beyond accumulating informative necessary knowledge. These pedagogic approaches are also linked to the preferable type of teaching: frontal teaching in which the teacher faces the class and lectures, or interactive teaching that features work in groups or whole-group discussion. In the first approach, the curriculum and its contents are central to pedagogic endeavors, while the interactive approach to students and their needs are at the center of endeavors and pedagogic thinking. Another question is whether to use only traditional teaching patterns: is there perhaps room to also use progressive teaching patterns such as creative drama, role playing, creating simulated choices, school trips, special civic ceremonies, and so on? And in our digital world, we must ask if we should rely solely on textbooks or if there is room for using more advanced technological means when teaching civics. Technological means allow access to additional civic spaces and make it possible to organize broader pedagogic activities. Should teachers focus on analyzing the Israeli system, or is it advisable to use comparative pedagogic methods examining similar and different political regimes worldwide? Using advanced technologies, comparative civics teaching can be performed in a better and more informed manner.

Perhaps the most central question in terms of awakening students' curiosity and interest concerns relevance—the extent to which the material is relevant or irrelevant to their world. It is the teacher's role, according to modern pedagogy, not just to teach and transmit knowledge, but to mediate it, so their students can choose the kind of knowledge they perceive to be relevant and significant for their existential world.

TOWARD A MORE ROBUST CIVICS EDUCATION IN ISRAEL

Though in the course of the years there has been a lot of improvement with revised curricula, it seems that the educational system in Israel enhances civics education rather than citizenship education.[27] Civics classes may teach the nuts and bolts of government and its functioning but they achieve very little in terms of developing in students any meaning of what it means to be a "good citizen"—other than, say, to vote. They perceive democracy mainly as "the rules of the game" rather than perceiving democracy as a core value and an integral part of the students' habitus.

When one examines the old curriculum and teacher's guide together with the new curriculum, the noticeable transition that occurred in teaching civics in Israel can be seen—the shift from an instrumental to a reflective approach. There is a new openness to integrating a range of teaching means, and positioning the students, with their needs and questions, at the center of educational efforts.

Refreshing changes like those are found in numerous schools and it is well worth encouraging the introduction into the curriculum of many non-formal indices and components. Various researchers have addressed the place of non-formal education in the process of teaching civics, and have underlined its substantial importance. Pinson [28] sees the advantages of presenting civic education via non-formal activities on the basis that they help to stimulate critical thought and encourage civil involvement. In comparison, Lemish is concerned that non-formal activities might encourage and reinforce narratives with an ethnocentric character, and thus weaken the civic education dimension. In other words, whereas Pinson stresses the cognitive aspect that can be enhanced through informal education (which functions as an open venue that enables deliberation and reflection), Lemish is concerned about the fact that sometimes the open space of informal education where the emotional aspects are cultivated might reinforce ethnocentric and unidimensional messages. Wahrman, who supports the inclusion of non-formal aspects in teaching, maintains that the impact of civics education conducted in a non-formal framework depends on the school's educational philosophy and the degree of dominance and centrality of non-formal education in the school's educational array. [29]

In research conducted on teaching the Holocaust in Israel, [30] I found that students considered the use of non-formal techniques as the secret of the subject's success, and among the principal reasons for this was that subject was perceived as significant; in my opinion, the comparative research conducted is equally relevant for civics teaching.

As I noted in a previous section, Jewish and Arab students receive civics education that reflects very different emphases. The former is particularistic and draws from a discourse of identity while the latter is universalistic and draws from a discourse of rights. A robust conceptualization of civics education will draw from both approaches. For Jewish students, effective civics teaching should undergo a gradual process and transition from the particularistic-ethnocentric approach and attitude toward a broader, universalist one. For Arab students, effective civics teaching must undergo a process of change and transition from a technical procedural discourse of rights toward a discourse of identity. In other words, a reconceptualization of civics education should be toward a discourse that includes a debate on the question of how the concept of civics integrates into and corresponds with the whole range of other identities in which humanity functions (religious identity, national identity, etc.) for all students. There is also room in public state education to consider deepening the political aspect, according to Lamm's perception, [31] instead of the neutral or ideological perception found in many Israeli schools.

Toward this end, I distinguish three main approaches to teaching the subject of civics. First is an approach contending that in civics education we must teach in an "objective," neutral manner that completely marginalizes conflicts. A second approach is to present disputes and conflicts, and then to present resolutions that match the school's prevailing ideology. A third approach suggests presenting a range of disputes and different political outlooks, and to let students choose, from a position of knowledge and after having received organized and methodical information, in a perception they find appropriate—even if it contradicts the teacher's opinion or the school spirit.

Avnon contends that changes in the curriculum must be performed "by conserving the principle of teaching a single language of civics for the entire schooling system that is budgeted by the State of Israel." [32] I take issue with Avnon's proposition that it is necessary to create a single language of civics in Israel, since that language will be the language of the ruling hegemony that enforces its perceptions, and does not permit a dialogue with different societal groups. I believe that the schooling system in a multicultural state like Israel should present its students with different languages of civics—that reflect the way in which the different and competing cultural narratives of minority groups impact on civil perceptions of members of the other groups in society—in order to allow a civil and multicultural discourse and dialogue.

Therefore, instead of proposing a uniform curriculum as matters stand in Israel, whose dominant narrative is a liberal one (as Wahrman maintains), [33] it would be better to present a curriculum that explicitly shows students the variety of civic perceptions found in society, the fundamental philosophical and ideological assumptions that underlie them, and more particularly to introduce, as Lamm [34] proposes, the interests that lie beneath the political rhetoric and efforts of different political-social groups. An approach of that kind to civics education will also make it possible to contain and present—alongside the dominant liberal perception—conservative and even non-liberal approaches that can be discussed in the classroom alongside radical and other approaches with a differential nature. The future of civics education in this multicultural, postmodern, troubled world depends to a great extent on flexibility, creativity and on attempts by its architects to lead this unique disciplinary field toward innovative pedagogic horizons—that are inclusive and different.

NOTES

1. Horowitz, D. and Lissak, M. 1990. *Trouble in Utopia: The Overburdened Polity of Israel*. Tel Aviv: Am Oved Publishers, 1990, p. 9.
2. Horowitz, D. and Lissak, M. *Trouble in Utopia: The Overburdened Polity of Israel*, 1990.
3. Ibid., p. 11
4. Ibid.
5. Ichilov, O. "Teaching Civics in a Divided Society: the Case of Israel." *International Studies in Sociology of Education*, vol. *13* (3), 2003, pp. 219–241.
6. Barak, M., and Ofarim, Y. "Chinuch Le-ezrachut, Le-democratia Ve-le-chayim Meshutafim: Mipui." [*Education for citizenship, democracy and shared living: An Overview*]. Jerusalem: The Van Leer Jerusalem Institute, 2009.
7. Kremnitzer, M., "To be Citizens—Civic Education to all Israeli Students," *A Report by the Commission Chaired by Prof. Mordechai Kremnitzer*. 1995. Pinson, H. "Inclusive Curriculum? Challenges to the Role of Civic Education

in a Jewish and Democratic State." *Curriculum Inquiry, vol. 37* (4), 2007, pp. 351–382.

8. Avnon, D., *Research and Policy in Civic Education in the High School Educational System in Israel,* 2013.

9. Kremnitzer, 1995 Commission Report, Section 4, p. 8.

10. The Law of Return is Israeli legislation passed in 1950 that grants all Jews the right to immigrate and live in Israel with full citizenship rights.

11. The status quo refers to the political understanding in Israel between secular and religious parties not to change agreed religious regulations (e.g., the Sabbath will be the official day of rest in Israel, etc).

12. Wahrman, H., *Citizenship between the lines A Critical look at civics studies in Israel.* Resling, Tel-Aviv, 2013. p. 101

13. Pedahzur, A. "The paradox of Civic Education in non-Liberal Democracies: The Case of Israel," *Journal of Education Policy,* vol. *16* (5), 2001, pp. 413–430, ibid., Gross, Z. Religious Zionist Attitudes towards the Peace Process. *International Journal of Public Theology, (IJPT), vol. 7*(1), 2013, pp. 174–196

14. Wahrman, *Citizenship between the lines A Critical look at civics studies in Israel pp.113–119.*

15. Ibid.

16. Curriculum, p. 269, cited in Ibid., p. 114.

17. Ichilov, O. Salomon, G. and Inbar, D. "Citizenship Education in Israel: A Jewish Democratic State," *Israel Affairs. Vol. 11* (2), 2005, pp. 303–323.

18. Ministry of Education 2002, p. 7 cited in Avnon, 2013, p. 27.

19. Schweid, E. "The Jewish Religion and the Israeli Democracy," *Democratic Culture,* vol. 1, 1999,pp. 181–188, Geiger,Y., "Patterns in Civics Education in a Jewish Nation-State," In Avnon, D. (ed.), *Civic Education in Israel,* 2013.

20. Wahrman, *Citizenship between the lines A Critical look at civics studies in Israel.*

21. Ibid., p. 230.

22. Lamm, Z. Types of Ideological Education in the Israeli School, in D. Bar-Tal, and A. Kelogman (eds.), *Special Issues in Psychology and Counseling in Education.* 1991. pp. 7–17.

23. Gross, Z. "Reflective Teaching as a Path to Religious Meaning Making and Growth," *Religious Education* vol. 105 (3), 2010c, pp. 265–282.

24. Willis, P., "Foot Soldiers of Modernity: The Dialectics of Cultural Consumption and the 21st-Century School," *Harvard Educational Review, vol. 73*(3), 2003, pp. 390–415.

25. Gutierrez, K. D., and Rogoff, B. Cultural Ways of Learning: Individual Traits or Repertoires of Practice. *Educational Researcher, vol. 32*(5), 2003, pp. 19–25.

26. McEntee, G. H., Appleby, J., Dowd, J., Grant, J., Hole, S., Silva, P., and Check, J. *At the Heart of Teaching: A Guide to Reflective Practice,* Teachers College Press, New York, 2003.

27. Gross, Z., "Reflective Teaching as a Path to Religious Meaning Making and Growth," *Religious Education,* Vol. 105 (3), 2010c, pp. 265–282.

28. Pinson, H., *Rethinking Israeliness: Citizenship Education and the Construction of Political Identities by Jewish and Palestinian Israeli youth.* Dissertation submitted for the degree of Doctor of Philosophy. School of Education: Cambridge, 2004.

29. Wahrman, *Citizenship between the lines A Critical Look at Civics Studies in Israel,* 2013.

30. Gross, Z. "Religious Education: Definitions, Dilemmas, Challenges And Future Horizons," *International Journal of Educational Reform IJER, vol. 20*(3) 2011b. pp. 256–276.

31. Lamm, Z., "Types of Ideological Education in the Israeli School," in D. Bar-Tal, and A. Kelogman (eds.), *Special Issues in Psychology and Counseling in Education*. The Ministry of Education, Jerusalem, pp. 7–17.
32. Avnon, D., *Research and Policy in Civic Education in the High School Educational System in Israel*. Jerusalem: The Israeli Association of Political Science, 2013, 6.
33. Wahrman, *Citizenship between the lines A Critical look at civics studies in Israel*, 2013
34. Lamm, Z. Types of Ideological Education in the Israeli School, in D. Bar-Tal, and A. Kelogman (eds.), *Special Issues in Psychology and Counseling in Education*. Jerusalem, The Ministry of Education 1991, (pp. 7–17).

9 On Hostipitality, Responsibility, and *Ubuntu*

Some Philosophical Remarks on Teaching and Learning in South Africa

Yusef Waghid and Nuraan Davids

INTRODUCTION

In this chapter, we focus on three constitutive aspects of democratic citizenship education: hostipitality (hospitality and hostility), responsibility, and *ubuntu* (humaneness). We argue, firstly, how and why hostipitality ought to be cultivated in South African public schools; secondly, how responsibility and humaneness (*ubuntu*) ought to be nurtured; and thirdly, what a politics of teaching and learning ought to look like if informed by dialogical encounters of a provocative, disruptive, and caring kind. We specifically show that teaching and learning can be advanced through critical education considering the country's break with its apartheid past. This past has led to dysfunctionality in public schooling and has to be combated through unsafe, provocative, and disruptive encounters—that is, through dialogues of distress and, more specifically, of provocation and disruption—ironically, the same type of protest and disturbance that led to the eventual downfall of apartheid.

Since 1996, teaching and learning in South African schools have been subjected to a plethora of education policy changes, most significantly a move away—at least symbolically—from the devastating ramifications of the segregationist apartheid education system. By 2003, the country's education system had already adopted an outcomes-based approach to education, which culminated in the National Curriculum Statement (NCS) of 2003 and eventually gave rise to the Curriculum Assessment Policy Statement (CAPS) in 2011 as a corollary of the pedagogical weaknesses identified in the NCS.[1] Whereas the NCS emphasized a teaching and learning methodology constituted of the implementation of learning outcomes in what we regard as a rather predetermined, mechanical way, CAPS was intended to couch the newly identified learning aims as pedagogical activities that can be internalized and acted upon by both teachers and learners as the educational agenda in public schools became overwhelmingly concerned with the country's democratization and equity agendas. It would not be unreasonable, then, to assert that CAPS was introduced to soften the prescriptive and highly mechanistic tone of the

NCS. Moreover, CAPS offered a more graceful bridge between the curriculum, which is highly centralized, and the surge of policy reform that swept the educational arena as the state endeavoured to address equity and redress via strong shifts toward decentralization.

And yet, as we see today, the move toward school-based management, in terms of which schools are expected to assume greater autonomy, and the establishment of school governing bodies (SGBs) has not only laid bare— through the vast differences in levels of parents' expertise, knowledge, and at times, literacy—the glaring inequalities between public schools, but has shown the policies to be more suited to functional and well-resourced schools and has had the unintended consequence of widening the existing rupture between privileged and under-privileged schools. On the one hand, democratization has in mind producing teachers and learners who can engage actively with one another in pedagogical processes, thus hopefully paving the way for fuller participation as citizens in multi-party democratic politics, along with building the economy. On the other hand, equitable redress aims to inculcate in learners greater societal awareness that hopefully can spawn just actions in attempts to remedy injustice, inequality, and the exclusion of marginalized groups in the wider South African society. Inasmuch as the aims of CAPS are laudable and perhaps difficult to critique, we contend that the current curriculum has a better chance of realizing its intended learning aims if, firstly, learners were to be initiated into a culture of hostipitality. In corroboration of this claim, and secondly, we shall argue that a culture of hostipitality cannot be engendered in public schools without teachers themselves becoming responsible beings enacting their humanity, before, thirdly, moving on to a defense of a provocative and disruptive politics of pedagogy.

UNDERSTANDING IN ORDER TO DISRUPT DYSFUNCTIONALITY

Attempts to avoid provocation and disruption in public schools have become synonymous with post-apartheid schooling, as it is often assumed that dysfunctionality in schools has and will be spawned by "unbecoming" provocative and disruptive action on the part of teachers and learners. Understandably, public schooling has been mandated by the post-apartheid state to remedy the suspicion and provocation associated with apartheid education, and rightfully so. However, after almost two decades since the abrupt separation with apartheid education, public schooling is still plagued by dysfunctionality, especially alarming increases in levels and types of violence.

One reason for this ongoing plague is that schools and schooling in South Africa can neither be divorced from their history nor from their context and environment. If schools are surrounded by a culture of gangsterism, drug abuse, violence, and other social ills, then how these schools are defined cannot be separated from the reality that the learners and community who constitute these schools are a part of the violence or social ill—whether as victims, or as perpetrators. Linked to the porous connection between the school and its community, no matter how disengaged that community might be, are the particular histories from which impoverished and apartheid-constructed schools have emerged. To this end, schools in the townships, especially, were considered and used as sites of protest against the apartheid government up to 1990. The particular educational and political discourse that permeated and shaped these schools was essentially one of remonstration, dissent, and violent objection. The introduction of new policies cannot undo this particular discourse, unless the curriculum itself offers the space for unrestrained pedagogical encounters. Furthermore, it would appear that the historical baggage of dysfunctionality and violence is not being countenanced by the provision of a new type of teacher training in post-apartheid South Africa.

In a recent study, Arends and Phurutse found that "beginner" teachers in South Africa "are thrust into classrooms without the necessary support and mentorship"; their (the teachers') expanded roles involve "more administrative duties instead of increased instructional time"; and school managers "may not be critical and reflective enough about their staff and this poses serious challenges to school improvement initiatives," such as "schools located in economically depressed areas . . . (producing) poor results."[2] However, what is disconcerting about their findings is that "violence is increasing both inside and outside of schools," making it practically impossible for beginner teachers to cope:

> In South Africa, many learners are also exposed to, or are themselves victims of, physical and sexual abuse, extreme poverty and HIV/AIDS. As a result of HIV/AIDS some young learners become heads of households. It is in such situations that teachers feel inadequate as effective educators, as the classroom and school situation demands more of them than teacher training prepared them for.[3]

To our mind, dysfunctionality is endemic to the public schooling system in South Africa and, although apartheid should be apportioned some blame in many instances, current schooling practices cannot be exonerated from exacerbating the dysfunctionality, which has now taken a somewhat unreflective and violent turn. And, to remedy the beleaguered public schooling system, South African schools require a provocative and disruptive response at all levels (most notably at the level of pedagogy) to counter escalating levels of dysfunctionality.

As alluded to, CAPS serves the purpose of equipping learners with the knowledge, skills and values necessary for "self-fulfilment, and meaningful participation in society as citizens of a free country."[4] Thus it seems as if CAPS would resonate with the democratizing of schooling in order to engender in learners competencies and skills to function in a democratic society. Here, CAPS encourages learners to engage in "active and critical learning"—that is, learners must be able to identify and solve problems and make decisions using critical and creative thinking; work effectively as individuals and with others as members of a team; organize and manage themselves and their activities responsibly and effectively; collect, analyse, organize, and critically evaluate information; communicate effectively using visual, symbolic, and/or language skills in various modes; use science and technology effectively and critically, showing responsibility toward the environment and the health of others; and demonstrate an understanding of the world as a set of related systems by recognizing that problem-solving contexts do not exist in isolation.[5] In this chapter, our interest is focused on CAPS's aim to ensure "meaningful participation" and "effective communication" in public schools—particularly between teachers and learners—as well as to show what a politics of teaching and learning ought to look like if informed by dialogical encounters of a provocative, disruptive, and caring kind.

From a cursory glance at CAPS, it does appear that meaningful participation and effective communication are couched in the notions of "dialogue," "debate," "negotiation," and "discussion." The Department of Basic Education (a division within the broader Department of Education) articulates dialogue as a participatory process aimed at arriving at "agreement" as its means of effective communication: "[dialogue refers to] . . . an exchange of ideas and opinions on a particular issue, esp. [sic] a religious or political issue with a view to reaching an amicable agreement or settlement."[6] Put differently, meaningful participation resonates with dialogue, and arriving at an agreement seems to be considered as an effective form of communication. In addition to conflating dialogue with debate, negotiation, and discussion, it appears as if dialogue is more appropriately practiced if learners were to be taken through mechanical steps of engagement with one another (i.e., dialogue is encouraged through very prescriptive and anticipated prompts with the aim, of course, to make learners reach consensus on pedagogical matters), meaning that the only concern appears to be that the teacher has taught the prescribed curriculum outcomes, and that the learner has hopefully achieved these outcomes.There appears little acknowledgement or space allowing for talking back, debate, or disagreement. In this regard, the DoBE, through CAPS, does not do much to reduce or attend to the conceptual misinterpretation of dialogue. Can dialogical pedagogical encounters really manifest if learners are mechanically policed with predetermined prods and reminders for when and how to express themselves? How deep is dialogue if it is used as some engineered stimulus to exhort learners to reach agreement or a settlement (often preconceived), so as to avoid disruption?

Of course, dialogue is not the same as debate, discussion, and negotiation. The split between being allowed to speak and being listened to is one that not only stunts classroom participation and deliberation, but also serves to fuel the often-encountered disconnection learners experience from their own learning. If one debates and has a discussion, the outcome is not inevitably agreement. Sometimes people debate and discuss issues with others without an agreement being reached, which of course does not make the dialogue redundant. Similarly, agreement cannot be a precondition for dialogue, for that would mark the end of dialogue. Rather, agreement—or disagreement, for that matter—evolves from a dialogue. If one engages with someone with the aim of reaching some kind of agreement, the possibility exists that the agreement might be plausible but, equally, also contrived, which possibly would render the consensus and even the dialogue a mechanical procedure, since the aim of the encounter would have been to teach consensus, rather than engagement. Instead, dialogue should be presented as a practice that allows learners to open up to one another, with the possibility that they (learners) might even come to some kind of disagreement among themselves, which of course would bode well for the cultivation of learners who can think independently and critically. The problem with a mechanical form of dialogue is that the possibility exists that the dialogue be "policed" by teachers, who would want to see that an agreement, often in their interest, is attained. In this way, learning to talk back might even be stunted, because the possibility exists equally that one's aspirations to be heard might be stunted prematurely because of an obligation to reach agreement. To this end, learners quickly learn that, while spaces might be created for their voices to be heard, these voices are not necessarily listened to.

Of course we are not suggesting that all forms of agreement are necessarily undesirable. Sometimes teachers and learners can agree beforehand to engage in a dialogical encounter in order to attain agreement—for instance, to combat bigotry. However, the agreement reached is rather the outcome of the dialogue than an agreement to reach consensus prior to the dialogue having begun. It perchance could happen that a predetermined agreement on how to undermine racial prejudice in schools, for example, is shared by most people (teachers and learners). But if agreement were to be the outcome of a shared compromise between teachers and learners, the possibility that the undesirable act of bigotry is countenanced in schools might just prove to be more meaningful than unspontaneous and artificial agreement on a fairly sensitive matter. So, what ought to happen to avoid fixed and pre-arranged agreements that have the potential to reduce dialogue to mere empty sound bytes?

CULTIVATING A CULTURE OF HOSTIPITALITY IN PUBLIC SCHOOLS

Seyla Benhabib offers an account of a provocative and disruptive dialogical encounter as tantamount to deliberative iteration—that is, teachers and learners engage in dialogue in which they exercise profound listening, reflection, and talking back to one another in an attempt to produce points of view that are well thought through—that is, speech acts that recognize the standpoints of the other.[7] She posits that, through deliberative iterations, teachers and learners engage in dialogue about their collective identity what she describes as free public spheres (which, as we have shown, is what schools ought to be)—that is, dialogues that challenge the assumption of the completeness of each culture by making it possible for the participants "to look at themselves from the perspective of others."[8] Simultaneously, such a provocative and disruptive dialogical encounter (iteration) also evokes what she refers to as "a dangerous indeterminacy or mutual suspicion" (hostipitality) through which participants in the encounter are initiated into becoming mutually suspicious of dystopias, such as forms of discrimination that might be evident in acts of racism and bullying.[9] For this reason, we find Benhabib's (2011) idea of hostipitality offers us a salient vehicle through which to address disruptive encounters that can result in the marginalization and exclusion of the other. After all, what is the use of provocative and belligerent dialogical encounters that have as a corollary further exclusion and alienation of the other?

In a way, public schooling requires a pedagogy of provocation and disruption that can contend with dysfunctionality, since ongoing attempts to transpose models of "functionality" onto these schools have been proven to be both ineffectual and lost in an environment where there is nothing to which to attach the "functionality." Studies conducted by Taylor reveal that, while approximately 80% of South African schools are essentially dysfunctional, thereby confirming that proper and effective education is not taking place, policies and administrative attempts to improve accountability, such as implementing Standard-based Assessment, capacity-building measures and support packages, have had no effect on dysfunctional schools.[10] There have been various recommendations to remedy the dysfunctionality at these schools, such as Jansen's[11] call for the reinstatement of the inspection system, as well as the implementation of an intervention program, the Education Action Zone (EAZ), which appeared to produce substantial and consistent improvements.[12] Smit and Oosthuizen, however, report that departments of education have been reluctant to take strong, emphatic action to enforce compliance.[13] Compounding, or possibly causing, this reluctance is the criticism voiced against EAZ, for example, namely that it is a crack unit with which to bully schools. To Smit and Oosthuizen, the reluctance to act decisively against dysfunctional schools suggests a profound misunderstanding of the principle of the rule of law:

> In other words, it is contended that by overtly allowing anarchy (lawlessness) and systematised unprofessionalism to prevail in schools, the education departments exhibit a fundamental misunderstanding of the democratic imperative to apply the law with relentless rigour in order to maintain a state based on the rule of law. To put it differently, if

the departments of education (and its officials) overestimate the political role that a teachers' union should be allowed to play, and if the departments of education misconceive the extent of the labour rights of educators, then the inevitable result is overpoliticisation of schools and systematised unprofessional conduct or dysfunctional behaviour by educators. Of course, a democracy is not anarchy, because the people agreed to and established the laws of the country. The political action by labour unions during the struggle against apartheid was understandable, because the previous regime was not democratic. However, with the attainment of democracy, political activism should no longer be the role and function of unions and their power should be restricted to labour matters. Therefore, by erroneously endorsing, permitting or condoning political activism by educator unions in schools, the education departments are acting contrary to the democratic principle of the rule of law.[14]

It does seem as if the Department of Basic Education's emphasis on agreement is targeted primarily at avoiding provocation and disruption in schools, as is evident from its insistence on securing "safe speech" through pedagogical encounters.[15] There are, however, are two issues at play here. On the one hand, given the centralized and prescriptive nature of an inspection system, and its inconsistency with a conception of hospitality, we would be as reluctant as the departments of education to re-instate this recommendation. On the other hand, it is doubtful that the reasoning informing the reluctance of the departments of education to adopt these recommendations are similar to ours. Our argument for the cultivation of hostipitality is not synonymous with the Department of Basic Education's advocacy for "safe speech"—which is how they have chosen to motivate their reluctance to heed these various recommendations. So, while the Department of Basic Education's advocacy for "safe speech" might work against its own demand for meaningful dialogue to unfold amongst teachers and learners, dysfunctionality, however, cannot be disregarded with the hope that functionality will prevail if people are treated with care through "safe speech." In this respect, the Department of Basic Education needs to afford to itself the same advocacy of "safe speech" that it affords to its teachers. This means that as an enactment of cultivation of hostipitality, the Department of Basic Education has to "talk back" to dysfunctionality, regardless if this iteration is viewed as hostile. The point we are trying to make here is that the cultivation of "safe schools" cannot be couched in a discourse of "safe speech," which is associated with a hesitancy to "talk back" or, worse, with a muted acceptance of dysfunctionality, as can be inferred from the department's reluctance to decisively address the continuing high levels of teacher absenteeism, or unpreparedness to teach. "Safe speech," as a practice of hostipitality, has to disturb dysfunctionality so that teachers are provoked into "talking back" so that they might engage with the dysfunctionality of high teacher absenteeism and unpreparedness. To this end, "safe speech," while provocative and unsafe, will serve to combat dysfunctionality.

In relation to the seminal ideas on dialogue as a provocative and distressful encounter, Eamon Callan avers that the purpose of meaningful communicative engagement is not an attempt "to achieve dialogical victory over our adversaries but rather the attempt to find and enact terms of political coexistence that we and they can reasonably endorse as morally acceptable."[16] Here, dialogue seems to be aimed at securing a space for reasonable and moral acceptance—a kind of shared compromise that emanates from the dialogue. For teachers, and learners (as well as the Department of Basic Education) to achieve such a shared compromise, they do not merely embark on "safe speech" because they are unwilling to confront one another's biases, but rather to disturb complacency or provoke doubts about the correctness of their moral beliefs or about the importance of the differences between what they and others believe (a matter of arousing distress), accompanied by a rough process of struggle and ethical confrontation—that is, belligerence.[17] If this happens, belligerence and distress eventually give way to moments of ethical conciliation, when the truth and error in rival positions have been made clear and a fitting synthesis of factional viewpoints is achieved.[18] Such a provocative and distressful dialogical encounter does not preclude anyone from dissent, and teachers and learners have a real chance of speaking their minds. When teachers and learners speak their minds, they announce themselves as reasonable and moral beings willing to engage with agreement and dissonance—that is, through agreement and dissent they endeavour to take one another on. However, when engaging with one another through provocation and distress, teachers and learners might begin to disrupt the notion of taken-for-grantedness, although the possibility also exists that excessive provocation might lead to more alienation amongst the participants as they set out to assert their voices in the dialogical encounter. This is a situation that public schooling can ill afford to let happen, as teachers and learners should always remain in conversation as they collectively proceed to remedy the distressing consequences of dysfunctionality.

Simply put, deliberations of a provocative and disruptive kind do not have predictable outcomes; and are marked by outcomes of vagueness and unpredictability. Although such a dialogical encounter does not constrain provocation and disruption, it recognizes that hostility and hospitality (that is, hostipitality) both can engender outcomes that might not have a predictable result. And, if the outcomes of dialogical encounters are difficult to work out, there is no reason to instigate over-excessive provocation and disruption that can result in irreconcilable relations between teachers and learners. The point being made here is that we should always guard against being too provocative and disruptive—a situation that could bring us nowhere. Rather, a hostipitable dialogical encounter has in mind placing a limit on provocation and disruption, which is different to a pre-defined set of constraints. And also that restraint ought to set in when we feel that we have actually done an injustice toward others, because a hostipitable dialogical encounter cannot occur at the expense of the loss of dignity of another. Therefore, a hostipitable dialogical encounter will always bring us into conversation with each other through provocation and disruption, without exceeding the limits—that is, without acting unjustly toward others. We can only know whether we have acted unjustly toward others when we recognize the other as seen from their vantage point—more specifically, when we become aware of the vulnerability of the other, upon which we then act. This brings us to a discussion of responsibility and humanity toward others in educative relations.

TOWARD ENGENDERING RESPONSIBILITY AND HUMANITY THROUGH PUBLIC SCHOOLING

Now what should be the responsibility of public schools in the quest to combat societal ills as our democratic state cries out for safety and security in schools and in society in general? Stanley Cavell cogently remarks "We are alone, and we are never alone," providing a clear indication that people are always in communal relations.[19] That is, one person is internally connected to another person and, by implication, is perceived as being answerable to or responsible for what happens to him or her, although such a person might not be tied homogenously to the other person. So, by virtue of being human, people have an internal connection to others, which makes them responsible to and for one another. Derrida considers the responsibility that one human being feels toward another as being born in her innate history of responsibility, that is in her culture, and in her ways of being.[20] To this end, knowing or stating that one has a responsibility is meaningless in the absence of practice or action. Following Cavell, the responsibility one human being has toward another is conceived of seeing the other from the other's point of view, with which one has to engage afresh.[21] Put differently, one cannot just approach the other by coercing the other to be like one, but rather recognizes the other for being an other with whom one should engage in order to connect with the other. It is through such a connection that the other presents herself to one, with all the other's differences and/ or similarities.

The point is, the possibility would always be there for one to engage with the other, and that one does not have to rebuke the other just on the grounds of difference. In other words, the other cannot be considered as a pariah undeserving of any form of engagement—an act that in itself would be a renunciation of one's responsibility. The point we are making is that, as human beings, we are responsible to other human beings without having to compromise our humanitarianism toward others—a matter of exercising our responsibility to them. And, following Derrida, schools, as constitutive of a "community of thinking," have to enact their responsibility toward learners by teaching them how to act with purpose and justice, so that they might learn that, as part of a "community of thinking," they have a responsibility to act against all types of dysfunctionality and dystopia.[22]

The Department of Basic Education is intent upon churning out teachers and learners who become vanguards of safety and security in public schools through its insistence that the production of both "safe" schools and classrooms, and "safe" environments in which they (the learners) live, is in fact the responsibility of teachers and learners. The thinking here appears to be that "safe schools" can be created and cultivated through "safe speech." What is even more disconcerting is when the DoBE endeavours to turn teachers and learners into active "vigilantes," particularly when having to deal with drug trafficking, gangsterism, and bullying, at the very least. But what can be so pernicious about teaching learners about the societal ills that undermine public schooling? There are two interrelated concerns here. Of course, education has social purposes, which are necessary for the cultivation of a socially just and safe society, but, firstly, to expect teachers and learners to extend their responsibilities beyond teaching and learning in public schools is a sad indictment of a democratic state's inability to deploy other societal resources to deal with unbearable societal troubles, such as the police and psychological services through its Ministries of Safety and Security and Home Affairs respectively. Secondly, it is unreasonable to expect teachers and learners to fulfil the roles of "safety officers" at schools; this is a demand that misdirects teaching and learning away from producing the critical minds so necessary to advance a legitimate course toward activist thinking that might engender better ways of dealing with crime and violence in South African society. While schools are indeed representations of society, and cannot be understood without taking cognizance of their society, teachers and learners cannot be expected to police and remedy that society.

It is teachers' responsibility to teach, and learners' responsibility to learn in order that a critical democratic citizenry be cultivated through public schooling. To this end, the purpose of schooling is to provide learners with the necessary skills to make the necessary choices, which will take them away from, rather than toward, acts of crime, violence, and social ills. It is certainly not the responsibility of schools to deploy teachers and learners as crime fighters in a fledgling democratic society where crime and violence continue to undermine any serious effort to cultivate critical pedagogy in schools. Instead, public schools, through critical teaching and learning, should produce activist minds that engage with others, so that reasonable ways and solutions are found to address societal harms and violence.

In demonstrating one's responsibility toward others there is an immediate acknowledgement of a connectedness and capacity for intimacy with others—thus limiting one's idiosyncratic privacy. It is for this reason that Cavell claims that "human beings do not necessarily desire isolation and incomprehension, but union or reunion, call it community."[23] Our private actions may lead to a betterment of our communal actions. I might privately contemplate to do something about combating dysfunctionality in public schools, but doing so autonomously without also penetrating the thoughts of other community members may not necessarily contribute toward a desired action. If one's privacy remains restricted to one, with the intention not to exercise one's responsibility to others, one's practices would remain unshared and separated from the people with whom one happens to live. So, one's privacy opens a door through which someone else can tap into one's thoughts—which might be of benefit to society. This is an activist role that is starkly different from assuming any direct role in combating crime and violence in society by assuming the role of vigilante to that end. In a Cavellian fashion, teachers and learners ought to be responsible human beings. This implies that they have to generate ideas about how to combat crime and violence without taking up the mantle of vigilantes—a matter of teachers and learners thinking differently about crime prevention, rather than doing the acts of crime prevention themselves. After all, public schooling, while not being expected to exceed their responsibilities, should be a space where matters of public concern are deliberated upon through provocative and disruptive dialogical encounters without succumbing to acts of vigilantism, which in any case undermine teachers' and learners' responsibility to be of service to other human beings. It is only through engaging in disruptive dialogical encounters with others that one can encounter the humanity of the other and engage from the perspective of the other without necessarily thinking that one needs to act on behalf of the other. After all, this is what *ubuntu* (human interdependence) has in mind: to think for and with the other, rather than performing acts of valour that can have devastating consequences for humanity.[24] What this means is that when we witness an injustice, such as learners not being afforded their right to an education, then to act and speak out against this injustice, is an act of *ubuntu*.

CONCLUSION: ON A REIMAGINED *UBUNTU* POLITICS OF TEACHING AND LEARNING

In extending and offering an enhanced conceptualization of citizenship, we include a conception of *ubuntu* as an enactment of humanness which, we believe, undergirds both acts of hostipitality and responsibility. In the context of (South) Africa, *ubuntu* is associated with a conception of human interdependence that is demonstrated through treating others with dignity—firstly in the cultural group to which one belongs, and secondly to all other human beings. The notion of *botho* or *ubuntu* is constitutive of African political, social, and ethical thought, often illuminating the communal interdependence of persons geared toward the cultivation of human flourishing in indigenous African societies.[25] *Ubuntu* is a practice that can enhance provocative, disruptive, just, responsible, and humane dialogical encounters as a consequence of its connection to a particular ethic of care.[26] So, a reimagined notion of *ubuntu* offers dialogical encounters as explained above, with a caring impetus. In African communities, one usually experiences the hospitality of the group, and participates in the activities of the group as a sign of respect. This practice is in line with the tribal social practices in which sharing and connecting with the group are seen as paramount. Yet, *ubuntu* contains a universalist element that starts from being interconnected with the group, which then extends to all other human beings:

> Ubuntu is very difficult to render into a Western language. It speaks to the very essence of being human. When you want to give high praise to someone we say, 'Yu, u Nobuntu'; he or she has Ubuntu. This means that they are generous, hospitable, friendly, caring and compassionate. They share what they have. It also means that humanity is caught up, is inextricably bound up, in theirs. We belong in a bundle of life. We say, 'a person is a person through other people' (in Xhosa *Ubuntu ungamntu ngabanye abantu* and in Zulu *Umuntu ngumuntu ngabanye*). I am human because I belong, I participate, and I share. A person with Ubuntu is open and available to others, affirming of others, does not feel threatened that others are able and good; for he or she has a proper self-assurance that comes with knowing that he or she belongs in a greater whole and is diminished when others are humiliated or diminished, when others are tortured or oppressed, or treated as if they were less than who they are.[27]

What follows is that *ubuntu*, first of all, is an acknowledgement by oneself that one is connected to a group, which in turn triggers a feeling of interconnectedness with others. Thus, the way one acts is governed by interconnectedness to the group to which one belongs, and then that same bonding is extended to every other human being on the grounds that one has had experience of affinity with one's group, and certainly that one has a desire to be treated in the way that one treats others. One cannot merely connect with others if one has not had prior experiences of a sense of interconnectedness with one's group. That is, it is necessary that one has internalized a sense of connectedness with the cultural group to which one belongs, which hopefully will be extended to universal others.[28] What it means to be a human being is therefore determined by a responsibility toward human beings about whom one cares deeply. Hence, *ubuntu* brings to a dialogical encounter the idea that participants who act provocatively, disruptively, responsibly, and justly do so caringly. Up to now, the Department of Basic Education has misunderstood an ethics with an equally limited understanding of a "safe speech"— believing that care is shown by not responding with hostility toward dysfunctionality. Yet, to care is to disrupt that which is wrong, so that teachers can be provoked and engage or debate in "safe speech."

Displaying *ubuntu* as an ethic of care to is to act against a perceived wrong, even though one knows that the outcome might lead to the disruption of another—in this case, holding accountable principals and teachers who do not fulfil their responsibility toward their learners, and hence toward others in society. One cannot lay claim to a conception of *ubuntu* when one does not enact one's responsibility in terms of what it means to act within an ethic of care. This brings us to a discussion of what it means to act caringly in provocative and disruptive dialogical encounters. Firstly, to act caringly (with *ubuntu*) toward others involves confronting and destabilizing oneself in relations with others. That is, when one recognizes that one might overstep the mark and cause undue hurt to someone else, one should not hesitate to constrain one's actions that might humiliate or rebuke others; secondly, a person acting with *ubuntu* can show remorse when violating the sanctity of others' lives—that is, one actually places a limit on one's capacity for inhumanity (performing acts of horror and other atrocities); and thirdly, acting with care always leaves open a door through which someone alienated on the grounds of having perpetrated heinous crimes can be encouraged to break with the past and open the possibility for a re-beginning.[29] In essence, any dialogical encounter that is provocative and disruptive can be caring as well—where caring refers to the capacity of humans to restrain their possible humiliation of others, restricting their own capacity to act inhumanely, and instigating opportunities for re-beginnings.

In sum, we have started off this chapter from the understanding that public schooling in South Africa is troubled by dysfunctionality, despite the well-intentioned curriculum to change teaching and learning in particular, because dysfunctionality cannot be remedied only through policy reform, especially not in a society in which being dysfunctional was synonymous with a form of protest against a dysfunctional apartheid system. We have argued that meaningful participation and effective communication have to be guided by provocative and disruptive dialogical encounters between teachers and learners, constituted by an ethics of responsibility, humanity, and dignity. And, if dialogical encounters were to countenance dysfunctionality in public schools successfully, they cannot be endorsed and exercised along the lines of untroubled "safe speech," and the expectation that teachers and learners ought to be held responsible as vigilantes to ensure safe and secure pedagogical environments in and beyond the public school classroom. "Safe speech" stands in contradiction to the purpose of CAPS, which encourages learners to engage in "active and critical learning," and it certainly undermines the purpose of equipping learners with the knowledge, skills, and values necessary for "self-fulfilment, and meaningful participation in society as citizens of a free country."[30] In other words, the notion of "safe speech" appears to be irreconcilable with the democratizing of schooling, or with cultivating a democratic agenda. Instead, the notion of *ubuntu* (human interdependence and humanness toward all others) engenders an ethic of care that can frame dialogical encounters along the lines of non-humiliation, thus paving the way for re-beginnings that can prevent people (teachers and learners) from being alienated from each other. Only then dysfunctionality in public schools might be remedied through provocative, disruptive, responsible, just, humane, and caring pedagogical encounters.

NOTES

1. DoE (Department of Education) Curriculum and Assessment Policy Statement: Further Education and Training (CAPS)—Grades 10, 11, and 12, Pretoria: Department of Education, 2011.
2. Fabian Arends and Makola Phurutse, Beginner teachers in South Africa: School readiness, knowledge and skills, HSRC Press, Cape Town, 2009, pp. 43–45.
3. Ibid., p. 44.
4. DoE (Department of Education) Curriculum and Assessment Policy Statement: Further Education and Training (CAPS)—Grades 10, 11, and 12, 2011, p. 2.
5. Ibid., p. 3.
6. DoBE (Department of Basic Education) A bill of responsibilities for the youth of South Africa, Pretoria: Government Printers, 2008.
7. Seyla Benhabib, Dignity in Adversity: Human Rights in Troubled Times, Oxford University, Oxford, 2011, p. 75.
8. Ibid., p. 76.
9. Ibid., p. 76.
10. Nick Taylor. Accountability and support in school development in South Africa. Paper presented to the 4th Sub-regional Conference on Assessment in Education hosted by Umalusi, Pretoria, 26–30 June, 2006, p. 2.
11. Jonathan Jansen, If I were Minister of Education . . . Key priorities to turning public schooling around.Improving Public Schooling Seminars. Umalusi, Pretoria, 2007.
12. Brahm Fleisch, "Bureaucratic accountability in the Education Action Zones of South Africa." South African Journal of Education, vol. 26, 2006, p.369–382.
13. Marius Smit and Izak Oosthuizen, (2011)" Improving school governance through participative democracy and the law. "South African Journal of Education, vol. 31(1), 2011, p. 64.
14. Ibid., pp. 64–65.
15. DoBE (Department of Basic Education) A Bill of Responsibilities for the Youth of South Africa, 2008, p. 16.
16. Eamon Callan, Creating Citizens: Political Education and Liberal Democracy, Oxford University Press, Oxford, 1997.
17. Ibid., p. 211.
18. Ibid., p. 212.
19. Stanley Cavell, The Claim of Reason: Wittgenstein, Skepticism, Morality, and Tragedy, Clarendon Press, Oxford, 1979, p. 440.
20. Jacques Derrida, Eyes of the University: Right to Philosophy 2. trans. J. Plug, Stanford University Press, Stanford, 2004, p. 155.

21. Cavell, The Claim of Reason, p. 441.
22. Derrida, Eyes of the University: Right to Philosophy 2, p. 148.
23. Cavell, The Claim of Reason, p. 463.
24. Yusef Waghid, African Philosophy of Education Reconsidered: On Being Human, Routledge, London, 2013, p. 2.
25. Matsephe Letseka, "African philosophy and educational discourse." In: Philip Higgs, Zola Vakalisa, Tobeka Mda and N'dri Assie-Lumumba (eds.) African voices in education. Juta, Lansdowne, 2000, p. 179.
26. Yusef Waghid and Paul Smeyers, "Reconsidering ubuntu: On the educational potential of an ethic of care." Educational Philosophy and Theory, vol. 44(S2), 2012, p. 6.
27. Desmond Tutu,(1999) No Future without Forgiveness, Image, New York, 1999, pp. 34–35.
28. Waghid and Smeyers, "Reconsidering Ubuntu: On the Educational Potential of an Ethic of Care." 2012, p.16.
29. Ibid., p. 18.
30. DoE (Department of Education) Curriculum and Assessment Policy Statement: Further Education and Training (CAPS)—Grades 10, 11, and 12, 2011, p. 2.

10 Citizenship Education in Colombia
Searching for the Political

Andrés Mejía

INTRODUCTION

It is supposed that the concepts of citizenship and of citizenship education must be, by definition, political. After all, the political is what has to do with the affairs of the *polis*, or the city. Nevertheless, the idea of the political as it has been used contemporarily goes beyond this simple definition, to represent a particular way of conceiving the relationship between the citizens and the state, as well as between the citizens themselves. In such a relationship, citizens are *political agents* who enter in conversation and conflict with others, over issues that are of public concern for the communities they belong to.[1] But then, not everything under the names of citizenship or civic education can be said to be political. When the political is left out of the conception of citizenship embedded in our educational practices—including public policy—we face the risk of promoting just a minimal and only superficially democratic engagement of the individuals as citizens in their various communities.

In this chapter, I intend to explore in what ways various dimensions of social life that constitute the political have been included in or excluded from the arguably most influential elements of public policy on citizenship education, currently in place at a national level in Colombia. The history of citizenship education in Colombia begins with the very origin of the country as an independent nation, in the early part of the nineteenth century. Our present arrangement in educational policy on this topic, however, is constituted by elements that have been formulated and implemented in a period of time that roughly spans the last two decades. These various elements have not always coincided in their ideological orientations and, as a result, we arguably now have a somewhat fragmented sense of citizenship education in practice.[2]

I firstly explain the idea of the political that my discussion will be based upon and its place in various conceptions of democracy. In this analysis I largely draw on the work of contemporary political philosopher Chantal Mouffe. Then I describe the arguably most important elements of public policy on citizenship education that are still in use today in Colombia, and discuss the places that the political has occupied in their conceptions of citizenship and of citizenship education. Lastly, I will present some of my conclusions concerning the significance of this analysis and the ways in which I take it that we could move forward.

I have to declare that I have been involved in the process of constructing some of these elements of policy, particularly the most recent ones, together with a number of other academics that come from disciplines such as law, political science, psychology, and sociology. I will leave it up to the reader to decide how this may have affected my own analyses.

CITIZENSHIP AND THE POLITICAL

Liberalism and Democracy

As pointed out earlier, etymologically the *political* refers to the affairs of the *polis*, that is, the city. The political, thus, has to do with issues that are of concern to the citizens. Now, the city is the space in which citizens live together, and this very fact must surely be the source or origin of the political. The challenges that living together poses for the citizens are multiple. A first one is peaceful coexistence: how the various individuals can share the same living space—physical or otherwise—without harming one another. This challenge involves the state in at least two different ways. Firstly, it must enforce the norms that guarantee coexistence, thus providing security to the citizens who must yield part of their freedom so that they obtain it. Secondly, it must restrain itself from exercising violence on the citizens except when it is necessary in order to maintain order and security, and always according to the law. Here we can find the liberal principles of the rule of law and of the rights and freedoms of the citizens, which stem at least from the *Declaration of the Rights of Man and of the Citizen* promulgated during the French revolution, but that have numerous predecessors, especially in Europe.

A second challenge for citizens who share some living space is that of how to decide on the issues that are of collective or public concern: the affairs of the *polis*. And in fact, it is in the activities related to this second challenge that we can locate the realm of *politics* and of *the political* proper. This idea can be traced back to the society which some take to have invented the very idea of citizenship in the West: Classical Greece.[3] As Arendt has pointed out following Aristotle, the location of the political is the space where citizens meet, agonistically, to show their worth in the pursuit of justice.[4] The *bios politikos* would be, precisely, life devoted to the affairs of the *polis*. Whilst the problem of peaceful coexistence is common to any group of individuals who share some living space, the problem of collective decision making is particularly relevant to those societies whose individuals can aspire to have some influence in such decisions. And of course this should be the case, although not exclusively, for societies which define themselves as democratic.

In order to better see what the idea of the political implies, one can begin by examining one form of citizenship that has been left devoid of any politics. As Mouffe remarks, this would be the case of a purely liberal arrangement. In her words, "Liberalism, in so far as it is formulated within a rationalistic and individualistic framework, is bound to be blind to the existence of the political and to delude itself with regard to the nature of politics."[5]

In such case, there is no need for any political activity. The citizens have a number of rights that, as pointed out previously, ultimately derive from the need to peacefully coexist while each pursues her own private ideals. These rights impose duties on them as well as on the state, namely those of respecting the rights of the other citizens. But there is no political activity here. The activities individuals engage in are of a private nature. Respecting the rights and liberties of others merely imposes some restrictions on those private activities—even if it is sometimes very difficult to make individuals attend to those restrictions—but it does not constitute any activity in itself. The spaces where citizens meet each other would be of a social, rather than a political, nature.[6] And the affairs of the state would merely become activities of *management*.

Nevertheless, the fact that liberalism does not directly involve a political dimension does not imply that it will necessarily exclude it in a straightforward way either. In fact, if democracy has this political nature, then a liberal democracy can be thought of as one instance of the possibility of keeping the rights and liberties of liberalism while at the same time incorporating the political dimension of democracy. However, as various authors have noted, the relation between liberalism and democracy is not an easy one.[7] In some respects, some of the rights and liberties of liberalism—such as freedom of conscience and of expression—are instrumental for a genuine democracy because they will guarantee that the citizens actually have the opportunity to participate in collective decision making processes. Additionally, some authors, including Mill, have argued that a democracy will be good for the protection of rights and freedoms because those in government will have a reason to do so, given their dependence on the citizens.[8] But, at the same time, their different natures put them in tension with each other on some occasions. One first tension can actually be argued to be beneficial: the institutionalisation of rights and freedoms can prevent some of the possible excesses of democracy, which might occur, for instance, when the majority might decide to somehow oppress or subordinate those who belong to a minority. A second one derives from the fact that liberalism is configured around the idea of difference in such a way that all the individuals are seen as unique, while democracy is established on the basis of equality. Curiously enough, by the very fact that liberalism does not distinguish one individual from another on the basis of who they are or the social groups they belong to, its emphasis on difference ends up in the postulation of a universal abstract individual with just the same rights and liberties as everybody else.[9]

This tension between liberalism and democracy would be, precisely, what can open up a space for the political to occupy, in liberal democracy. In Greaves' words, "certain concepts, ideals, and practices exist at the interstice between democracy and liberalism, deriving their roots from one or both yet in conflict with some element of either liberal or democratic foundational principles."[10] Those interstitial concepts, practices, and ideals are then always open to debate and conflict, and thus provide the content for political struggle. Exclusions are created by treating all the individuals in the same way and not acknowledging the difference that belonging to a particular social group can make for an individual. But, at the same time, any definitions of groups will inevitably establish some boundaries by producing an interpretation of liberal and democratic principles—concepts, ideals, and practices—that creates new exclusions. This is why Mouffe argues that politics in a liberal democracy will be marked by a continuous struggle over interpretations and practices about ideals for society, by social groups whose identity is fluid and dynamic and therefore changes through time. What is important, then, is to not close off the possibilities for conflict to emerge so that the political can always be maintained in a liberal democracy.

Participation and Representation

The political, so conceived, makes itself present in different ways in different sorts of democratic activity. For instance, the traditional distinction between participation and representation also configures a different form for the political. In a representative democracy, political struggle only occurs in the attempt, by the political parties, to get the votes of the citizens. Political parties and their candidates construct some interpretation of the problems and exclusions in society from a particular ideological perspective, and then citizens simply vote to choose one from them. Political agency is here relegated to the indirect mechanism of representation, and the political duties of the citizen are limited to a basic understanding of the issues of public concern, so that then she can vote appropriately.

In representative democracy, therefore, the political has a limited scope. Even if no ideological censorship is established for political parties, citizens do not have to produce their own interpretations but choose from a number of them that some candidates construct. Following Dewey's characterisation of democracy in terms of a way of life that maximises interactions between its members,[11] a representative democracy will look like an unnecessary reduction of the possibilities for a society to construct their own present and future.

In a participatory democracy, citizens are expected to take a more active part in processes of collective decision making in all domains of life: family, the school, the workplace, the neighbourhood, and even in the relation with the state.[12] In the Deweyan terms just mentioned, interaction with others is enhanced in which the citizens advance their own interpretations and assess those of others, and in which they attempt to gain support by other fellow citizens to press the adoption or implementation of certain actions at the same time that they are the object of others' similar moves. This way, political agency will certainly be of a broader scope than in a representative democracy, but it will depend on the actual possibilities that the citizen has for associating with others, constructing a voice, making it be heard by others, and acquiring some power to allow her to actually influence the decisions taken and the actions carried out. Now, when assessing how wide this agency can be, it has to be taken into account that the traditional institutional channels for participation are usually insufficient, as are the usual presumably purely rational methods of decision making. This way, the political requires an opening of channels of expression, instances of decision making, and action. Furthermore, the political is agonistic; it is defined by conflict. And, in Mouffe's words, it requires that democracy be radical.[13]

Of course, representative democracy can live side by side with participatory democracy. The number of instances of collective decision making can be large in a truly democratic society. But, of course, this position directly contradicts the postulates of the champions of representative democracy and their Schumpeterian stance, according to which citizens should elect their representatives and then give them a free hand to take decisions so that the government's actions will not be hindered by the interference that might be expected of citizens making too many and too exacting demands on the state.[14]

THE POLITICAL WITHIN AND WITHOUT CURRENT POLICY ON CITIZENSHIP EDUCATION IN COLOMBIA

In what follows, I will present and discuss those elements of public policy at a national level in Colombia which directly concern citizenship education, have some element of compulsoriness, and are still applied today. These criteria require me to look back at some norms of a general nature, which set the frame for citizenship education, but to mostly concentrate on the last decade in which various more concrete elements have been produced. I have grouped these elements of public policy roughly according to a chronological criterion. Given that such elements tend to share their underlying political ideology with others that were produced close in time, I take it that this grouping will more clearly show the various conceptions of citizenship and political ideologies that have been influential in their production. As mentioned in the introduction, my analysis will be focused on the place of the political in the kind of citizenship education promoted by them, referring to the encounters in democracy in which citizens, either as individuals or as social actors, meet with others to deliberate and negotiate decisions concerning the public in a broad sense.

Citizenship Education in Colombia before 1991

The origins of citizenship education in Colombia date back to the very beginning of Colombia as a sovereign state, after it became independent from the Kingdom of Spain in 1819. A three-part instruction in the form of a catechism was developed which included urbanity, morality, and civics. The latter was mostly devoted to honouring the national symbols of the newly created country and to learning the new independent state's version of recent history as a means of constructing a Colombian national identity.[15] This was particularly important, as the Colombian independence wars were not exactly waged in the name of some nationhood with ethnic or cultural characteristics that could be clearly distinguishable from those of the Spaniards. Colombia had then a fragmented population composed of Spanish whites, local whites (mostly of Spanish ascendency but born in the new lands), mestizos, aborigines, and blacks. The wars of independence were mostly an initiative of the local whites, who resented the fact that they did not have any access to political power and were underprivileged in comparison with the Spaniards. According to Riveros, still at the end of the nineteenth century and during a large part of the twentieth century, religious and civic education were articulated under the single purpose of constructing a national identity, using as a model narrative the messianic story of a hero who becomes a martyr by trying to save the rest of us from some kind of evil forces.[16]

It should suffice to say that these initial proposals of citizenship mostly based in the construction of a common national identity finally gave way with the advent of a new constitution.

The New Constitution and the General Settings for Citizenship Education in 1991–1994

In 1991, a new Constitution was promulgated in Colombia, replacing the previous one from 1886, which was a long-lasting one, especially compared to the short-lived ones of the nineteenth century. It is widely acknowledged that the new Constitution changed in a radical way the official understanding of the nation and the state, producing important changes—though not all the expected ones—in the actual conduct of politics and in the dynamics of participation.[17] Various aspects characterise this Constitution that are relevant for my discussion on citizenship education in Colombia:

- In the very first sentence of the Constitution, Colombia is declared an "Estado social de derecho"[18] (i.e., a state guided by the rule of law, with a social responsibility).

- Human rights are included in the Constitution. The whole society is held responsible for their protection, although the state is given a special responsibility in this concern. These rights include various liberal political, civil and personal freedoms as well as other social and community rights such as access to education, health, culture, and a healthful environment.
- Colombia is acknowledged as a multicultural country with a plurality of religions, languages, and cultures in general, and composed of a plurality of peoples with different histories and different ideals for the future. This overturns the drive towards a unified national identity, with a very close connection with the Roman Catholic Church, which characterised the previous constitutions.[19]
- Democratic processes are encouraged by means of giving communities a role in decision making processes in various dimensions of social life, including education.
- Some mechanisms are introduced for direct citizen participation in decisions which are of general national concern, such as the *referendum* and the *plebiscite*.
- Another mechanism, the *tutela*, is established that allows citizens to demand from a judge in a quick and efficient way the protection of a fundamental right that has been violated or is in imminent risk.
- Differences between different social groups in society are acknowledged, which allows for some laws that followed in which special treatment was given to women (in terms of their participation in public office posts) and to indigenous peoples (concerning a special legal jurisdiction that allowed them to be guided by their own legal norms in a wide range of cases, as well as their participation in Congress).

I claim that it is important to understand the nature of the Colombian Constitution because many of the main elements of educational policy that concern citizenship education spring from those political commitments declared in it. This does not mean, however, that there is only one way to interpret it. In fact, it is in the interpretive spaces left open here and in the interstices between the liberal and the democratic principles of the Constitution that, as argued in the previous section, the political can emerge.

Apart from the substantive political commitments expressed in the Constitution, it also established citizenship education as compulsory: "In all educational institutions, public or private, the study of the Constitution and civic instruction are compulsory."[20] In 1994, this was materialised in the form of a requirement on the classes imparted by schools, by means of a decree that specified that, in order to be able to graduate from school, "any student must take at least 50 hours of Constitutional Studies."[21] There was no such specification of how to comply with the constitutional command in the case of higher education, though in practice universities decided to follow the requirement for schools and included a new course in their curricula for this purpose.

Shortly after the Constitution was promulgated, a General Law of Education followed in 1994 with a decree that operationalised some aspects of it.[22] This law attempted to provide some general guidelines for the domain of education that would follow political ideological lines similar to those of the Constitution. As regards citizenship education, two main elements should be highlighted. First, there is a definition of the general ends of education. In its 5th article it included the following:[23]

- An education to respect life and all the human rights, peace and the principles of democracy, of coexistence, pluralism, justice, solidarity and equity, as well as of tolerance and freedom.
- An education to facilitate the participation by all in those decisions that affect the life of the nation in respect of the economic, the political, the administrative, and the cultural.
- An education to respect legitimate authority and the law, national culture, Colombian history, and the national symbols.
- The study and a critical understanding of national culture and the ethnic and cultural diversity of our country, as the grounds for national unity and identity.

The second element concerns the establishment of a mechanism of participation at the level of educational institutions. It consisted in the creation of student and parent councils, and the inclusion of representatives of the students, of the teachers (or lecturers) and of the wider community in the administrative board of all educational institutions. This mechanism was based on the idea that there are—or there should be—educational communities composed by all these actors, which effectively have a right as well as a responsibility for the decisions in various aspects of education in schools and universities. One such aspect has a wide scope, given that it concerns the definition of the kind of education that any particular institution is to offer, which certainly touches on the even wider issue of the general purposes of education. The educational community of every educational institution, then, must collectively construct an Institutional Educational Project (PEI) which specifies the institution's identity in terms of the means and ends of education that it chooses to follow. Even though the PEI must be constructed within the frame provided by the goals stated in the Law of Education, the latter's breadth in their definition effectively gives plenty of autonomy to educational communities for deciding their own identity and future.

Colombia was not the first country to establish this mechanism; but it can be said to clearly reflect a progressivist concern for the promotion of a participatory democracy. Such sort of democracy, as an ideal, suggests that people should have the opportunity to decide on matters which affect them, collectively, in all dimensions of human life such as their neighbourhoods, educational institutions, or workplaces, as well as in their relations with the state.[24]

It is hard to estimate the effects that this mechanism has had on the actual events and behaviours in schools and universities. According to some researchers,[25] it has been difficult to genuinely create a democratic culture in the way that it was envisaged in the Constitution and the Law of Education. Nevertheless, arguably, some concepts were effectively introduced into the general public vocabulary about education, which were central to this purpose. This suggests that the intervention was not only legal-normative, but also symbolic.

To synthesise, the basic tenets of citizenship education as promoted by the Constitution and the Law of Education clearly denote the bases of a liberal democracy. Moreover, the liberal rights and liberties established in the Constitution—which every citizen is supposed to learn in formal education—as well as the mechanisms for demanding their protection, such as the *tutela*, are here assumed to prevent democracy from producing a tyranny of the majority; that is, even if the majority were to democratically decide to implement policies or actions that might go against a minority, the fact that the rights are declared in the Constitution would set a limit to such decisions. This constitutes one of the important aspects of the relationship between liberalism and democracy.

Assessment Enters the Scene— The New Policies Introduced in 2003–2005

In 2003, there was an important new impulse given to citizenship education, framed within the general policy implemented by the Minister of Education at that time, which consisted of the introduction of assessment as a critical mechanism for the advancement of education. In particular, the Minister decided to implement standardised national tests in a number of disciplinary areas at different levels in schools, as well as for students who were about to graduate from university programs at an undergraduate level. Before then, there was only a test for students attending their final year in school (grade 11).[26] The office in charge of the construction of those tests was the National Institute of Assessment (ICFES). Those tests for school grades 5 and 9 (SABER 5 and SABER 9) included a module of citizenship competencies, and were applied for the first time in November 2003, and then irregularly in subsequent years until 2009 without substantial changes. One year after the first application of the tests, the *National Standards of Citizenship Competencies* were published,[27] and in 2005 a book was released containing what can be understood as the theoretical framework that laid the foundations for both the standards and the tests.[28] This order comes as a sort of surprise, as a rationalistic logic would have suggested that one would first define what citizenship and citizenship education are about (the theoretical framework), then one would establish some goals for various ages or grades, and then one would construct the tests. The reverse order that was actually taken speaks volumes for the importance attributed to assessment by the Ministry of Education. A colleague and I have provided a detailed critique of these policies elsewhere.[29] Here I will summarise and develop that critique, with my eyes set on the place of the political in the underlying conception of citizenship.

The National Standards of Citizenship Competencies comprised three main dimensions of citizenship: peaceful coexistence; participation and democratic responsibility; and plurality, identity, and the valuing of difference. The tests contained questions in the three dimensions, but vastly focused on peaceful coexistence. The theoretical framework again showed this ladenness towards the first dimension, but of course developed all three dimensions.[30] In this respect, it is also significant that the preface to the Standards, written by the Minister of Education, is titled "Learning to coexist," and makes no mention of the other two dimensions.[31]

A look at these three elements of policy reveals a number of underlying assumptions which point to a certain conception of citizenship that can be described as psychologistic, formalistic and largely apolitical. Arguably, a great advancement was made in depicting the skills and attitudes required of individuals for a non-violent society. This approach was psychologistic in the sense that, as Mejía and Perafán put it, an assumption was made that "social relations at a macro level are the total sum of social relations at a micro level (of personal interaction)."[32] With their ladenness towards peaceful coexistence, much of these elements of policy revolved around dealing with possible conflicts that arise between individuals, and concentrated on emotional and attitudinal aspects. That is, it was arguably assumed that the psychological characterizations of aggression, which are defined in terms of psychological processes and emotional and mental states, are just as good to understand those forms of "aggression" that occur between social groups. In doing so, structural forms of oppression[33]—which may in some cases lead to physical aggression between individuals—and their differential effects on social groups were effectively ignored altogether. But, of course, neither level of analysis can be reduced to the other.

As concerns democratic participation, this conception of citizenship was also formalistic. It privileged knowledge of the formal procedures for participation in schools and in society in general, as established by the law. It did not mention any alternative forms of democratic participation or the actual opportunities and obstacles for the conduct of politics in the actual settings that citizens encounter at various levels. This way, democratic processes are implicitly taken to take place only through the formal channels that have been established by the law, such as student councils in educational institutions, and procedures of direct democracy. As various authors have argued, however, democracy can be displayed in manifold spaces and domains of action, making use of various forms of interaction between different groups of people.[34]

Lastly, by saying that the conception of citizenship implicit in these policies is largely apolitical, I want to direct attention to the fact that the strong emphasis on peaceful coexistence may reflect the fact that a grave concern in a country such as Colombia is that of violence.[35] But it also shows a minimization of the political role of the citizens, whose duty, as argued in the earlier discussion on liberalism, becomes to respect the rights of others and not do any harm to them. Moreover, it also suggests a particular conception of the roots of violence as lying inside the individual.[36] All in all, actually these three characteristics of citizenship presented or implied in the framework, standards and tests, all express a retreat of the political from citizenship.

A Change of Emphasis—The 2012 Reformulation of the Citizenship Tests

Before I begin this description, I remind the reader that I have participated in the construction of the new policy, which is what I will be referring to in what follows. Therefore it is understandable that my analysis is regarded with some scepticism. I leave it for the reader to decide whether I have been able to be critical enough.

The last tests of citizenship competencies within the framework depicted in the previous section were administered in 2009, before new tests, with a new conceptual framework, started to be constructed in 2011. These new citizenship competencies tests were applied in grades 5 and 9, as before, but also to undergraduate students in their programme's final year (SABER PRO). Nevertheless, some parts of the old tests have been kept in the new ones for grades 5 and 9. The National Standards of Citizenship Competencies have not been reformed, though, but a new document with a conceptual framework is being elaborated at the time of writing this chapter. Curiously enough, the same reversal of the logical order in respect of what would be expected from a rationalistic point of view was followed in this case, just like it happened in the 2003 policy elements.

The new tests were administered in 2012 for the first time. The structure of the part that is common to all the tests (SABER 5, 9 and PRO) consists of four main components: knowledge of the Constitution, argumentation, multiperspectivism, and systemic thinking. The latter three are considered different kinds of dimensions, or *tools*, of critical thinking, roughly following Bermúdez's conceptualisation.[37] Knowledge of the Constitution refers to what it says about rights and duties, structure and organisation of the State, and mechanisms for democratic participation. Argumentation refers to the skills needed to analyse and evaluate assertions, arguments and discourses about issues of social concern. This component is closely related to critical thinking as it is conceptualised by the critical thinking movement. Multiperspectivism is the "capacity to analyse a problem situation from different perspectives,"[38] as well as to understand the various interests and perspectives in a conflict situation, recognizing their differences as legitimate. And lastly, systemic thinking refers to the "capacity to identify and relate the different aspects that constitute or determine a problem situation in the social domain."[39]

The rationale behind this choice is explained by ICFES in terms of the competencies needed for democratic participation:

> The exercise of citizenship is understood here as more than the exercise of rights and duties, for it also includes active participation in the community that one belongs to. This way, a competent citizen knows his social and political context, knows his rights and duties, has the ability to reflect on social problems, is concerned about the issues of his society, participates in the search for solutions to social problems, and seeks the general well-being of his community.[40]

Again, I have elaborated my arguments in detail elsewhere,[41] and here I will simply present a summary of the main conclusions. In that article, I was interested in identifying the conception of citizenship that is implicit in these new tests,[42] and in the ways in which certain practical decisions close off the open space left by the tensions between democracy and liberalism; in other words, the place that the political occupies in such a conception. In particular, my analysis was centred on five decisions that define the tests and that have implications for the configuration of a particular kind of citizenship. The first of these was to have a standardised test that would be applied at a national level. An implication of this decision is that citizenship is taken to be and mean the same for everyone in the country. Nevertheless, while this is true at the abstract level of the definition of the fundamental human rights and liberties— for which all the citizens are equal—as well as of the specification of formal mechanisms for participating in democracy, it is certainly not so when it concerns the obstacles and opportunities for effectively using those participation mechanisms or reclaiming the protection of one's rights and liberties. Belonging to one or another social group makes a difference in this respect. But, then, a purely egalitarian view will only serve to mask those differences in opportunities and obstacles.

The second decision that was considered was to have a paper-and-pencil test comprised of multiple choice items. Those items are constructed in such a way that four alternative answers are presented and the student must choose the only one option that is uncontroversially correct. This decision imposes a reduction on the level of complexity that the items can handle, for otherwise answers might be controversial. The consequence is that citizenship is implicitly regarded as uncontroversial, just in the same way that, as already argued, liberalism takes the political to rest on a minimal consensus and pushes all possibly controversial issues back to the realm of the private.[43]

The third decision regards the emphasis on an understanding of the *what* of the public rather than of the *how* of politics. That is, the tests ask the student to critically appraise arguments, situations, decisions or institutions, but the problem of *how* actual participation can occur, how a citizen can associate with others to enhance their political agency, use mass or other media to express herself, take advantage of the connectivity of social networks, use the arts to mobilise her own desires as well as those of other fellow citizens, deal with politicians in an effective way, or in general everything that the citizen needs to consider about the conditions of possibility for her political agency to be deployed,[44] is simply ignored altogether. A critical appraisal of issues of public concern, then, is implicitly assumed as being enough for participation. But this is only the case when participation is reduced to the election of representatives by means of voting.

The fourth and fifth decisions—the adoption of a minimalist and of a formalist strategy, respectively—can arguably be seen as strategies adopted in the construction of test items with the intention of avoiding accusations of ideological bias. Minimalism consists in only using items whose correct answer will not favour any political ideology, apart from what can clearly be taken to be directly derived from the Constitution. Interestingly, while such ideological bias will be avoided in particular items, the strategy will produce another bias when the test is looked at as a whole. Effectively, the implicit conception of citizenship will also be a minimalist one, for reasons similar to those that I have already espoused in the discussion about the requirement to have uncontroversial items.

Formalism consists in assessing, not the opinions that students have, but the cognitive skills that they employ in order to arrive at them. The main manifestation of this strategy can be seen in the general structure of the tests: the critical thinking components—argumentation, multiperspectivism, and systemic thinking—are defined in terms of cognitive skills and not in terms of beliefs. Nevertheless, this separation between what someone believes and how she came to believe, with differential effects on the possibility of bias, is hard to sustain. This effect can be seen at least in the intrinsic valuing of pluralism that underlays multiperspectivism as well as the importance—or, actually, lack of it—that is attributed in systemic thinking to the analysis of social and economic structures such as those that maintain structural forms of oppression.

With the analysis of these five decisions we can now delineate a certain conception of citizenship which seems to be implicit in the tests. It is largely liberal, focusing on the individuals but not in groups, with a minimal political space for democratic conflict, and privileging representation over actual participation. Of course, assessing the cognitive tools or skills for a critical understanding of issues of public concern is certainly an improvement on the mere knowledge of the formal mechanisms for participation. But the political has been reduced, at any rate, to the minimal expression of a representative liberal democracy.

CONCLUSION

Our present landscape is a mixture of elements of policy that come from different times and conceptions of education and citizenship. The various institutions and mechanisms being enacted and used today open certain possibilities for citizenship education in different and not completely complementary ways. They span from a pure liberal view devoid of politics to forms of representative democracy at local (school and university) and macro levels, in which the political is assigned a minimal place anyway. If one is to take seriously the need to maintain and promote the existence of a variety of channels of expression and participation—of forms of democracy, or, as Boaventura de Sousa Santos has called it, a demodiversity[45]—as well as a variety of positions that interpret and enter in conflict over the inclusions and exclusions of the institutions and mechanisms by means of which citizenship is expressed, then this mixture is, in itself, valuable for the promotion of a healthful citizenship.

Nevertheless, in spite of this variety, as I have tried to show the political has been largely left out of the conceptions of citizenship promoted, or deployed, by these elements of policy. A first step in the direction of allowing for the political to play a role in citizenship is to promote its emergence in other contexts; perhaps, acknowledging and fostering those that have already emerged. Laws, documents of conceptual frameworks, standards, and tests produced officially must be prevented from becoming hegemonic. One important step in this direction concerns self-criticism and making explicit the limitations and conceptions in the tests, standards, frameworks, and even in the formal mechanisms for participation. It is to this purpose that this work mainly attempts to contribute.

NOTES

1. Dominique Leydet, "Citizenship," in E. Zalta (ed.), *The Stanford Encyclopedia of Philosophy*, 2011, http://plato.stanford.edu/archives/fall2011/entries/citizenship/ (09/2013).
2. For a general analysis of this in education, see Mónica S. Orduz, *Análisis de la incidencia de evaluaciones y objetivos de desempeño implementados nacionalmente frente a la autonomía escolar curricular, a la luz de la ley 115 de 1994 en dos instituciones educativas de Bogotá (Estudios de caso)*, unpublished Master's thesis, Universidad de los Andes, 2006.
3. Paul Magnette, *Citizenship: The history of an idea*, ECPR Press, Colchester, 2005; Christopher Lyle Johnstone, "Rhetoric, civic consciousness, and civic

conscience: The invention of citizenship in Classical Greece," *Advances in the History of Rhetoric*, vol.5 no.1, pp.1–9.

4. Hannah Arendt, *The Human Condition*, The University of Chicago Press, Chicago, 1998.
5. Chantal Mouffe, *The Return of the Political*, Verso, London, 2005, p.140.
6. Hannah Arendt, *The Human Condition*.
7. See, for instance, Giovanni Sartori, *¿Qué es la democracia?*; and Chantal Mouffe, "Carl Schmitt and the paradox of liberal democracy," *Canadian Journal of Law and Jurisprudence*, vol.10, no.1, pp.21–33, 1997.
8. Penny Enslin, "Education for liberal democracy: Universalising a Western construct?," *Journal of Philosophy of Education*, vol. 33, no.2, pp.175–186, 1999. Frank Cunningham, *Theories of Democracy: A critical Introduction*, Routledge, London, 2002.
9. For the idea of a social group, see Iris Marion Young, *Justice and the Politics of Difference*, Princeton University Press, Princeton, 1990.
10. Wilfrid Greaves, "The intervention imperative: Contradictions between liberalism, democracy, and humanitarian intervention," *Innovations: A Journal of Politics*, vol.8, pp.59–72.
11. John Dewey, *Democracy and Education*, Redford, Wilder Publications.
12. Frank Cunningham, *Theories of Democracy*.
13. Chantal Mouffe, "Democracy, Power, and the 'Political,'" in Seyla Benhabib (ed.), *Democracy and Difference: Contesting the Boundaries of the Political*, Princeton University Press, Princeton. See also Iris Marion Young, *Justice and the Politics of Difference*, 1996.
14. Frank Cunningham, *Theories of Democracy*.
15. Martha Cecilia Herrera, "Políticas públicas en educación ciudadana en Colombia y América Latina: La arena de lucha del campo intelectual en la historia reciente," *Historia de la Educación—Anuario*, vol.9, 2008.
16. Andrés Riveros, *De-efectos-de: textos escolares de educación religiosa escolar como lugarización de lo nacio-religioso*, Universidad de los Andes, Bogotá, 2013.
17. Rodolfo Arango, *Derechos, constitucionalismo y democracia*, Universidad Externado de Colombia, Bogotá, 2004.
18. *Constitución Política de Colombia*. Available at http://www.mincultura. gov.co/?idcategoria=6545# (08/2013).
19. Rodolfo Arango, *Derechos, constitucionalismo y democracia*.
20. *Constitución Política de Colombia*, article 41, my translation.
21. Decreto 107 de 1994, article 1, my translation. Available at *http://www. mineducacion.gov.co/1621/articles-104562_archivo_pdf.pdf* (08/2013).
22. Ley 115 de 1994. Available at *http://www.mineducacion.gov.co/1621/ articles-85906_archivo_pdf.pdf* (08/2013). Decreto 1860 de 1994. Available at http://www.mineducacion.gov.co/1621/articles-172061_archivo_pdf_ decreto1860_94.pdf (08/2013).
23. Ley 115 de 1994, article 5, my translation.
24. Frank Cunningham, *Theories of Democracy*.
25. Rafael Ávila and Marina Camargo, *La utopía de los PEI el laberinto escolar*, Colciencias-UPN-Anthropos, Bogotá, 1999.
26. There was a previous test at an international level in which Colombia took part: the 1999 Civic Education Study (CIVED). Nevertheless, it does not constitute public policy in the sense of influencing the life of the citizens. A decade later, Colombia also took part in the International Civics and Citizenship Education Study (ICCS). There were twenty-eight participating countries in the CIVED study and thirty-eight in ICCS. See Judith Torney-Purta and Jo-Ann Amadeo, "The contributions of international large-scale studies

in civic education and engagement." In Matthias Von Davier, Eugenio Gonzalez, Irwin Kirsch and Kentaro Yamamoto (eds.), *The Role of International Large-Scale Assessments: Perspectives from Technology, Economy, and Educational Research*. Springer, Dordrecht, 2013.

27. *Estándares Nacionales de Competencias Ciudadanas. Formar para la ciudadanía . . . ¡Sí es posible!* Available at http://www.mineducacion.gov.co/1621/articles-75768_archivo_pdf.pdf (08/2013). It was during this period that the expression "citizenship competencies" was adopted as defining the form that educational goals should take regarding citizenship. This was in line with one of the main changes in the restructuring of the standardized assessment that had taken place in Colombia four years earlier, in 1999.

28. Alexánder Ruiz Silva and Enrique Chaux, *La Formación de Competencias Ciudadanas*, Ascofade, Bogotá, 2005.

29. Andrés Mejía and Betsy Perafán, "Para acercarse al dragón, para amansarlo, es necesario haberlo amansado primero: Una mirada crítica a las competencias ciudadanas," *Revista de Estudios Sociales*, 2006, no.23, pp.23–35. Available at http://res.uniandes.edu.co/pdf/descargar.php?f=./data/Revista_No_23/04_Dossier2.pdf (08/2013).

30. Ibid.

31. Ministerio de Educación Nacional, *Estándares Nacionales de Competencias Ciudadanas*.

32. Andrés Mejía and Betsy Perafán, "Para acercarse al dragón para amansarlo, es necesario haberlo amansado primero." p.28, my translation.

33. Iris Marion Young, *Justice and the Politics of Difference*.

34. Boaventura de Sousa Santos, "Enriquecer la democracia construyendo la plurinacionalidad," in Miriam Lang and Alejandra Santillana (eds.), *Democracia, participación y socialismo. Bolivia—Ecuador—Venezuela*, Fundación Rosa Luxemburg, Quito. See also Iris Marion Young, *Justice and the Politics of Difference*.

35. Martha Cecilia Herrera, "Políticas públicas en educación ciudadana en Colombia y América Latina."

36. Andrés Mejía and Betsy Perafán, "Para acercarse al dragón para amansarlo, es necesarion haberlo amansado primero."

37. Ángela Bermúdez. *Thinking Critically Together: The Intellectual and Discursive Dynamics of Controversial Conversations*. Harvard University Press, Boston, 2008.

38. ICFES, *Módulo de Competencias Ciudadanas SABER PRO 2013—12013*, p. 4, my translation. Available at https://.icfes.gov.co%2Fexamenes%2Fcomponent%2Fdocman%2Fdoc_download%2F406-guia-de-competencias-ciudadanas-2013–1%3FItemid%3D&ei=4KtXUvyWO7TI4AO-n4CwDg&usg=AFQjCNG3sWt8Uncz_9bmu6jIGOC4yhL_HQ&bvm=bv.53899372,d.dmg

39. Ibid.

40. Ibid.

41. Andrés Mejía, "The Open Space of Liberal Democracy: The Case of the Tests of Citizenship Competencies in Colombia," in press.

42. The idea of an implicit conception is to be treated as analogous to that of an implicit assumption, in the theoretical developments of the critical thinking movement. An implicit assumption must be distinguished from a made assumption in terms of the latter corresponding to a decision made by the person advancing some argument, while the former is a reconstruction of the logical implications that need to be assumed so that the argument is correct and makes sense. See Robert Ennis, "Identifying Implicit Assumptions," *Synthese*, vol.51, pp.61–86, 1982.

43. Chantal Mouffe. "Democracy, Power, and the 'Political'."
44. Martha Cecilia Herrera, "Políticas públicas en educación ciudadana en Colombia y América Latina."
45. Boaventura de Sousa Santos, *Enriquecer la democracia construyendo la plurinacionalidad*, Luxemburg, Quito. See also Iris Marion Young, *Justice and the Politics of Difference*.

11 Citizenship Education in Mexico[1]

Maria-Eugenia Luna-Elizarraras

INTRODUCTION

This chapter describes the general characteristics of citizenship education in Mexican "basic education" (which includes primary school, from grades 1–6, and secondary school, from grades 7–9). Highlighted is the preponderant role played by the formal curriculum in defining the content of citizenship education that all schools should promote. This curriculum proposes to locate school-based citizenship education at the forefront of pedagogical initiatives that insist on the necessity of forging a critical, participatory democratic perspective that is congruent with the challenges of global citizenship and based on universal values and human rights.

The tension between this curriculum and everyday school practices is also analyzed. It is in this context that one can identify the various difficulties faced in the implementation of recent initiatives for a citizenship education that would transcend traditional civics instruction and contribute instead to the development of actual citizenship competencies. Most of these difficulties are attributed to the lack of adequate strategies for in-service teacher education. However, in this chapter I argue that schools' organizational and administrative conditions provide the greatest difficulties insofar as they limit or impede the emergence of experiences of democratic community, as well as practices that would overcome the formalism that has characterized school-based civic education. Indeed, the pertinence of the matter of school administration and organization for civic education, and for the benefit of other domains of learning, has not been linked to civic education initiatives per se. Based on the analysis presented here, I provide suggestions for linking the forms of citizenship education comprising the curriculum with the practices that make up the real organizational conditions of schools in Mexico.

MEXICAN SOCIOPOLITICAL CONTEXT FOR CITIZENSHIP EDUCATION

Formally, Mexico is a federation of states organized in a democratic republic that was constituted as an independent country at the beginning of the nineteenth century, when it became independent from the Spanish crown after three centuries of colonial life. Currently, Mexico possesses a predominantly mixed race population, and 6% of the population speaks one of the eighty-nine indigenous languages.[2]

Throughout its history, Mexico has been characterized by its centralized and authoritarian governments. While the nineteenth century represented an arduous process of conformation of the laws and institutions that would consolidate the current form of republican government, the twentieth century witnessed the rise of a system of democratic government in which the same party—the Partido Revolucionario Institucional (PRI), or "Institutional Party of the Revolution"—assumed the presidency for seventy consecutive years.

In this period, the practice of political power was characterized by the application of authoritarian measures such as limiting the viability of other party options. The most relevant and viable party presence was the right-wing Partido Acción Nacional (PAN, "National Action Party") which in the year 2000 finally obtained the presidency and governed for two consecutive periods. Earlier, still under the PRI, numerous acts of repression and political prosecution took place against social movements of peasants, workers, teachers, and students, in diverse moments between 1950 and 1970: disappearances, clandestine killings, and massacres.[3]

According to Favela, as Mexico has tried to constitute itself as a lawful state, the mechanisms to deal with social protest have become more flexible, with a greater disposition to negotiation, while other resources have been put into practice to contain and inhibit the opposition.[4] Thus, for example, in recent years the neutralization of collective actions and protests has been achieved by promoting participation in institutional and bureaucratic processes. At the same time, the state has been led to open itself up and diversify the channels for citizen participation beyond the mere casting of votes.

The 2000 change of party in the presidency had to do in great measure with protests and organization among several sectors of society. Indeed, since 1988, when popular opposition was first expressed about the suspicion of fraudulent presidential election results, the citizen, particularly organized in and through civil society, generated continuous movements around the opening of participatory spaces, and to ask for an accounting of federal, state, and municipal governments. In a diverse manner, the citizen finally took on her role as a political subject.[5] The creation in 1997 of the Comisión Nacional de Derechos Humanos (National Human Rights Commission), the constitutional acknowledgement of Mexico as a multicultural nation in 1992, the creation of accountability mechanisms for public services, and the recognition of citizens' right to access public information and hold accountable government actions all constitute examples of the opening and diversification of state institutions as a response to citizens' demands.[6]

As noted, in the 2000 elections, for the first time in seventy years, a change in the party that held the presidency of the country took place: the PAN defeated the PRI in democratic elections. This party alternation represented, for a good portion of the citizenry, a possibility to exercise their rights by casting a vote and trusting the institutions responsible for the regulation of electoral processes. Besides, it constituted an opportunity for citizens to participate and positively value their power to influence decisions, at least with regards to who rules the country.

The PAN, as an opposition party for fifty years, questioned the authoritarianism of numerous PRI governments, as well as the patronage system and corrupt practices that were performed at the federal, state, and municipal levels. Notwithstanding, the twelve years of the PAN government did not consolidate various aspects of its political agenda; on the contrary, it has been often accused of the same vicious practices of PRI governments.

In this brief overview of Mexican political life, it is possible to situate the rise and development of a notion of citizenship with clear communitarian aspects, that is, one clearly identified with the "collective" ideal of the Mexican nation.[7] As with the majority of modern—particularly Latin American—nation-states, the organization of republican institutions was supposed to be accompanied by the formation[8] of a citizenry that would know how to use them. Yet this communitarian vision was translated rather abstractly and distantly into nationalistic values, such as love of fatherland, independence, and justice, which would fill the speeches of presidents and other political figures throughout nearly all of the twentieth century.

During this period, what prevailed was a kind of state paternalism centered on the figure of the president; citizen participation was limited to voting in elections, and for this reason independent political organization and participation was discouraged. Even though it may be true that in Mexico, unlike other Latin American countries, there was never a military dictatorship as such, the exercise of political power did have a strongly authoritarian cast.

What eventually contributed to generating new kinds of relations, characterized by a liberal orientation,[9] between government and citizenry, were diverse internal social processes, such as the oppositional social movements in Mexico during the second half of the twentieth century; the influence of mobilized social organizations and the entirety of civil society in those countries that did suffer military dictatorship; and the need for our country to participate more actively in the international markets. In this context, individual rights and freedoms acquired greater weight. At the same time, as already mentioned, the greater attention to human rights, participatory citizenship, and the political right to demand accountability from government representatives has required us to think in terms of a competent citizenry active in decisions of public interest.

Mexico is an unequal country in which the market liberalization of the 1980s translated neither into national economic development nor the elimination of economic disparities. Such differences are expressed in various spheres of social life: wealth distribution, political participation, access to education and high-quality health services, as well as differentiated opportunities for men and women, among the principal concerns.[10] Even as the concept of citizenship that prevails nowadays has been moving closer to a viewpoint in which citizens should act politically well beyond electoral periods, this viewpoint still faces great difficulties in fostering political practices that are coherent with both the exercise of human rights and the disposition to contribute to the common good. In certain respects, citizenship constitutes a reference point around which we might highlight those social features that can generate cohesion between a population as unequal as Mexican society is, in economic, social, cultural, and political terms.

On the other hand, the recent recognition of our country's multicultural reality has required a more inclusive notion of citizenship that implies appreciating the diversity of our (mostly indigenous) languages and cultures, as well as making the effort to comprehend that the better part of our mestizo population represents the "other" for the members of these cultures. In this way, citizenship acquires a broader quality that includes diverse cultural categories.

The actual forms of citizenship practiced today in Mexico serve to question the perspectives on citizenship governed by the extremes of liberalism and communitarianism and commonly wielded in political discourse. The problems that the citizenry needs to solve in our country must thus be rooted in an understanding of citizenship that goes well beyond the "merely juridical *status* granted by a state; it also implies a reciprocally engaged *relationship* between persons in the public sphere."[11]

HISTORICAL ASPECTS OF CITIZENSHIP EDUCATION IN BASIC EDUCATION

Since the time that Mexico was founded as an independent nation, schools were given the task of forging citizens with a strong feeling of national identity and identified with the institutions and laws that began to regulate their organization. Through the subjects of history and geography, mainly, a basic knowledge about the characteristics of the country was promoted, as well as the understanding of the main historical process that led to its formation as an independent country. In this way, citizenship education had a strong nationalistic character that was translated into the study of geography and national history.[12]

These attempts, whose origins date back to the end of the nineteenth century, contrasted with the social and political environment that prevailed in the earlier years of independence, where foreign invasions by France and the United States took place, as well as internal wars due to the process of separation of state institutions from the church and attempts of the Conservative party to establish an empire headed by the European archduke Maximilian. Also, the idea of a national state ruled by laws and institutions ran into serious obstacles such as the exercise of local political power in several regions of the country, where inherited colonial practices prevailed and where the owners of estates reoccupied their properties and exerted influence over the local governments.[13]

The first known proposals for civil education were based on the teaching model that was generated by religious catechism.[14] This approach induced pupils to memorize phrases that were related to what was considered to be a good citizen. Starting from a question with a predetermined answer, students repeated definitions from memory about the characteristics of a good citizen. At the same time that contents that would foster patriotic love in nursery school children were discussed in the first pedagogic congresses at the end of the nineteenth century, moral primers focused on good behavior, conventional social norms and proper customs also proliferated.[15]

By the end of the 1910 Revolution, public education received another big impulse to incorporate large sectors of the population into primary schools. Educational projects, especially those of civic education, gradually acquired new emphases that expressed the ideals of social justice and formal democracy that had been brandished during the revolutionary movement. Notwithstanding, it is possible to identify that during the main part of the twentieth century, the principal axis of citizenship education was constructed around nationalism linked with formal democracy.[16] This kind of citizenship education promoted a formal treatment of public life: an emphasis on the formal structure of government, the political administrative organization, and the political constitution. These elements scarcely made reference to pupils' life. On the contrary, they maintained a distance between students and the social and political life of the country and the world, by means of a conception of citizenship as exclusive of the adult world and centered in government actions, where citizens' participation was kept limited to the casting of votes and to established institutional channels.[17]

Up until 1971, there existed the subject of civic education in the syllabus of basic education. Between 1974 and 1993, civics was incorporated into the social studies area.[18] In 1993, the subjects of civic education in primary and civics in secondary were restored and a distinct feature of their incorporation was the inclusion of topics related to human rights, particularly those of children, and education in values. In this 1993 reform, the programs included nationalism-related elements, which were considered to be an important aspect of civic education and civics, and denominated "Strengthening of National Identity."

In 1999, topics on ethics and human development were incorporated into the new subject of civics and ethics education, in the secondary school syllabus. In this project, Ethics was introduced in an outstanding manner, and as an important aspect of citizen's formation. With this, the autonomous margin of decision of individuals with respect to public affairs became explicit. Besides, material related to the conditions and possibilities of adolescents was introduced as a starting point from which students would reflect and make decisions concerning their life as citizens.

In this way, secondary-level civics and ethics education currently promotes the development of a "citizenship morality that establishes criteria that belong to an Aristotelian heritage, with respect to its communitarian sense, where individuals in a society must respond to the exigencies of a political community. And we also think of another with a Kantian hue that appeals to the freedom of the subject, who is capable of dictating laws for oneself."[19]

In this new subject of civic and ethical education the SEP made clear its desire to bring into closer contact the personal lives of students—as legal minors with particular needs and interests—with the sphere of public and collective life. The need to re-conceive citizenship education was enriched by a participatory perspective on democracy, the recognition that individuals develop multiple levels of belonging (local, regional, national, and global), and an accompanying perspective on interculturalism as "an alternative that provokes one to re-ground and organize the social order, because it insists on fair communication between cultures as world figures . . . that recognize the other as different. The other is neither erased nor isolated; rather, there is a search for understanding, dialoguing, and respecting him."[20]

Beginning in 2000, education based on competencies (a perspective that sought to ensure the presence of learning experiences in real contexts where students develop) derived in a complete reformulation of the program of civic and ethics education in secondary, and its introduction at the level of elementary schools. In both programs, eight civic and ethic competencies were outlined: (1) knowledge and care of oneself; (2) self-regulation and the responsible practice of freedom; (3) respect and appreciation of diversity; (4) sense of belonging to the community, the nation and humankind; (5) handling and resolution of conflicts; (6) social and political participation; (7) sticking to legality and a sense of justice; (8) understanding and appreciating democracy. This program for secondary education was published in 2006[21] and that of primary in 2008.

By means of the competencies that were defined for this subject, the curricular programs introduced topics that were associated with the acknowledgement of the prevailing cultural diversity in Mexico, as well as the development of interculturalism[22] as a path for developing positive attitudes and values toward those who express differences of varying kinds, but especially ethnic and cultural. On the other hand, such programs included topics related to a participative democracy, in which a more active role is conferred to the citizen in democratic societies, which goes beyond casting a vote in electoral processes, a trait of the formal perspective of representative democracy in previous syllabi.

In the year 2000, the Secretary of Education of Baja California initiated "Cultura de la Legalidad" (Culture of Lawfulness) in secondary schools of the north region of the country. This program was generated in the United States as part of a policy to fight corruption and organized crime from schools. It then became wide-spread in the northern states of Mexico and was later incorporated into the curricular space of state subject, and is applied in the entities where it is considered necessary.[23]

In 2007, the Safe School Program was generated, which constituted a part of the so-called "Limpiemos Mexico" ("Let's clean Mexico") government strategy against drug traffic. This later changed into "Vivir mejor" ("Living better"). This program, in contrast with its predecessors, did not propose curricular contents but a series of actions to be carried out by directive personnel in order to propitiate safety conditions for students, mainly in those regions of the country with high levels of crime.

Since the late 1990s, besides those programs initiated by the Ministry of Public Education, other public institutions developed programs that were targeted to children and adolescents from elementary and secondary, with the aim to promote an initial knowledge to the work of public institutions, as well as to contribute to the development of participation and the acknowledgement of their rights. The Federal Electoral Institute has started out consultancies with kids since 1997, in which adolescent girls and boys participate. Also, the legislative power organizes annually the so-called "Kids' Parliaments," in which primary schools students from all over the country participate.

EFFORTS TO BRING CITIZENSHIP EDUCATION CLOSER TO CITIZENS' REAL NEEDS AND PRACTICES

Throughout this journey of the different projects of citizenship education, it is possible to note the development of a nationalist project that turned each time more intercultural, universal and cosmopolitan. The latter applies to the discourse of programs and syllabi in which different perspectives around the citizen were expressed. While turning from a colonial society into a centralized one, in the nineteenth century, and with a paternalist and authoritative state, a citizenship education was not required beyond informing students about some aspects of institutions and their functions. For that purpose, a history that fed national identity sufficed: a unique history for all the country, in which revolutionary governments appeared as its end and climax of the country's political development, and identified with the love for a large and generous nation.

In this manner, citizenship education was centered in the development of trust in governors and institutions. Its contents have spun around the importance of a representative democracy that focuses on a citizen which lays the responsibility of decision making in public life on the representatives they elect. In this way, the commitment of vote casting was outlined as the only mechanism of democratic participation that was fostered during most of the twentieth century.

The observation and vigilance by the citizen over governments´ performance as well as the demonstrations and pacific social protests were not an issue for citizenship education until the appearance of programs and the publishing of textbooks in the twenty-first century. For this reason, participative democracy is a new element in citizenship education, gaining legitimacy as a facet of citizen performance in the 1988 electoral process, in which a great number of citizens expressed their lack of satisfaction with PRI governments. In this period, there was also a great citizen participation in the vigilance and realization of elections. Also, the 1994 *zapatista* movement was featured by its pacifism and demonstrated the importance of mass media as a complement to citizen participation to spread the movement in the national and international contexts.

As was pointed out before, the 1993 syllabus was the one that introduced contents related to human rights and the National Commission of Human Rights—an institution created in 1992. Its presence in the programs of civic education and civics distinguished them from constitutional rights, which had already been a matter of study in these subjects since the 1960s. The latter gave way to the incorporation of children´s rights and the promotion of a vision that extended far beyond the electoral processes: the defense of the rights that all people are granted by birth.

With the appearance of the party transition that took place in the year 2000, a possibility was opened, inside and outside SEP, to generate several proposals that were oriented toward the formation on values and citizenship education. In each state of the country there appeared proposals from approaches.[24] SEP had to "contain" these emerging proposals and to organize one of its own through which guidelines were given for citizenship education all over the country. Also, when faced with traditional civics, which was imprinted with an authoritarian perspective about the "must be" of citizens, the official syllabus had to incorporate other elements that acknowledge other subjects and processes favoring the development of a citizenship culture. This change of perspective in citizenship formation at the basic education level responds to a generalized acknowledgement, in the social and political life of the Mexican society, that the political culture of citizens is configured in non-formal spaces, beyond the context of governmental institutions.

Foundations of Citizenship Education

It was in this context of liberalization that citizenship education was structured on a foundation which brought in multiple disciplinary influences, thereby providing a cornerstone for conceiving of different ways to shape children and adolescents through basic schooling. Among the disciplinary influences one could recognize first and foremost was philosophy and its diverse areas, including ethics, axiology, and political philosophy. In this fashion, a curriculum framework was created which could include: rational knowledge from diverse moral perspectives, the substance and nature of ethical values, and political thought about the relationship between individuals and the state.[25]

With these elements in place it was possible to establish a citizenship education that would include the socio-moral dimension along with an understanding of the functioning of government institutions and the role of citizenship vis-à-vis government action. Such reference points fostered a conception of citizenship education as a process that should be promoted from childhood on, generating values oriented to an interest in the common good, mutual responsibility, and political and social participation.[26]

Currently, in political and educational discourse, a conceptualization is made of the following characteristics:

- Interested on local, state, national, and international public affairs.
- Capable of self-informing and critically judging the quality of information that circulates through the media and information and communication technologies.
- Committed to causes that contribute to common well-being.
- Participative and exigent before the actions of the government and of other sectors of society whose decisions affect the rights and well-being of all the population.
- Shows disposition to organization with persons or groups, in a responsible manner, in order to solve problems and to improve well-being conditions.
- Capable of exchanging points of view in a respectful dialog, in which there is room for the right to dissent.
- Aware about his/her rights.
- Interested in taking advantage of participatory spaces and citizen resources to address authorities.[27]

These features are present in regulatory documents and in the curricular program of basic education. We can now characterize such features in terms of a citizenship education rooted in the life experiences of students, in the contexts where they learn and grow, so that from such experiences we can move them toward an understanding of the moral and sociopolitical dimensions of the world around which we can develop skills, values, and attitudes.

THE CITIZENSHIP EDUCATION PROGRAM OF STUDY AND THE IDEAL OF CITIZENSHIP THAT IT SUSTAINS

The citizen program in basic education expresses a group of expectations and ideals that, in good measure, are congruent with the characteristics of a democratic education around everyday practices. This program starts from kindergarten and continues through elementary and secondary school, that is, throughout the entirety of basic education.

First, the syllabus of basic education—which includes kindergarten, primary, and secondary, as pointed out—is organized into various "fields of formation," which go through these three levels. The field that is more

directly involved with citizenship education is named "personal development and coexistence." In this field of formation, the course of study known
as "personal and social development" occupies pre-school education, while
the subject of "civic and ethical education" is studied in both primary and
secondary schools.

In the following section, the characteristics of citizenship education in
each of these educational levels are described.

PRE-SCHOOL EDUCATION

This education, addressed to children between three and five years old, is
comprised of a course of study organized into five formative fields.[28] The
field that is more closely related to citizenship education is that of "social
and personal development," which covers "the attitudes and processes of
construction of personal identity and emotional and social competencies;
comprehension and regulation of emotions, and the ability to establish interpersonal relationships. It also promotes self-regulation by agreeing on limits to behaviors."[29] At this early level, citizenship education emphasizes the
immediate interactive context and encourages students, on the one hand,
to identify their own ability to regulate their emotions and personal reactions, taking into account their effects on other people. With this emphasis,
the foundations are laid for students to begin recognizing shared interests,
which in later years will be broadened toward the public interest and the
identification of their personal position in relation to the public interest—a
constant aspect of citizenship with respect to the events of public life.

This field is divided into two aspects: personal identity and interpersonal
relationships, and each one contemplates the development of certain competencies. Thus, some aspects from liberal and communitarian perspectives
are visible in this educative level.

Personal Identity establishes the following as competencies: "Acknowledges his/her qualities and capacities, and develops a sensibility for others'
needs and qualities," and, "Gradually acts with greater confidence and control, according to external criteria, rules and conventions that regulate his
behavior in the different contexts of participation."

These competencies also contemplate the achievement of expected learning
outcomes that are related to citizenship education. Among the more notable
of such learning outcomes are students' knowledge of their own tastes, interests, feelings, and motivations, as well as the effort required to reach their
goals; and their capacity to confront challenges and strategize ways to deal
with them, both individually and collectively. Also included is the ability to
express disappointment when their opinions are neither heard nor accepted,
as well as the consideration of others' opinions in order to live harmoniously.
Finally, such competencies include the inclination to offer support to those
who need it and to learn how to take care of and respect oneself.

Another group of learning outcomes refers to the student's ability to identify the consequences of the language s/he uses to participate with others, as well as his/her capacity to control his behavior with regard to the care and respect that others deserve. Altogether then, personal identity expresses many features of the liberal perspective on citizenship.

The other part of this formative field, interpersonal relationships, establishes the following competencies: "Accepts his classmates as they are, and learns to act according to the necessary values for life in a community, putting them into practice in daily life," and, "Establishes positive relationships with others, based on understanding, acceptance and empathy."[30] In this aspect the communitarian conception of citizenship is most evident, especially through the allusion to values articulated in Article Three of the Constitution, which establishes the ethical orientation of all basic education: freedom, equality, justice, democracy, solidarity, love of country, sovereignty, respect for human dignity, and respect for diversity.

As part of these competencies, the learning outcomes that are highlighted include those related to the identification of those capacities common to both girls and boys for engaging in diverse activities, as well as confronting situations that are unjust or in which rights are not respected; and their disposition for assuming responsibility and collaborating on individual and collective tasks, as well as the ability to interact with children with different qualities and interests. Other learning outcomes include the acceptance and application of rules based on equality[31] and respect, and the identification of the diversity of ethnic, linguistic, physical, and gender characteristics— and the importance of the participation of everyone in the life of society.[32]

As can be appreciated from the expected learning outcomes that correspond to the four competencies promoted at this educational level, the personal and interpersonal dimensions constitute the starting point for reflection about the society and the place students have in it. The reference to the context of daily coexistence of students bestows importance on the practice of competencies.

Primary and Secondary Education

In both levels of elementary education, the subject of civic and ethical formation promotes the development of eight civil and ethic competencies whose development is fostered in a gradual manner. Such competencies include: knowledge and care of oneself; self-regulation and the responsible exercise of freedom; respect and appreciation of diversity; sense of belonging to the community, the nation, and humankind; handling and resolution of conflicts; social and political participation; adherence to legality and sense of justice; comprehension and appreciation for democracy. These competencies are developed throughout primary and secondary education and it is through them that the combination of communitarian and libertarian elements are expressed; these, in turn, start in the students' personal sphere and move out toward broader processes in social life, as indicated in the following diagram.

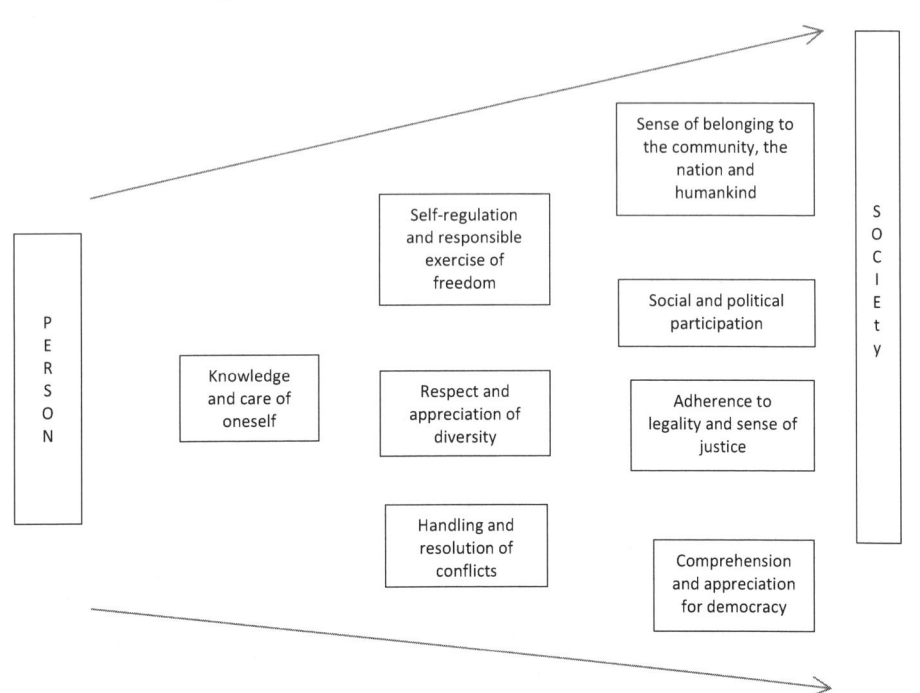

The curriculum of civic and ethical education for both primary and second-ary schools is developed through five units in each grade (See Appendix 1), thereby allowing them to unfold in the established timeframe. In Appendix 1, one can observe that in each grade the curriculum follows a trajectory starting with themes rooted in the students' personal sphere—this is the case for Unit 1 in every grade—in order to move from there to the exercise of freedom and responsibility in Unit 2. Unit 3 takes up the sense of belong-ing to different social groups, cultural diversity, and interculturalism. In Unit 4, themes related to the role of citizenship in a democratic state are addressed, as well as the function of laws in protecting rights and regulat-ing the actions of government. Finally, Unit 5 explores the resolution of conflicts across diverse spheres of social life.

In the case of primary education, besides the work derived from this subject and mainly developed in the *classroom*, other dimensions are con-sidered to promote civic and ethic education:

The *cross-curricular work* is a series of themes in which knowledge is brought together by students across a variety of subjects in order to face sit-uations of social and ethical relevance. Some of the proposed themes are:

- Environmental education for sustainability
- Education for peace and human rights
- Intercultural education

- Gender perspective
- Health education
- Sexual education
- Ethical consumption
- Financial and economic education
- Road safety education
- Transparency and accountability
- Culture for prevention of drugs addictions
- Rational and ethical use of technology[33]

The *school social environment, or climate,* is another dimension concerned with the daily coexistence within the classroom and the diverse school spaces. It is considered that such an environment has an impact in the formation of students through practice and relationships with others, which bear values and attitudes. Among the aspects of the school environment to be considered for civic and ethic formation, the following relate most directly to citizenship education:

- The respect for people's dignity
- Conflict resolution and negotiation of personal and community interests
- Equity and inclusion
- Participation
- The existence of clear and democratically constructed rules

Students' daily life is another dimension for the consideration of coexistence experiences that pupils have beyond the school context, in other groups like the family, the community, friends and other organizations. The aspects that are considered as valuable in this dimension for civic and ethic formation are:

- Care of oneself, identity and personal and family expectations
- Rights and responsibilities at home, in the community and the country
- Respect and value of diversity, participation and conflict resolution
- Understanding of relationships among students, family and mass media

Other components of this proposal are the so-called formative proceedings mechanisms, which consist of central strategies for civil and ethic formation in any of the contexts in which they develop. Dialogue, empathy, decision making, comprehension and critical reflection, development of ethic judgment, work projects and participation remain central to citizenship education. Such mechanisms, while articulated as dispositions to be developed in students, consist of specific learning strategies for civic and ethical.[34]

These mechanisms also suggest the promotion of constant attention to students' experiences in their most immediate everyday contexts of sociability. In this way, the programs suggest the possibility that students will analyze the functions of law in social life and the manner in which they can be justly applied. To achieve this, the programs start in the first years of primary school with the recognition of how norms are applied in everyday life, thereby facilitating the identification of the values and attitudes necessary for respecting such norms and following them as shared agreements.

CHALLENGES AND ACHIEVEMENTS OF THE CITIZENSHIP EDUCATION CURRICULUM

The subjects of citizenship education have notably been transformed with respect to the first proposals raised in the nineteenth century, and that were then also validated throughout the better part of the twentieth century by focusing on the formal knowledge of government institutions and the laws of the country. Through the concept of civic and ethical competencies, the current programs of study advocate a change in the conception of the personal-individual sphere toward a personal-social sphere by means of the practice of ethical reflection. With this practice, bridges are built in which the students can perceive the relationship that the exercise of political power and political participation has with their lives, that is, their needs and interests as children and adolescents.

In this way, the nationalist perspective that lent both content and form to the prior collectivistic emphasis on citizenship has been enriched by a broader vision of civic identity that today no longer gets reduced to an abstract picture of the country. On the contrary, identity now is recognized as being the result of a constant process that may have multiple referents— region, national, all of humanity—and that also surpasses the older notion of *mestizaje* ('mixed race') that had the practical effect of negating the truly pluriethnic and multicultural character of our country.

Additionally, the liberal component of citizenship has been included in new programs for citizenship education by recognizing the rights and liberties of all people, in particular the rights of children. Moreover, such education has been enriched with pedagogical practices that make feasible the possibility for students to develop the capacity to make decisions and deliberate over their ensuing consequences as one way of further developing their own autonomy.

Currently, syllabi offer a wider view of citizenship and citizenship formation in several aspects, as mentioned in the following:

- Consideration of the needs, interests, and conditions of students[35]
- Acknowledgement of multiculturalism and the need to build intercultural relationships to overcome a homogenizing perspective, based on the idea of crossbreeding
- The distinction of citizenship as a formal status and citizenship as a series of competencies, which has allowed children and adolescents to exert diverse attitudes, commitments and citizen knowledge

- The acknowledgement that citizenship is built-up by a series of practices that in order to be developed, requires the constant exertion in spaces where students coexist daily

In several studies of school work that has been generated through current programs of civic and ethic formation, a series of practices can be identified which overcome the work centered on note dictation, memorization of concepts and constitutional precepts, as well as the abstract treatment of formal aspects of civics. Among those practices, the following remain important:

- Incorporation of brief research tasks into the daily work of students, incorporating information derived from the environment in which they live
- The recovery of ideas and experiences of students as illustrative examples, or as analysis of situations in order to contrast them with diverse information
- The elaboration of questions that seek the generation of debate among students, as well as the manifestation of their opinions, due to the fact that those questions admit several answers, while opening the opportunity for students to formulate arguments to which they can apply information of several types
- The approximation of concepts to the experiences of students, as well as their application to formulate explanations about what is taking place in their daily surroundings
- The promotion of actions of social participation to improve the surrounding conditions through tasks that are accessible to all students, as well as the negotiation of proposals through mechanisms of citizenship such as group debates, the taking of polls, the publication of texts that express shared ideas and sentiments, and the writing of petitions directed to particular authorities, all within the context of school and community life, and with the support of educators

These changes in the approach to classroom work around citizenship education, though subtle, represent advances in the conceptions and practices that are starting to be perceived in basic education schools. The classroom practices show significant advances with respect to those identified ten years ago, in various close-ups to the implementation of civic and ethic education. Some of the most frequent difficulties among educators were: their lack of knowledge to take advantage of students experiences as an starting point to confront several aspects of citizenship; the tendency to indoctrinate students with their adult perspective before several points of view submitted by students; the use of formal and abstract explanations that became distant from the reality of pupils.[36]

With respect to the teaching methods that educators must apply in order to achieve the expected learning outcomes, the changes that were required can be perceived as a simple matter of didactic resources and strategies, that is, as a methodological problem. However, it also represents an issue of perspective with respect to citizenship and the path already walked by students in their formation as citizens, even though they do not bear this legal status.

Also, the contents of the current syllabus suggest challenges to school work as a coexistence space, and therefore, to its formative potential. Specifically, aspects related to the school environment identify challenges that question the way in which primary and secondary schools are organized and function to work.

This way, from the syllabus the need is outlined for schools to: offer students participation spaces; apply democratic forms for decision making which pertain to the whole school community; prevailing of full respect to human rights; and that the practice of discipline by adult authority respects students as worthwhile persons.

Notwithstanding, in several approaches to school practices of civil formation, the existing tension is emphasized among a series of organization guidelines that give school an authoritative hue, which is characterized by the following features:

- School management is centered in adult decisions, with scarce margin and opportunities to define and decide collective issues in which students could and should be taken into account.
- Actions that are promoted for the school as a whole, derived from the subject of civic and ethic formation, or from other programs, (as those activities promoted by other institutions, like the ones from the Instituto Federal Electoral (Federal Institute for Elections),[37] are usually confined to the activities of the subject itself and the responsibility for their application is delegated to the educators that teach them.
- Closely related to the prior characteristic, the development of competencies for citizen is not part of the agenda of collegiate encounters of educators. Citizenship education does not constitute a priority either for teachers to generate agreements about the way to act or solve any conflict. Often, educators think about the need to promote values when they deal with disruptive students' behavior, in order to reinforce disciplinary measures..
- The limited use of spaces that are created for student participation such as, the school assembly, the bulletin board and the society of alumni. Such spaces are usually defined in their contents and the way to utilize them by educators, but with a very limited margin for students to express their interests, needs, proposals and opinions within them.
- Due to the fact that the actions and contents which are proposed in the programs of civic and ethic formation are more general, since they invite to the incorporation of particular interests of each school, their realization is usually minimized or simply nullified. Its abandonment is also due to the lack of a prescribed schedule to carry them out.

Due to this final constraint, the written proposal of the syllabus of Citizenship Education runs into a series of breaks and discontinuities that, occasionally, oppose its guiding principles and thereby complicate its concrete application in the classrooms and schools. The aforementioned issue, which is a frequent quality of the relationship between the written programs and school practices, shows the persistence of citizenship education approaches that are still rooted in an abstract coverage of curricular content, thereby eclipsing the possible relationship between such content and students' real lives both in and out of school.

CONCLUSION

This proposal, orientated toward the development of competencies implies for the main users of programs (i.e., the educators) the need to have the availability of administrative and organizational school conditions that allow the display of teaching approaches that are congruent with the pedagogical principles that guide civic and ethic education. Among others, the following needs can be highlighted.

A shared evaluation among educators, principals, and educational assistants in each school, of the sense of citizenship in the integral education of students is needed. The latter suggests the approval of a collegiate discussion to define concrete actions around the aspects of school coexistence that can contribute to citizenship education.

This requires the appropriate functioning of the School Board (Consejo Técnico Escolar), since citizenship education is not only a teachers' responsibility, but it is also a task for all the people who work at schools: principals and supervision personnel.[38] This way, it will be possible to develop common criteria and strategies to propitiate alumni participation, to solve conflicts that arise among them and other members of schools, to establish and modify rules that are related to attributions, rights and responsibilities of those who integrate the school community.

On the other hand, it is necessary to have conditions for teachers to grant the necessary time to the application of activities such as research, team and group discussion, the collaborative work among students and the tasks that are oriented to social participation inside and outside school. These are activities that are frequently undervalued and are usually substituted by note taking of teachers' explanations, questionnaires to be solved with information from textbooks, as well as the answering of written exercises with these materials. These activities imply less time and a lesser action of students inside and outside the school.

Citizenship formation requires appreciation in schools as an opportunity to analyze the dynamics of social life and the school itself. That is why educators have to generate within schools spaces of dialog and formation in which they can test various forms to regulate students' behavior at school and to acknowledge that the adult authority must be exerted from other perspectives.

The school as a whole, as a space of coexistence, far from being a simple extension of citizenship education, requires to be valued as the immediate ground where students can test the knowledge in the lessons of civic and ethic education. The palpable validity of the respect for human rights at schools, the equal treatment, the rejection of discriminatory attitudes and gender equality, constitute conditions that educators and directive personnel need to take care of in order to have students experience their viability and benefits for personal and collective well-being.[39] If the importance of the school environment is not acknowledged in citizenship education, a risk arises that students will consider it as an academic discourse that has no validity with their reality and, in the worst scenario, a simulation game.

The recognition of the role of school administration and organization for the citizenship formation of children and adolescents acquires a greater relevance in light of the results obtained by Mexico in the International Civic and Citizenship Education Study (ICCS 2009), in which the fact that programs by themselves will not ensure an adequate development of citizenship competencies, as the ones evaluated by that research.[40]

Therefore, it is necessary that the Public Ministry of Education provide an impulse to the development of citizenship formation through the environment and school coexistence, by means of guidelines and materials addressed to School Technical Councils. Through these mechanisms, it is mandatory for schools to have the availability of technical and pedagogical capacities in order to take decisions about the measures that must be set out to advance the strengthening of such formation, which is present in the syllabus, but requires collective resonance in the daily school life.

The current citizen syllabus is at risk of becoming simply a formality if students do not set out the civic and ethic competencies outlined in it. The isolated work by some teachers, mainly in secondary schools, limits possibilities for students to experience life at school as a community. Also, daily schedules require a certain degree of flexibility for the development of formative activities that occasionally require a longer time, or the intervention of several educators or school staff.

In this manner, citizenship education needs to be established as a point in the agenda of School Technical Councils, for the importance that formation has in the students' lives and for schools to achieve their educational purposes.

One must always bear in mind that certain practices, values, and attitudes are acknowledged by the syllabus, while others that have current and authentic validity for students are excluded. In citizenship education, the attention to these practices that occur in the daily life of each school is crucial to start out a meaningful formation for the children and adolescents of the twenty-first century, their communicational and socialization experiences overflow any attempts of formalization through the syllabus.

Appendix 1 Syllabus of Civic and Ethic Education for Primary and Secondary Education

Grade	Unit I	Unit II	Unit III	Unit IV	Unit V
PRIMARY EDUCATION					
1°	I know and take care of myself	I express myself, take responsibility, and learn to decide	I know and respect people that surround me	We build rules to coexist and live better	Dialoguing to solve differences and improve our surroundings
2°	Girls and boys that grow and take care of themselves	My responsibilities and limits	We all need from each other	Rules for harmonic coexistence	Building up agreements and solving conflicts
3°	Careful, cautious, and protected girls and boys	I learn to express my emotions, set goals, and fulfill agreements	The care for the environment and appreciation of cultural diversity	Laws that regulate coexistence and protect our rights	We learn to organize ourselves and solve conflicts
4°	Girls and boys that take care of their health and personal integrity	The exercise of my freedom and respect to my own rights and others' rights	Mexico, a diverse and plural country	Mexico, a regulated country by laws	Citizen participation and pacific coexistence
5°	Girls and boy that build their identity and prevent risks	Girls and boys that learn to be free, autonomous, and fair	Girls and boys that work for equity, against discrimination and for the care of the environment	Democratic life and government	Conflict solution without violence and linked to human rights
6°	From childhood to adolescence	Making decisions according to ethical principles for a better future	The challenges of societies now	The pillars of democratic government	Social events that demand citizenship participation
SECONDARY EDUCATION					
2°	Civic and ethics education in social and personal development	Adolescents and their coexistence environments	The civic and ethic dimension of coexistence	Principles and values of democracy	Toward the identification of ethic commitments
3°	The challenges of personal and social development	Thinking, making decisions, and acting for the future	Identity and interculturalism for a democratic citizenship	Participation and democratic citizenship	Toward an informed, committed, and participative citizenship

Source: SEP (2011) *Agreement No. 592.*

NOTES

1. I want to thank Professor Bradley A. Levinson for his valuable comments to this manuscript.
2. INEGI, Population and residence census 2010 (Censo de Población y vivienda 2010):http://cuentame.inegi.org.mx/poblacion/lindigena.aspx?tema=P#uno, (consulted on 14/07/2013). According to the 2010 census, México possesses a population of 112,336,538 inhabitants.
3. Sergio Aguayo, *The tray: A history of the intelligence services in México (La Charola. Una historia de los servicios de inteligencia en México)*, México, Grijalbo; Ramírez, Ramón (1969) *The mexican student movement (El movimiento estudiantil mexicano)*, (México, Era, 2001).
4. Margarita Favela, "Political System and Social Protest: From Authoritarianism to Plurality" ("Sistema político y protesta social: del autoritarismo a la pluralidad"), en Ordorica, Manuel y Jean François Prud'homme (Eds.) *Great Mexican Problems. Abridged Edition. (Los grandes problemas de México. Edición abreviada)*, V. 2, (México, El Colegio de México, 2012) 89–92.
5. Carlos Monsiváis, *Free Admission: A Chronicle Of A Society That Organizes Itself (Entrada libre, crónicas de la sociedad que se organiza)*, México, Era 1987).
6. However, according to Favela, during the PAN federal governments (2000 to 2012), and protected by a discourse of "institutional modernization," the regime not only has reduced social rights by issuing new legal dispositions against pensions and social security, but it has also started out a process of contraction of individual rights, shielded by a discourse against insecurity" (Favela, M. *Op. Cit.*, p. 92.)
7. Even republican France also found itself with the challenge of developing sentiments and faculties tied to the new order. Cfr. Rosanvallon, Pierre, *La consagración del ciudadano. Historia del sufragio universal en Francia [The acknowledgment of citizenship. Universal suffrage in France]*, México, Instituto Mora, 1999.
8. The term "formación" in Spanish is notoriously difficult to translate into English. Similar to the term *bildung* in German, it refers to the broad shaping of human habits, values, and desires. Formación is often used alongside citizenship in Spanish-speaking contexts, in order to indicate that citizenship "education" requires much more than knowledge or skill. Here I will sometimes translate term as "education," when it is used quite similarly to the well-known English phrases "civic or citizenship education," but occasionally I will preserve the broader meaning of the term as "formation."
9. By liberalism I mean a political perspective based on freedom and individual rights as the cornerstone of political action and of the relationship between individuals and the state and its institutions. (Cfr. Puig, Josep María, *Prácticas morales. Una aproximación a la educación moral [Moral Practices. An Approach to Moral Education]*, Buenos Aires, Paidós, 2003.). It's important to note that some aspects of this kind of liberalism were present alongside collectivist nationalism; witness the fact that throughout the nineteenth century the struggle for constitutional reform centered on the fight for religious freedom and the secular state, with the attendant separation of church property from the state, and precisely the Liberal Party played an important role in this. Nonetheless, the exercise of individual rights and freedoms in everyday life remained severely limited, and they were even confounded with "modern" social norms and conventions.

10. Fernando Cortés and Orlandina de Oliveira (Coor.), "Social Inequality: Introduction" ("Desigualdad social. Introducción"), in Ordorica, Manuel y Jean François Prud'homme (Coor.) *Op. cit.*, 19–21.
11. Bradley Levinson citado en Adriana Acevedo and Paula López, *Ciudadanos inesperados. Espacios de formación de la ciudadanía ayer y hoy [Unexpected Citizens. Spaces of Citizenship Formation Yesterday and Today]*, México, El Colegio de México/Cinvestav, 2012, 21.
12. Josefina Vazquez, *Nationalism and education (Nacionalismo y educación)*, (México, El Colegio de México, 1975); Maria Eugenia Luna, "On formation with a national (ist) sense to the citizen of a global village" ("De la formación con sentido nacional (ista) a la ciudadanía de la aldea global"), in Alba et al, *Civic and Ethics education in Basic Education: challenges and possibilities in the context of a globalized society (La Formación Cívica y Ética en la Educación Básica: retos y posibilidades en el contexto de la sociedad globalizada)*, (México, SEP-AFSEDF, 2011), 110–118.
13. Fernando Escalante, *Imaginary Citizens: Memorial of the Efforts and Misfortunes of Virtue and an Apology of the Triumphant Vice in the Mexican Republic: A Treatise of Public Moral (Ciudadanos imaginarios. Memorial de los afanes y desventuras de la virtud y apología del vicio triunfante en la República mexicana: tratado de moral pública)*, (México, El Colegio de México, 1992).
14. Eugenia Roldán, "The nineteenth-century Mexican school as a ceremonial initiation to citizenship: norms, catechisms and public exams" ("La escuela mexicana decimonónica como iniciación ceremonial a la ciudadanía: normas, catecismos y exámenes públicos"), in Acevedo, Ariadna y Paula López (Coor.) *Unexpected citizens. Spaces of citizen formation yesterday and today (Ciudadanos inesperados. Espacios de formación de la ciudadanía ayer y hoy)*, (México, El Colegio de México-CINVESTAV, 2012).
15. *Mexican Simon. Reading Book for Schools*, (*El Simon Mexicano. Libro de lectura para uso de las escuelas*), (Mexico, Antigua Imprenta de Murguia, 1868); L. H.B.V. A. *Civic Instruction for Children (Instrucción cívica para uso de los niños)*, (México Antigua Imprenta de Murguia, 1892).
16. In 1921, the Ministry of Education (Secretaria de Educacion Pública [SEP]) was founded and since then has had in charge the design of a national curriculum for pre-school, primary and secondary education.
17. Maria-Eugenia Luna, "Citizenship Education in the Latin American Region," *34th Annual Pacific Circle Consortium Conference*, Ashland, Oregon, 2010.
18. In 1974, two syllabus plans were established: one of them was organized by subjects and the other was structured in thematic areas. In the latter, the social studies area integrated the subjects of history, geography, and civics.
19. Maria Eugenia Luna, "Citizenship Education in Mexico," in John J. Cogan and David. Grossman, *Creating Socially Responsible Citizens. Cases from the Asia-Pacific Region*, Charlotte, Information Age Publishing, 2012, 136.
20. SEP, *Políticas y fundamentos de la educación intercultural bilingüe en México [Policy and Basis of Intercultural and Bilingual Education in Mexico]*, México, 2007, 40, 41.
21. The program was published as part of the Secondary School Reform, which was of curricular character.
22. As indicated above, it was in the final decade of the twentieth century that the multicultural nature of Mexico was finally recognized; such recognition was tied to the actions of the Zapatista Army of the state of Chiapas, a non-violent indigenous movement which made visible the living conditions of the indigenous people in that region of the country.

23. In Mexico, there is a national syllabus for basic education which provides an elective space in secondary schools, in which educational authorities from each state propose regional contents. Currently, in this space, there exist state programs inscribed in the field of Citizenship Education and the so-called "Culture of Lawfulness." The opening for this state space was introduced in 1993 under the name of Elective Subject.

24. Bradley Levinson and Margaret Sutton, "Civic Education Reform for Democracy. U. S. Models in Mexico and Indonesia, in Doyle Stevick and Bradley Levinson (Eds.) *Advancing Democracy Through Education?*, (North Carolina, Information Age Publishing, 2008).

25. Victoria Camps, *Los valores de la educación* [*Values of education*], Madrid, Anaya, 1996; Carlos Cullen, *Autonomía moral, participación democrática y cuidado del otro* [*Moral Autonomy, Democratic Participation and Care of Others*], Buenos Aires, Novedades Educativas, 2004; Risieri Frondizi, *¿Qué son los valores?* [*What are values?*], México, Fondo de Cultura Económica (Breviarios, 135), 1972; José Fernández, *Filosofía política de la democracia* [*Political Philosophy of Democracy*], México, Fontamara, (Biblioteca de Ética, Filosofía del Derecho y Política, 43), 1997.

26. Bernard Crick, *En defensa de la política* [*In Defence of Politics*], México, Tusquets Editores/IFE, 2001; Monserrat Payá, *Educación en valores para una sociedad abierta y plural. Aproximación conceptual* [*Education in values for an open and plural Society*], Bilbao, Desclée de Brouwer, 2000; Luis Salazar and José Woldenberg, *Principios y valores de la democracia* [*Principles and Values of Democracy*], México, Instituto Federal Electoral, (Cuadernos de Divulgación de la Cultura Democrática, 1), 1997.

27. SEP, *2011 Program. Basic Education (Plan de Estudios 2011. Educación Básica)*, (México, SEP,2011), 58.

28. These fields are language and communication, mathematical reasoning, exploration and knowledge of the world, personal and social development, and artistic expression and appreciation.

29. SEP (2011) *Agreement No, 592*, 46.

30. SEP, Ibid.

31. The kind of equality that is referenced in the programs of study is that which individuals have before the law, as well as their equality in dignity and rights. As mentioned previously, economic equality is a still unresolved matter in Mexican life.

32. Ibid.

33. SEP, *2011 Curriculum programs. A guide for teachers. Basic Education. Secondary. Civic and ethic Education (Programas de estudio 2011. Guía para el maestro. Educación Básica. Secundaria. Formación Cívica y Ética)*, (Mexico, SEP, 2011); SEP, (*2011 Curriculum programs. Guide for teachers. Basic Education. Primary. First grade (Programas de estudio 2011. Guía para el maestro. Educación Básica. Primaria. Primer grado)*, (México, SEP, 2012).

34. There now exists in the Ibero-american context an extensive pedagogical literature which includes strategies whose names are linked to the types of dispositions that are sought to be cultivated amongst students. Cfr.: María Rosa Buxarrais *et al*, *La educación moral en primaria y secundaria*, México, SEP, 1999; Greta Papadimitriou and Sinú Romo, *Capacidades y competencias para la resolución no violenta de conflictos. Educación para la Paz y los Derechos Humanos*, México, MxGraw-Hill, 2005; Josep Puig y Xus Martín, *La educación moral en la escuela. Teoría y práctica*, Barcelona, EDEBE.

35. Lilian Alvarez and Maria Eugenia Luna, "Civic education in the transition to the new century" ("La educación cívica en la transición al nuevo siglo"), in

Democracy and Civic Education (Democracia y educación cívica), (México, Electoral Institute of Distrito Federal, 2007), 59–84.

36. Luna, M. E. ("Mexican secondary schools: conditions and possibilities for the development of citizenship culture." Paper presented at the XXV Annual Conference of the Pacific Circle Consortium, Christchurch, 2001)

37. This program consists on the realization of surveys among students, within primary and secondary schools, about the conditions in which they live their rights and the situations that impair their respect and fulfillment.

38. SEP *Guidelines for organization and functioning of School Councils (Lineamientos para la organización y el funcionamiento de los Consejos Técnicos Escolares)*, (México, SEP, 2013), 11. The school councils are composed of teachers and key administrative personnel in each school. Such councils make both pedagogical and administrative decisions about what activities will be conducted throughout the school year.

39. Levinson, We Are All Equal: *Students Culture an Identity at a Mexican Secondary School, 1888–1998* (Durham, NC, Duke University Press, 2001).

40. W. Schulz, J. Ainley, J. Fraillon, D. Kerr, B. Losito, *ICCS 2009 International Report: Civic knowledge, attitudes, and engagement among lower-secondary school students in 38 countries*, (Amsterdam, IEA, 2010).

12 Tertiary Education and Critical Citizenship

Peter Roberts

INTRODUCTION

What role can tertiary education play in fostering critical citizenship?[1] This chapter considers this question in relation to the New Zealand context. I begin with a brief history of tertiary education in New Zealand from 1984 to 2008, before turning to more recent policy developments. I argue that neoliberal ideas have exerted a strong influence over directions taken in the tertiary sector, with an emphasis on performance, accountability, relevance, and economic advancement. Knowledge has been treated as a commodity and competition within and between tertiary education institutions has been encouraged. In the final part of the chapter I problematize these trends, arguing that they rest on an unhelpfully narrow view of citizenship, and offer an alternative way of thinking about the nature and purposes of tertiary education. I stress the importance of ontological, epistemological, ethical, and political questions in preparing students to become not merely consumers and competitors in a global economic market but critical participants in democratic life.[2]

NEOLIBERALISM AND TERTIARY EDUCATION REFORM IN NEW ZEALAND, 1984–2008

To understand contemporary tertiary education policy, it is helpful to have some sense of where we have travelled over the years. The path New Zealand has taken is similar to the one followed by many other countries in the Western world: over much of the last quarter of a century, under both Labour and National governments, New Zealanders have witnessed the progressive application of neoliberal principles in the tertiary education sector.[3] There is no *one* neoliberalism; rather, what we have seen is variations on a theme, with a mix of ideas applied in different ways at different times. Mark Olssen observes that neoliberalism as it evolved in the New Zealand context blended aspects of monetarism, Human Capital Theory, Public Choice Theory, Agency Theory, and Transaction Cost

Economics.[4] The monetarist element drew its inspiration from the political and economic liberalism of Milton Friedman and Frederich Hayek. Friedman argued for a "quantity theory of money," with the control of inflation as a central strategy in securing a stable economy.[5] This economic approach was complemented by Hayek's identification of political factors (e.g., the influence of trade unions, cumbersome bureaucracies, unnecessary government interference) as impediments to the free operation of markets. Human Capital Theory, promoted in its modern form by figures such Theodore Schultz, E.F. Denison and Gary Becker, reasserted a pivotal role for education as a driver of economic growth. The human capital of a nation is "the sum of skills, talents and knowledge embodied in its population," and education is one contributing factor to this (other influences include nutrition, medical care and job training).[6] Human Capital Theorists distinguish between private rates of return and social rates of return. Under neoliberalism, the emphasis in considering the role of education is on the former; education is seen as private good rather than a public good. It is assumed that individuals who invest in education will enhance their cognitive capacity, thereby increasing their productivity and their earnings.[7] Education is also seen as means for building a competitive edge through innovation, change, and the application of technology. The neoliberal application of Human Capital Theory promotes the ideal of perfect competition in a free market, without government subsidies, as the basis for an efficient and effective education system.[8]

Public Choice Theory, as promulgated by James Buchanan in particular, contests the assumption that the public good is best served by government and its agencies. Politicians and bureaucrats, it is argued, tend to serve their own interests, neglecting the rights of consumers; in so doing, they make a mockery of the notion a public good. The answer, public choice theorists suggest, is to focus on the individual and his or her wants and choices. Unlike Hayek, Buchanan did not believe in the spontaneous ordering of markets through a process of social evolution; this, he felt, could lead to social chaos. Instead, he saw a place for both a "protective" state (law and defense) and a "productive" state. The positive arm of the productive state, Olssen notes, "effectively extracts compliance from individuals in order to engineer a market order."[9] Agency Theory proceeds from a construction of work relations as a hierarchical series of contracts between "principals" and "agents" linked by chains of authority and command. Thus, "a single person will be principal to those further down the chain of command and agent to those further up."[10] The process of ensuring that the agent acts in accordance with the wishes of the principal is based not a "broad job description" with notions such as responsibility and professional autonomy at its heart; rather, the focus is on the contractual fulfillment of managerial demands, with clear lines of accountability, for which the agent receives a specific reward or sanction depending on his or her performance. As principals will not always be in a position to observe the behavior of agents, systems for monitoring, motivating and assessing performance need to be in place.[11] Transaction Cost Economics is closely linked to Public Choice Theory and Agency Theory. It "seeks to analyse and account for the efficiency costs of transacting business and the effect these have on organisational form."[12] Transaction Cost Economists evaluate different institutional arrangements and governance structures with a view to finding the most efficient method for facilitating transactions in a given market context.[13]

With these theoretical points in mind, what can be said about the practice of neoliberal reform in New Zealand? Politically, the starting point was the election of the fourth Labour government in 1984. After years of former Prime Minister Muldoon's interventionism, Roger Douglas, Minister of Finance in Labour's 1984–1987 term, was eager to make changes in quantum leaps, at great speed, not allowing interest groups to mobilize.[14] Reform did not come quickly enough for Douglas (who was removed from his Finance portfolio by Prime Minister Lange shortly after Labour was re-elected) but over time, industries were deregulated, tariffs and subsidies were reduced or removed, state assets were partially or fully privatized, and managerialist practices were implemented in public institutions.

When National returned to power in 1990, attention turned to the social portfolios of education, health and welfare. Cuts were made to benefits, market rates were introduced for state housing tenants, and hospitals became Crown Health Enterprises. A number of tasks that previously had been undertaken by public servants were contracted out, and there was an expressed commitment (even if this often did not eventuate in practice) to the idea of leaner, more efficient bureaucratic structures. For an increasing range of services that had hitherto been government funded, the principle of "user pays" now applied. "Enterprise" and "entrepreneurialism" became buzzwords not just within the commercial domain but across the social sector. There was much talk also of the need for institutions to establish, assess and meet "performance indicators," and to extract ever greater efficiencies from systems and employees, if proper accountability for the use of public money was to be assured.[15]

From the mid-1990s onward, tertiary education was expected to operate along market lines. "Choice" and "competition" became the foundation stones on which policy was built. Students were recast as "consumers" and institutions became "providers." Underlying this approach was the ontological construct *homo economicus*: the rational, autonomous, utility-maximizing, interest-serving individual.[16] The model of the market was employed in depicting the ideal social and economic context for individual decision making and behavior. In tandem with this, knowledge came to be seen as a commodity, to be traded in the same way as any other good or service in a marketized world. As David Harvey observes, "[t]o presume that markets and market signals can best determine all allocative decisions is to presume that everything can in principle be treated as a commodity. Commodification presumes the existence of property rights over processes, things, and social relations, that a price can be put on them, and that they can be traded subject to legal contract."[17] The market, conceived in this light, becomes "an appropriate guide—an ethic—for all human action."[18] Consistent with these market-based principles, gaining a degree or any other tertiary qualification came to be seen principally as a form of private benefit, and students were required to pay a growing portion of the costs associated with their education. The preferred systems of governance within universities became those consistent with a "Board of Directors" model from the world of business. Under the student loans scheme, debt grew rapidly. Incentives for the further growth of private tertiary education were put in place. The total number of tertiary education institutions and organizations increased dramatically and there was a proliferation of new qualifications.[19]

When the Labour-Alliance coalition government was formed in 1999, some of the excesses of the "more market" era of the 1990s were reduced. The mantra of "choice, choice, and more choice" was no longer recited, a more prominent role for government in steering the system was asserted, and greater recognition was given to the distinctive experiences and aspirations of Māori and Pacific students. Influenced by Tony Blair's "Third Way" policy program in Britain, a new central motif emerged: the role of tertiary education in promoting New Zealand's development as a "knowledge society and economy." In some respects, however, key aspects of the neoliberal agenda of the 1990s became more entrenched through the Labour-led years of 1999–2008. While some attempts were made by government to foster collaboration between researchers (e.g., with the Centres of Research Excellence), other developments—notably, the emergence of a Performance-Based Research Fund (PBRF)—intensified the ethos of competition within and between institutions. The PBRF, along with the rise of export education, has pushed the commodification of knowledge in new directions. The logic of performativity continued to prevail, with seemingly endless forms to complete, assessments to be made, and targets to be met. Throughout the first decade of the new century, universities and other tertiary institutions have marketed themselves aggressively, seeking to distinguish their "brand" from offerings elsewhere.

The notion of adapting almost everything we do to adhere to the rules of the market was central to the 1990s reforms but was pursued less dogmatically in the Labour-led years of 1999–2008. Nonetheless, "Third Way" politics, both in the UK and in New Zealand, represented less an abandonment of neoliberalism than a reconfiguration of it. The Third Way was intended to be neither dogmatic "Old Left" socialism nor rampant New Right capitalism. As Anthony Giddens, Tony Blair's "guru", envisaged it, the Third Way was not merely a compromise between these two positions—a kind of pragmatic mid-point—but a genuine alternative in social and economic thinking.[20] It would acknowledge the reality of globalization in its myriad dimensions—economic, technological, political, and cultural—while also paying serious attention to the need for social inclusiveness, cohesiveness and fairness. Education, technology and creativity would have key roles to play, with knowledge as the component central to all three. Yet, in practice, the market, by this stage very much a crucible for competition between multinational companies mediated by national policy initiatives, came to dominate over social goals. The Third Way, as a number of critical policy analysts have argued, was neoliberalism with a "softer face."[21] In the New Zealand context, it did not take long to realize that the "society" element of the "knowledge society and economy" ideal was very much secondary to the economic imperatives associated with new forms of information capitalism, new means of communication, new systems of exchange.[22] Tertiary education remained harnessed to the broader goal of advancing New Zealand's standing in a competitive, sophisticated, technologically advanced world.

How, then, have we fared in the post-2008 years? As the next section shows, during this more recent period there has been a strengthening of neoliberal resolve on the part of the New Zealand government. I shall argue that what we now have is an excessively narrow conception of tertiary education, premised upon a correspondingly restrictive view of contemporary citizenship. Tertiary education, as portrayed in the New Zealand government's current *Tertiary Education Strategy*, is intended to prepare people who will create and value wealth, meet the demands of employers, and minimize wastage on "irrelevant" activities. Such citizens will seek continuous increases in performance and, consistent with the principle of accountability, will expect to be monitored and assessed on a regular basis. Against this, I shall propose an alternative: tertiary education for critical citizenship. This approach places the human being, rather than the economy, at the center of our tertiary education endeavors; it values the arts and humanities for their role in allowing us to address ontological, epistemological, ethical, and political questions of longstanding significance; it emphasizes trust and responsibility over monitoring and accountability; and, it upholds the importance of critique, questioning, and the active investigation of alternatives. Tertiary education for critical citizenship does not merely accept a neoliberal, globalized world for what it is; it does not allow us to remain altogether comfortable in the assumptions and beliefs that govern our lives. This approach acknowledges that tertiary education may unsettle and disturb us, changing forever the way we view ourselves, others and the world.

RELEVANCE, PERFORMANCE AND ECONOMIC ADVANCEMENT: CONTEMPORARY TERTIARY EDUCATION POLICY

The current New Zealand government's vision for tertiary education is set out in the *Tertiary Education Strategy 2010–15*.[23] It is for "a world-leading education system that equips all New Zealanders with the knowledge, skills and values to be successful citizens in the 21st century." Such a system is "an important first step toward a productive and growing economy that delivers greater prosperity, security and opportunity for all New Zealanders."[24] The government wants tertiary education to be "relevant" and "efficient," with "high quality" qualifications that meet the needs of students, their families and the economy.[25] The expectation is that the tertiary system will:

- Provide New Zealanders of all backgrounds with opportunities to gain world-class skills and knowledge
- Raise the skills and knowledge of the current and future workforce to meet labor market demand and social needs
- Produce high-quality research to build on New Zealand's knowledge base, respond to the needs of the economy and address environmental and social challenges
- Enable Māori to enjoy education success as Māori[26]

With the global economic downturn, government income has been reduced while welfare costs and demand for tertiary education have increased. To make best use of public funds under these circumstances, the government will target priority groups, seek improvements in the performance of the tertiary education system, and strengthen the contribution research makes to innovation and economic productivity.[27] Tertiary institutions will have to do more with fewer resources, develop other revenue streams, and become more responsive to the demands of students, employers, and industry.[28] The government intends to meet its goals by:

- Increasing the number of young people (aged under 25) achieving qualifications at levels four and above, particularly degrees
- Increasing the number of Māori students enjoying success at higher levels
- Increasing the number of Pasifika students achieving at higher levels
- Increasing the number of young people moving successfully from school into tertiary education
- Improving literacy, language, and numeracy and skills outcomes from levels one to three study
- Improving the educational and financial performance of providers
- Strengthening research outcomes[29]

If the performance of the sector is to improve it will be necessary to:

- Enhance quality assurance
- Provide better incentives for providers to respond to students and market signals, by:
    - Making provider-level performance information publicly available
    - Linking funding more closely to performance

- Support and encourage student performance
- Strengthen collaboration and shared resources for greater efficiency
- Continue to build international linkages[30]

"Performance" will be a fundamental principle across the tertiary sector: "To encourage efficient and high-quality provision, high performing providers will attract more resources, particularly through performance-linked funding."[31]

According to the *Strategy*, the government is adopting a long-term view of its investment in research. It is noted that under the Performance-Based Research Fund (PBRF), improvements in the quality of research and number of research degree completions have been made.[32] The *Strategy* points out, further, that good teaching should be informed by research, in both "academic" and "applied" settings: "This enables the development of human, social and cultural capital, as tertiary education institutions play a key role in spreading knowledge and in transferring technology through teaching."[33] Research is also crucial in stimulating innovation and driving economic growth. It not only builds New Zealand's knowledge base but also allows that knowledge to be taken up for commercial use and applied in addressing social and environmental problems. In a constrained funding environment, however, the government needs to ensure that public money invested in research provides a good economic return. Tertiary institutions will "need to work more closely with business to ensure that research meets the needs of the economy."[34] Indeed, the government expects "the entire sector to supply skills that are relevant to the labor market. Tertiary providers need to make better connections with industry and ensure they are aware of the likely demand for skills."[35] Research in universities should combine "excellence with impact."[36]

BEYOND THE ECONOMY? TERTIARY EDUCATION AND CRITICAL CITIZENSHIP

What are we to make of the language and substance of a document such as New Zealand's *Tertiary Education Strategy*? The short answer is that under the current government, the neoliberal thread that had linked most major initiatives in tertiary education in the preceding two decades has remained unbroken. But there is a longer, more complicated answer as well, with wider international significance for citizenship education. It has to do with the way we talk about ourselves, govern ourselves, organize our institutions, conceive of the educational process, and, ultimately, understand ourselves as human beings. Policy does not determine practice in precise detail but it does set parameters within which decisions can be made and actions taken. So, what are those parameters? The emphasis, more than ever, is very much on the economic dimensions of tertiary education. This is so in several senses. First, the costs of funding a public tertiary education are stressed, and these are, as the *Strategy* suggests, significant. In its *Briefing to the Incoming Minister* in December 2011, the Tertiary Education Commission (TEC) notes that it allocates some $2.8 billion in funding each year to more than 800 tertiary education organizations. Nearly half of this funding goes to universities.[37] Second, the wider context for tertiary education reform is conceived principally in economic terms. The global economic downturn is cited as a reason for tightening up on funding and expecting more to be achieved with less. Third, and most importantly for present purposes, the primary goals for, and benefits of, tertiary education are seen as economic in nature. Tertiary education, we are told, should lead to greater productivity, innovation in the workplace, and higher export returns. It is also regarded as a means for improving social mobility, the development of workplace skills and knowledge, and personal prosperity. If the tertiary education system is succeeding, we will, it is hoped, become progressively more competitive on the world economic stage, and not only enhance our standing among OECD nations (on league tables of economic performance) but make our mark more broadly as a small, "smart," entrepreneurial, forward-thinking country punching above its weight internationally.

The views expressed in the *Strategy* have been reinforced by subsequent government statements and by the decisions made and actions taken by ministers and officials. In articulating its vision for the sector at the end of 2011, the Tertiary Education Commission noted as its first and main claim that "tertiary education is a key contributor to our economic future." Realizing this vision, the Commission added, "will require ambition and stronger steering."[38] The government appears to have needed little convincing on this point. The steering has been firm and clear, as exemplified by a recent statement from the Minister responsible for tertiary education, Steven Joyce, who called for the University of Auckland to increase the number of engineering students. "If they want us to be more directive, I'm more than willing," Mr Joyce said: "I'm watching them really closely to make sure they do respond to what the market wants, and if they don't, I can go and tell them how many they should enrol for each department."[39] The reference to making tertiary education more "relevant," a key theme in the last *Tertiary Education Strategy* produced under Labour, remains to the fore for National—but now some of the ambiguity associated with that term has been removed: institutions will be made, by direct or indirect means, in both their teaching and research, to fit in with the needs or demands of industry, work more closely with businesses, exploit more fully the commercial potential of the knowledge they produce, and minimize wastage on "irrelevant" programs.

The implied view of citizenship here is excessively narrow. Citizens are constructed as self-interested individuals in a world driven by the logic of production and consumption. It is taken as given that economic prosperity will be a primary goal, perhaps *the* primary goal, for all New Zealanders.

Tertiary education is seen as a means for preparing people to perform effectively in a competitive global market, and the areas of research and teaching deemed most important are those geared toward the demands of employers. The process of economic globalization is seen as inevitable, and the question of whether capitalism should be favored over other modes of production is never even put on the table. Protests against, for example, world trade discussions are tolerated provided they can be dismissed as the actions of an extremist few. Similarly, citizens are not prevented from raising concerns about the environmental impact of new developments, as long as this does not disrupt the overall process of relentless global capitalist expansion. Indeed, such concerns can be turned to good economic effect, with the economic discourse of "sustainability" often serving as a profitable standpoint from which to pitch new ventures and industries, especially when appealing to overseas buyers and tourists. Citizens are expected to conform to this model of the world, not because they are forced to do so but because it is portrayed as the only rational, realistic way forward for the country.

The emphasis on economic imperatives is now so marked that policy makers and politicians appear to run out of words when trying to say anything else meaningful about tertiary education. In the *Strategy*, comments on the wider benefits of tertiary education are largely confined to one section of an Appendix on "Context and Trends." There it is noted:

> An effective tertiary education system will underpin New Zealand's ability to prosper economically and build a strong society into the future. The skills and knowledge people gain through tertiary education improve their chances of employment and increase their earnings. Higher education levels have been linked to better general well-being, better health and greater social mobility. Tertiary-educated people are more involved in the community and are more likely to vote and stand for public office.[40]

Even here, there is a rapid return to the main agenda. This section goes on to stress the significance of tertiary education in supplying skilled labor for a productive economy, generating ideas that lead to new products and services, and facilitating infrastructure improvements. By building New Zealand's skills base, the *Strategy* continues, tertiary education enhances production volumes and efficiencies, raises our gross domestic product, and enables us to compete more effectively on the international economic stage. The tertiary education system also "links New Zealand to the outside world, both through the exchange of knowledge and skills, and through the flow of students."[41] Tertiary education provides direct economic gains through the employment of staff, and students have a significant impact on the life of communities in which they are based.[42] International students generate substantial export earnings.[43] The remaining benefits of tertiary education are captured within a few sentences:

Tertiary education plays a vital role in democracy by promoting freedom of thought and expression. New Zealand's culture is enriched through tertiary education's role in theatre, dance, music, literature and art. Tertiary education helps to transmit the wider culture, including ähuatanga Mäori and tikanga Mäori, within society and between generations. It can serve to raise the consciousness of the population about the environment.[44]

Few of us would disagree with the sentiments expressed here. The point is, however, that with so little said about the social and cultural value of tertiary education, the words become nothing more than rhetoric, and marginalized rhetoric at that. It is as if the whole process of tertiary education has become *dehumanized* in a quite specific sense. For the statements that carry weight in the official discourse on tertiary education, it is scarcely necessary to refer to human beings at all. As long as the system *performs*, the particulars of human thinking, feeling and willing, of relationships and contexts, become largely irrelevant. It might be overstating the case to say that we have simply become fodder for an economic machine, but there are certainly some features of tertiary education life that have a machine-like quality to them. Under the PBRF, for example, almost every aspect of research has been reconceived in terms of the language of "outputs." The Tertiary Education Commission has pushed the case for performance-based funding not only in relation to research but more broadly, noting that such models have gained currency internationally as a way of responding to both funding constraints and growing student "consumerism."[45] Funding, the Commission suggests, can be tied in part to course and qualification completions and can target key "momentum" points such as first-year retention. The Commission also raises the idea of "compacts" between government and large tertiary education organizations: long-term agreements that support "high-level strategic initiatives, in tandem with more mechanistic funding of 'throughput' at an individual student level."[46]

The approach to citizenship suggested by these developments has some disturbing implications. Tertiary education becomes a means for evaluating and processing people in an efficient, systematic, standardized manner. Both tertiary education students and academic staff become part of this relentless production process. As participants in the tertiary system, both students and staff learn to accept certain forms of monitoring and assessment as part of their very reason for being. We learn that for something to count, it must be measurable, forgetting that much of what makes tertiary education most valuable, most significant in transforming human lives, is immeasurable. The obsession with monitoring and measurement within the tertiary sector is replicated more broadly in New Zealand society, with ever more intrusive surveillance of citizens. As this chapter is being written, legislation that will allow the Government Communications Security Bureau (GCSB) to spy on New Zealand citizens and pass on information to international agencies is being advanced through parliament. The concerns raised by New Zealanders about these changes mirror the deep sense of unease felt by many people elsewhere in the world following revelations of possible monitoring by the U.S. government of web-based activities across the globe. As citizens, we have increasingly been encouraged to not merely tolerate such intrusions but embrace them—as necessary steps to ensure our security in a terror-ridden world.[47]

The phenomenon of heightened surveillance (and its acceptance) as a condition of citizenship is closely related to the culture of distrust that underpins neoliberal reform. Under neoliberalism, the language of accountability replaces the notion of responsibility. Regimes of accountability tend to be more formal, more hierarchical, and more linear than relationships of responsibility. Accountability is often tightly linked with regular, systematized assessments of performance, where those who fall short can be disciplined and/or required to undergo professional development. Accountability is often compliance-driven; responsibility is more a matter of morality. The development of a strong sense of responsibility, I wish to argue, is a key feature of critical citizenship. Critical citizenship relies on an prevailing ethos of trust, where participants in any democratic social sphere, whether this is within a university or within a country, are granted considerable autonomy to get on with their jobs and are expected to do them well. With trust comes responsibility but this must be more than externally generated. A sense of responsibility comes from within; it is a quality we uphold when no one is looking. In a tertiary education environment, it works in conjunction with academic freedom: the right to address any scholarly question or problem, and to advance views or adopt perspectives that may be controversial, without fear of interference or suppression by others in positions of power within or beyond one's institution. Responsibility in tertiary education is also evident in the long hours academics commit to the job, the integrity demonstrated in the use of scholarly sources (including proper acknowledgement of others' work), and the commitment shown to professional and community groups outside one's institution. Accountability is imposed on us; responsibility arises from a sense of inner conviction and commitment.[48]

Tertiary education for critical citizenship also places a premium on questioning, critique, and the active exploration of alternatives. The notion of critique has largely disappeared from policy discourses on tertiary education in the neoliberal age, not only within New Zealand but internationally. Where references are made at all to being "critical," the language and assumptions are typically those associated with the "critical thinking" movement. Critical thinking is seen as a skills-based activity. Critique has an overt *political* dimension. It is not merely the ability to analyze texts or delineate key premises in an argument, important though those abilities are; it also implies a willingness to problematize the status quo, question authority, and place ideas in their broader social, cultural, and historical contexts. Of course, the apparent "neutrality" of critical thinking as depicted in prevailing policy discourses is anything but; often it is tied in with rhetoric about the need for creativity and innovation—not for their own sake but for economic advancement. Critique need not mean simply finding fault with the way the world is; it can also involve the constructive task of pondering and building *better* worlds.[49] Creativity has an important role to play in that process as well, but the forms of creative thought needed in taking the possibility of better worlds seriously do not simply appear as if by magic; they require time and appropriate educational conditions to develop. The current New Zealand government is prioritizing the young in its tertiary education policy. Over recent years, funding for informal adult and community education initiatives has been cut, despite continuing rhetoric about the importance of lifelong learning. Those who are under 25 now in New Zealand have known nothing other than neoliberalism as the ideology underpinning everyday social and economic life. It is hardly surprising, then, that when possibilities for alternative forms of social organization are raised in university classrooms, academics are sometimes met with perplexed stares or expressions of polite disinterest.

That said, if we look a little further afield, there are some signs that neoliberalism is lessening its hold over the hearts and minds of the young. The Occupy movements that started in places such as Wall Street in the United States and subsequently swept around the world provide grounds for legitimate hope that the forms of subtle control so essential to neoliberalism will not be guaranteed safe passage. The deep social divisions created by global neoliberal capitalism have spawned a new sense of shared responsibility in many quarters, including pockets of the academy. University students are among those who, as Henry Giroux puts it, "tell us that the social visions embedded in casino capitalism and deeply authoritarian regimes have lost their ability to normalize their values as well as their power to intimidate and silence through threats, coercion, and state violence."[50] Many of these students recognize that they have come to be seen as disposable servants of late capitalist economies. They have built up huge debts seeking the gains promised to them by higher education and they have been let down. They see the hypocrisy in politicians making cuts to public spending, while providing tax breaks for the wealthy few.[51] These young people, protesters of today, are in some cases the professors of the future.

Universities have an important ongoing role to play in examining these movements, setting them in their broader historical and political contexts, and showing how they are connected to other struggles against greed and the commodification of everyday life. Researchers cannot remain neutral in the face of this push for change. "Why," Giroux asks, "do so many academics cling to a notion of disinterested and objective scholarship and publish and make a claim to pedagogy that allegedly decries any relationship to politics, power or interest in larger social issues?"[52] The answer, he says, is that "for all intents and purposes, too many academics who make a claim to objectivity, and, in some cases, reject the presence of the military-industrial-academic complex on campus, have become irrelevant to offering any viable defense of the university as a democratic public sphere, or, for that matter, even defending to a broader public the very conditions that make their work possible."[53] Giroux's concern here, as I interpret it, is not so much with particular individuals and their refusal to examine the politics of their own academic decisions or actions; rather, it is with the prevalence of such avowed neutrality as a widespread phenomenon at the very time when such a stance seems most absurd. That the university is a political institution has never been more obvious, with commercial interests playing a more dominant and intrusive role in determining what forms of teaching and research are supported than ever before; yet, at precisely this moment, the tendency to retreat to the safe haven of scientific or scholarly "objectivity" is making a resurgence. Robust debate of these questions often fails to materialize in exactly those contexts where it is most needed. This is not to say that academics set out to deliberately undermine the democratic and critical ideals the university is meant to uphold; it is more a matter of such questions not being raised. Giroux wants us, at the very least, to *listen* to what is being said by those involved in resistance movements. He would acknowledge, I think, that there is more than one way to take a principled political stance as an academic. Getting involved may mean marching on the streets or occupying a public space in protest, but a contribution can also be made through critical teaching, "risky" research, and a willingness to enter into dialogue with those positioned as "Others" in neoliberal times.

If we take the idea of tertiary education for critical citizenship seriously, economic considerations do not disappear. A key role of tertiary education *is* the preparation of people for employment, and those seeking to enter the workforce must be realistic in assessing economic impediments and opportunities. An understanding of the economics of education is imperative in any robust, well rounded account of schooling and tertiary systems. It must also be recognized that finances are always limited; difficult decisions need to be made in determining what is to be taught, by whom, and for whom. Every country, if it is to serve its citizens well, must at the very least provide the basic material resources necessary for survival. But an economic perspective is not enough on its own. Martha Nussbaum notes that a narrow focus on economic growth not only has the effect of marginalizing and devaluing the arts and humanities; it also does not deliver the gains it promises in health and education. Healthy democracies, she maintains, need people who are critical and imaginative, who care for others and value diversity, and who can place local problems in broader perspective.[54] In tertiary education for critical citizenship, economic concerns are seen as intimately intertwined with other questions of a metaphysical, ontological, epistemological, ethical, and political kind: What does it mean to be a human being? What is the nature of reality? What is "knowledge" and how do we come to know? What ought we to do? (How should we live? How should we structure our society?) What are the impediments to the realization of our ideals? These questions need not ever be uttered in exactly the form indicated here, but they can nevertheless inform everything else we do in tertiary education institutions.[55] Answers to all of them are provided, tacitly, by neoliberals, but if our aim is critical citizenship those answers will be placed into active, rigorous conversation with other perspectives, other modes of life.[56]

The approach supported here places human beings, not economic growth, at the center of tertiary education. It rests on the assumption that tertiary education should make us uncomfortable; it should trouble us, shake us from our slumbers, leaving us feeling a little "on edge." Thus conceived, tertiary education poses inherent risks, not just in an economic sense, as the New Zealand government makes clear, but in existential terms. With the development of a reflective, critical consciousness comes the possibility of not just discomfort but *despair*.[57] In committing to tertiary education for critical citizenship, we acknowledge that there is no "going back"—no way of returning to our previous ways of understanding ourselves and the world. Tertiary education seen in this light makes us, as Paulo Freire would put it, a little less certain of our certainties, but no less committed for that.[58] Knowledge becomes not a commodity to be traded on world markets but something we strive to pursue in seeking to more deeply understand the human condition, the problems we face, and the possibilities open to us. Through this kind of critical tertiary education, we come to not merely tolerate immeasurability but celebrate it. We move from the logic of relentless, machine-like production to the far more complicated, less precise, more unpredictable processes of contemplation, participation, and creation. The arts and humanities become essential parts of a well-rounded tertiary education system, not trifling extras to be supported only after priority has been given to the STEM subject domains of science, technology, engineering, and mathematics.

CONCLUSION

For more than two decades, tertiary education in New Zealand has been dominated by neoliberal ideas, the logic of performativity, and the overriding goal of economic advancement. In this chapter, I have suggested that it need not be this way. There are alternative ways of understanding ourselves and the world we live in, and active consideration of such alternatives is an important part of tertiary education for critical citizenship. Making the case for a broader approach to tertiary education does not make it so, and those committed to this must be prepared to settle in for the long haul. Opening up new ways of thinking about the nature and purpose of tertiary education is a process of struggle—both externally and internally. Rubbing against the grain in our teaching and research, in meetings, and in our engagement with government policy tests our resolve and can leave us feeling exhausted. But part of the shift I am arguing for here is a move away from competitive individualism to more a collegial, cooperative approach in tertiary education. Solidarity with others, based not on blind allegiance but a spirit of intellectual friendship, provides sustenance for our own ongoing development as critical citizens.

NOTES

1. In New Zealand, the term "tertiary education" refers to all post-schooling education and includes universities, polytechnics, *wananga* (indigenous higher education institutions), adult and community education, and industry training organizations. It is now uncommon for key New Zealand policy documents to distinguish between "higher education" and "further education."
2. For a wide-ranging collection of essays on globalization, neoliberalism, and citizenship in a single volume, see Michael A. Peters, Alan Britton, and Harry Blee (eds.), *Global Citizenship Education: Philosophy, Theory and Pedagogy* (Rotterdam: Sense Publishers, 2008).
3. The closest equivalent political parties internationally are Labour and the Conservatives in Britain. In both Britain and New Zealand, traditional distinctions between "progressive" and "conservative" or "left" and "right" parties have become blurred over recent decades. In New Zealand, Labour is sometimes portrayed as center-left and National as center-right, but these labels too can be contested. Overall, there has been a much stronger movement toward the center-right than the center-left.
4. Mark Olssen, *The Neo-liberal Appropriation of Tertiary Education Policy in New Zealand: Accountability, Research and Academic Freedom* (Palmerston North: New Zealand Association for Research in Education, 2001). See also David Harvey, *A Brief History of Neoliberalism* (Oxford: Oxford University Press, 2005).
5. Ibid., 8.
6. Ibid., 10.
7. Ibid., 10–11.
8. Ibid., 12.
9. Ibid., 16.
10. Ibid., 16.
11. Ibid., 16–17.
12. Ibid., 18.
13. Ibid., 18.
14. Roger Douglas, *Unfinished Business* (Auckland: Random House, 1993).
15. For a critique of related developments in the United States, see Henry A. Giroux, "Neoliberalism, Corporate Culture, and the Promise of Higher Education: The University as a Democratic Public Sphere," *Harvard Educational Review* 72, no. 4 (2002): 424–463.
16. Michael Peters and James Marshall, *Individualism and Community: Education and Social Policy in the Postmodern Condition* (London: Falmer, 1997).
17. Harvey, *A Brief History of Neoliberalism*, 165.
18. Ibid., 165.
19. See further, Michael Peters and Peter Roberts, *University Futures and the Politics of Reform in New Zealand* (Palmerston North: Dunmore Press, 1999).
20. Anthony Giddens, *The Third Way and Its Critics* (Cambridge: Polity Press, 2000).

21. John Codd, "The Third Way for Tertiary Education Policy: TEAC and Beyond," *New Zealand Annual Review of Education* 10 (2001): 31–57; Peter Roberts and Michael A. Peters, *Neoliberalism, Higher Education and Research* (Rotterdam: Sense Publishers, 2008).
22. Roberts and Peters, *Neoliberalism, Higher Education and Research.*
23. Ministry of Education, *Tertiary Education Strategy, 2010–15* (Wellington: Ministry of Education, Office of the Minister for Tertiary Education, 2009).
24. Ministry of Education, *Tertiary Education Strategy*, 6.
25. Ministry of Education, *Tertiary Education Strategy*, 6, 13.
26. Ibid., 6.
27. Ibid., 10.
28. Ibid., 10, 13, 18.
29. Ibid., 10.
30. Ibid., 14.
31. Ibid., 18.
32. Ibid., 16.
33. Ibid., 7.
34. Ibid., 7.
35. Ibid., 18.
36. Ibid., 16.
37. Tertiary Education Commission, *Briefing to the Incoming Minister* (Wellington: Tertiary Education Commission, December 2011): 47.
38. Ibid., 1, 3.
39. Simon Collins, "Skills crisis: Minister's threat to uni on funding," *New Zealand Herald*, 19 November 2012.
40. Ministry of Education, *Tertiary Education Strategy*, 24.
41. Ibid., 24.
42. Ibid., 24.
43. Ibid., 24, 25.
44. Ibid., 24.
45. Tertiary Education Commission, *Briefing to the Incoming Minister*, 9.
46. Ibid., 9.
47. On the resurgence of new discourses on patriotism and citizenship in a post-9/11 educational world, see the various essays in Bruce Haynes (ed.) *Patriotism and Citizenship Education* (Oxford: Wiley-Blackwell, 2009).
48. For a range of perspectives on discourses of accountability, see Ming Ching, "Accountability and Professionalism: A Contradiction in Terms?" *Higher Education Research and Development* 31, no. 6 (2012): 785–795; Barbara Romzek, "Dynamics of Public Sector Accountability in an Era of Reform," *International Review of Administrative Sciences* 66, no. 1 (2000): 21–44; Martin Trow, "Trust, Markets and Accountability in Higher Education: A Comparative Perspective," *Higher Education Policy* 9, no. 4 (1996): 309–324; Jeroen Huisman and Jan Currie, "Accountability in Higher Education: Bridge Over Troubled Water?" *Higher Education* 48 (2004): 529–551; Lesley Vidovich and Roger Slee, "Bringing Universities to Account? Exploring Some Global and Local Policy Tensions," *Journal of Education Policy* 16, no. 5 (2001): 431–453; Andreas Hoecht, "Quality Assurance in UK Higher Education: Issues of Trust, Control, Professional Autonomy and Accountability," *Higher Education* 51 (2006): 541–563; Tatiana Suspitsyna, "Accountability in American Education as a Rhetoric and a Technology of Governmentality," *Journal of Education Policy* 25, no. 5 (2010): 567–586; William M. Zumeta, "What Does it Mean to be Accountable? Dimensions and Implications of Higher Education's Public Accountability," *The Review of Higher Education* 35, no. 1 (2011): 131–148.

49. Peter Roberts and John Freeman-Moir, *Better Worlds: Education, Art, and Utopia* (Lanham, MD: Lexington Books, 2013).

50. Henry A. Giroux, "Beyond the Limits of Neoliberal Higher Education: Global Youth Resistance and the American/British Divide," article posted by the Campaign for the Public University, November 7, 2011: 12. (Online: http://publicuniversity.org.uk/2011/11/07/beyond-the-limits-of-neoliberal-higher-education-global-youth-resistance-and-the-americanbritish-divide/).

51. Henry A. Giroux, "Why Faculty Should Join Occupy Movement Protesters on College Campuses," *Truthout*, 19 December (2011): 1–2. (Online: http://www.truth-out.org/why-faculty-should-join-occupy-movement-protesters-college-campuses/1324328832)

52. Giroux, "Why Faculty Should Join Occupy Movement Protesters on College Campuses," 3.

53. Ibid., 3.

54. Martha Nussbaum, *Not for Profit: Why Democracy Needs the Humanities* (Princeton: Princeton University Press, 2010).

55. An interesting comparison here is with the work of Veugelers, who distinguishes between open, moral and social-political global citizenship. Wiel Veugelers, "The Moral and the Political in Global Citizenship: Appreciating Differences in Education," *Globalisation, Societies and Education* 9, nos. 3–4 (2011): 473–485.

56. On the need to consider alternative ontological and epistemological traditions when addressing the question of global citizenship, see Karen Pashby, "Cultivating Global Citizens: Planting New Seeds or Pruning the Perennials? Looking for the Citizen-Subject in Global Citizenship Education Theory," *Globalisation, Societies and Education* 9, nos. 3–4 (2011): 427–442.

57. Some of the thinkers who demonstrate a connection between reflective consciousness and despair include Søren Kierkegaard, *The Sickness Unto Death*, trans. A. Hannay (London: Penguin, 1989); Fyodor Dostoevsky, *Notes from Underground*, trans. R. Pevear and L. Volokhonsky (New York: Everyman's Library, 2004); Arthur Schopenhauer, *The World as Will and Representation*, vol. 1, trans. E.F. Payne (New York: Dover, 1969); Miguel de Unamuno, *The Tragic Sense of Life in Men and Nations*, trans. A. Kerrigan (Princeton, NJ: Princeton University Press, 1972); and Simone Weil, *Gravity and Grace*, trans. A. Wills (Lincoln: Bison Books, 1997). See also Peter Roberts, "Happiness, Despair and Education," *Studies in Philosophy and Education* 32 (2013); Peter Roberts, "Education, Faith, and Despair: Wrestling with Kierkegaard," *Philosophy of Education Yearbook 2013* (Urbana, IL: Philosophy of Education Society, 2014).

58. Paulo Freire, *Pedagogy of the Heart* (New York: Continuum, 1997); Paulo Freire, *Pedagogy of Freedom* (Lanham, MD: Rowman & Littlefield, 1998); Paulo Freire, *Teachers as Cultural Workers: Letters to Those Who Dare Teach* (Boulder, CO: Westview Press, 1998).

Epilogue
Reading Citizenship Education in Neoliberal Times

Aaron M. Kuntz and John E. Petrovic

INTRODUCTION

In their recent interrogation of scholarship on citizenship education, Nicoll et al.[1] point out that practices of citizenship are ubiquitous—always already enacted—even if they go unrealized or unrecognized by citizens and researchers alike. Further, the ever-present practices of citizenship take on myriad and protean forms: "citizenship is not universal or unified; it is discursive, heterogeneous, dynamic, fragmented and historically changeable."[2] And yet, citizenship practices do not spontaneously appear out of nowhere—they draw meaning and articulation from an equally vast array of "dynamic, fragmented and historically changeable" events and policies that extend simultaneously from local and global contexts (and everywhere in-between). Indeed, it is the pervasive, fluid development of citizenship that requires critical examination at simultaneously local and global levels—keeping a critical eye on how the immediate context intermingles with larger social processes that persist regardless of national boundaries.

In this way, space and time intersect, as historical developments imprint on localized contexts making possible an array of citizenship practices, some recognized as legitimate, others not. Take, for example, the unique circumstances of Hong Kong (outlined in Chapter 2) in which the transfer of sovereignty from Britain to China initiated an entirely new series of citizenship practices even as others were cast as superfluous to the production of the legitimate citizen. Similarly, South Africa's emergence from apartheid (contextualized in Chapter 9) made possible new considerations for "safe speech" within educational and governmental institutions. And, of course, both circumstances require critical engagement in order to reveal the underlying epistemological and ontological assumptions that govern newly emergent practices of citizenship or assertions of what is (un)safe speech. Equally important are the more micro, daily events that collude towards new understandings and practices of citizenship. Indeed, newly emergent conceptions and enactments of citizenry are revealed in the dynamic interplay of localized practices and larger discursive formations; our critical interrogation of citizenship generally, and citizenship education more specifically, must remain attuned to the interconnection of daily practices, policy formation, and more globalized assumptions concerning what we know and how we come to know.[3]

Such historical circumstances are not easily contained by national borders, however. Consequently, critical examination of citizenship education within any locale must remain attuned to contemporary international assertions of globalization, especially the globalization of a neoliberal ethos, with their own concomitant assertions of values and assumptions regarding legitimate acts and practices of citizenship. As the chapters in this volume detail, formal declarations of citizenship education (what it is, how it should be taught, who should be the object of its enactment) make possible an array of citizenship practices, identities, and values that occur in both formal and informal spaces. Importantly, however, each chapter also observes how formal declarations can and have occluded other possibilities. Indeed, sometimes this is the intent, as Gross[4] points out in her discussion of apolitical approaches in Israel (and as we pointed to in the Prologue's presentation of the Texas curricular battles).

Given this, it was important that each of the previous chapters make sense of citizenship education through specific analyses of historical policies, tracing the imprint of their implementation on educational practices in specific locales along with the respective sociocultural values and assumptions that undergird such practices and allow them to "make sense." In this way, citizenship education, in its multiple and varied forms, is shown in all its discursive materiality—extending from historical claims regarding what it means to be a citizen, the purposes of education, and the material realities of enacting both citizenship and education. This is perhaps best seen in Kanako Ide's example of Amerasians in Okinawa, Japan. Here, Amerasians extend from an historical legacy of World War II that produced children of Japanese mothers and American solders. Amerasians thus call in to question key cultural assumptions about what it means to be a citizen both locally (within Okinawa as well as the larger nation of Japan) and more globally (born of parents from two distinct cultural settings, yet residing within the auspices of one national boundary). Consequently, the material presence of Amerasians within Japan disrupts the assumption that Japan is a homogenous society, bound by a common history and ancestry.

As a means for understanding and expanding upon the international forms of citizenship education presented in this volume, we begin from the production of the neoliberal citizen within a context of globalization, a contextual background informing all of the previous chapters. We read this particularly material and discursive formation through an interpretation of citizenship education as an emerging curriculum expressing particular theories of interest and experience. Through this critical reading, the specter of "the citizen" takes on unique shape, informed by the uniquely dynamic intersection of local practices and global discourses. Further, the interrogation of the citizen generally, and citizenship education more specifically, affords the possibility for developing strategies to counter regressive educational practices that have become normalized in an international array of contexts. Through productive critique new change is possible.

Though certainly each of the chapters in this volume details locally unique historical contexts that contribute to contemporary formations of citizenship education within their respective locales, they also offer a window into an overlapping array of issues and themes that exceed the geographical and historical contexts of the nation-state. These overlapping themes extend from a unique series of provocative questions—first articulated in the this book's Prologue—that are meant to open up discussion regarding what it means to be a citizen, how acts of citizenry are conceived and articulated, the implications for education within the neoliberal order, and the inherent tensions involved in striving to achieve a degree of patriotism even as one participates in international formations of globalization. As the chapter authors in this volume demonstrate, citizenship education thus serves as a useful entry point into key cultural questions and anxieties that have endured for centuries.

Further—and perhaps more importantly—each chapter offers a uniquely critical means for engaging with the specter of citizenship education; chapters present particular philosophical frames through which to interpret and act within seemingly fixed and stable discourses of what it means to be a citizen on local and global scales. Therefore, in this concluding chapter, we want to engage with both the thematic content of the previous writings and the means by which the authors articulate and analyze such content. The former provides a window to the values and principles that assert themselves globally even as they emerge from local contexts. The latter is important given that critical engagement with citizenship education is always already political; both what we know and how we come to know matter.

WHY CITIZENSHIP EDUCATION MATTERS

In many ways, citizenship education (in all its local and international formations) offers an assumptive view of the world that reveals otherwise hidden ideological formations of what it means to be a recognized, legitimate, and productive human within select sociohistorical contexts. As these assumptions are integrated into curricular structures within the educational system as well as more informal practices of citizenship without, they govern particular ways of acting and knowing. In this sense, articulations of citizenship education are alike in form to Henry Giroux's recognition of the role of theory: "theory does more than structure one's selection of the facts that shape one's world. Theory also plays a vital role in reproducing a reality that includes tacit common sense assumptions about what society and history are all about." [5] As detailed in all of the chapters in this volume, citizenship education remains a vital battleground for claims regarding whose "common sense" matters and how we are to connect (or not) within local, national, and international contexts.

As such, the chapters in this volume might be understood as engaging in theoretical analyses aligned with Peter McLaren's notion of *theories of interest* and *experience*, respectively. [6] As McLaren notes, it remains important for productive social critique to consider both "theories of interest" and "theories of experience" when interrogating curricular systems and pedagogical practices. "Theories of interest" extend from questions regarding whose interest specific curricula serve. In this sense, knowledge (for our purposes those ways of knowing and coming to know that inform citizenship education) extends from and works to legitimize particular worldviews and remains inherent in the production of common sense. Specific to the chapters in this volume, authors may be seen to critically engage with theories of interest as they extend from local sociohistorical contexts. Whose interests, for example, does "safe language" serve in South Africa? Or, whose interests does the subordination of citizenship education to civics education, as explicated by Martinez and Prats, serve?

Citizenship curricula the world over seems intent on developing neoliberal citizens capable of remaining competitive within the globalized world order. Whose interests are served, then, through the commodification of knowledge, the production of citizenship education as a "thing" every legitimate citizen must encounter and, ultimately, own? Marx' conceptualization of reification as "thingification" is a useful way to consider this. In thingifying, the object of analysis is taken ahistorically, ripped from sociohistorical context as simply being or having been from nowhere. If, for example, you ask someone from the U.S. or England to define, say, "third world," you are likely to elicit a static description of poverty, backwardness, a failure to adequately compete on the world stage, and a general sense of lack. Ignoring the ethnocentrism entailed in such descriptions, what is assumed is that a "third world" simply exists as an objective marker absent any conception of how it was brought into being as a historically produced category, mainly through economic, cultural, and physical terrorism. Thingification of the third world, then, simply leads to fix-it, patriarchal approaches to dealing with third world concerns which, in typical neoliberal fashion, do more harm than good given that neoliberalism serves the interests of the most economically dominant nations. Thus to "fix" the "third world," this neoliberal rationality assumes, means to confect an environment that foregrounds economic values of efficiency, production, and discreet individuals regardless of local contexts and history. [7] In short, this "thing," the "third world," connotes a problem in need of attention by the "first world" which, given its dominant status, holds the solution to "third world" problems.

What, then, occurs when select processes such as citizenship education become reified? Might conceiving of citizenship education as a "thing" make possible a type of "vulgar patriotism" in which citizens are given static forms of information meant to produce unity through state-based indoctrination? Although not all of the chapters in this volume explicitly invoke neoliberalism in globalization, together they offer insights into how neoliberalism manifests in different contexts and, thus, inform critical analyses of citizenship education. Further, the authors of the preceding chapters push theories of interest to consider whose interests might be productively included in alternative formations of citizenship education as, for example, a series of practices and engagements in critical thinking and the imaginative possibility for a more progressive society.

Alongside analyses that foreground theories of interest, McLaren posits the necessity of developing "theories of experience" that recognize the impact of curricular formations on how students understand their experiences in the world. As McLaren writes, "curriculum implies a picture of how to live" and "is deeply implicated in the production and organization of student experiences within historically produced social forms."[8] In this sense, it remains important to consider the types of experiences students have in formal and informal educational contexts as they encounter citizenship education. How are students pedagogically encouraged to understand their experiences in particular ways, according to particular formations of citizenship and citizenship education? How do contemporary curricular formations encourage power-laden interpretations of the world in which we live? One might ask, for example, how experiences of a professed apolitical education shape students' ideals and actions of citizenship (see the example of Israel as explicated by Gross). Or, as Mejía offers from the case of Colombia, in what ways does standardized assessment shape the citizenship curriculum and how does this inform pedagogy? In other words, assessment is, itself, a form of experience. Our argument is that the chapters in this volume must all be read through a neoliberal frame, the dominant discourse of our times, that informs citizenship practices generally and conceptions of citizenship education more specifically. Though some chapters overtly name and describe neoliberal processes in their descriptions of local sociohistorical practices and processes, others allude to the governing values and assumptions of neoliberalism without invoking the term directly. As such, processes of globalization, dominated by a neoliberal ethos, inform and accelerate the implementation and acceptance of neoliberal values, assumptions, and assertions of "common sense." Given this contemporary reality, it perhaps makes good sense to revisit three overarching questions first offered within our Prologue, paying special attention to the normative claims of the neoliberal context.

In the Prologue, we noted that, when read together, the chapters address a series of complex, dynamic questions that extend from deeply held philosophical assumptions regarding education. To begin, we asked, "What is the good or productive citizen?" Simply stated, in neoliberal terms the productive citizen is one who remains economically viable, contributing to an expanding economy, and whose work helps the nation-state keep abreast or accelerate economically within the incessant processes of globalization. This citizen draws identity from his/her occupation—the very means with which s/he contributes to the economy and engages in processes of consumption. Even in communist-ruled China, the new socialist citizenship is driven by the market, as noted by Zhu and Camicia. As an even more specific example, we again note the discussion of standardized assessment in Mejía's chapter. Standardization reflects neoliberal notions of accountability such that the potential productivity of individuals can be measured.

Our second question draws from the assumptions of the first: "How should citizenship education be conceptualized?" In this sense, the production of citizenship education extends from assumptions regarding what a productive citizen looks like; policies governing citizenship education gain commonsensical traction from beliefs regarding the "legitimate citizen." In many ways, citizenship education is asserted within the neoliberal context as a means to erase *negative* difference in the name of national unity (Cf. the chapters on Japan and Canada) while, at the same time, asserting one's individuality as the freedom to engage in the economic market as a consumer as just noted. In this sense, citizenship education has come to play a pivotal role in making absent cultural histories that might challenge hegemonic norms and distract the citizenry from a fixation on becoming productive players on the economic market. Consider the example of the United States, in which Heybach and Sheffield explicate the erasure of the Trail of Tears against the immensity of a shared cultural history invoked by the looming force of Mount Rushmore. Here, the slaughter of Native Americans on behalf of an imperialistic nation is made absent in favor of an educational discourse surrounding "bold" visions of citizenship extending from the mythos of American Exceptionalism.[9]

Lastly, we asked in the Prologue, how does the local sociopolitical context affect conceptualizations of the good citizen and citizenship education? Importantly, neoliberal values and assumptions pervade local contexts and exacerbate extant challenges to implementing robust articulations of citizenship. For example, we might read the dysfunctionality that Waghid and Davids document in South Africa, as exacerbated by neoliberal policy approaches. Specifically, the assumed greater autonomy of schools via SGBs increases local inequalities between resource-rich and under-resourced schools as differences between parent expertise, technological opportunities, etc. are laid bare. We might couch the policy of increased autonomy in South Africa in increasingly individualistic and competitive terms such that schools must vie for increasingly scarce resources. Heybach and Sheffield raise a similar concern in their discussion of Race to the Top and other policy initiatives in the United States. Given these circumstances, the culture of the school is such that citizenship education necessarily reflects that sociohistorical context—the experience that students receive is imbued in competition, accountability, and measurable academic productivity. To change this, Waghid and Davids defend the notion of hostipitality, which reclaims in productive ways student resistance.

In other words, what this example demonstrates is that there remains the possibility that some acts of citizenship (such as hostipitality) remain unrecognized, extending as they do from rationales that are not neoliberal. These are citizenship practices that occur outside economically determined claims of "common sense." In order for such practices to inform our beliefs for who a citizen is and what a citizen does, we must imagine alternative possibilities governed by alternative rationalities.

THE PURPOSES OF EDUCATION IN NEOLIBERAL TIMES

In this volume's Prologue we presented four broad purposes of education: *economic, social, political,* and *intellectual.* The analysis of these purposes might usefully frame a critical interrogation into the questions just offered. The governing values of neoliberalism lay claim to legitimated formations of these purposes. *Economically,* the purpose of education has taken a decided turn towards legitimated identity formations based on individual earning power and symbols of accumulation. Here, the individual stands in proxy for the larger nation-state—individual accumulation and economic prosperity exist as patriotic symbols of achievement. Similarly, within our contemporary context the *social* purposes of education seem to extend from assimilationist desires to display national unity outwards towards the international community while depicting simplistic formations of diversity and/or multiculturalism. In this sense, the neoliberal frame promotes diversity (increasing the number of underrepresented groups in educational systems, for example) but does so in the interest of creating a larger and more economically productive workforce. As a consequence, diversity is over-simplified and represented as, perhaps, percentages of different ethnic backgrounds in select schools, and with the overarching goal of assimilating all students into the neoliberal ideals and values that have come to dominate curricula the world over. This is diversity in the name of economic interests.

Given these *economic* and *social* purposes of education, what then does it mean to be a *political* citizen and how might educational systems encourage particular formations of political subjectivities even as they constrain others? Again, given the neoliberal context, political formations of education remain driven by economic values and priorities. Thus, to engage politically is actually, a la Gross, to be apolitical and, instead, to, once again, engage in an economic politicality that reaffirms the individual as both a producer and a consumer. In contrast, the contributors to this volume all conceive of political citizenry as a distinct challenge to and intervention within this status quo. Educating for political citizenry, then, would necessarily mean developing the critical thinking skills and dispositions that allow learners to reflect on contemporary contexts leading to the imagination of possibilities for a more socially just future. This speaks to the intellectual purposes of education.

What *intellectual* purposes of education have taken shape in our contemporary contexts? Critically, the intellectual purposes of education actively work against wholly technocratic ideals of education-as-procedure with predictive outcomes and prescribed pedagogical techniques. And yet, as noted by Michael Apple, current educational values have given rise to a type of new managerialism that emphasizes the ability to employ predetermined procedures and techniques in order to maintain capitalist systems. [10] As a consequence, one might claim that the only way to maintain current vestiges of democracy is to sustain or perpetuate the managerial middle class and highlight their necessary (and limited) activities within educational systems.[11] This, we argue, is a bastardized formation of the intellectual purpose of education, as it requires sedentary and passive acceptance of procedurized, static content, with little opportunity for engagement and change.

Importantly, each and every chapter in this volume refuses the normalized and legitimated purposes of education just outlined. In this way, the authors seek renewed claims for what education is and what it can (and should) do in relation to citizenship. Through examining the historical production of present-day citizenship education in local and international contexts, the authors offer pointed interventions into the production of the citizen through their critique of existing educational systems and practices. Taking a cue from Nicoll et al.'s call for "opening discourses of citizenship education to the possibility of other ways of thinking,"[12] chapter authors point to the possibility for thinking and acting otherwise. This is engaged political critique aimed at creating the possibility for both new acts of citizenship and the recognition of those citizenship practices that are already enacted but not always recognized by students, teachers, administrators, and scholars alike.

Thus it is that in order to counter starkly neoliberal educational policies in New Zealand, Roberts advocates for a critical citizenship built on a sense of shared responsibility, critique, and the active examination of alternatives to the status quo. This is citizenship education that productively foregrounds the intellectual and political purposes of education from a critical perspective. Similarly, Martinez and Prats argue that the sociohistorical context of Spain necessitates education for citizenship as the explicit exploration of the possibilities inherent in radical democracy. This is citizenship education as both examining and, perhaps more importantly, *enacting* radical democratic practices. Likewise, the example of England posits the need to create an educational infrastructure that makes possible democratic environments both within formal institutions of education and without.

As a means to recalibrate the very meaning of citizenship, Gross advocates for a reconceptualization of citizenship education in Israel that shifts from technical and procedural discussions of rights to human identities. Perhaps read as an example of this move towards reconceiving of human identity, Waghid and Davids offer a South African conception of citizenship education as *Ubuntu*, with an emphasis on one's interconnectedness to a larger group and the determination to promote positive social transformation through disrupting normative sensibilities through an allegiance to provocative care.

These chapters point to the possibilities inherent in understanding citizenship and citizenship education differently, according to newly productive rationalities and assumptions not dependent on the neoliberal model. Within each lies a contextually specific answer to the question of why citizenship education matters, and each informs a global ideal. As a consequence, it makes good sense to consider the consequences (for good and for ill) of how we understand citizenship and the ways in which such understandings lead to particular practices and select dispositions.

BEYOND COMMODIFICATION: RETHINKING CITIZENSHIP AND CITIZENSHIP EDUCATION

In order to intervene within neoliberal formations of citizenship education one must engage in productive critique—interrogating the present system as one's analyses offer the possibility for thinking, acting, and being otherwise. Inherent in the chapters throughout this book is the authors' refusal to understand citizenship as a product or commodity—a "thing" that one possesses or gives to another. Citizenship-as-commodity develops alongside deficit models of education; the assumption that education exists as a means to overcome what students inherently lack. Unfortunately, the "thingification" of knowledge in education remains commonplace in our contemporary times (one need only look to the incessant production of standards-based education to witness the procedurization of knowledge-as-thing in educational systems the world over). As Nicoll et al. note, all-too-often politicians and educators alike situate citizenship education as addressing "the problem of not enough citizenship."[13] The "problem of not enough" situates learners as always already in deficit and teachers as in the role of overcoming inherently deficient students, filling knowledge-gaps with identifiable and fixed educational points.

This particular formation of deficit thinking, though certainly commonplace, is striking in relation to citizenship education. For, what does it mean to gain more knowledge and become *more* of a citizen? Might becoming more of a citizen simply mean increasing one's legitimacy within the eyes of the state and/or the international community? Conversely, what does it mean to lack citizenship, educationally speaking? More than the necessary papers to prove one's position as a citizen, the preceding chapters offer citizenship education as a means to overcome a series of contemporary anxieties and concerns regarding diversity, national unity, and construction of an economically productive workforce capable of maintaining pace with the speed of globalization. Thus, to be deficient within the realm of citizenship perhaps means to lack the skills and dispositions to contribute to the international economic market all the while maintaining a fidelity to the more localized nation-state. Of course, such a push-pull relation between micro-level cultural values and more macro-oriented assumptions of neoliberalism is not without its own challenges and contradictions. In this scenario, then, citizenship education might be read as national and/ or state attempts to negotiate such tensions—to normalize strategies for overcoming the possible contradictions of responding to local and global contexts and values simultaneously. "Deficit" here might be understood as lacking economically productive skills and sensibilities as well as the necessary cultural/national allegiances and knowledges that collude to maintain a static national identity, one that is always already "imagined."[14] In this way, the citizen becomes a measurable, divisible, and differentially valued commodity constructed through a similarly produced and thingified notion of citizenship education; deficit thinking makes commodities of us all.

Further, the rationale that undergirds the deficit model emphasizes individual accountability and removes the possibility of more collective responsibility from the equation; more structural issues of power are not held accountable or even raised as a possible place for critique within the deficit model. After all, if one is deficient in a particular area, s/he simply needs to participate in those activities that remove the deficit. Individual students are thus responsible for their own deficits even as individual teachers are held accountable for "fixing" the inherent lack in their students' citizenship knowledge. Thus, deficit-level thinking extends from the same values and rationalities that govern the neoliberal frame. In this sense, citizenship education is aimed at those subjects who are "not enough" citizens, who have simply not encountered "enough" citizenship education. Education exists as a means to "make-up" for a citizenship deficit.

Equally important, the deficit model overlaps with neoliberal values of economic production, there remains a significant number of every population that will never be "enough" of a citizen—these are the elderly, the disabled, the incarcerated, and others whose material realities preclude them from engaging in work activities that would otherwise label them "productive citizens." Add to these those whose social circumstances keep them out of the workforce, constituting what Karl Marx deemed the "reserve army of the unemployed"[15]—individuals cast outside the workforce until the market expands and their (often-remedial) labor is needed once more.[16] Such examples point once again to citizenship as a series of sociohistorical processes constructed of an overlapping array of contexts that are simultaneously local and global in origin.

What then becomes of citizenship education if understood beyond the confines of deficit thinking? Further, what becomes of the citizen? These are the questions imaginatively addressed in the latter portions of each preceding chapter as their respective authors point to the possibility of enacting citizenship education—and, ultimately, citizenry—in newly productive ways. This is citizenship education as possibility; as intervention into the incessant (re)production of the neoliberal order in our globalized times whether through hostipitality or a reconceptualization of civics to citizenship, or interculturalism, or cosmopolitanism.

Nicoll et al. note two contemporary issues inherent in scholarship on citizenship education: situating students as lacking citizenship and therefore outside the local community and a failure to conceive of and engage with the "discursive and material support for citizenship activity."[17] They raise these concerns with the assumption that scholars have perhaps missed those citizenship activities that exist beyond the deficit model assumed by the former even as they maintain an overly narrow and individualistic focus on context that excludes the latter. As a means to avoid the trap of turning a blind eye to the productive possibilities inherent in all social circumstance, we turn next to the overlapping contexts that both make possible the neoliberal, deficit-based formation of citizenship education and, importantly, the possibility for existing otherwise.

IN WHAT CONTEXTS?

As the chapters throughout this volume note, citizenship education operates within particular contexts of globalization and neoliberalism. These contexts offer and encourage particular subject formations—of teachers, students, citizens, etc.—even as they foreground particular formations of knowledge.

In response, the authors in this volume understand citizenship education and the citizen itself as a practice, a less-than-stable series of subjectivities and activities. Kisby's examination of citizenship education in England asserts citizenship "as an activity, rather than a status." Further, Martinez' and Prats' overview of citizenship education in Spain calls for a reconstituted notion of citizenship that resists the static, closed offerings of neoliberalism. In its place, Martinez and Prats call for the recognition of citizenship as a "notion which is open and under construction." In such formations, the citizen, and the knowledges that mark citizenship, are not easily defined, contained, or measured. In this sense, citizenship might be seen to operate against the educational movement of our times. As a consequence, citizenship and citizenship education takes on a particularly critical political role for intervening in educational discourse at local and global levels, with skills that are not easily quantifiable, tracked, or tested. This is citizenship education as a disruptive force, a series of practices that productively challenge the assumptive values and logics of our contemporary times.

As all of the chapters articulate, citizenship education develops within particular contemporary contexts, particularly that of neoliberalism. What, then, is the neoliberal citizen and how does it operate within local and global contexts? To begin, the neoliberal citizen is measurable—its qualities are accounted for by multiple procedures and institutions. More specifically, the neoliberal citizen is shown in New Zealand policy documents, as Roberts shows, as self-interested and driven by logics of production and consumption. These dispositions receive their commonsensical traction through the assertion of neoliberalism as enabling the progressive forma- tion of the country given contemporary contexts of globalization. Thus, in order to allow New Zealand to compete on the world stage, the citizen must evolve as an independent, rational, individual who draws value from his/her relation to the market.

In concert with the neoliberal citizen is the globalized context that both enables and extends the specter of the neoliberal citizen. As processes of globalization collapse the boundaries between nations and cultures, neo- liberal values and assumptions extend to a normative logic unbound by traditional geographic barriers. Globalization thus speeds up the produc- tion of neoliberal citizenry. Within the context of England, for example, globalization is articulated as "increased interconnectedness and interde- pendence of individuals and societies across the world affecting economic, social, cultural, environmental, security and political matters and aspects of life."[18] More than simply connections across national borders, the con- text of globalization serves as a backdrop upon which neoliberal policies and procedures regarding citizenship are built. As noted in the chapter on England, the overarching acceptance of globalization as a commonsensical reality leads to the justification for implementing neoliberal policies across social institutions. In this way, globalization provides the context in which neoliberal rationalities might emerge and thrive.

Given this contemporary context of globalization, it makes good sense to revisit the initial claims we made in the Prologue regarding the inter-re- lationship of the nation-state and international community via the citizen. Is the nation-state still usefully claimed as conceptually prior to a more global society? Or, might the specter of the globalized, neoliberal citizen overwhelm the easy distinction between nation-states and more global society? This is not to say that the boundaries of the nation-state have dis- solved or have otherwise been rendered absent. Instead, it perhaps points to the ease with which national identities are subsumed by more globally oriented assertions of economic production and values. That is, as the globalized context continues, neoliberal rationalities become increasingly commonsensical, regardless of the geographical boundaries of nation or state. Perhaps this makes space for the globalized nation-state—an entity bound within the entanglement of the globalized context and neoliberal rationale. Thus, though cultural customs and traditions may remain dis- tinct, they continue to be read according to like values of individualism, economic rationality, and market-based accountability. These overarch- ing assertions of neoliberal values as the square upon which all acts of citizenry are understood and interpreted have created a series of contem- porary anxieties that both plague the modern nation-state and, often, drive the momentum for changes within formal and informal manifesta- tions of citizenship education.

CONCLUSION: FACING ANXIETIES

As nations seek to maintain or advance their standing within this global-ized, neoliberal context, specific anxieties emerge concerning their ability to keep up or remain apace this hyper-individualized context. As the chap-ters in this volume attest, citizenship education becomes an institutional mechanism to counter specific concerns regarding the ability to develop economically productive citizens on the "world stage." Thus citizenship education emerges through the production of the citizen against or as a response to particular uncertainties. Most often, these anxieties seem to extend from the often-contradictory notion of maintaining an inward-looking patriotism and outward-moving positioning within the global (eco-nomic) order.

In this juxtaposition, citizenship education most often seems to be employed as a means for increased and more definitive social cohesion (often expressed as the production, articulation, and maintenance of patriotism or patriotic ideals) and as a consequent strategy to overcome the "problem" of diversity which is assumed to negatively impact citizens' ability to be productive. At times, these tensions perhaps result in the formation of social contradictions, as seen in the example of China. Nationalism within the Chinese context was to express both strong patriotism and allegiance to the ruling party. Cosmopolitanism, or the allegiance to an internationally defined humanity, disrupts nationalistic rhetoric within the globalized world order. So, the cos-mopolitanism required of the context of globalization encounters a history of nationalism that often is assumed and remains unquestioned.

It might thus prove useful to consider the "problem" that citizenship education is invoked and/or employed to counter—what is citizenship edu-cation meant to fix? As a consequence, critical interrogations of citizenship education as it develops in local and more global contexts, reveals much about the assumptions regarding what it means to be an active and produc-tive citizen in our contemporary context.

Importantly, a key element for engaging with the formation and enact-ment of citizenship via citizenship education is sustained interrogation of the intersection of local practices and more macro-level global discourses. In this way, critical examination of citizenship and citizenship education reveals multiple tensions and anxieties inherent in contemporary forma-tions of the nation-state as well as the anxieties and concerns that lead to the production and regulation of citizenship and educational activities. Broadly, citizenship education can be read as responding to anxieties that extend from the assumed values of neoliberalism and the imagined momen-tum of globalization. These broad anxieties uniquely develop within select local contexts.

Given the articulated tension between local patriotism and more global anxieties regarding economic competition, it remains important to develop analyses that similarly link local contexts with more macro discourses—something emphasized in each of the chapters in this volume. In the end, alternative practices of citizenship are there. Perhaps they go unrecognized or perhaps they are otherwise rendered illegitimate, but they exist. As an assumptive frame, neoliberalism cannot reconcile all acts; daily practices of citizenship extend beyond the bounds of governing rationalities. Therefore, a conceptualization of global citizenship cannot be global, it must emanate by taking account of local contexts, histories, etc. that inform citizenship education to develop citizens who can read through dominant discourses, neoliberal or otherwise with the aim of instigating progressive social change.

NOTES

1. Nicoll, K., Fejes, A., Olson, M., Dahlstedt, M., and Biesta, G., "Opening Discourses of Citizenship Education: A Theorization with Foucault," *Journal of Education Policy*. 2013.
2. Ibid., p. 12.
3. In the sense that the chapters within this volume are educative, they may well be examples of enacting the *intellectual* purposes of education, originally explicated in the Prologue to this volume.
4. All authorial references made without citation stem from chapters within this volume.
5. Henry Giroux, *Teachers as Intellectuals: Toward a Critical Pedagogy of Learning*, Bergin Publishers, Wesport, CT, 1988, 47.
6. Peter McLaren, *Critical Pedagogy and Predatory Culture: Oppositional Politics in a Postmodern Era*, Routledge, New York, 1995.
7. The lending practices of the International Monetary Fund (IMF) are a good example of this as countries are given large-scale loans to allow them to better manage economically even as these same loans come with specific punitive measures aimed to bring economically behind nations more in-line with neoliberal economic norms. For a critique of IMF lending practices and other "world" organizations driven by "first world" interests see Richard Peet, *Unholy trinity: The IMF, World Bank, and WTO*, Zed Books, NY, New York, 2003.
8. McLaren, *Critical Pedagogy and Predatory Culture*, p. 40.
9. Contrary to the advent of the term as invoked by writers such as Alex de Tocqueville's (1840) *Democracy in America*, "American Exceptionalism" has come to connote an assumed moral authority within the world. Whereas the former pointed to the historical development of the United States as a democracy rich in resources, the latter presents a rather ahistorical assertion of the United States as a predestined leader in world affairs, based, we might add, largely on a felt sense of economic prowess. Interestingly, Russian Prime Minister Vladimir Putin recently penned an opinion piece in the *New York Times* that critiqued the view that the U.S. citizens saw themselves as unique within the world order.
10. Michael Apple, *Educating the "Right" Way: Markets, Standards, God, and Inequality (2ⁿᵈ ed.)*, Routledge, New York, 2006.
11. For an example of the new managerialism within higher education, see Gildersleeve, R., Kuntz, A., Pasque, P., & Carducci, R. The role of critical inquiry in (re)constructing the public agenda for higher education: Confronting the

conservative modernization of the academy. *The Review of Higher Education, 34*(1), 2010, 85–121.

12. Nicoll et al., "Opening Discourses of Citizenship Education," p. 6.
13. Ibid., p. 1.
14. Benedict Anderson, *Imagined Communities: Reflections on the Origin and Spread of Nationalism*. Verso, New York, 1991.
15. Karl Marx, *Capital, Volume I: A Critique of Political Economy*, Penguin Editions Press, New York, 1992 (1976).
16. For an examination of education-as-skills-training in response to the whims of the neoliberal economic market, see Kuntz, A., Gildersleeve, R., and Pasque, P., Obama's American Graduation Initiative: Race, Conservative Modernization, and a Logic of Abstraction. *Peabody Journal of Education, 86*, 2011, 488–505.
17. Nicoll et al., "Opening Discourses of Citizenship Education," p. 1.
18. Kisby, this volume.

Contributors

Steven P. Camicia is an associate professor of social studies education. His research focuses on curriculum and instruction in the areas of perspective consciousness, postcolonial theory, queer theory, global education, and social justice as they relate to democratic education and decision making processes. Along with book chapters and articles, he is currently writing a book entitled *LGBTQ Curriculum and Heteronormativity in the Classroom: Democratic Education as Social Change*. Steven is a former elementary school teacher. His research has been published in scholarly journals such as *Theory and Research in Social Education, the Social Studies, Social Studies Research and Practice, International Journal of Social Studies Research, Journal of Teaching and Teacher Education, the Journal of Public Deliberation, and the London Review of Education*.

Nuraan Davids is lecturer of philosophy of education in the Department of Education Policy Studies, Faculty of Education at Stellenbosch University. Her recent book is, *Women, Cosmopolitanism and Islamic Education: On the virtues of engagement and belonging* (London: Peter Lang, 2013).

Dianne Gereluk is Associate Dean of Undergraduate Programs in Education at the University of Calgary, and Associate Professor in Educational Studies in Leadership, Policy and Governance. Her research examines primarily religious and cultural parameters in a pluralist society. She has taught in the areas of philosophy of education, educational policy and politics, and secondary social studies. She is author of *Education and Community* (Continuum, 2006), *Symbolic Clothing in Schools* (Continuum, 2008), *Education, Extremism and Terrorism* (Bloomsbury, 2011). Her most recent book (coauthored with Dr. Lynn Bosetti), *Understanding School Choice in Canada*, will be forthcoming in spring 2014 (University of Toronto Press).

Zehavit Gross is the head of The UNESCO/Burg Chair in Education for Human Values, Tolerance and Peace and serves as the head of graduate program of Management and Development in Informal Education Systems in the School of Education, Bar-Ilan University, Israel. Her main area of specialization is socialization (civic, religious, national) processes among adolescents. For 18 years she is a facilitator of a conflict management course between Israeli Arab and Jewish students at Bar- Ilan University. She is currently involved in four international research projects all over the world. Her book together with Lynn Davies (Birmingham University) and Khansaa Diab (an Israeli Arab scholar) entitled: Gender, Religion and Education in a Chaotic Post Modern World was published in 2013 by Springer. Her book together with Lynn Davies entitled: The Contested Role of education in Conflict and Fragility will be published by Sense Publishers.

Jessica A. Heybach is an Assistant Professor of Education at Aurora University. Her scholarly interests lie at the intersection of curriculum theory, visual culture, and philosophy of education. She has published journal articles in *Education and Culture, Critical Questions in the Education, and Philosophical Studies in Education.* Also, she recently coedited the book *Dystopia and Education: Insights into Theory, Praxis, and Policy in an Age of Utopia-Gone-Wrong* with Eric C. Sheffield.

Kanako Ide is an Associate Professor in the Faculty of Education at Soka University, Tokyo, Japan. Her main research interests are in democratic education, peace education, and patriotic education from a philosophical perspective. She has also been working with French artist Fabrice Lemire, an artistic director of Cirque du Soleil, to explore the embodiment of democracy in dance and contemporary performing arts. She actively participates in the International Network of Philosophers of Education, is currently a member of the committee on the Status of Women in the Profession in the Philosophy of Education Society of the United States.

Liz Jackson is Assistant Professor in the Division of Policy, Administration, and Social Sciences Education at the University of Hong Kong, Faculty of Education. Jackson received her PhD from the University of Illinois (Urbana-Champaign), and has worked in education policy development in South Africa and the United Arab Emirates. Her research interests include global and comparative studies in education, philosophy of education, and citizenship and multicultural education. Her latest research project examines the representations of religion and ethnic minorities in Hong Kong Liberal Studies textbooks and other curricular resources, and is being funded under the Early Career Scheme of the University Grants Committee of Hong Kong. Her book entitled *Islam and Muslims in U.S. Public Schools: Reconsidering Multiculturalism* will be published with Routledge in 2014.

Ben Kisby is a Senior Lecturer in Politics in the School of Social and Political Sciences at the University of Lincoln. He has taught at the University of Bristol, at Queen Mary, University of London and at the University of Sheffield, where he was an Economic and Social Research Council postdoctoral Research Fellow. Ben is a Fellow of the Royal Society of Arts and a member of the UK Political Studies Association (PSA), and co-convenes the PSA Young People's Politics specialist group with James Sloam and Jacqui Briggs. Ben's research interests include British politics, comparative public policy, social capital, political participation, citizenship theory, and comparative citizenship education. He has published a number of papers on citizenship education and his monograph analyzing why and how Labour introduced citizenship education as a compulsory subject in the National Curriculum in England, *The Labour Party and Citizenship Education: Policy Networks and the Introduction of Citizenship Lessons in Schools*, was published in 2012.

Aaron M. Kuntz is Associate Professor of Educational Studies at the University of Alabama, where he currently serves as Program Coordinator for the PhD in Educational Research. His research interests include critical qualitative inquiry, academic activism and citizenship, critical geography, and philosophy of education. He grounds his methodological theorizing in empirical questions about the production of inquiry in the K–16 arena, faculty work and activism in postsecondary institutions, and the impact of the built environment on learning. Dr. Kuntz's publications appear in such diverse journals as *Qualitative Inquiry, Educational Action Research, Cultural Studies*↔*Critical Methodologies,* the *Journal of Language and Politics, Educational Studies, The Journal of Higher Education*, the *Peabody Journal of Education*, and others. Currently, Dr. Kuntz is completing a book on educational inquiry, methodological responsibility, and social justice practices entitled *Critical Qualitative Work: Methodology, Truth-Telling, Activism.*

Maria-Eugenia Luna-Elizarraras is a primary education teacher with experience at teaching at the secondary and tertiary levels. She works as an independent consultant on citizenship education, human development, and mentoring. She worked in the Secretariat of Public Education in Mexico as Deputy Director of civic and ethic training, coordinating the design of curriculum for primary and secondary education in these fields. She is also heavily involved in teacher education, designing courses and diplomas for teachers on topics such as values, the study of the social sciences, and sex education as well as conducting qualitative and ethnographic studies on processes related to teacher education and the construction of values in the daily life of schools and the classrooms. She has contributed to the development of projects related to the implementation of the curriculum, as well as evaluation of citizenship skills (ICCS 2009).

Miquel Martínez is Professor of Theory of Education and member of the Research Group on Education for Democratic Values and Moral

Development (GREM) at the University of Barcelona. His academic activity is focused on citizenship and values education, educational policy and prospective, and in particular learning and ethics in higher education. He has spoken at various universities and participates as a consultant and evaluator in different projects, agencies, institutions, government and educational organizations and universities in Spain and abroad. He has been Director of the Institute of Education Sciences, Dean of the Faculty of Education and Vice Chancellor of the University of Barcelona. He is currently the coordinator of the Program of improvement and innovation in teacher training of the Interuniversity Council of Catalonia. He is the author and editor of several books and papers on education and has conducted various projects of innovation and educational research.

Andrés Mejía presently works at the Centre for Research and Training in Education (CIFE), at the University of Los Andes, in Bogotá, Colombia. He is a founding member of the Latin American Association of Philosophy of Education (ALFE), and editor of the journals *Voces y Silencios* and *Ixtli: Revista Latinoamericana de Filosofía de la Educación*. His research interests in philosophy of education span such diverse topics as critical pedagogy, critical thinking, citizenship, ethics, educational research, and systems thinking. His approach is frequently interdisciplinary, as is his background. He has recently collaborated with the National Institute for Assessment in Education in Colombia (ICFES) in the conceptualization and construction of the tests of citizenship competencies.

John E. Petrovic is Professor of Educational Philosophy and Policy Studies and Program Coordinator for the Social and Cultural Studies in Education PhD at the University of Alabama. His research interests lie primarily in how liberal political theory informs educational policy. In this vein, he has written articles on a range of issues and topics from Dewey, to heterosexism, to language policy. He has published in such journals as *Educational Theory, Educational Studies, Journal of Language and Politics*, and the *International Multilingual Research Journal*. He is editor of *International Perspectives on Bilingual Education: Policy, Practice, and Controversy* (IAP, 2010). He is currently completing a book in which he develops a post-liberal theory of language policy in education.

Enric Prats is Professor of International Education at University of Barcelona, and member of the Research Group on Education for Democratic Values and Moral Development (GREM) at the same university. His research has focused on intercultural education and mediated citizenship. His academic interest is also focuses on supranational and international education, in prospective and comparative perspective. He is a member of the Commission of Ethical Code of the Catalan Federation of NGOs. He is the author and coeditor of several books and papers.

Peter Roberts is Professor of Education at the University of Canterbury in New Zealand. His primary areas of scholarship are philosophy of education and educational policy studies. He has published widely in international journals. His most recent books include *Paulo Freire in the 21st Century: Education, Dialogue, and Transformation* (2010), *The Virtues of Openness: Education, Science, and Scholarship in the Digital Age*, with Michael Peters (2011), and *Better Worlds: Education, Art, and Utopia*, with John Freeman-Moir (2013). Professor Roberts is Director of the Educational Theory, Policy and Practice Research Hub at the University of Canterbury, and President of the Philosophy of Education Society of Australasia (PESA). In 2008, he was made a Fellow of PESA in recognition of his 'outstanding service to the Society and to the discipline of Philosophy of Education'. In 2010 he was a Canterbury Fellow at the University of Oxford, and in 2012 he was an inaugural Rutherford Visiting Scholar at Trinity College, Cambridge.

David Scott is a PhD candidate in the Faculty of Education at the University of Calgary. His research examines how teachers in Alberta are interpreting and pedagogically addressing a curricular mandate in the province to engage social studies from Aboriginal and Francophone perspectives. He is a recipient of the prestigious Joseph-Armand Bombardier Canada Doctoral Scholarship. Prior to this, David taught social studies and language arts at the junior high and high school level for nine years.

Eric C. Sheffield is a Professor in the Reading, Foundations, and Technology Department housed in the College of Education at Missouri State University. His research interests include peace education, community service learning, democratic education, the role of religion in education, and dystopian educational theory. Eric is the Assistant Director of the Academy for Educational Studies and serves as the founding editor for the academy's national peer-reviewed online journal, *Critical Questions in Education*. In addition to numerous journal articles, Eric has written/coedited several books, including most recently *Dystopia and Education: Insights into Theory, Praxis, and Policy in an Age of Utopia-Gone-Wrong* (2013), coedited with Jessica A. Heybach; *"Strong" Community Service Learning: Philosophical Perspectives* (2011); and *The Role of Religion in 21st Century Public Schools* (2009), coedited with Steven P. Jones.

Yusef Waghid is Professor of Philosophy of Education in the Faculty of Education at Stellenbosch University. His most recent books are *Education, Democracy and Citizenship Reconsidered: Pedagogical Encounters* (Stellenbosch: Sun Media Press, 2010), and *Conceptions of Islamic* *education: Pedagogical Framings* (New York: Peter Lang, 2011), and *African Philosophy of Education Reconsidered: On Being Human* (London: Routledge, 2013). In 2011, he was honored with the prestigious National Research Foundation (NRF) Special Recognition Award, "Champion of Research Capacity Development at Higher Education Institutions in South Africa," as recognition for his influence and significant contribution towards the transformation of the social science community in South Africa.

Juanjuan Zhu is an assessment specialist for English language learners. Her research interests include the broad areas of social studies education, language education, critical theory, postmodern theory, and cosmopolitanism. She did her dissertation on deconstructing the concept of good citizenship embedded in foreign language curriculum in China and the U.S. She has also published in the fields of foreign/secondary language education and human rights education. Her experience as a former college teacher in China further educated in the U.S. facilitates her to conduct research in comparative, critical, and power-conscious ways.

Index

A

accountability, xx, 48, 68, 76, 77, 84, 170, 199, 220, 221, 224, 230, 242, 246, 248

assimilation, x, 23, 24, 35, 40, 57, 115, 129, 130, 131, 132, 133, 150, 243

B

bilingual, 96, 134, 135, 136, 137

C

capitalism, xii, xv, 19, 28, 51, 74, 77, 82, 223, 224, 228, 231

civics education (as different from citizenship education), x, xviii, xix, 78, 87, 91, 151, 160, 197, 204, 240, 247; defined in Israel, 153

colonialism, 24, 116

communitarian, xviii, 2, 5, 71, 111, 199, 200, 202, 206–207

competencies, xx, 168, 188, 189, 190, 191, 195, 197, 202, 206, 207, 210, 212, 213, 214, 256

consumer (ist, ism), x, xvi, 1, 7, 15, 48, 58, 69, 82, 113, 220, 222, 229, 242, 243

corporate order, xv

cosmopolitan (cosmopolitanism), xvii, xix, xx, 2, 12, 13, 22, 27, 43, 45, 46, 47, 49, 51, 54, 56, 58, 59, 93, 97, 98, 203, 247, 249

critical thinking, xi, xvii, xxi, 2, 12, 13, 28, 30, 31, 190, 192, 230, 241, 243

D

democracy, xii, xiv, xvi, xx, 2, 3, 4, 12, 14, 27, 28, 29, 30, 31, 32, 51, 58, 69, 72, 80, 88, 90, 93, 94, 99, 102, 107, 123, 143, 153, 154, 155, 156, 157, 160, 171, 180, 182, 183, 184, 187, 188, 189, 191, 193, 201, 202, 203, 204, 207, 208, 215, 229, 244

dialogue, 4, 23, 29, 38, 39, 70, 73, 87, 101, 102, 106, 111, 129, 141, 142, 143, 162, 165, 166, 168, 169, 170, 171, 172, 209, 232

discourse, ix, xvi, xvii, xix, 1, 10, 11, 14, 43, 45–60, 82, 92, 110, 132, 144, 152, 154, 161, 162, 167, 171, 205, 214, 228, 229, 230, 231, 238, 239, 241, 242, 244, 247, 249, 250; defined, 46

diversity, xii, xvi, xviii, xix, 5, 12, 13, 23, 27, 35, 90, 102, 106, 113, 120, 129, 131, 133, 134, 135, 137, 139, 141, 142, 144, 145, 187, 200, 202, 207, 208, 209, 215, 232, 243, 245, 249

E

economic rationalism, 73–75

entrepreneurship, xii, 28, 56, 58, 59, 74, 97, 106, 137, 222, 227

equity, 12, 13, 100, 105, 119, 120, 121, 132, 165, 166, 187, 209, 215

ethnocentric, 29, 46, 47, 133, 154, 161

F

free market, xii, xiii, xvii, 16, 19, 69, 129, 221

freedom, xii, xix, 6, 27, 44, 58, 59, 60, 74, 75, 76, 88, 89, 94, 105, 121, 134, 140, 141, 181, 182, 186, 187, 189, 202, 207, 208, 215, 216, 229, 230, 242

G

global economy, xviii, 1, 9, 14, 15, 69, 70, 77, 78, 81, 117

globalization (globalisation), xiv, xv, xvi, xvii, 1, 2, 10, 27, 28, 32, 36, 38, 39, 45, 46, 47, 53, 101, 113, 116, 117, 121, 223, 228, 238, 239, 241, 242, 245, 247, 248, 249; defined, 7

H

hegemony, x, 45, 48, 74, 136, 162, 221

human capital, x, 48, 74, 136, 221; defined, 48, 221

human rights, 7, 12, 15, 27, 29, 47, 72, 93, 94, 96, 98, 99, 113, 143, 154, 186, 187, 191, 197, 199, 200, 201, 204, 208, 212, 215

hyperglobalization (hyperglobalisation), xvi, 9, 10, 11, 14; defined, 7–8

I

identity, xvii, xviii, xix, 5, 13, 15, 22, 26, 28, 30, 32, 34, 37, 39, 40, 47, 75, 90, 91, 111, 112, 113, 114, 115, 118, 120, 121, 122, 123, 124, 128, 129, 130, 131, 132, 136, 137, 139, 142, 143, 144, 154, 161, 170, 183, 187, 189, 206, 207, 209, 210, 215, 242, 243, 244

ideology (ideological), xi, xii, xiv, xv, xvii, xviii, xix, 16, 22, 24, 28, 29, 31, 40, 43, 44, 46, 48, 50, 55, 68, 69, 72, 73, 74, 75, 76, 81, 87, 90, 92, 93, 94, 96, 97, 99, 106, 107, 128, 135, 150, 151, 154, 156, 157, 158, 159, 161, 162, 180, 183, 184, 187, 192, 231, 239

imagined community, xii, 47

individualism, xx, 48, 234, 248

intercultural education (interculturalism, intercultural civic education), xvii, xix, 23, 38, 39, 40, 129, 137, 139, 141, 142, 143, 144, 202, 203, 206, 210, 214, 247

L

liberal (liberal democratic/democracy), xiv, xvii, xviii, xix, xx, 1, 2, 3, 22, 25, 27, 31, 32, 36, 37, 69, 71, 72, 73, 74, 120, 128, 129, 133, 134, 137, 138, 139, 140, 143, 145, 153, 155, 157, 162, 181, 182, 183, 186, 188, 190, 191, 192, 193, 199, 200, 206, 207, 210, 221; defined, 216

M

moral (moral education, moral civic education, morality), x, xvi, xx, 2, 4, 5, 23, 25, 28, 29, 30, 31, 33, 35, 37, 39, 45, 48, 49, 51, 52, 53, 54, 59, 71, 72, 74, 76, 77, 81, 82, 96, 101, 102, 103, 106, 112, 122, 132, 141, 142, 143, 144, 158, 172, 185, 201, 202, 204, 205, 230

multicultural (multiculturalism), xviii, xix, 2, 23, 35, 36, 37, 38, 68, 110, 111, 113, 118, 119, 120, 121, 122, 128, 129, 132–145, 162, 186, 198, 200, 210, 243

N

national identity, x, 22, 25, 27, 30, 32, 34, 36, 37, 39, 47, 118, 120, 130, 132, 138, 151, 161, 185, 186, 187, 200, 201, 203, 246

nationalism, xi, xv, xvii, 24, 28, 43, 44, 45, 46, 47, 49–56, 58, 59, 92, 116, 129, 150, 201, 249

nation-state, xiii, xiv, xv, 8, 9, 10, 12, 22, 27, 28, 34, 37, 56, 120, 129, 130, 145, 151, 199, 239, 241, 243, 246, 248, 249

neoconservative (neoconservativism), xv, xvii, 69, 71, 73, 74, 75, 76, 83, 98; defined, 72

neoliberal, x, xv, xvi, xvii, xix, xxi, 1, 8, 10, 11, 16, 43, 45–51, 54–59, 69, 73, 74, 75, 76, 83, 129, 136, 137, 138, 139, 145, 220, 221, 22, 223, 224, 226, 230, 231, 232, 233, 238–250; defined, 16, 47–48, 74

P

participatory, xx, 4, 29, 87, 93, 99, 105, 106, 168, 183, 184, 187, 197, 198, 199, 205

patriotism, xv, xvii, 3, 5, 35, 39, 45, 47, 51, 52, 53, 68, 70, 82, 91, 92, 144, 239, 240, 249 pluralism, 3, 14, 27, 102, 137, 145, 156, 187, 192

political education, xix, 3, 28, 94, 157; defined, 3, 158

prejudice, 35, 133, 136, 144, 145, 100

public (as in public sphere, arena, etc), xi, 4, 8, 16, 24, 70, 74, 88, 91, 93, 112, 120, 122, 130, 141, 143, 144, 150, 151, 155, 170, 180, 181, 183, 185, 192, 199, 200, 201, 202, 203, 206, 221, 232

R

racism, 35, 111, 133, 136, 170

reform, xvii, xviii, xx, 6, 26, 28, 32, 44, 45, 55, 71, 74, 87, 89, 92, 93, 94, 95, 96, 97, 98, 112, 121, 136, 137, 166, 177, 192, 201, 222, 223, 227, 230

republican (republicanism), 2, 3, 5, 15, 198, 199

responsibility (as in civic responsbility), xix, 4, 5, 12, 53, 74, 88, 100, 112, 141, 142, 165, 168, 173, 174, 175, 176, 177, 185, 186, 189, 205, 207, 208, 212, 213, 215, 221, 224, 230, 231, 244, 246

rights (human rights, collective rights), xvi, xix, 2, 3, 5, 7, 11, 12, 13, 14, 15, 22, 27, 29, 37, 39, 45, 47, 48, 72, 75, 77, 88, 92, 93, 94, 96, 98, 99, 102, 104, 111, 113, 121, 134, 135, 136, 137, 139, 141, 143, 145, 154, 156, 161, 181, 182, 183, 186, 187, 188, 190, 191, 197, 199, 200, 201, 204, 205, 208, 209, 210, 212, 213, 214, 215, 222, 244

S

security, xv, 7, 49, 55, 56, 76, 77, 78, 79, 94, 173, 174, 181, 230, 248

service learning, 95, 106

shared-fate citizenship, xii, xiv, 23, 25, 39; defined, xiii, 26

social capital, 4, 5, 100, 101; consensus, 87, 157

social justice, xvii, 12, 13, 15, 47, 80, 129, 132, 133, 136, 137, 138, 201

socialism, xii, 28, 30, 52, 54, 71, 223

sovereignty, xvi, 7, 25, 26, 44, 56, 115, 121, 207, 237

status quo, xvii, 56, 59, 80, 154, 230, 243, 244

surveillance, x, 68, 229, 230

T

technology, xi, 7, 8, 11, 14, 96, 110, 168, 209, 221, 224, 226, 233

theory of experience, xvi, 240, 241

theory of interest, xvi, 240

W

welfare state, 73, 99, 137

World Trade Organization, xvii, 44, 53, 55